European Financial Markets and Institutions

Written for undergraduate and graduate students of finance, economics, and business, this textbook provides a fresh analysis of the European financial system. Combining theory, empirical data, and policy, it examines and explains financial markets, financial infrastructures, financial institutions, and challenges in the domain of financial supervision and competition policy.

Key features:

- Designed specifically for courses on European banking and finance
- Clear signposting and presentation of text with learning objectives, boxes for key concepts and theories, chapter overviews, and suggestions for further reading
- Broad coverage of the European financial system – markets, infrastructure, and institutions
- Explains the ongoing process of financial integration, in particular the impact of the euro
- Examines financial systems of new Member States
- Uses up-to-date European data throughout

A companion website can be found at www.cambridge.org/de_Haan with exercises and freely downloadable solutions.

JAKOB DE HAAN is Professor of Political Economy at the University of Groningen. He is also a fellow of CESiFo (Munich, Germany) and Editor of the *European Journal of Political Economy*.

SANDER OOSTERLOO is Senior Policy Advisor at the Netherlands Ministry of Finance. He received his PhD from the University of Groningen and is affiliated with its Faculty of Economics and Business.

DIRK SCHOENMAKER is Professor of Finance, Banking, and Insurance at the VU University Amsterdam, and Director of European Affairs, Competition, and Consumer Policy at the Netherlands Ministry of Economic Affairs. Before that, he was Deputy Director Financial Markets Policy at the Netherlands Ministry of Finance.

European Financial Markets and Institutions

Jakob de Haan

Sander Oosterloo

Dirk Schoenmaker

CAMBRIDGE
UNIVERSITY PRESS

CAMBRIDGE UNIVERSITY PRESS

Cambridge, New York, Melbourne, Madrid, Cape Town, Singapore, São Paulo, Delhi

Cambridge University Press
The Edinburgh Building, Cambridge CB2 8RU, UK

Published in the United States of America by Cambridge University Press, New York

www.cambridge.org
Information on this title: www.cambridge.org/9780521709521

First published 2009

Printed in the United Kingdom at the University Press, Cambridge

A catalogue record for this publication is available from the British Library

ISBN 978-0-521-88299-6 hardback
ISBN 978-0-521-70952-1 paperback

Contents

Boxes

Figures

x

Tables

Countries

Member states of the European Union

	Country	Official abbreviation	Year of accession
1	Austria	AT	1995
2	Belgium	BE	1951
3	Bulgaria	BG	2007
4	Cyprus	CY	2004
5	Czech Republic	CZ	2004
6	Denmark	DK	1973
7	Estonia	EE	2004
8	Finland	FI	1995
9	France	FR	1951
10	Germany	DE	1951
11	Greece	EL	1981
12	Hungary	HU	2004
13	Ireland	IE	1973
14	Italy	IT	1951
15	Latvia	LV	2004
16	Lithuania	LT	2004
17	Luxembourg	LU	1951
18	Malta	MT	2004
19	Netherlands	NL	1951
20	Poland	PL	2004
21	Portugal	PT	1986
22	Romania	RO	2007
23	Slovakia	SK	2004
24	Slovenia	SI	2004
25	Spain	ES	1986
26	Sweden	SE	1995
27	United Kingdom	UK	1973

The European Union (EU) consists of 27 Member States as of 2009 (EU-27). Before the accession of the New Member States in 2004 and 2007, the EU consisted of 15 Member States, which are usually indicated by EU-15. The 10 New Member States in 2004 are indicated by NMS-10 and the total of 12 New Member States in 2004 and 2007 are indicated by NMS-12. EU-25 refers to the EU-15 and NMS-10.

Countries in the euro area

	Country	Year of accession
1	Austria	1999
2	Belgium	1999
3	Cyprus	2008
4	Finland	1999
5	France	1999
6	Germany	1999
7	Greece	2001
8	Ireland	1999
9	Italy	1999
10	Luxembourg	1999
11	Malta	2008
12	Netherlands	1999
13	Portugal	1999
14	Slovakia	2009
15	Slovenia	2007
16	Spain	1999

Abbreviations

ABS	Asset-Backed Securities
ABP	Algemeen Burgerlijk Pensioenfonds
ALM	Asset and Liability Management
AMF	Autorité des Marchés Financiers
ATM	Automated Teller Machine
BaFin	Bundesanstalt für Finanzdienstleistungsaufsicht
BHB	Bond Home Bias
BIS	Bank for International Settlements
BME	Bolsas y Mercados Españoles
CALPERS	California Public Employees Retirement Scheme
CAPM	Capital Asset Pricing Model
CB	Central Bank
CEBS	Committee of European Banking Supervisors
CEEC	Central and Eastern European Countries
CEIOPS	Committee of Insurance and Occupational Pensions Supervisors
CESR	Committee of European Securities Regulators
CCP	Central Counterparty
CD	Certificate of Deposit
CDC	Collective Defined Contribution
CDO	Collateralised Debt Obligation
CDS	Credit Default Swap
CEA	Comité Européen des Assurances
CEO	Chief Executive Officer
CFO	Chief Financial Officer
CLS	Continuous Linked Settlement
CRA	Credit Rating Agency
CRD	Capital Requirements Directive
CRO	Chief Risk Officer
CSD	Central Securities Depository

DB	Defined Benefit
DC	Defined Contribution
DG	Directorate General
DTB	Deutsche Terminbörse
EBA	Euro Banking Association
EBC	European Banking Committee
EBRD	European Bank for Reconstruction and Development
EC	European Commission
ECB	European Central Bank
ECFI	European Court of First Instance
ECJ	European Court of Justice
ECN	European Competition Network
ECOFIN	Economic and Financial Affairs Council
ECSC	European Coal and Steel Community
ECU	European Currency Unit
EEA	European Economic Area
EEC	European Economic Community
EFA	European Financial Agency
EFAMA	European Fund and Asset Management Association
EFCC	European Financial Conglomerates Committee
EFR	European Financial Services Round Table
EHB	Equity Home Bias
EIOPC	European Insurance and Occupational Pensions Committee
EMI	European Monetary Institute
EMS	European Monetary System
EMU	Economic and Monetary Union
EOE	European Options Exchange
EONIA	Euro Overnight Index Average
EP	European Parliament
EPC	European Payments Council
EPM	ECB payment mechanism
ERC	European Repo Council
ERM	Exchange Rate Mechanism
ESC	European Securities Committee
ESCB	European System of Central Banks
ESFS	European System of Financial Supervisors
EU	European Union

EURATOM	European Atomic Energy Community
EUREPO	Repo Market Reference Rate for the Euro
EURIBOR	Euro Inter-Bank Offered Rate
FDI	Foreign Direct Investment
FRA	Forward Rate Agreement
FSA	Financial Services Authority
FSAP	Financial Services Action Plan
FSC	Financial Services Committee
FSF	Financial Stability Forum
FSR	Financial Stability Review
FX	Foreign Exchange
GDP	Gross Domestic Product
GMI	Governance Metrics International
GVA	Gross Value Added
HI	Herfindahl Index
IAS	International Accounting Standards
IASB	International Accounting Standards Board
ICI	Investment Company Institute
ICMA	International Capital Market Association
ICSD	International Central Securities Depository
IFRS	International Financial Reporting Standards
IMF	International Monetary Fund
IPO	Initial Public Offering
IRS	Interest Rate Swap
ISD	Investment Services Directive
ISDA	International Swaps and Derivatives Association
IT	Information Technology
LI	Lerner Index
LIFFE	London International Financial Futures and Options Exchange
LoLR	Lender of Last Resort
LSE	London Stock Exchange
LTCM	Long-Term Capital Management
LVPS	Large Value Payment System
M&As	Mergers and Acquisitions
MBS	Mortgage-Backed Securities
MFI	Monetary Financial Institution
MIF	Multilateral Interchange Fee

MiFID	Markets in Financial Instruments Directive
MoU	Memorandum of Understanding
MRO	Main Refinancing Operation
MTF	Multi-Trading Facility
MSCI	Morgan Stanley Capital International
NCA	National Competition Authority
NCB	National Central Bank
NMS	New Member States
NYSE	New York Stock Exchange
OECD	Organisation for Economic Cooperation and Development
OFT	Office of Fair Trading
OIS	Overnight Interest Rate Swap
OMX	OfficeMax
OTC	Over-the-Counter
PAYG	Pay-As-You-Go
P&C	Property and Casualty
PCA	Prompt Corrective Action
PSD	Payment Services Directive
PvP	Payment versus Payment
RAROC	Risk Adjusted Return On Capital
REB	Regional Equity Bias
RBB	Regional Bond Bias
ROE	Return On Equity
RTGS	Real-Time Gross Settlement
SCP	Structure-Conduct-Performance
SEA	Single European Act
SEC	Securities and Exchange Commission
SEPA	Single Euro Payments Area
SETS	London Stock Exchange's premier Electronic Trading System
SIV	Structured Investment Vehicle
SMEs	Small and Medium Enterprises
SOFFEX	Swiss Options and Financial Futures Exchange
SPO	Secondary Public Offering
SPV	Special Purpose Vehicle
SRO	Self Regulatory Organisation
SSP	Single Shared Platform
SSNIP	Small, but Significant Non-transitory Increase in Prices

TARGET	Trans-European Automated Real-Time Gross Settlement Express Transfer System
TFEU	Treaty on the Functioning of the EU
UCITS	Undertakings for Collective Investments in Transferable Securities
UK	United Kingdom
US	United States
VaR	Value-at-Risk

Preface

As a team of authors we have followed the building of the European financial system from different angles. We have contributed to the academic literature on this topic. Moreover, one of us has been teaching a course on European Financial Integration, from which this book has emerged. On the policy side, two of the authors have been directly involved in the work of national administrations (i.e., the Ministry of Finance and the Ministry of Economic Affairs in the Netherlands) as well as the European institutions (i.e., the Council and the European Commission). As part of our job, we have participated in many meetings in Brussels discussing the future of European financial markets and institutions and negotiating new European financial services directives.

How does this textbook compare with other books?

Different from other textbooks, *European Financial Markets and Institutions* has a wide coverage dealing with the various elements of the European financial system supported by recent data and examples. This wide coverage implies that we treat not only the functioning of financial markets where trading takes place but also the working of supporting infrastructures (clearing and settlement) where trades are executed. Turning to financial institutions, we cover the full range of financial intermediaries from institutional investors to banks and insurance companies. Based on new data, we document the gradual shift of financial intermediation from banks towards institutional investors, such as pension funds, mutual funds, and hedge funds. In this process of re-intermediation, the assets of institutional investors have tripled over the last two decades. As to policy making, we cover the full range of financial regulation and supervision, financial stability, and competition. We deal with the challenges of European financial integration for nationally based financial supervision and stability policies. Competition is a new topic for a finance textbook.

The existing textbooks in the field of financial markets and institutions generally describe the relevant theories and subsequently relate these theories to the general characteristics of financial markets. An excellent example of such a more in-depth textbook is *The Economics of Financial Markets* by Roy E. Bailey. The broad coverage of our book is comparable to the widely used textbook *Financial Markets and Institutions* by Frederic S. Mishkin and Stanley G. Eakins. Whereas our book focuses on the EU, Mishkin and Eakins analyse the US financial system. The early European textbooks (e.g., *The Economics of Money, Banking and Finance – A European Text*, by Peter Howells and Keith Brain) typically contain chapters on the UK, French, and German banking systems, but do not provide an overview of European banking. More advanced textbooks that do discuss the specifics of the European financial system mostly do this in the context of monetary policy making.

Finally, the excellent *Handbook on European Financial Markets and Institutions* edited by Xavier Freixas, Philipp Hartmann, and Colin Mayer has been published recently. This handbook has a broad coverage of the European financial system, but deals with topics on a stand-alone basis in separate chapters and is not constructed as an integrated textbook. Nevertheless, it contains very useful material for further study of a particular aspect of the European financial system.

How to use this book

European Financial Markets and Institutions is an accessible textbook for both undergraduate and graduate students of Finance, Economics, and Business Administration. Each chapter first gives an overview and identifies learning objectives. Throughout the book we use boxes in which certain issues are explained in more detail, by referring to theory or practical examples. Furthermore, we make abundant use of graphs and tables to give students a comprehensive overview of the European financial system. At the end of each chapter we provide suggestions for further reading. Cambridge University Press provides a supporting website for this book. This website contains exercises (and their solutions) for each chapter. The website also provides regular updates of figures and tables used in the book, and identifies new policy issues.

A basic understanding of finance is needed to use this textbook, as we assume that students are familiar with the basic finance models, such as the standard capital asset pricing model (CAPM). The book can be used for third-year undergraduate courses as well as for graduate courses. More advanced material for graduate students is contained in special boxes marked by a star (*). Undergraduate students can skip these technical boxes.

Jakob de Haan
Sander Oosterloo
Dirk Schoenmaker

Part I

Setting the Stage

1

Functions of the Financial System

OVERVIEW

Having a well-functioning financial system in place that directs funds to their most productive uses is a crucial prerequisite for economic development. The financial system consists of all financial intermediaries and financial markets and their relations with respect to the flow of funds to and from households, governments, business firms, and foreigners, as well as the financial infrastructure.

The main task of the financial system is to channel funds from sectors that have a surplus to sectors that have a shortage of funds. In doing so, the financial sector performs two main functions: (1) reducing information and transaction costs, and (2) facilitating the trading, diversification, and management of risk. These functions are discussed at length in this chapter.

The importance of financial markets and financial intermediaries differs across Member States of the European Union (EU). An important question is how differences in financial systems affect macroeconomic outcomes. Atomistic markets face a free-rider problem: when an investor acquires information about an investment project and behaves accordingly, he reveals this information to all investors, thereby dissuading other investors from devoting resources towards acquiring information. Financial intermediaries may be better able to deal with this problem than financial markets.

This chapter discusses these and other pros and cons of bank-based and market-based systems. A specific element in this debate is the role of corporate governance, i.e. the set of mechanisms arranging the relationship between stakeholders of a firm, notably holders of equity, and the management of the firm. Investors (the outsiders) cannot perfectly monitor managers acting on their behalf since managers (the insiders) have superior information about the performance of the company. So there is a need for certain mechanisms that prevent the insiders of a company using the profits of the firm for their own benefit rather than returning the money to the outside investors. This chapter outlines the various mechanisms in place.

While there is considerable evidence that financial development is good for economic growth, there is no clear evidence that one type of financial system is better for growth than another. However, various recent studies suggest that differences in financial systems may influence the type of activity in which a country specialises. The reason is that different forms of economic activity may be more easily provided by one financial system than another. Likewise, there is some evidence suggesting that in a market-based system households may be better able to smooth consumption in the face of income shocks. However, there is also evidence indicating that a bank-based system is better able to provide inter-temporal smoothing of investment.

Finally, the chapter discusses the 'law and finance' view according to which legal system differences are key in explaining international differences in financial structure. According to this approach, distinguishing countries by the efficiency of national legal systems in supporting financial transactions is more useful than distinguishing countries by whether they have bank-based or market-based financial systems.

LEARNING OBJECTIVES

After you have studied this chapter, you should be able to:
- explain the main functions of the financial system
- differentiate between the roles of financial markets and financial intermediaries
- explain why financial development may stimulate economic growth
- explain why government regulation and supervision of the financial system is needed
- describe the advantages and disadvantages of bank-based and market-based financial systems
- explain the various corporate governance mechanisms
- explain the 'law and finance' view.

1.1 Functions of a financial system

The financial system

This section explains why financial development matters for economic welfare. To understand the importance of financial development, the essentials

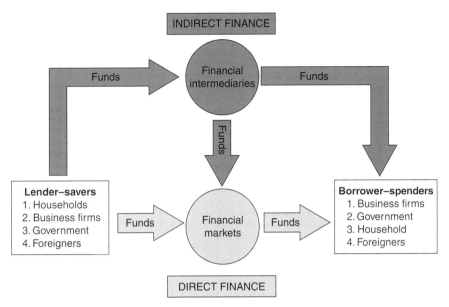

Figure 1.1   Working of the financial system
Source: Mishkin (2006)

of a country's financial system will first be outlined. The *financial system* encompasses all financial intermediaries and financial markets and their relations with respect to the flow of funds to and from households, governments, business firms, and foreigners, as well as the financial infrastructure. *Financial infrastructure* is the set of institutions that enables effective operation of financial intermediaries and financial markets, including such elements as payment systems, credit information bureaus, and collateral registries.

The main task of the financial system is to channel funds from sectors that have a surplus to sectors that have a shortage of funds. Figure 1.1 offers a schematic diagram explaining the working of the financial system.

Sectors that have saved and are lending funds are at the left, and those that must borrow to finance their spending are at the right. *Direct finance* occurs if a sector in need of funds borrows from another sector via a financial market. A *financial market* is a market where participants issue and trade securities. This direct finance route is shown at the bottom of Figure 1.1. With *indirect finance*, a financial intermediary obtains funds from savers and uses these savings to make loans to a sector in need of finance. *Financial intermediaries* are coalitions of agents that combine to provide financial services, such as banks, insurance companies, finance companies, mutual funds, pension funds, etc. (Levine, 1997). This indirect finance route is shown at the top of Figure 1.1.

In most countries, indirect finance is the main route for moving funds from lenders to borrowers. These countries have a *bank-based system*, while countries that rely more on financial markets have a *market-based system*.

The financial system transforms household savings into funds available for investment by firms. However, the importance of financial markets and financial intermediaries differs across Member States of the EU, as will be explained in some detail in this chapter. Also the types of assets held by households differ among the various European countries. Despite all these differences, there is one feature that is common to all the financial systems in these countries and that is the importance of *internal finance*. Most investments by firms in industrial countries are financed through retained earnings, regardless of the relative importance of financial markets and intermediaries (Allen and Gale, 2000).

The past 30 years have seen revolutionary changes in the structure of the world's financial markets and institutions. Some financial markets have become obsolete, while new ones have emerged. Similarly, some financial institutions have gone bankrupt, while new entrants have emerged. However, the functions of the financial system have been more stable than the markets and institutions used to accomplish these functions (Merton, 1995). This first chapter of the book discusses at length the functions of the financial system. The later chapters discuss the changes in the financial markets and financial institutions in Europe.

Having a well-functioning financial system in place that directs funds to their most productive uses is a crucial prerequisite for economic development. If sectors with surplus funds cannot channel their money to sectors with good investment opportunities, many productive investments will never take place. Indeed, cross-country, case-study, industry- and firm-level analyses suggest that the functioning of financial systems is vitally linked to economic growth. Specifically, countries with larger banks and more active stock markets grow faster over subsequent decades, even after controlling for many other factors underlying economic growth (Levine, 2005). Box 1.1 discusses some studies coming to this conclusion.

Main functions

Let us focus on the two main *functions of the financial system*, i.e. (1) reducing information and transaction costs, and (2) facilitating the trading, diversification, and management of risk, to explain why the financial sector may stimulate capital formation and/or technological innovation, two of the driving forces of economic growth.

Box 1.1 Financial development and economic growth

King and Levine (1993a, b) were among the first to argue that financial development is related to economic development. King and Levine (1993b) suggest that current financial depth can predict economic growth over the consequent 10–30 years and conclude that 'better financial systems stimulate faster productivity growth and growth in per capita output by funnelling society's resources to promising productivity-enhancing endeavours' (King and Levine, 1993b, p. 540).

Rajan and Zingales (1998) argue that financial development should be most relevant to industries that depend on external finance and that these industries should grow fastest in countries with well-developed financial systems. They therefore focus on 36 individual industries in 41 countries and analyse the influence of the interaction between the external financial dependence of those industries and the financial development of the countries on the growth rates of those industries in the different countries over the period 1980 to 1990. Using various measures of financial development of a country (the ratio of market capitalisation to GDP, domestic credit to the private sector over GDP, and accounting standards), they report a strong relation between economic growth in different industries and countries and the interaction of financial development of countries and the financial dependence of industries. Rajan and Zingales (1998, p. 584) conclude that their results 'suggest that financial development has a substantial supportive influence on the rate of economic growth and this works, at least partly, by reducing the cost of external finance to financially dependent firms'.

Papaioannou (2008) points out that evidence based on cross-country cross-sectional regressions faces various problems in establishing causality. First, it is almost impossible to account for all possible factors that may foster growth. Second, the effect of financial development may be heterogeneous across countries. Third, there can be reverse causation: financial development can be both the cause and the consequence of economic growth. Finally, the indicators of financial development as generally used in these studies (such as private domestic credit to GDP and market capitalisation as a share of GDP) lack a sound theoretical basis.

Other important studies include Levine *et al.* (2000), who address the endogeneity problems inherent in finance and growth regressions, and the papers in Demirgüç-Kunt and Levine (2001) that use a number of different econometric techniques on datasets ranging from micro-level firm data to international comparative studies. All these studies, and many others, report evidence that financial development stimulates economic growth (Levine, 2005; Papaioannou, 2008).

However, some other studies voice concerns about this conclusion. For instance, Driffill (2003) questions the robustness of some well-known studies, arguing that a number of results hinge on the inclusion of outliers, while the inclusion of regional dummies, especially those for the Asian Tigers, also renders coefficients on financial development insignificant. Trew (2006) argues that most empirical evidence on the finance-growth nexus is disconnected from theories suggesting why financial development affects growth.

Reducing information asymmetry and transaction costs

The financial system helps overcome an information asymmetry between borrowers and lenders. An information asymmetry can occur ex ante and ex post, i.e., before and after a financial contract has been agreed upon. The ex-ante information asymmetry arises because borrowers generally know more about their investment projects than lenders. Borrowers most eager to engage in a transaction are the most likely ones to produce an undesirable outcome for the lender (*adverse selection*). It is difficult and costly to evaluate potential borrowers. Individual savers may not have the time, capacity, or means to collect and process information on a wide array of potential borrowers. So high information costs may keep funds from flowing to their highest productive use. Financial intermediaries may reduce the costs of acquiring and processing information and thereby improve resource allocation (see chapters 6, 7, 8, and 9). Without intermediaries, each investor would face the large fixed cost associated with evaluating investment projects. Also financial markets may reduce information costs (see chapter 3). Economising on information-acquisition costs facilitates the gathering of information about investment opportunities and thereby improves resource allocation. Besides identifying the best investments, financial intermediaries may boost the rate of technological innovation by identifying those entrepreneurs with the best chances of successfully initiating new goods and production processes (Levine, 2005).

The information asymmetry problem occurs ex post when borrowers, but not investors, can observe actual behaviour. Once a loan has been granted, there is a risk that the borrower will engage in activities that are undesirable from the perspective of the lender (*moral hazard*). Financial markets and intermediaries also mitigate the information acquisition and enforcement costs of monitoring borrowers. For example, equity holders and banks will create financial arrangements that compel managers to manage the firm in their best interest (see section 1.2 for more details).

Furthermore, the financial system reduces the time and money spent in carrying out financial transactions (*transaction costs*). Financial intermediaries can reduce transaction costs as they have developed expertise and can take advantage of economies of scale and scope. A good example of how the financial system reduces transaction costs is *pooling*, i.e., the (costly) process of agglomerating capital from disparate savers for investment. By pooling the funds of various small savers, large investment projects can be financed. Without pooling, savers would have to buy and sell entire firms (Levine, 1997). Mobilising savings involves (a) overcoming the transaction costs associated with collecting savings from different individuals, and (b) overcoming the informational asymmetries associated with making savers feel comfortable in relinquishing control of their savings (Levine, 2005).

By reducing information and transaction costs, financial systems lower the cost of channelling funds between borrowers and lenders, which frees up resources for other uses, such as investment and innovation. In addition, financial intermediation affects capital accumulation by allocating funds to their most productive uses. However, higher returns on investment ambiguously affect saving rates, as the income and substitution effects work in opposite directions. A higher return makes saving more attractive (substitution effect), but fewer savings are needed to receive the same returns (income effect). Similarly, lower risk – to which we will turn below – also ambiguously affects savings rates. Thus, the improved resource allocation and lower risk brought about by the financial system may lower saving rates (Levine, 2005).

Trading, diversification, and management of risk

The second main service the financial sector provides is facilitating the trading, diversification, and management of risk. Financial systems may mitigate the risks associated with individual investment projects by providing opportunities for trading and diversifying risk which – in the end – may affect long-run economic growth. In general, high-return projects tend to be riskier than low-return projects. Thus, financial systems that make it easier for people to diversify risk by offering a broad range of high-risk (like equity) and low-risk (like government bonds) investment opportunities tend to induce a portfolio shift towards projects with higher expected returns. Likewise, the ability to hold a diversified portfolio of innovative projects reduces risk and promotes investment in growth-enhancing innovative activities (Levine, 2005).

One particular way in which financial intermediaries and markets reduce risk is by providing *liquidity*, i.e., the ease and speed with which agents can convert assets into purchasing power at agreed prices (Levine, 1997). Savers are generally unwilling to delegate control over their savings to investors for long periods so that less investment is likely to occur in high-return projects that require a long-term commitment of capital. However, the financial system creates the possibility for savers to hold liquid assets – like equity, bonds, or demand deposits – that they can sell quickly and easily if they seek access to their savings, simultaneously transforming these liquid financial instruments into long-term capital investments. Without a financial system, all investors would be locked into illiquid long-term investments that yield high payoffs only to those who consume at the end of the investment. Liquidity is created by financial intermediaries as well as financial markets. For instance, a bank transforms short-term liquid deposits into long-term illiquid loans, therefore making it possible for households to withdraw deposits without interrupting industrial production. Similarly, stock markets reduce liquidity risks by allowing stock holders to trade their shares, while firms still have access to long-term capital.

Risk measurement and management is a key function of financial intermediaries. The traditional role of banks in monitoring the credit risk of borrowers has evolved towards the use of advanced models by all types of financial intermediaries to measure and manage financial risks. Progress in information technology has facilitated the development of advanced risk-management models, which rely on statistical methods to process financial data (see chapters 7 and 9 for more details).

Securitisation is an important means for the financial system to perform the function of trading, diversification, and management of risk. *Securitisation* is the packaging of particular assets and the redistribution of these packages by selling securities, backed by these assets, to investors. For instance, an intermediary may create a pool of mortgage loans (bundling) and then issue bonds backed by those mortgage loans (unbundling). Securitisation thereby converts illiquid assets into liquid assets. While residential mortgages were the first financial assets to be securitised, many other types of financial assets have undergone the same process. A recent example are so-called catastrophe bonds (also known as cat bonds). If insurers have built up a portfolio of risks by insuring properties in a region that may be hit by a catastrophe, they could create a special-purpose entity that would issue the cat bond (see chapter 8 for more details). Investors who buy the bond make a healthy return on their investment, unless a catastrophe, like a hurricane or an earthquake, hits the region because then the principal initially paid by the investors is forgiven and is used by the sponsors to pay their claims to policy holders.

Role of government

A well-functioning financial system requires particular government actions. First, government regulation is needed to protect *property rights* and to *enforce contracts*. Property rights refer to control of the use of the property, the right to any benefit from the property, the right to transfer or sell the property, and the right to exclude others from the property. Absence of secure property rights and enforcement of contracts severely restrict financial transactions and investment, thereby hampering financial development. If it is not clear who is entitled to perform a transaction, exchange will be unlikely. As the financial system allocates capital across time and space, contracts are needed to connect providers and users of funds. If one of the parties does not adhere to the content of a contract, an independent enforcement agency (for instance, a court) is needed, otherwise contracts would be useless.

Second, government regulation is needed to encourage proper information provision (*transparency*) so that providers of funds can take better decisions on how to allocate their money. Government regulation can reduce adverse selection and moral hazard problems in financial systems and enhance their efficiency by increasing the amount of information available to investors, for instance by setting and enforcing accounting standards. Although government regulation to increase transparency is crucial to reducing adverse selection and moral hazard problems, borrowers have strong incentives to cheat so that government regulation may not always be sufficient, as various recent corporate scandals, such as WorldCom, Parmalat, and Ahold, illustrate.

Third, in view of the importance of financial intermediaries, government should arrange for regulation and supervision of financial institutions in order to ensure their *soundness*. Savers are often unable to properly evaluate the financial soundness of a financial intermediary as that requires extensive effort and technical knowledge. Financial intermediaries have an incentive to take too many risks. This is because high-risk investments generally bring in more revenues that accrue to the intermediary, while if the intermediary fails a substantial part of the costs will be borne by the depositors. Government regulation may prevent financial intermediaries from taking too much risk. Depositors may also be protected by introducing some deposit-insurance system, but this may provide the intermediary with an even stronger incentive for risky behaviour. Finally, there is a risk that a sound financial intermediary may fail when another intermediary goes bankrupt due to taking too much risk (*contagion*). Since the public cannot distinguish between sound

Investors can use several tools to ensure that the management of a firm acts in their interest. The most important of these are the appointment of the board of directors, executive compensation, the market for corporate control, concentrated holdings, and monitoring by financial intermediaries (Allen and Gale, 2000).

By appointing the board of directors,[4] shareholders have an instrument to control managers and ensure that the firm is run in their interest. The way that boards are chosen differs across countries. In many countries the management of the firm effectively determines who is nominated for the board, so that an incestuous relationship may blossom between boards of directors and management (Jensen, 1993). Boards may, for instance, approve various protection mechanisms that reduce the attractiveness of a takeover, one of the mechanisms in the market for corporate control (see below).

A second method of ensuring that managers pursue the interests of shareholders is to structure executive compensation appropriately. By making managers' compensation depend on the firm's performance, shareholders can provide incentives for the management of the firm. Examples include direct ownership of shares, stock options, and bonuses dependent on the share price. However, contingent compensation may also have a less desirable effect. If the managers' compensation is sensitive to the performance of the firm, they will have an incentive to take excessive risks as they benefit greatly from good performance, while the penalties for poor performance are limited (Allen and Gale, 2000).

Probably the most important mechanism to control firm management is the market for corporate control that can operate in three ways: proxy contests, friendly mergers and takeovers, and hostile takeovers. In *proxy contests*, a shareholder tries to persuade other shareholders to act in concert with him and force the management of the firm to change course or even to unseat the board of directors. Whether proxy contests work depends, among other things, on the dispersion of shareholding. Friendly *mergers and takeovers* occur when the management of both firms agree that combining the firms would create additional value. The transaction can occur in various ways, such as an exchange of stock or a tender offer by one firm for the other firm's stock (Allen and Gale, 2000).

The potentially most important device in the market for corporate control forcing managers to behave in accordance with the interests of stock holders is a hostile takeover. A *takeover bid* is an attempt by a potential acquirer to obtain a controlling block of shares in a target firm, and thereby gain control of the board and, through it, the firm's management. If a firm does not exploit all of its growth potential, some outsiders may consider the firm an attractive takeover target. After a takeover, they will try to improve the performance of the firm by replacing the current management. This threat gives managers the right incentives to behave in the interest of current stock holders. However, a takeover threat may not be effective for various reasons. First, a takeover threat may not work well due to the information asymmetry between insiders and outsiders: ill-informed outsiders will outbid relatively well-informed insiders for control of firms only when they pay too much. Second, there may again be a free-rider problem. If an outsider spends resources obtaining information, other market participants will observe the results of this research when the outsider bids for shares of the firm. Third, firms often take various actions that deter takeovers and thereby weaken the market as a disciplining device. For instance, a firm may issue rights to existing shareholders to acquire a large number of new securities.

Since the market for corporate control may not always ensure that managers behave in accordance with the interest of shareholders, proponents of a bank-based system argue that monitoring by financial institutions may be more effective in this regard. The agency problem is solved by financial institutions' acting as the outside monitor for firms (Allen and Gale, 2000). The main characteristics of this system are a long-term relationship between banks – but potentially also other financial intermediaries like institutional shareholders (see chapter 6) – and firms, the holding of both equity and debt by the financial intermediary, and the active intervention by the financial intermediary should the firm become financially distressed.

The case for a market-based system focuses on the problems created by powerful banks. While firms with close ties to a 'main bank' have greater access to capital and are less cash constrained than firms without such a bank, the dependence on an influential bank may have various negative effects. Bankers act in their own best interests, not necessarily in the best interests of all stakeholders. For instance, banks with power can extract part of the expected future profits from potentially profitable investments, which may reduce the firm's effort to undertake innovative investments. Influential banks may also prevent outsiders from removing inefficient managers if these managers are particularly generous to the bankers. Bank managers may also be more reluctant to bankrupt firms with which they have had long-term ties (Levine, 2005).

Furthermore, there may be difficulties in governing banks themselves. The information asymmetries between bank insiders and outsiders may be larger than with non-financial corporations. Therefore, banks are even more likely than non-financial firms to have a large, controlling owner.

Finally, proponents of market-based financial systems claim that markets provide a richer set of instruments to manage risks. While bank-based systems may provide inexpensive, basic risk-management services for standardised situations, market-based systems provide greater flexibility to tailor make products.

Types of activity

While there is considerable evidence that financial development is good for economic growth, there is no clear evidence that one kind of financial system is better for growth than another. For instance, Levine (2002) finds that the quality of the financial services produced by the entire financial system (intermediaries and markets) matters for economic growth. However, various recent studies suggest that differences in financial systems may influence the type of activity in which a country specialises. The reason is that different forms of economic activity may be more easily provided by one financial system than the other. Box 1.4 summarises a study providing support for this view.

Box 1.4   Does the financial system matter after all?

To pursue the hypothesis that different financial systems might favour industries with different kinds of characteristics, Carlin and Mayer (2003) examine the inter-relation between types of systems, the nature of different industries, and the levels of activity in those industries in different countries. They evaluate whether there is a relationship between the growth rates of industries in different countries and the interaction between country structures (e.g., the degree of market and bank orientation of their financial systems) and industry characteristics (the dependence of industries on external equity or bank-debt sources of finance and inputs of skilled labour). The sample comprises 14 OECD countries and 27 industries over the period from 1970 to 1995. The financial structure of different countries is measured by the size of their stock markets, accounting standards, the ratio of bank credit to GDP, and the degree of bank ownership of corporate equity. The structure of corporate systems is captured by the degree of concentration of ownership and by the extent of pyramid ownership. The characteristics of legal systems are measured by indicators of legal protection of investors or creditors and by the common- or civil-law origin of the legal system as indicated by its source in English, German, Scandinavian, or French law. Carlin and Mayer report strong evidence of a relation between industry growth rates in different countries and the interaction of country financial structures with industry characteristics. Market-oriented financial systems are associated with high growth of external equity-financed and skill-intensive industries. The effect comes through investment in R&D rather than fixed capital expenditures.

Economies of scale in monitoring make banks more efficient monitors than individual market participants. However, securities markets have the advantage of aggregating diverse views of a large number of market participants and are therefore more likely to support activities where there is a high degree of uncertainty in production, while banks are more likely to support activities in which uncertainty is low but gestation periods are long (Carlin and Mayer, 2000). Banks may be effective at eliminating duplication of information gathering and processing, but may not be effective gatherers and processors of information in new, uncertain situations involving innovative products and processes, in which case securities markets work better. Similarly, Dewatripont and Maskin (1995) argue that banks will find it difficult to credibly commit not to renegotiate contracts in the case of long-run contacts with firms. The credible imposition of tight budget constraints may be necessary for the funding of newer, higher-risk firms.

Other differences

In practice, financial systems are always a mixture of financial markets and financial intermediaries. In a recent study, the IMF (2006) classifies financial systems using the degree to which financial transactions are conducted on the basis of a direct (and generally longer-term) relationship between two entities, usually a bank and a customer, or are conducted at 'arm's-length', where parties concerned typically do not have any special knowledge about each other that is not available publicly. The IMF has constructed a new Financial Index, ranging between 0 and 1, with a higher value representing a greater 'arm's-length' content in the financial system (i.e., it is more market-based).[5] Figure 1.4 shows the IMF Financial Index.

The Financial Index suggests that despite an increase in the arm's-length content of financial systems across advanced economies, important differences remain. Indeed, the increase in the index has generally been larger for those countries with relatively high values already in 1995. Thus, there is little evidence of convergence. This variation in the Financial Index across countries is indicative of important differences in the way financial systems perform their intermediation function. In countries with more arm's-length content, a larger share of household and firm financing takes place through financial markets.

According to the IMF (2006), the degree of arm's length transactions in a financial system may affect household behaviour. A large body of empirical

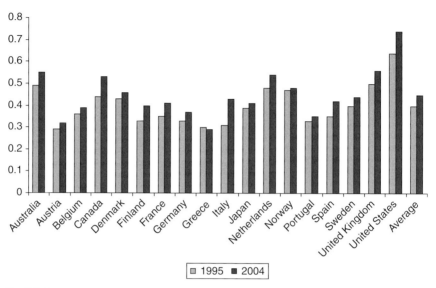

Figure 1.4   The IMF Financial Index for industrial countries, 1995 and 2004
Source: IMF (2006)

evidence shows that private consumption is sensitive to changes in current income, contrary to the implications of the permanent income hypothesis. This finding of 'excess sensitivity' of consumption to current income has most often been attributed to borrowing constraints faced by households, implying that as borrowing constraints ease, consumption can be expected to become less sensitive to current income. In a more arm's-length financial system, households may be better able to smooth consumption in the face of income shocks. In such systems, investors can price collateral more effectively in a liquid market and acquire financial claims on a diversified pool of borrowers. The IMF (2006) provides some evidence that countries with more arm's-length systems tend to exhibit a lower correlation between consumption and current income growth, suggesting a greater degree of consumption smoothing. Figure 1.5 is reproduced here from the IMF study. The figure shows the correlation between consumption and current income growth and the Financial Index. There is a negative relationship that is significant. This finding is consistent with the notion that consumers in countries with a more arm's-length financial system are better able to smooth consumption in the face of changes in their income.

The IMF (2006) also presents evidence that the degree of arm's-length transactions in a financial system may affect investment behaviour. During normal business-cycle downturns, financial systems with a lower degree of arm's-length transactions (and a higher degree of relationship-based lending)

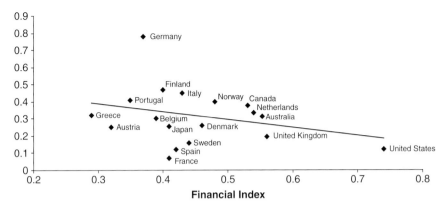

Figure 1.5   Consumption-income correlations and the Financial Index, 1985–2005
Source: IMF (2006)

could be expected to give greater weight to the long-term gains from main-taining an existing relationship with a borrower by providing short-term assurance that financing will be available in the event of a temporary disruption in cash flow, particularly as the lender's own balance sheet is on average more exposed to the borrower. Providing financing to ride out such temporary downturns may not be in the interest of the borrower only but also of the lender. The capital buffer of the bank (as lender) then absorbs part of the losses caused by the downturn. Allen and Gale (2000) also argue that a bank-based system is better able to provide inter-temporal smoothing of investment (and thereby the wider economy) than a market-based system. This is illustrated in Figure 1.6, also taken from the IMF study (2006). The response of the business investment to business cycles is smoother for countries in the lower half of the Financial Index (more relationship-based).

Complements

Some authors argue that financial markets and financial intermediaries may provide complementary growth-enhancing financial services to the economy. Intermediaries may be necessary for the successful functioning of markets. A historical perspective shows that financial markets did not develop spontaneously. The earliest financial transactions involving loans were handled by financial intermediaries. It was not until the Amsterdam Bourse was founded at the start of the seventeenth century that anything like a formal financial market existed (Allen and Gale, 2000). Stock markets may complement banks by spurring competition for corporate control and by offering alternative

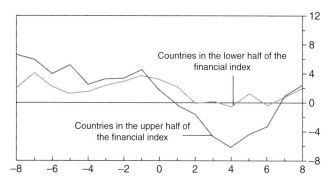

Figure 1.6   Business investment response to business cycles (per cent change year-on-year; constant prices), 1985–2005
Source: IMF (2006)

means of financing investment, thereby reducing the potentially harmful effects of excessive bank power. Indeed, banks have increasingly moved away from their traditional deposit-taking and lending role into fee-generating activities, such as the securitisation of loans and the sale of risk-management products (see chapter 7). Financial markets, of course, also compete with banks. Consumers can invest directly in securities (government and private bonds, and stocks) rather than leaving their money in savings accounts, while borrowers can go to the capital markets rather than to banks. This is often called *dis-intermediation*.

Allen and Santomero (1998) forcefully argue that financial intermediaries reduce what they call *participation costs*, i.e., the costs of learning about effectively using financial markets as well as participating in them on a day-to-day basis. As financial markets have become increasingly complex over time, financial intermediaries offer various services to the uninformed investors, such as providing information, investing on their behalf, or offering a fixed-income claim against the intermediary's balance sheet. Investors get access to financial markets through the intermediary's services, which add value to the transaction by reducing the (perceived) participation costs of uninformed investors. Allen and Santomero argue that the increase in the breadth and depth of financial markets has been the result of greater use of these instruments by financial intermediaries and firms. The increased size of financial markets has coincided with a dramatic shift away from direct participation by individuals in financial markets towards participation through various kinds of intermediaries. The importance of different types of intermediary has also undergone a significant change. While the share of assets held by banks has fallen, that of institutional investors has dramatically increased in size (see chapter 6 for a further analysis). Also in countries with a bank-dominated financial system, like France and Italy, the role of institutional investors has increased. As a consequence, institutional investors have also become more dominant in corporate-governance issues.

Legal system

Finally, some recent research suggests that legal system differences are key in explaining international differences in financial structure. In this approach, the financial system is a set of contracts that is defined and made more or less effective by legal rights and enforcement mechanisms. A well-functioning legal system facilitates the operation of both financial markets and intermediaries. According to this literature, distinguishing countries by the efficiency of national legal systems in supporting financial transactions is more useful than distinguishing countries by whether they have bank-based or market-based financial systems. La Porta *et al.* (1997) argue that financial systems offer different levels of creditor and shareholder protection depending on the origin of the legal rules in place, i.e., English, French, German, or Scandinavian origin. Common-law countries of the English tradition protect both shareholders and creditors the most, French civil-law countries the least, and German and Scandinavian civil-law countries somewhere in the middle. La Porta *et al.* (1997, p. 1149) find that 'civil law, and particularly French civil law, countries, have both the weakest investor protections and the least developed capital markets, especially as compared to common law countries'.

Table 1.2 summarises some of the measures as developed by La Porta *et al.* (1997) and extended and updated by Djankov *et al.* (2006; 2007) for the EU Member States. Column (2) shows the legal family to which the country belongs. The rationale of the other measures is as follows. Those who control a firm, whether they are managers, controlling shareholders, or both, can use their power to deliver firm wealth to themselves, without sharing it with the other investors. The measures quantify the extent to which various investors are protected. Column (3) presents a creditor-rights index that measures powers of secured lenders in bankruptcy (Djankov *et al.* 2007). The creditor-rights index varies between 0 (poor creditor rights) and 4 (strong creditor rights). For their full sample, Djankov *et al.* report that the index of creditor rights for 2003 is lowest in French legal-origin countries and highest in German legal-origin ones.

Table 1.2 Indicators of investor and creditor protection, 2003

(1)	(2)	(3)	(4)	(5)
Country	Law family	Creditor rights	Shareholders' rights	Anti-self dealing index
Austria	German	3	2.5	0.21
Belgium	French	2	2	0.54
Bulgaria	German	n.a.	4	0.66
Czech Republic	German	3	4	0.34
Denmark	Scandinavian	3	4	0.47
Finland	Scandinavian	1	3.5	0.46
France	French	0	3	0.38
Germany	German	3	2.5	0.28
Greece	French	1	2	0.23
Hungary	German	1	2	0.20
Ireland	English	1	4	0.79
Italy	French	2	2.5	0.39
Latvia	German	3	3	0.35
Lithuania	French	2	4	0.38
Luxembourg	French	n.a.	1	0.25
Netherlands	French	3	3	0.21
Portugal	French	1	2.5	0.49
Slovakia	German	2	3	0.29
Slovenia	German	3	n.a.	n.a.
Spain	French	2	5	0.37
Sweden	Scandinavian	1	3.5	0.34
United Kingdom	English	4	5	0.93
Average German		2.57	3.00	0.33
Average French		1.63	2.78	0.36
Average English		2.50	4.50	0.55
Average Scandinavian		1.67	3.67	0.42

Note: n.a. means not available
Source: La Porta *et al.* (1997), Djankov *et al.* (2006, 2007)

Column (4) shows an index reflecting shareholder rights. The original index, reported in La Porta *et al.* (1997), has been criticised by a number of scholars for its ad-hoc nature, for mistakes in its coding, and for conceptual ambiguity in the definitions of some of its components. Therefore, Djankov *et al.* (2006) came up with a revised and extended index that is shown in column (4) of Table 1.2. This index is available for 72 countries and is based on laws and regulations applicable to publicly traded firms in May 2003. The index summarises the protection of minority shareholders in the corporate decision-making process, including the right to vote. This index varies between 0 (poor shareholder rights) and 6 (strong shareholder rights). For their full sample, Djankov *et al.* report that the index of shareholder rights is lowest in French legal-origin countries and highest in English legal-origin ones.

A recent alternative measure of shareholder protection quantifies their rights against expropriation by corporate insiders through self-dealing (see Djankov *et al.*, 2006). Various forms of such self-dealing include executive perquisites to excessive compensation, transfer pricing, self-serving financial transactions such as directed equity issuance or personal loans to insiders, and outright theft of corporate assets. This index ranges between 0 (poor protection) and 1 (high protection) and is shown in column (5) of Table 1.2. For their full sample, Djankov *et al.* report that the index is lowest in French legal-origin countries and highest in English legal-origin ones.

Various conclusions can be drawn from Table 1.2. First, the EU Member States clearly have different legal traditions. So, if the finance and law view is correct (see Box 1.5 for some discussion), financial differences in the EU are likely to remain in place, despite attempts to create one single financial market

---

Box 1.5 Legal origin or political institutions?

According to the law and finance literature, the financial development of countries can be traced back to their legal origins (La Porta *et al.*, 1997). There is some evidence in support of this view. Beck *et al.* (2001) investigate the relative effects of political arrangements, legal origin, and different historical factors on financial development. They conclude that legal origin offers a substantially stronger explanation of financial development than political conditions. However, Keefer (2007) challenges this conclusion. He uses total credit extended to the private sector by banks and other financial institutions as a measure of financial-sector development. This is the preferred way of Beck *et al.* (2001) to measure financial development. Keefer reports that various political variables, including his measure of political checks and balances (i.e., how many political actors can block proposed legislation, therefore tracking whether formal institutions exist that potentially impose constraints on arbitrary behaviour by the executive branch) and newspaper circulation (a proxy for the extent of voter information), have a significant influence on financial-sector development. More importantly, these variables remain significant determinants of financial-sector development, even controlling for legal origin. In fact, the legal-origin variables often become insignificant once political variables are included in the regression model.

(see chapter 2 for further details on the various policy initiatives to create such a single market). Second, the various indicators vary widely across the EU Member States, suggesting that the degree that investors are protected differs substantially across these countries. For instance, the creditor rights index ranges between 0 (France) and 4 (the UK), while the shareholder index ranges between 1 (Luxembourg) and 5 (Spain and the UK).

1.3 Conclusions

The financial system encompasses all financial intermediaries and financial markets and their relations with respect to the flow of funds to and from households, governments, business firms, and foreigners (including the financial infrastructure). The main task of the financial system is to channel funds from sectors that have a surplus to sectors that have a shortage of funds. The importance of financial markets and financial intermediaries differs across Member States of the European Union. However, most investments by firms in the EU are financed through retained earnings, regardless of the relative importance of financial markets and intermediaries.

The financial system helps overcome an information asymmetry between borrowers and lenders. An information asymmetry can occur ex ante and ex post, i.e., before and after a financial contract has been agreed upon. The ex-ante information asymmetry arises because borrowers generally know more about their investment projects than lenders. The ex-post information asymmetry arises because borrowers, but not investors, can observe actual behaviour. Furthermore, the financial system reduces the time and money spent in carrying out financial transactions.

A well-functioning financial system requires particular government actions. First, government regulation is needed to protect property rights and to enforce contracts. Second, government regulation is needed to encourage proper information provision so that providers of funds can take better decisions on how to allocate their money. Third, government should arrange for regulation and supervision of financial institutions in order to ensure their soundness. Finally, governments are responsible for competition policy to ensure competition.

An important question is how differences in financial systems affect macroeconomic outcomes. Atomistic markets face a free-rider problem: when an investor acquires information about an investment project and behaves

Table 1.3 Bank-based vs. market-based financial systems

	Bank-based	Market-based
Economic growth	++	++
High-uncertainty investment	– –	++
Low-uncertainty investment	++	– –
Consumption smoothing	–	+
Investment smoothing	+	–

accordingly, he reveals this information to all investors, thereby dissuading other investors from devoting resources towards acquiring information. Financial intermediaries may be better able to deal with this problem than financial markets.

Another element in the debate on the pros and cons of bank-based vs. market-based systems refers to corporate governance, i.e., the set of mechanisms arranging the relationship between stakeholders of a firm, notably holders of equity, and the management of the firm. Investors (the outsiders) cannot perfectly monitor managers acting on their behalf since managers (the insiders) have superior information about the performance of the company. So there is a need for certain mechanisms that prevent the insiders of a company using the profits of the firm for their own benefit rather than returning the money to the outside investors.

While there is considerable evidence that financial development is good for economic growth, there is no clear evidence that one kind of financial system is better for growth than another. However, various recent studies suggest that differences in financial systems may influence the type of activity in which a country specialises. The reason is that different forms of economic activity may be more easily provided by one financial system than the other. Likewise, there is some evidence suggesting that in financial systems characterised by a greater degree of arm's-length transactions, households seem to be able to smooth consumption more effectively in the face of unanticipated changes in their income, although they may be more sensitive to changes in asset prices. By contrast, financial systems characterised by a greater degree of relationship-based lending are able to smooth business investment more effectively in the face of changes in the business cycle. Table 1.3 summarises these issues.

Some authors argue that financial markets and financial intermediaries provide complementary growth-enhancing financial services to the economy. Intermediaries are necessary for the successful functioning of markets.

Finally, according to the 'law and finance' view, legal-system differences are key in explaining international differences in financial structure. Therefore, distinguishing countries by the efficiency of national legal systems in supporting financial transactions is more useful than distinguishing countries by whether they have bank-based or market-based financial systems.

NOTES

1. Whether competition increases depends on the entry strategy of foreign intermediaries. For instance, if a foreign intermediary acquires various domestic intermediaries and merges them, competition may decrease.
2. Various studies examine this issue. A good example is Petersen and Rajan (1994) who, on the basis of a large-scale sample of US firms with less than 500 employees, found evidence that relationships increase the availability and reduce the price of credit to firms. The empirical results suggest that the availability of finance increases as the firm spends more time in a relationship, as it increases ties to a lender by expanding the number of financial services it buys from it, and as it concentrates its borrowing with the lender.
3. While the median is over 50 per cent for the overall group of 374 companies in Germany, the median for the 30 large companies in the DAX30 is only 11 per cent. Similarly, the relatively low median reported for France relates only to the 40 large companies in the CAC40 (Becht and Roëll, 1999).
4. There are two main types of board of directors. The UK and the US have a so-called one-tier board, which consists of a mix of outside (non-executive) directors and inside (executive) directors, who are the top executives of the firm. The role of management is to implement the business policies that the board has determined. Continental European countries apply the two-tier board system with a supervisory board and a management board. The supervisory board is the controlling body and elected by the shareholders (and sometimes also by the employees). The management board is appointed by the supervisory board.
5. The interested reader is referred to Appendix 4.1 of IMF (2006) for further details.

SUGGESTED READING

Allen, F. and D. Gale (2000), *Comparing Financial Systems*, MIT Press, Cambridge (MA).

Carlin, W. and C.P. Mayer (2003), Finance, Investment and Growth, *Journal of Financial Economics*, 69(1), 191–226.

Papaioannou, E. (2008), Finance and Growth. A Macroeconomic Assessment of the Evidence from a European Angle, in: X. Freixas, P. Hartmann, and C. Mayer (eds.), *Handbook of European Financial Markets and Institutions*, Oxford University Press, Oxford, 68–98.

REFERENCES

Abiad, A. and A. Mody (2005), Financial Reform: What Shakes It? What Shapes It?, *American Economic Review*, 95(1), 66–88.

Allen, F., L. Bartiloro, and O. Kowalewski (2006), The Financial System of EU 25, in: K. Liebscher, J. Christl, P. Mooslechner, and D. Ritzberger-Grünwald (eds), *Financial Development, Integration and Stability in Central, Eastern and South-Eastern Europe*, Edward Elgar, Cheltenham, 80–104.

Allen, F. and D. Gale (2000), *Comparing Financial Systems*, MIT Press, Cambridge (MA).

Allen, F. and A. M. Santomero (1997), The Theory of Financial Intermediation, *Journal of Banking and Finance*, 21, 1461–1485.

Becht, M. and A. Roëll (1999), Blockholdings in Europe: An International Comparison, *European Economic Review*, 43, 1049–1056.

Beck, T., A. Demirgüç-Kunt, and R. Levine (2001), Law, Politics and Finance, World Bank, Policy Research Working Paper 2585.

Bekeart, G., C. R. Harvey, and C. Lundblad (2005), Does Financial Liberalization Spur Growth? *Journal of Financial Economics*, 77, 3–55.

Carlin, W. and C. P. Mayer (2000), How Do Financial Systems Affect Economic Performance?, in: X. Vives (ed.), *Corporate Governance: Theoretical and Empirical Perspectives*, Cambridge University Press, Cambridge (UK), pp. 137–168.

Carlin, W. and C. P. Mayer (2003), Finance, Investment and Growth, *Journal of Financial Economics*, 69(1), 191–226.

Demirgüç-Kunt, A. and Levine, R. (eds.) (2001), *Financial Structure and Economic Growth: A Cross-Country Comparison of Banks, Markets and Development*, MIT Press, Cambridge (MA).

Dewatripont, M. and E. Maskin (1995), Credit Efficiency in Centralized and Decentralized Economies, *Review of Economic Studies*, 62, 541–555.

Djankov, S., R. La Porta, F. Lopez-de Silanes, and A. Shleifer (2006), The Law and Economics of Self-dealing, working paper.

Djankov, S., C. McLiesh, and A. Shleifer (2007), Private Credit in 129 Countries, *Journal of Financial Economics*, 84, 299–329.

Driffill, J. (2003), Growth and Finance, *The Manchester School*, 71, 363–80.

European Central Bank (2006), *Financial Stability Review* (December), ECB, Frankfurt am Main.

European Central Bank (2007), *Financial Integration in Europe*, ECB, Frankfurt am Main.

Fernandez, R. and D. Rodrik (1991), Resistance to Reform: Status Quo Bias in the Presence of Individual-specific Uncertainty, *American Economic Review*, 81, 1146–1155.

Governance Metrics International (2006), *Ratings on 3800 Global Companies*, GMI, New York.

International Monetary Fund (2006), *World Economic Outlook*, chapter 4, IMF, Washington DC.

Jensen, M. (1993), The Modern Industrial Revolution, Exit, and the Failure of Internal Control Systems, *Journal of Finance*, 48, 831–880.

Jensen, M. and W. Meckling (1976), Theory of the Firm: Managerial Behavior, Agency Costs, and Capital Structure, *Journal of Financial Economics*, 3, 287–322.

Keefer, P. (2007), Beyond Legal Origin and Checks and Balances: Political Credibility, Citizen Information and Financial Sector Development, World Bank Policy Research Working Paper 4154.

King, R. G. and R. Levine (1993a), Finance and Growth: Schumpeter Might Be Right, *Quarterly Journal of Economics*, 108, 717–737.

King, R. G. and R. Levine (1993b), Finance, Entrepreneurship, and Growth: Theory and Evidence, *Journal of Monetary Economics*, 32, 513–542.

La Porta, R., F. Lopez-de-Silanes, A. Shleifer, and R. Vishny (1997), Legal Determinants of External Finance, *Journal of Finance*, 52, 1131–1150.

Levine, R. (1997), Financial Development and Economic Growth: Views and Agenda, *Journal of Economic Literature*, 35, 688–726.

Levine, R. (2002), Bank-Based or Market-Based Financial Systems: Which is Better?, *Journal of Financial Intermediation*, 11, 398–428.

Levine, R. (2005), Finance and Growth: Theory, Mechanisms and Evidence, in: P. Aghion and S. N. Durlauf (eds.), *Handbook of Economic Growth*, Elsevier, Amsterdam, 865–923.

Levine, R., N. Loayza, and T. Beck (2000), Financial Intermediation and Growth: Causality and Causes, *Journal of Monetary Economics*, 46, 31–77.

Merton, R. C. (1995), Financial Innovation and the Management and Regulation of Financial Institutions, *Journal of Banking and Finance*, 19, 461–481.

Mishkin, F. S. (2006), *The Next Great Globalization*, Princeton University Press, Princeton.

Papaioannou, E. (2008), Finance and Growth. A Macroeconomic Assessment of the Evidence from a European Angle, in: X. Freixas, P. Hartmann, and C. Mayer (eds.), *Handbook of European Financial Markets and Institutions*, Oxford University Press, Oxford, 68–98.

Petersen, M. A. and R. G. Rajan (1994), The Benefits of Lending Relationships: Evidence from Small Business Data, *The Journal of Finance*, 49 (1), 3–37.

Rajan, R. and L. Zingales (1998), Financial Dependence and Growth, *American Economic Review*, 88, 559–586.

Trew, A. (2006), Finance and Growth: A Critical Survey, *The Economic Record*, 82, 481–490.

2

European Financial Integration: Origins and History

OVERVIEW

The European Union consists of 27 Member States at the time of writing and has supranational and intergovernmental forms of co-operation. The EU has its origins in the European Coal and Steel Community (ECSC) formed by six European countries in 1951. Since then, it has grown in size through the accession of new Member States, while it has also increased its powers by the addition of new policy areas to its remit.

This chapter describes the major steps towards monetary and financial integration in the European Union. In addition, it explains the most important EU institutions (European Commission, Council of the EU, European Council, the European Parliament, and the European Court of Justice) and legal instruments (like directives and regulations).

A major step in the history of European integration was the publication of the report of the Committee for the Study of Economic and Monetary Union in 1989. In this so-called Delors Report, named after the chairman of this committee, a three-phase transition towards monetary unification was proposed. The main conclusions of the Delors Committee were incorporated in the 1992 Treaty on European Union and finally led to the introduction of the single currency as well as the European Central Bank (ECB).

An important milestone for financial integration was the launch of the Financial Services Action Plan (FSAP) by the European Commission in May 1999. The purpose of the FSAP was to remove regulatory and market barriers that limit the cross-border provision of financial services and the free flow of capital within the EU, and to create a level playing field among market participants.

LEARNING OBJECTIVES

After you have studied this chapter, you should be able to:
- outline the various steps in the process of European monetary and financial integration
- describe the fundamental principles underlying the financial integration process
- explain the functioning of the most important EU institutions and their responsibilities
- describe the various EU legal instruments.

2.1 European integration: introduction

Although the idea of economic integration of European countries was proposed earlier, it was put into practice only after the Second World War. The major impetus was the Schuman plan of May 1950 that foresaw the establishment of the so-called European Coal and Steel Community. It was very much inspired by political considerations as the ECSC was seen as the basis for Franco–German reconciliation. To ensure that reconstruction in the western part of Germany would not endanger peace, the ECSC intended to integrate the coal and steel sectors, which were at the time considered to be of central importance for the defence industry. The main objective of the ECSC was the elimination of barriers and the encouragement of competition in these sectors.

The ECSC that started in 1951 was in many ways characteristic for the European integration process of the years to come. First, its membership was limited. Only Belgium, Germany, France, Italy, Luxembourg, and the Netherlands were members. The United Kingdom and various other European countries remained outside the organisation. It was only in 1973 that Denmark, Ireland, and the UK joined what was then called the European Communities, to be followed by Greece (1981) and Spain and Portugal (1986). Austria, Finland, and Sweden became members in 1995. After the collapse of communism at the end of the 1980s, various Eastern- and Central-European countries became candidate members of what was by then called the European Union. In 2004, Cyprus, the Czech Republic, Estonia, Hungary, Latvia, Lithuania, Malta, Poland, Slovakia, and Slovenia acceded to the EU, followed in 2007 by Bulgaria and Romania.

Second, much of the organisational structure of the EU as we know it today (see section 2.2) is very similar to that of the ECSC. For instance, the High Authority, the ECSC's supranational executive organ, was the predecessor of

---

Box 2.1 The role of treaties

Treaties form the basis of the European integration process. The basic treaty is the *Treaty of Rome* (1957) establishing the European Economic Community. The Treaty of Rome contains the legal basis for most decisions taken by the institutions of the European Union (see section 2.2) and is still the main source of communitary legislation. The original Treaty of Rome has been amended by subsequent treaties.

A first major amendment is the *Single European Act* (1986) completing the internal market. The chief objective of the Single European Act was to add new momentum to the process of European integration. An important innovation was that it moved away from the principle of unanimity for the harmonisation of legislation. Another major amendment is the *Maastricht Treaty on European Union* (1992) launching Economic and Monetary Union. The Maastricht Treaty also created the European Union.

Next, the Treaty of Rome was amended by the *Treaty of Amsterdam* (1997). The Amsterdam Treaty puts a greater emphasis on security and justice matters and contains the beginning of a common foreign and security policy. A further amendment is contained in the *Treaty of Nice* (2001). The Nice Treaty deals with reforming the institutions so that the EU could continue to function effectively after its enlargement to 25 Member States in 2004 and subsequently to 27 Member States in 2007. The Treaty of Nice also changed the number of votes, as specified in Table 2.1.

The final amendment is the *Treaty of Lisbon* (2007), which is (subject to ratification) scheduled to enter into force in 2009. The Lisbon Treaty further streamlines the institutions of the EU and upgrades the powers of the European Parliament (see Box 2.2).

---

the European Commission. The first president of this High Authority was Jean Monnet. Other institutions of the ECSC were the Council of Ministers (representing member governments), the Assembly (composed of 68 delegates from the national parliaments, later transformed into the European Parliament), and the European Court of Justice.

With the entering into force of the Treaty of Rome in 1958, the European Economic Community (EEC) and the European Atomic Energy Community (Euratom) came into being (see Box 2.1 on the role of treaties). Of the three communities (i.e., the ECSC, the EEC, and Euratom), the EEC was by far the most important in terms of scope and instruments.[1] The Treaty paved the way for the creation of a common market where goods, services, labour, and capital could move freely. It directed Europe towards a single financial market, but it was not until the 1980s that major steps were taken in this direction.

In 1985, the European Commission published a White Paper on the Completion of the Internal Market, which provided for the free circulation of persons, goods, services, and capital in the European Union. Economies of scale and scope would result from decreased border controls, unified technical standards, reduced distribution and marketing costs, and standardised rules and regulations in the manufacturing and services sectors. To provide an economic underpinning of the Internal Market Project, the Cecchini Report (1988) calculated the costs of nationally fragmented markets, i.e., the costs of 'non-Europe', and estimated the benefits of the Internal Market at approximately 4–7 per cent of GDP. The White Paper led to the adoption of the so-called Single European Act (SEA) in 1986 that aimed at completing the internal market by 1992.

Another major step in the history of European integration was the publication of the report of the Committee for the Study of Economic and Monetary Union in 1989. In the *Delors Report* – named after the chairman of this committee and then-president of the European Commission, Jacques Delors – a three-phase transition towards monetary unification was proposed. The main conclusions of the Delors Committee were incorporated in the 1992 Treaty on European Union, better known as the Maastricht Treaty, named after the Dutch city where the final negotiations took place. As a consequence, the Economic and Monetary Union (EMU) started on 1 January 1999 with the irrevocable fixing of the exchange rates of the then 11 participating countries and the start of the common monetary policy by the ECB. Euro notes and coins were introduced in January 2002.

In May 1999, the European Commission launched the Financial Services Action Plan. The purpose of the FSAP was to remove regulatory and market barriers that limit the cross-border provision of financial services and the free flow of capital within the EU, and to create a level playing field among market participants.

This chapter outlines the most important steps taken towards European financial integration. The next section goes on to explain the most important European institutions and the legal instruments used to shape integration. As full financial integration requires monetary integration, section 2.3 describes first how monetary integration has evolved. Section 2.4 sets out the major steps towards financial integration.

2.2 European institutions and instruments

There are two basic approaches towards integration. In the *supranational* approach, an international institution that is independent from national governments is responsible for policy making, while in the *intergovernmental* approach an international institution basically fulfils a secretariat role for the governments and has no real power. The key difference in the two approaches is the transfer of sovereignty from the Member States to that institution. Whereas in the intergovernmental approach no sovereignty is transferred, in the supranational approach Member States lose their power to enact legislation. Interestingly, in the EU both types of integration exist (Craig and De Burca, 2007).

Institutions

The *European Commission* is the EU institution that is most independent from the Member States. Its most important task is to initiate legislation. Only the Commission can come up with formal proposals for legislation (the so-called right of initiative). The Council and Parliament, to be explained below, are only able to request legislation. The formal legislative process starts with the presentation of a proposal by the European Commission to the European Parliament and the European Council, after which the process of negotiation between the latter parties starts. Currently, the Commission consists of 27 Commissioners, one from each Member State, who are appointed for a five-year term (see Box 2.2 for the changes once the Lisbon Treaty is in force). Commissioners are expected to detach themselves from national interests. The President of the Commission and the other Commissioners are first nominated by the European Council and are officially approved by the European Parliament. The Commission has its own staff, sometimes referred to as 'the Brussels bureaucracy'. Although this name suggests otherwise, the size of the Commission staff is relatively small – in 2008 the Commission employed just over 24,000 officials. Each Commissioner is responsible for a particular policy area, and politically responsible for a Directorate General (DG).[2] The most important DGs for financial services are DG Internal Market and Services, DG Economic and Financial Affairs, and DG Competition.

The *Council* of the European Union consists of representatives of each Member State at the ministerial level. When the Council meetings comprise ministers of economics and finance, it is known as *Ecofin*. Decision making in the Council is on the basis of unanimity, simple majority, or qualified majority. In most cases, the Council votes on issues by qualified majority, meaning that there must be a minimum of 255 votes out of 345 and a majority of Member States. Table 2.1 indicates that the number of votes of the Member

limited than that of national parliaments. Still, over time, the influence of the EP has increased. Currently, it has 785 members, but that number will be reduced to 750 when the Treaty of Lisbon enters into force. The EP has veto power over the appointment of the Commission. It can also dismiss the Commission. The EP also has the right to reject the EU Budget. It plays an important role in legislation, which may go through different procedures. Under the *consultation procedure*, the EP only gives its opinion. Under the *co-operation procedure* it has the right to amend or even reject legislation, but these decisions may be overruled by the Council. Under the *co-decision procedure*, acceptance by the EP is necessary. The Commission presents a proposal to Parliament and the Council, then the EP sends amendments to the Council, which can either adopt the text with those amendments or send back a 'common position'. That proposal may be approved or further amendments may be tabled by the EP. If the Council does not approve those, a 'Conciliation Committee' is formed that seeks agreement. Finally, under the *assent procedure* the Council is required to obtain the European Parliament's assent before certain important decisions are taken. The assent principle is based on a single reading. The EP may accept or reject a proposal but cannot amend it. If the EP does not give its assent, the act in question cannot be adopted. The assent procedure applies mainly to the accession of new Member States, association agreements, and other fundamental agreements with third countries. It is, among others, also required with regard to the specific tasks of the ECB and amendments to the Statutes of the European System of Central Banks (ESCB) and the ECB. Parliament's assent is given by a majority of votes cast, but a majority of Members is also required in case of the accession of a new Member State and the electoral procedure.

The *European Court of Justice* (ECJ) consists of 27 judges (one judge per Member State) and 8 advocates-general. Judgments of the ECJ on matters relating to the interpretation and application of European law have been of great importance for the development of the EU. As the supreme court of the EU, the ECJ gives a coherent and uniform interpretation of Community law and ensures compliance by the Member States. The ECJ has rejected protectionism in many judgments and thus contributed significantly to the realisation of the internal market.

Legal instruments

Legislative measures in the EU are proposed by the European Commission and – in the case of nearly all the measures under the Financial Services Action Plan (see section 2.4) – are adopted by co-decision under which the Council and the European Parliament consider, amend, and agree on the final content of each legislative measure. These measures are published in the *Official Journal of the European Union* and can take the form of:

- *regulations* – a regulation is binding in its entirety and directly applicable in all Member States, and does not require transposition into the respective national laws (although there may be changes required in Member States' law to achieve the full effect of the regulation);
- *directives* – a directive is binding upon each Member State to which it is addressed, but gives national authorities the choice of form and methods. In other words, directives must be incorporated in the national law of each Member State, generally by introducing or amending national laws, within a deadline of usually 18 or 24 months after publication.

In addition to regulations and directives, the Commission or the Council can take *decisions* which are binding upon those to whom they are addressed. The Commission and the Council can also formulate *recommendations* or deliver *opinions*. These are not legally binding, although politically they can be important. The various instruments have a different impact on integration (see also Box 2.3). A regulation fosters full integration, because of its direct

---

Box 2.3 Dynamics of integration

The combination of the choice of the decision-making procedure (supranational or intergovernmental) and the choice of legal instrument (regulation or directive) determines to a large extent the degree of integration. In the area of competition policy and monetary policy, the EU has chosen for regulations to ensure uniformity across the EU. A good example is the Regulation on the Introduction of the Euro (EC/974/98), according to which the national currencies participating in the euro could only be converted into the euro in a uniform way. If the euro denomination of the German D-Mark, for example, were calculated differently across countries, there would be scope for arbitrage. A supranational institution (the European Central Bank; see section 2.3) is responsible for policymaking. The money market shows that the ECB has been successful in adopting a uniform monetary policy across the euro area as the money-market rates in the various euro-area countries have fully converged (see chapter 4).

In the area of financial services policy, the EU has often opted for directives. These directives are mostly implemented in a different way by each Member State. An example is the definition of 'capital' under the Banking Directive (2006/48/EC). This directive determines how much capital banks must maintain in view of the risks that a bank faces. All 27 Member States use their own definition of capital. Moreover, banking supervision is executed by national supervisory authorities. Banking groups that have cross-border operations in the EU sometimes complain about the differences in rules and approach taken by national supervisors.

application. Basically, the rules are uniform and overrule national legislation, to the extent that the latter is not consistent with the regulation. By contrast, a directive needs to be implemented by the Member States, leaving scope for minor or major differences. The rules are then harmonised and are generally not uniform.

The adoption or implementation of legal instruments is only the first element of the legislative framework. The second element is the putting in place of the relevant administrative arrangements to ensure that the new rules are observed. The third element, sometimes referred to as enforcement, is ensuring that the new rules work effectively and are complied with across the EU.

2.3 Monetary integration

During the initial phase of European integration, the emphasis was on integration of goods markets. As far as monetary issues were concerned, the Rome Treaty described exchange-rate policies as a matter of 'common concern', but did not offer substantive contents as to its meaning. It was only at the summit in 1969 in The Hague that the European governments agreed on monetary union. Pierre Werner, prime minister of Luxembourg at the time, was appointed to chair a committee that was to draw up a plan. The Werner Report was completed in 1970. It called for the completion of a monetary union by 1980. The Werner Committee proposed a three-stage approach towards monetary union, leading eventually to fixed exchange rates and a common monetary policy.

Although the Council adopted the plan, the turmoil in the currency markets at the time made it falter. The mid-1970s can be characterised as a low point in European monetary integration. However, at the end of the 1970s the then French president Valéry Giscard D'Estaing and German chancellor Helmut Schmidt took the initiative for the European Monetary System (EMS). The aim of the EMS was to create a 'zone of monetary stability' in Europe. The core was the so-called Exchange Rate Mechanism (ERM). Currencies participating in the ERM were supposed to fluctuate vis-à-vis one another within a band of plus and minus 2.25 per cent around agreed-upon central rates. These central rates could be adjusted. Although this system brought some stability for the participating currencies, there were, at times, frequent adjustments of the central rates. Within the system, the German D-Mark functioned as the anchor. Countries that pegged their currency to the

German one had little room for manoeuvre in monetary policy making. If the German monetary authorities decided to change their interest rates, the other countries had to follow if they wanted to maintain their peg. Various countries, notably France, felt that the German-dominated ERM did not always serve their interests as the German monetary authorities, in deciding on interest rates, took into account only the economic situation in Germany. A monetary union was considered the proper answer to this problem.

During the 1980s, the discussion therefore focused again on monetary integration. There is no doubt that the signing of the Single European Act in 1986 and the commitment to complete the internal market by 1992 were important in furthering monetary union. Initially regarded as rather modest in nature, the SEA succeeded in developing renewed momentum for European integration, not least by establishing a clear deadline for completion of the internal market. It was argued that in order to reap the full gains from the internal market, exchange-rate risks and transaction costs were to be banished by introducing a common currency. This view is apparent from the title of an important study by the European Commission: 'One Market, One Money' (Emerson *et al.*, 1992). Although many economists do not subscribe to the view that fixed exchange rates are needed to fully capture the gains from the Single Market, the argument gained popularity under policy makers.

At the Hannover summit in June 1988, the European Council decided to establish a committee that should propose concrete stages leading to Economic and Monetary Union. The committee was chaired by Jacques Delors. A year later the committee presented its report. Although it did not offer a specified timetable, the committee proposed a gradual process towards EMU, eventually leading to monetary union, but stressed that the timing of each stage required a political decision. In the final stage, there would be a single currency under a new central bank's authority. Although not strictly necessary for the creation of monetary union, the Delors Committee argued in favour of a single currency as this would demonstrate the irreversibility of the union. The countries participating were not only supposed to have a common currency but would also co-ordinate their economic policies, notably fiscal policy. That is why the system is called Economic and Monetary Union.[3]

Subsequent negotiations eventually led to the adoption of the 1992 Treaty on European Union, signed in Maastricht where the leaders of the EU countries met to take a decision on EMU. The negotiations were difficult as the United Kingdom had strong reservations about moving towards an

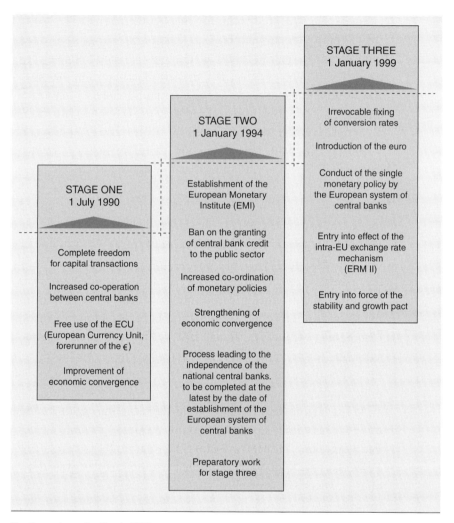

Figure 2.1   The three stages leading to EMU
Source: ECB

EU-wide currency union. The compromise that was reached was to give the UK a so-called 'opt-out clause', i.e., even if the UK meets the convergence criteria for entering the euro area as stipulated in the Maastricht Treaty, it is up to the UK government to decide about entry.

Many of the suggestions of the Delors Committee found their way into the Treaty, including a three-stages approach (see Figure 2.1). As suggested in the Delors Report, the first stage of EMU started on 1 July 1990 with the liberalisation of capital controls (see section 2.4 for further details).

However, ratification of the Treaty turned out to be difficult. Denmark rejected the Maastricht Treaty at a referendum in June 1992.[4] The rejection, with a slight majority, came as a huge shock. In France, where the Maastricht Treaty was put to a referendum after the Danes initially had said no, the majority in favour was a wafer-thin 51 per cent. Ratification was tortuous and contentious in some other countries too.

Perspectives for EMU became dim when serious currency crises occurred in 1992/1993 that forced governments to broaden the ERM fluctuation band to plus and minus 15 per cent. Many sceptics asked what hope there could be for a monetary union among countries unable to keep national currencies aligned. Sometimes EMU was perceived as an ambitious project that would never fly, just like the emu, the large Australian bird. For instance, the then prime minister of the UK, John Major, wrote in *The Economist* that continuing 'to recite the mantra of full economic and monetary union . . . will have all the quaintness of a rain dance and about the same potency'. Although the currency crises for some time led to lingering doubts, with the start of the second stage of EMU on 1 January 1994 it became clear that EMU was becoming more and more likely.

At the beginning of 1998, the European Council decided that 11 of the then 15 EU Member States could join the currency union. This decision was based on the so-called convergence criteria as outlined in the Maastricht Treaty that refer to inflation, long-term interest rates, exchange rate stability, and the public deficit and debt-to-GDP ratios.

On 1 January 1999 Europe entered a new era with the adoption of a single currency – the euro – by 11 Member States of the EU. Greece joined the euro area in 2001 and Slovenia in 2007, while Cyprus and Malta introduced the euro in 2008 and Slovakia in 2009. It was the first time that countries of anything like this number, size, or global economic weight had gathered together on a voluntary basis to share a currency and to pool their monetary sovereignty.

With the start of EMU, participating countries no longer had their own monetary sovereignty. As of 1 January 1999, monetary policy in the euro area was delegated to the ECB. The *Governing Council of the ECB* is responsible for taking monetary policy decisions. This Council consists of the Executive Board of the ECB – made up of the president, the vice-president, and four other members – and the central-bank governors from the countries in the euro area. Box 2.4 explains the decision-making procedures of the ECB's Governing Council. Together with National Central Banks (NCBs), the ECB is part of the European System of Central Banks. While the ECB is responsible for policy decisions, NCBs play a role in implementing monetary policy. The

Box 2.4 Decision making within the ECB Governing Council

Under the Maastricht Treaty, the ECB Governing Council takes monetary policy decisions by a simple majority of the votes cast by the members who are present in person. Each member has one vote. The principle of 'one member, one vote' reflects that all the members of the Governing Council, including the governors of the NCBs, are appointed in their personal capacity and not as representatives of their Member States. At some point in time, the new EU Member States will join the euro area. Furthermore, three 'old' EU Member States that are currently not members of the euro area – the United Kingdom, Sweden (that does not meet the convergence criteria), and Denmark – could decide to adopt the euro. So membership in the Eurosystem might increase to 27. The size of the ECB Governing Council could therefore increase to 33, making it by far the largest monetary policy-making institution among OECD countries. Due to this increase in membership, discussion and voting procedures would likely become more time-consuming and complicated.

The Treaty of Nice therefore called for a revision of the decision-making procedures for the ECB. It contained a so-called enabling clause which, in essence, enabled the Council to amend Article 10.2 of the ECB Statute on a recommendation from either the ECB or the Commission. In December 2002, the Governing Council of the ECB adopted a proposal for reform of the ECB after enlargement of the monetary union. This proposal was adopted by the Council. Under the new rules, there is a limit of 15 NCB governors exercising a voting right, although all members of the Governing Council (with and without voting rights) may participate in the policy meetings.

If the euro area increases to more than 15 countries, there will be two groups with rotating voting rights. The first group will consist of the 5 governors of the Member States that occupy the highest positions in the country rankings on the basis of a so-called composite indicator of 'representativeness'. They share 4 voting rights. The second group will consist of all other governors, who will share 11 voting rights. The principal component of the 'representativeness' indicator will be the Member State's GDP. The second component will be the total assets of the aggregated balance sheet of monetary financial institutions (TABS-MFI) within the territory of the Member State concerned. The relative weights of the two components are 5/6 for GDP and 1/6 for TABS-MFI.

Once there are 22 euro-area members, there will be three groups with rotation. The allocation of central banks to the groups will be based on a ranking according to the composite indicator. The rotation scheme is as follows. The first group, which will have 4 votes, will be composed of the 5 central bank governors from the euro-area Member States which occupy the highest positions (the 'big five'). The second group, with 8 voting rights, will consist of half of all national central bank governors selected from the subsequent positions in the ranking. The third group will be composed of the remaining governors. They will share 3 voting rights.

The new decision-making rules have met considerable criticism from academic observers (see De Haan *et al.*, 2005 for a discussion). Apart from critique on the size of the Governing Council, Gros (2003) argues that the new rules give up 'the principle of equality of Member States, thus potentially undermining the idea that all members of Governing Council should forget the particular interests of their home country and act only in the interest of the entire euro area'. Gros also argues that the rules are not transparent because they are too complicated. Furthermore, there are arbitrary elements: the weight given to the indicator of the size of financial markets (1/6) is not motivated in any way and seems designed to ensure a better position of one country (Luxembourg). According to Gros, Luxembourg will have a larger weight than Finland (a country with about 10 times the population and 6 times the GDP of Luxembourg). The third group with the lowest voting power would consist exclusively of new Member States.

central banks of the EU Member States that do not participate in the euro area are members of the ESCB but they do not take part in the decision making on the single monetary policy for the euro area and the implementation of such decisions.

The ECB's primary objective as laid down in the Maastricht Treaty is price stability. The ECB has announced its interpretation of price stability (maintaining inflation in the euro area below but close to 2 per cent in the medium term) and has developed a monetary-policy strategy to accomplish this objective (see De Haan *et al.*, 2005 for further details). Although the primary objective is to maintain price stability, there are explicit references in the Treaty to financial regulation and supervision. For instance, the Treaty states that the ESCB has to promote the smooth operations of payment systems. According to Article 105 (5), the ESCB shall contribute to the smooth conduct of policies pursued by the competent authorities relating to the prudential supervision of credit institutions and the stability of the financial system. Similarly, Article 105 (6) of the Treaty states that the Council may confer upon the ECB specific tasks concerning policies relating to the prudential supervision of credit institutions and other financial institutions with the exception of insurance undertakings. However, the Treaty is explicit on the principle of decentralisation and allocation of regulatory and supervisory powers to national central banks. Only in very special circumstances, and with unanimity in the European Council, will the ECB be allowed to regulate and supervise financial institutions.

2.4 Financial integration

The Treaty of Rome of 1957 identified the 'creation of a unified economic area with a common market' as a task of the Community. As for the creation of a single market for financial services, policy primarily focused on the banking system in the first decades. The first step towards harmonisation of prudential standards for supervision of banks was set with the First Banking Directive (77/780/EEC). This directive required full harmonisation of relevant banking standards, such as solvency, liquidity, and internal controls. But the national approaches to basic prudential standards, including capital requirements, continued to diverge. Major subsequent steps were taken under the Internal Market Programme and the Financial Services Action Plan.

The Internal Market

As pointed out in section 2.1, in the second half of the 1980s completion of the internal market was high on the agenda of European policymakers. In the context of banking, the European Commission called for a single banking licence and home-country control. Accordingly, the Second Banking Directive (89/646/EEC) determines that a credit institution that is authorised in any EU Member State is allowed to establish branches or supply cross-border financial services in the other EU Member States. Such a *single banking licence* is necessary and sufficient for cross-border provision of banking services and the establishment of branches in other Member States. The single banking licence has therefore significantly contributed to stimulating cross-border banking in Europe. However, the main limitation of the Second Banking Directive is that the single licence does not extend to subsidiaries in host Member States. This is unfortunate, as the process of cross-border European banking more often takes place via subsidiaries, especially when the cross-border operations involve major banking operations (see chapter 7).

Importantly, the Second Banking Directive also introduced the principle of *home-country control* in supervision of branches with few limited exceptions, notably the supervision of branch liquidity. The authorities in the home country are responsible for supervision on solvency that extends to the bank itself, its foreign and national subsidiaries, which have to be consolidated for supervisory purposes, and its foreign branches. The authorities in the host state retain the right to regulate a foreign bank's activities in that state only to the extent that such regulation is necessary for the protection of 'public interest'. Also in emergency situations, the host-country supervisor may take precautionary measures necessary to protect depositors, investors, and others to whom services are provided (Dermine, 2006).

The European legal framework incorporates the international banking standards of the Basel Committee on Banking Supervision (see Box 2.5). An important element in banking supervision are the so-called *capital adequacy requirements*, i.e., regulations on the minimum amount of capital that banks have to provide for. The Solvency and Own Funds Directives (89/647/EEC and 89/299/EEC) that laid down the solvency rules for banks were based on the 1988 Basel Capital Accord (see Box 2.5).

An important principle underlying European financial integration is *minimum harmonisation*. Instead of fully harmonising rules, a common minimum is defined that Member States have to implement. However, they are free to

---

Box 2.5 Basel Committee on Banking Supervision

The Basel Committee on Banking Supervision provides a forum for regular cooperation on banking supervisory matters. Its objective is to enhance understanding of key supervisory issues and improve the quality of banking supervision worldwide. It seeks to do so by exchanging information on national supervisory issues, approaches, and techniques, with a view to promoting common understanding. At times, the Committee develops guidelines and supervisory standards in areas where they are considered desirable. Examples include Standards on Capital Adequacy (Basel I and Basel II; see below), the Core Principles for Effective Banking Supervision, and the Concordat on cross-border banking supervision.

The Committee's members come from Belgium, Canada, France, Germany, Italy, Japan, Luxembourg, the Netherlands, Spain, Sweden, Switzerland, the United Kingdom, and the United States. Countries are represented by their central bank and also by the authority with formal responsibility for the prudential supervision of banking business where this is not the central bank. At the time of writing the Chairman of the Committee is Nout Wellink, President of the Netherlands Bank. The Committee's Secretariat is located at the Bank for International Settlements in Basel, Switzerland.

One of the issues that the committee frequently discusses is minimum capital requirements for banks. In 2004, an agreement was reached, generally referred to as the *Basel II Accord*. It uses a three-pillars concept: (1) minimum capital requirements, (2) supervisory review, and (3) market discipline. Its predecessor, the Basel I accord of 1988, dealt with only parts of each of these pillars. Basel II seeks to improve on the existing rules by aligning regulatory capital requirements more closely to the underlying risks that banks face (see chapter 10 for an in-depth discussion of the Basel II framework).

move beyond this minimum. A good example of this approach is the Directive on Deposit Guarantee Schemes (94/19/EEC) that was accepted by the Council in 1994. This directive provides for mandatory coverage per depositor with a minimum of €20,000. The directive does not deal with funding, so that the financing has to be arranged at the national level (e.g., ex-ante or ex-post funding). Deposits of a branch are covered by the deposit-insurance system of the home country. All EU countries have now adopted an explicit deposit-insurance scheme with compulsory participation, but the minimum coverage limit currently falls short in some of the new EU Member States that are under transitional arrangements following their recent accession. However, practical arrangements with respect to coverage limits, funding, and coinsurance differ substantially across EU Member States. While the coverage limit in some of the new Member States is below the EU minimum, the UK deposit insurance scheme covers up to £35,000 and Italy has the highest coverage limit, at €103,000 (Wajid *et al.*, 2007).

So far, this section has discussed banking integration under the internal market programme. Similar developments have taken place in the fields of insurance and securities. The Third Insurance Directives (92/49/EEC and 92/96/EEC) and the Investment Services Directive (93/22/EEC) also adopted the principles of a single licence, home-country control, and minimum harmonisation of standards.

Another important milestone for European financial integration was the Directive on Liberalisation of Capital Flows (88/361/EEC). Starting from 1 July 1990 – i.e., the start of the first phase of EMU – capital controls were, as a rule, no longer allowed. Only in the case of large, speculative movements could the European Commission authorise capital controls.

The Financial Services Action Plan

The European Council of Cardiff in 1998 underlined the importance of financial market integration as a political priority. In reaction, the European Commission published a Communication entitled 'Financial Services: Building a Framework for Action' which set out a series of measures to strengthen integration. This document recognised the crucial role of financial services in the EU's economy, and aimed to complement the introduction of the euro by creating the right conditions for the financial sector to strengthen integration. The overall objective was to create deeper and more liquid capital markets and remove remaining barriers to cross-border provision of financial services. Financial integration was not perceived as a goal in itself but rather as

The Financial Services Action Plan has four objectives:

- single EU wholesale market
- open and secure retail markets
- state-of-the-art prudential rules and supervision
- optimal single financial market

Figure 2.2   Objectives of FSAP

a means to deliver economic growth. The Communication was discussed at the European Council meeting in 1998 in Vienna, whereupon the Council called for a 'concrete and urgent working programme'. This resulted in May 1999 in the launch of the *Financial Services Action Plan* by the European Commission. The purpose of the FSAP, endorsed by the European Council in March 2000, is to remove regulatory and market barriers that limit the cross-border provision of financial services and the free flow of capital within the EU, and to create a level playing field among market participants. It consists of a set of 42 measures to fill gaps and remove remaining barriers to provide a legal and regulatory environment that supports the integration of financial markets across the EU.

The FSAP has four objectives (see Figure 2.2). The first objective is a single EU wholesale market. The Markets in Financial Instruments Directive (MiFID, 2004/39/EC) is, to a large extent, the cornerstone of the FSAP. This directive provides securities firms with an updated EU passport, allowing them to offer a range of financial services across Member States on a 'home-country control' basis (Haas, 2005). Under the passport principle, a firm licensed to provide financial services in its home country has the right to provide these same services throughout the EU, without the need for an additional licence. MiFID applies the passport to a broader range of financial instruments and significantly extends the list of financial services that can be 'passported' across European countries. A major innovation is the introduction of new trading venues. While the Investment Services Directives (ISD) restricted securities trading to regulated markets (i.e., stock exchanges), MiFID also allows trading on multilateral trading facilities (MTFs), i.e., systems that bring together multiple parties (e.g., retail investors or other investment firms) that are interested in buying and selling financial instruments and enable them to do so. MiFID also facilitates in-house matching (i.e., matching a buyer and a seller within the same firm). Under certain conditions regarding pre-trade transparency and best execution, banks are allowed to 'match' customer trades internally. MTFs and in-house matching are expected to be major competitors of the more traditional exchanges.

The objective of MiFID is to foster the emergence of a single, more competitive, cross-border securities market across the EU. The directive promotes, and often prescribes through detailed rules, European-wide legislative harmonisation for key components of the provision of financial services along the following central principles (Haas, 2007): increased competition, a level playing field, increased market efficiency, and better investor protection.

The second objective of the FSAP is open and secure retail markets. The Commission acknowledged that certain barriers prevented consumers and suppliers from reaping the single-market benefits of increased choice and competitive terms. In order to develop open and secure markets for retail financial services the Commission therefore aimed to:

- promote enhanced information, transparency and security for cross-border provision of retail financial services;
- expedite speedy resolution of consumer disputes through effective extrajudicial procedures; and
- balance application of local consumer-protection rules.

Examples of FSAP-Directives in the domain of retail financial services include the Distance Selling Directive and the Insurance Mediation Directive (see the Appendix to this chapter).

The third objective of the FSAP is state-of-the-art prudential rules and supervision. The Capital Requirements Directive (CRD), comprising Directive 2006/48/EC and Directive 2006/49/EC, lay down these new capital-adequacy rules for banks and is based on the 2004 Basel II Capital Accord (see Box 2.5). Under these directives investment firms and credit institutions are allowed to use internal models for risk management to calculate their capital requirement.

Capital-requirements rules stipulate the minimum amounts of own financial resources that credit institutions and investment firms must have in order to cover the risks to which they are exposed. The aim is to ensure the financial soundness of these institutions – in particular to ensure that they can weather difficult periods, thereby protecting depositors and clients, and fostering the stability of the financial system. Under the CRD, capital requirements will be more comprehensive than in the past. In particular they will cover the so-called 'operational risk', which is the risk of loss from inadequate or failed internal processes, people, or systems, or from external events. The CRD introduces capital requirements to ensure that institutions are resilient to such risks.

The final objective of the FSAP is related to wider conditions for an optimal single financial market, e.g. addressing disparities in tax treatment and creating an efficient and transparent legal system for corporate governance.

In 2004, the European Commission concluded that the Financial Services Action Plan was delivered on time, with 40 out of 42 measures being adopted before the 2005 deadline (see the Appendix for various examples). These include a directive on the reorganisation and winding up of credit institutions, a regulation on the application of international accounting standards, a directive on European Company Statute, and a directive on the taxation of savings income in the form of interest payments.

In December 2005, the European Commission published a White Paper on financial services policy over the period 2005–2010, which focuses on implementing existing rules and enforcing co-operation rather than proposing new laws. The focus of the White Paper is on:

- consolidation of existing legislation, with few new initiatives;
- ensuring the effective transposition of European rules into national regulation and more rigorous enforcement by supervisory authorities;
- continuous ex-post evaluation whereby the Commission will monitor carefully the application of these rules in practice and their impact on the European financial sector.

The European Commission has indicated again and again that the new strategy has a strong focus on delivering the benefits of European integration and on getting things done correctly. Instead of proposing new legislative measures there is a strong focus on market-led initiatives. There are nevertheless a number of targeted areas where the Commission will propose new initiatives. For example, in order to complete unfinished business, the Commission in 2007 proposed new capital and supervisory rules for insurers and re-insurers, also known as 'Solvency II' (see the Appendix). Moreover, while significant progress has been achieved to integrate wholesale markets, financial services offered to consumers remain deeply fragmented. That is why the Commission has announced new initiatives to improve competitiveness of retail financial services and increase consumers' access to them. Among other things, the Commission proposed initiatives in the domain of mortgages, bank account mobility, product tying, and consumer education.

Finally, the European Central Bank and the European Commission aim to achieve a Single Euro Payment Area (SEPA) by 2010. The vision for the SEPA is that all euro-area payments should become domestic and reach a level of safety and efficiency at least on a par with the best-performing national payment system. The Commission has contributed to SEPA by providing a

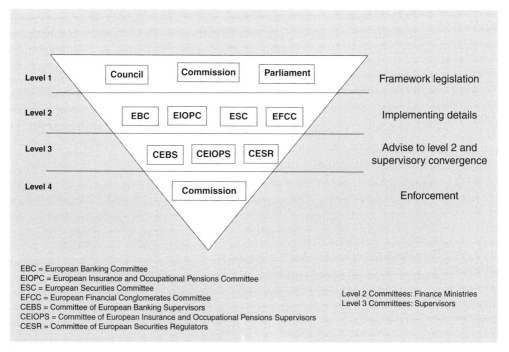

Figure 2.3   The Lamfalussy structure of supervisory committees in the EU

coherent legal framework for cross-border payments by means of the Payment Services Directive (PSD) (see chapter 5).

Lamfalussy process

Under the FSAP a new approach was introduced – the so-called *Lamfalussy framework* – for the development and adoption of EU financial services legislation. Its objective is to speed up the legislative process, deliver more uniform and better technical regulation, and facilitate supervisory convergence. The Lamfalussy framework was proposed in 2001 by the Committee of Wise Men on the Regulation of European Securities Markets, chaired by Alexandre Lamfalussy. The European Council endorsed the approach at its 2001 Stockholm Summit. The Lamfalussy approach was originally applied to the securities markets only, but it was extended to the banking and insurance sectors in 2005.

Under the Lamfalussy framework, financial regulation is passed at two levels (see Figure 2.3). At level 1, the basic principles and implementing powers are laid down in directives and regulations co-decided by the Council and the European Parliament on the basis of Commission proposals.

At level 2, implementing measures (containing technical details) for level 1 legislation are adopted. They are to ensure that the EU regulatory framework keeps up with market developments. This is done by the European Commission, after the vote of a relevant committee (the level 2 committees). At level 3, the committees consisting of the representatives of national supervisory authorities (the level 3 committees) advise the Commission on level 2 measures. Another aim of the supervisory committees is to contribute to consistent and convergent implementation of EU directives by securing more effective co-operation between national supervisors and the convergence of supervisory practices. To date, the level 3 committees have put major efforts into performing their tasks concerning supervisory convergence. Finally, at level 4 the European Commission enforces the timely and correct transposition of EU legislation into national law.

2.5 Conclusions

The EU has its origins in the European Coal and Steel Community, formed by six European countries in 1951. Since then, the EU has grown in size through the accession of new Member States, while it has also increased its powers by the addition of new policy areas to its remit. At the time of writing, the European Union consists of 27 Member States and has supranational and intergovernmental forms of co-operation.

Legislation has been the main mechanism for fostering economic integration. Treaties are the milestones in the integration process. An example is the Maastricht Treaty establishing the European Central Bank. Within the broader framework of these treaties, legislative measures are proposed by the European Commission and adopted by the Council and the European Parliament. These legislative measures include regulations, which apply directly in each Member State, and directives, which need to be incorporated in the national law of each Member State. While regulations ensure a uniform regulatory framework throughout the EU, the implementation of directives by Member States leaves scope for differences.

Monetary integration is characterised by two major steps. In 1979, the European Monetary System was introduced. A key element of the EMS was the Exchange Rate Mechanism, within which the currencies of participating countries were supposed to fluctuate within a band of plus and minus 2.25 per cent. In the early 1990s, the EMS was strained by the differing economic policies and conditions of its members and the band of fluctuation was subsequently widened to plus and minus 15 per cent. In 1999, the European Central Bank took over responsibility for monetary policy making and a common currency, the euro, was introduced in 11 of the 15 EU Member States.

Financial integration is a more gradual process. In 1992, the EU created an internal market by a system of laws which apply in all Member States, guaranteeing the freedom of movement of people, goods, services, and capital. In the area of financial services, the internal market introduced a single licence and home-country control for financial institutions. With a licence from the home country, financial institutions can expand throughout the EU. To strengthen financial integration further, the Commission launched the Financial Services Action Plan in 1999 with the purpose of removing any remaining barriers that limit the cross-border provision of financial services. The FSAP measures are complemented by a system of supervisory committees to enhance convergence of supervisory standards and practices across the EU. Financial supervision is the responsibility of national supervisory agencies. It is important not only to have common rules but also to apply these rules in a similar way to achieve financial integration. Only then can a level playing field between countries be achieved.

Appendix: Examples of FSAP in action

Objective: a single EU wholesale market

European Company Statute (2157/2001/EC)

The European Company Statute aims to provide for the formation of a type of company ('Societas Europaea' or 'SE') that can operate on an EU-wide basis and be governed by a single law directly applicable in all Member States. This new form of company is available to commercial bodies with operations in more than one Member State; its use will be entirely voluntary. The corporate form that emerged from the Statute is an EU public limited-liability company, registered in one Member State, with capital divided into shares and having legal personality.

International Accounting Standards (1606/2002/EC)

International Accounting Standards (IAS) – now referred to as International Financial Reporting Standards (IFRS) – aim to provide a single set of high-quality and comparable global accounting standards. The standards are issued by the International Accounting Standards Board (IASB), which co-operates with national accounting standard setters to achieve convergence in accounting standards around the world. Although the IASB has no formal authority to require compliance with its standards, EU Member States agreed in July 2002 that all publicly traded companies in the EU must prepare their consolidated accounts on the basis of IFRS, as adopted for use in the EU.

Market Abuse Directive (2003/6/EC)

This directive aims to ensure the integrity of financial markets in the EU, to establish and implement common standards against market abuse throughout the EU, and to enhance investor confidence in these markets. It introduces a comprehensive EU-wide market-abuse regime, harmonising rules on the prevention of insider dealing and market manipulation in securities markets. The directive defines a common, EU-wide approach to areas such as the standards of care to be observed and the disclosures to be made by those producing and disseminating research; safe-harbour provisions concerning share buy-backs and stabilisation; guidelines for determining accepted market practices; insider information on commodity derivative markets; the maintenance of lists of those who have access to inside information by issuers; and the obligation for persons arranging transactions professionally to report suspicious transactions.

Prospectus Directive (2003/71/EC)

This directive aims to enable corporate issuers to raise finance on competitive terms on an EU-wide basis and to provide investors and intermediaries with access to all markets from a single point of entry. It sets out the initial information and disclosure obligations for issues of securities that are offered to the public or are admitted to trading on a regulated market in the EU.

Market in Financial Instruments Directive (2004/39/EC)

This directive replaces the Investment Services Directive (93/22/EEC), regulating the authorisation, behaviour, and conduct of business of securities firms and markets. The directive aims to provide for an integrated securities market in the EU and for the effective cross-border provision of investment services, whilst enhancing the protection of investors and market integrity.

Objective: open and secure retail markets

Distance Marketing Directive (2002/65/EC)

This directive aims to protect retail customers who deal with a financial services firm or acquire a financial product through the exclusive use of distance means such as telephone, Internet, fax or post. It ensures that retail customers are given minimum specified information about financial services or products before contracting and have the right to cancel some types of contracts after entering into them.

Insurance Mediation Directive (2002/92/EC)

This directive aims to improve choice and reinforce protection for customers whilst helping insurance intermediaries (like insurance brokers and banks) to market their services cross-border in the EU. The directive sets common minimum standards across the EU for the regulation of the sale and administration of insurance. It provides rights for an insurance intermediary established in one Member State to operate in another Member State.

Unfair Commercial Practices Directive (2005/29/EC)

This directive aims to clarify consumers' rights and to simplify cross-border trade. Common rules and principles will give consumers the same protection against unfair practices and rogue traders whether they are buying from their corner shop or purchasing from a website based abroad. It also means that businesses will be able to advertise and market to all 480 million consumers in the EU, in the same way as to their domestic customers. The aim is thus to boost consumer confidence and give business a uniform and transparent EU-wide set of rules.

Objective: state-of-the-art prudential rules and supervision

Conglomerates Directive (2002/87/EC)

This directive aims to introduce an enhanced prudential regime for the supervision of financial conglomerates, which are groups with significant activities in the banking and/or investment sectors on the one hand, and the insurance sector on the other. It does this by setting out how to calculate capital-adequacy requirements for financial conglomerates to eliminate double-counting capital and excessive leveraging; requiring that financial conglomerates have enough capital to meet a binding capital-adequacy test; and requiring groups to have adequate systems and controls to monitor intra-group exposures and risk concentrations across sectors.

Occupational Pension Funds Directive (2003/41/EC)

This directive aims to allow occupational pension funds to operate on an EU-wide basis. It provides a common framework across the EU for pension schemes, relating to funding, regulation, and information to members, and allows institutions for occupational retirement provision established in one Member State to be sponsored by employers in other Member States.

Capital Requirements Directive (2006/48/EC and 2006/49/EC)

This directive updates the existing capital adequacy rules for banks and investment firms. It provides a better alignment of regulatory capital to risk and creates incentives for better risk management. The directive adopts a three-pillar approach.

Proposal for Solvency II Directive (COM/2007/361)

This draft directive – which was proposed after the FSAP to complete unfinished business – introduces more sophisticated solvency requirements for insurers, in order to guarantee that they have sufficient capital to withstand adverse events, such as floods, storms, or big car accidents. This will help to increase their financial soundness. Currently, EU solvency requirements cover insurance risks only, whereas in the future insurers would be required to hold capital against market risk, credit risk, and operational risk as well. The Solvency II proposal draws on the experiences from banking and follows the three-pillar approach of the Capital Requirements Directive.

Objective: wider conditions for an optimal single financial market

Savings Directive (2003/48/EC)

This directive aims to enable interest on savings received in one Member State, by individuals who are resident for tax purposes in another Member State, to be made subject to effective taxation in accordance with the laws of the latter Member State. It establishes automatic exchange of information as the way of combating cross-border tax evasion on savings income.

Sources: HM Treasury (2004) and European Commission

NOTES

1. The three communities were merged in 1967. Since then, one often referred to the European Communities, later to be changed in European Community. Since the Maastricht Treaty one generally refers to the European Union.
2. Sometimes a Commissioner is responsible for more than one DG.

3. So EMU does not mean European Monetary Union. Unfortunately, this is how the abbreviation is often explained, sometimes also in academic publications.
4. After Denmark attained a similar position to the UK, the Danes voted again about the Treaty in a second referendum in 1993, in which 57 per cent of the voters favoured ratification.

SUGGESTED READING

Decressin, J., H. Faruqee, and W. Fonteyne (eds.) (2007), *Integrating Europe's Financial Markets*, IMF, Washington DC.

De Haan, J., S.C.W. Eijffinger, and S. Waller (2005), *The European Central Bank: Centralization, Transparency and Credibility*, MIT Press, Cambridge (MA).

Dermine, J. (2006), European Banking Integration: Don't Put the Cart before the Horse, *Financial Markets, Institutions & Instruments*, 15 (2), 57–106.

REFERENCES

Cecchini, P. (1988), *The European Challenge, 1992*, The Benefits of a Single Market, Gower, Aldershot.

Craig, P. and G. De Burca (2007), *EU Law: Text, Cases, and Materials*, 4th edition, Oxford University Press, Oxford.

De Haan, J., S.C.W. Eijffinger, and S. Waller (2005), *The European Central Bank: Centralization, Transparency and Credibility*, MIT Press, Cambridge (MA).

Dermine, J. (2006), European Banking Integration: Don't Put the Cart before the Horse, *Financial Markets, Institutions & Instruments*, 15 (2), 57–106.

Emerson, M., D. Gros, A. Italianer, J. Pisani-Ferry, and H. Reichenbach (1992), *One Market, One Money*, An Evaluation of the Potential Benefits and Costs of Forming an Economic and Monetary Union, Oxford University Press, Oxford.

Gros, D. (2003), Reforming the Composition of the ECB Governing Council in View of Enlargement: How Not to Do It!, Briefing paper for the Monetary Committee of the European Parliament, February.

Haas, F. (2005), The Integration of European Financial Markets, in: *Euro Area Policies: Selected Issues*, IMF Country Report 05/266, IMF, Washington DC.

Haas, F. (2007), Current State of Play, in: Decressin, J., H. Faruqee, and W. Fonteyne (eds.), *Integrating Europe's Financial Markets*, IMF, Washington DC.

HM Treasury (2004), *The EU Financial Services Action Plan: Delivering the FSAP in the UK*, HM Treasury, London.

Wajid, S.K., A. Tieman, M. Khamis, F. Haas, D. Schoenmaker, P. Iossifov, and K. Tintchev (2007), *Financial Integration in the Nordic-Baltic Region: Challenges for Financial Policies*, IMF, Washington DC.

Part II

Financial Markets

European Financial Markets

OVERVIEW

This chapter starts off by reviewing the functions that financial markets perform. First, financial markets release information to aid the price-discovery process. Second, markets provide a platform to trade. The main trading mechanisms, i.e., quote-driven and order-driven markets, are discussed. Finally, markets provide an infrastructure to settle trades. The remainder of the chapter describes the main financial markets in the EU (the money market, bond markets, equity markets, and derivatives markets).

The euro money market is the market for euro-denominated short-term funds and related derivative instruments. It consists of various segments, including unsecured deposit contracts with various maturities, ranging from overnight to one year, and repurchase agreements (so-called repos, i.e., reverse transactions secured by securities) also ranging from overnight to one year. Credit institutions account for the largest share of the euro money market. The ECB has a major influence on the money market via its use of various monetary policy instruments (reserve requirements, standing facilities, and open-market operations). There are three main market interest rates for the money market: EONIA (euro overnight index average), EURIBOR (euro interbank offered rate), and EUREPO (the repo market reference rate for the euro).

The bulk of euro-denominated bonds (i.e., debt securities with a maturity of more than one year) is issued by euro-area issuers. Although the share of private-sector securities (corporate bonds) in all euro-denominated debt securities outstanding has risen, securities issued by public authorities (government bonds) still form the most important market segment. The introduction of the euro in 1999 created a pan-European capital market, making government-debt managers small to medium-sized players in a larger European market, instead of being the dominant player in the national market. Although long-term interest rates have become more similar in the euro area, differentials vis-à-vis the German yield vary considerably across countries, while for each country the yield differential varies considerably over time. The issuance of so-called asset-backed securities has increased rapidly during the last decade.

The importance of equity finance in the EU is growing, although there are large differences across exchanges. The market capitalisation of Euronext and the London Stock Exchange (LSE) are much higher than those of other exchanges in the EU. Measured by trading activity, the LSE and Euronext together account for nearly 60 per cent of stock-market turnover in the EU. Despite the increase in equity finance, public equity markets play a limited role as a source of new funds for firms that raise external financing generally via bank loans or debt securities. Still, the number and value of initial public offerings (IPOs) grew spectacularly from the mid-1990s.

Finally, the chapter discusses derivatives, i.e., financial instruments whose value is derived from the value of something else. They can be based on different types of assets (such as equities or commodities), prices (such as interest rates or exchange rates), or indexes (such as a stock market index). They are traded on organised exchanges or over-the-counter (OTC). Derivatives can provide a source of income but are also important risk-management tools. The most important derivatives are futures, forwards, options, and swaps.

LEARNING OBJECTIVES

After you have studied this chapter, you should be able to:
- explain the purpose and structure of financial markets
- describe the essentials of the euro money market, including its functions and main interest rates
- explain how the monetary policy of the ECB affects the money market
- discuss the most important developments in the money market since the start of the monetary union
- discuss the most important developments in the bond markets since the start of the monetary union
- discuss the most important developments in the equity markets since the start of the monetary union
- describe the essentials of the derivatives markets.

3.1 Financial markets: functions and structure

Functions

A *financial market* is a market where individuals issue and trade securities. *Securities* are fungible, negotiable instruments representing financial value, and are broadly categorised in debt securities and equity securities. In financial markets, funds are channelled from those with a surplus, who buy securities, to those with a shortage, who issue new securities or sell existing securities (see chapter 1). A financial market can be seen as a set of arrangements that allows trading among its participants. The following functions are performed by a financial market depending on the phase of trading (Bailey, 2005):

- Price discovery: the market facilitates the dissemination of information. This enables participants who want to buy or sell to find out the prices at which trades can be agreed upon (pre-trading phase).
- Trading mechanism: the market provides a mechanism to facilitate the making of agreements. There must be a means by which those who want to sell can communicate with those who want to buy (trading phase).
- Clearing and settlement arrangements: the agreements are executed. The market must ensure that the terms of each agreement are honoured (post-trading phase).

Price discovery involves the incorporation of new information into asset prices (O'Hara, 2003). Securities represent a promise of future payments. The value of a security depends on expectations of the size and the risk of these future payments. New information can affect these expectations. In an efficient market, prices reflect all (publicly) available information.[1] Markets also provide liquidity. Market liquidity refers to the matching of buyers and sellers (O'Hara, 2003). Liquidity is intertemporal in nature as buyers and sellers may enter the market at different points in time. The trading mechanism is the means of matching those buyers to sellers. Below we discuss the main trading mechanisms in more detail. Finally, clearing and settlement arrangements include: 1) confirmation of the terms of the transactions; 2) clearing of the trades to establish the obligations of buyers and sellers; 3) settlement of the accounts to finalise the delivery of securities against payment of money. These post-trading arrangements are discussed in chapter 5.

The functions of a market are performed by its participants (Bailey, 2005). The participants in financial markets can be classified into various groups, according to their motive for trading:

1. Public investors, who ultimately own the securities and who are motivated by the returns from holding the securities. Public investors include private individuals and institutional investors, such as pension funds and mutual funds.
2. *Brokers*, who act as agents for public investors and who are motivated by the remuneration received (typically in the form of commission fees) for the services they provide. Brokers thus trade for others and not on their own account.
3. *Dealers*, who do trade on their own account but whose primary motive is to profit from trading rather than from holding securities. Typically, dealers obtain their return from the differences between the prices at which they buy and sell the security over short intervals of time.

In practice the three groups are not mutually exclusive. Some public investors may occasionally act on behalf of others; brokers may act as dealers and hold securities on their own, while dealers often hold securities in excess of the inventories needed to facilitate their trading activities. The role of these three groups differs according to the trading mechanism adopted by a financial market.

Another important group of firms active on financial markets are the credit rating agencies (CRAs) that assess the credit risk of borrowers (see Box 3.1).

Trading mechanisms

Financial markets use a trading mechanism for matching buyers to sellers. As the trading mechanism is a defining characteristic, financial markets are often classified by their trading mechanism (Harris, 2003). The two main types are quote-driven markets and order-driven markets, while hybrid markets use some combination of the two.

Quote-driven markets

In *quote-driven markets* (also known as dealer markets), dealers quote *bid* and *ask prices* at which they are prepared to buy or sell, respectively, specified amounts of the security (Bailey, 2005). Quote-driven markets require little formal organisation, but need mechanisms for publishing the dealers' price quotations and for regulating the conduct of dealers. Stock exchanges normally grant dealers (or market makers) privileged access to certain administrative procedures or market information. In return for these privileges, dealers have particular obligations, most importantly to quote 'firm' bid and

Box 3.1 Credit rating agencies

Credit rating agencies, such as Fitch, Moody's, and Standard & Poor's, assess the credit risks of borrowers (governments, financial, and non-financial firms). Their ratings are expressed on a scale of letters and figures. The Standard & Poor's rating scale is, for example, as follows: AAA (highest rating), AA, A, BBB, BB, B, CCC, CC, C, D (lowest rating). The agencies are paid by the issuers of these instruments to publish a rating. Ratings play an important role in financial markets as investors use them to evaluate the credit risks of financial instruments. The assessment of these instruments requires specific knowledge and is highly time-consuming, making it attractive for individual investors to rely on the ratings of the credit rating agencies. The ratings also have an important influence on the interest rate that borrowers have to pay. A downgrading generally leads quickly to higher interest rates on loans. It should be stressed, however, that a rating refers only to the credit risk; other risks, like market or liquidity risk, are not covered.

The financial crisis of 2007/2008 gave rise to calls for more regulation and overall improvements in the rating process. According to the Financial Stability Forum[2] (2008), poor credit assessments of complex structured credit products (such as asset-backed securities and collateralised debt obligations) by CRAs contributed to both the build-up and the unfolding of the financial crisis. CRAs assigned high ratings to complex structured sub-prime debt based on inadequate historical data and in some cases flawed models. Moreover, once the problems in the sub-prime market came to light, CRAs responded with a considerable time lag, i.e., ratings were not immediately downgraded. In response to this the FSF issued the following recommendations:

- CRAs should improve the quality of the rating process and manage conflicts of interest related to the issuer-pays model. Although the latter is an issue for the rating process in general, the Committee of European Securities Regulators (CESR, 2008) stresses that the nature of structured credit means that issuers can bring repeat business to the CRAs. This feature might drive CRAs to favour business volume instead of rigorousness and independence and hence to 'overrate' transactions in order to maintain a profitable flow of business.
- CRAs should differentiate ratings on complex structured credit products from those on 'regular' bonds as these ratings have different risk properties. Next to this, CRAs should expand the initial and ongoing information provided on risk characteristics of structured products.
- CRAs should enhance their review of the quality of the data received from issuers and of the due diligence performed on underlying assets by all parties involved.

The turbulence in financial markets showed that some investors had relied too heavily on ratings and in some cases had fully substituted ratings for independent assessments and due diligence (while ratings do not cover the full range of risks that investors face). The FSF (2008) therefore stressed that investors should address their over-reliance on ratings.

ask prices at which they guarantee to make trades of up to specified volumes. Anyone who wants to trade in a quote-driven market must trade with a dealer. Either the investors negotiate with the dealers themselves or their brokers negotiate with the dealers.

When a security is traded, the buyer pays the ask price, p_a, and the seller receives the bid price, p_b. The difference is the *bid–ask spread*: $s = p_a - p_b$ received by the dealer. The dealer typically holds an inventory of securities during the day to be able to sell (and buy) immediately. From his return (i.e., the bid–ask spread), the dealer has to cover the costs of holding his inventory (e.g., interest costs of financing the securities inventory) and the risks (e.g., prices may move while the securities are in the inventory). While bid and ask prices are published, dealers may negotiate special prices for large transactions. The spread could be broader for particularly large transactions (i.e., block trades) to cover the price risk of such block trades before the dealer can sell on (or buy) the bought (sold) securities to (from) other dealers in the market.

Order-driven markets

In *order-driven markets* (also known as auction markets), participants issue orders to buy or sell at stated prices, which can be modelled as 'double auctions'. Participants issue instructions that specific actions should be taken in response to the arrival of publicly verifiable price observations. The price is then adjusted by an 'auctioneer' until the total orders to buy equal the total orders to sell (Bailey, 2005). There are different forms of order-driven markets. In call markets, the price is determined at a limited number of specified times. In that way, orders can be collected and the auction takes place at the specified time. This type of auction is widely used for new issues of government debt (see section 3.3) and initial public offerings of equity (see section 3.4). The call-market mechanism has disappeared in secondary markets for bonds and equity and has been replaced by continuous trading systems.

In continuous auction markets, public investors send their instructions ('orders') to buy or sell to brokers. There are different sorts of order. The most well-known are the *limit order*, which specifies purchase or sale at maximum buying prices or minimum selling prices, respectively, and the *market order*, which specifies purchase or sale at the best available price. The outstanding limit-orders are generally listed in a limit-order book. The existence of a limit-order book implies automatic trade matching, though in practice some element of discretion remains (e.g., in setting the priority of orders). Order-driven markets are highly formalised as the auction rules for matching trades have to be specified in great detail to ensure an orderly and fair trading process.

Hybrid markets

Trading mechanisms are often compared with respect to transparency and liquidity (Bailey, 2005). In terms of fundamental principles, quote-driven markets and order-driven markets should result in the same market prices if all trades are made public. But in practice quote-driven markets tend to be more fragmented. Dealers quote different bid and ask prices, and deals that have been executed are not necessarily public information or may be published with some delay (to allow dealers some time to off-load large trades in the market). Thus, order-driven markets tend to be more transparent than quote-driven markets.

Liquidity does not depend only on the trading mechanism. In a call market, investors must wait until the next price fixing takes place. By contrast, they can trade immediately in continuous order-driven markets. The price, however, depends on the availability of sufficient orders (liquidity) on the other side of the market. Investors may therefore sometimes prefer the opportunity to negotiate individual agreements with dealers in quote-driven markets. Also, quote-driven markets may allow a delay of publication so that deals can be kept secret, if only for a limited time.

In practice, we observe *hybrid markets*, which combine characteristics of quote-driven and order-driven markets. Advances in IT have spurred the development of order-driven markets, in particular for equity trading. The combination of smart trading rules (software) with fast computers (hardware) allows an almost instantaneous matching of orders. Euronext, for example, applies an order-driven trading mechanism with a centralised electronic order book. Nevertheless, Euronext also enables small and medium-sized listed companies to hire a designated market maker to act as 'liquidity provider' in their stock. Similarly, the London Stock Exchange's premier electronic trading system (SETS) combines electronic order-driven trading with liquidity provision by market makers. While stock exchanges are becoming more order-driven, bond markets tend to be more quote-driven (making use of dealers). Sections 3.3 and 3.4 discuss the main bond markets and stock exchanges in more detail.

Overview of financial markets

The principal financial markets that we discuss in the remainder of the chapter are:
- the money market – this is the market for short-term funds up to one year. In particular, banks use the money market for the management of their short-term liquidity positions;

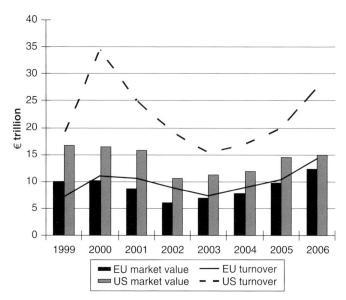

Figure 3.1   Size of the equity markets, annual turnover, and year-end market value (€ trillion), 1999–2006
Source: World Federation of Exchanges

- the bond markets – these are the most important segment of the market for debt securities with a maturity of more than one year. Governments and firms issue bonds to raise medium- and long-term debt against a fixed or flexible interest rate;
- the equity markets – firms may raise funds by issuing equity that grants the investor a residual claim on the company's income;
- the derivatives market – derivatives are financial instruments whose value is derived from the value of something else. Derivatives are important risk-management tools.

Figures 3.1 and 3.2 compare the size of the main funding markets, the equity and bond markets, in the EU and the US. These figures demonstrate the fundamental difference between the financial systems of the EU and the US (see also chapter 1). The US financial system is primarily market-based. The annual turnover on US equity markets in 2006 (€27 trillion) was twice that of EU equity markets (€14 trillion), which confirms that the US markets are deeper and more liquid than the EU markets. Nevertheless, the importance of equity finance is growing in the EU. The equity market capitalisation increased from €10 trillion in 1999 to €12 trillion in 2006.

At the time of the introduction of the euro, the EU bond market amounted to €9 trillion compared with €15 trillion in the US (see Figure 3.2). The EU

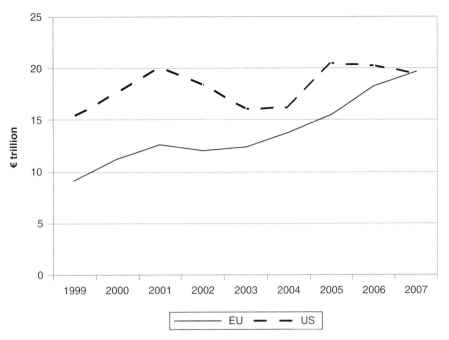

Figure 3.2   Bond markets, amounts outstanding year-end (€ trillion), 1999–2007
Source: Bank for International Settlements, Quarterly Reviews

bond market has experienced spectacular growth since then so that the EU and US bond markets have become similar in size, with the outstanding value of bonds equal to €20 trillion in 2007.

3.2 Money market

In a broad sense, the *money market* consists of the market for short-term funds, usually with maturity up to one year. The *'euro money market'* is the market for euro-denominated short-term funds and related derivative instruments (i.e., contracts, such as options and futures, whose value is derived from the value of the underlying instrument). Credit institutions (i.e., banks) account for the largest share of the euro money market. As will be explained below, these institutions rely on the euro money market for the management of their short-term liquidity positions and for the fulfilment of their minimum reserve requirements. Other important market participants are money-market funds, other financial intermediaries (such as investment funds other than money-market funds), insurance companies and pension funds, as well as large non-financial corporations (ECB, 2008a).

The most important money-market segments are the unsecured deposit markets (with various maturities, ranging from overnight to one year) and the secured repo markets (often called repos) with maturities also ranging from overnight to one year.[3] A *repurchase agreement* is an arrangement whereby an asset is sold while the seller simultaneously obtains the right and obligation to repurchase it at a specific price on a future date or on demand. Such an agreement is similar to collateralised borrowing of cash (ECB, 2008b). The most important difference between the secured and the unsecured segments is the amount of risk involved. When providing unsecured interbank deposits, a bank transfers funds to another bank for a specified period of time during which it assumes full counterparty credit risk. In the secured repo markets, this counterparty credit risk is mitigated as the bank that provides liquidity receives collateral (e.g., bonds) in return. In the event of a credit default, the liquidity-providing bank can utilise the collateral received to satisfy its claim against the defaulting bank. Because of this lower credit risk, secured repo rates are usually somewhat lower than unsecured deposit rates (ECB, 2008a).

Apart from transactions with the central bank, money-market participants trade with each other to take positions in relation to their short-term interest rate expectations, to finance their securities trading portfolios (bonds, shares, etc.), to hedge their more long-term positions with more short-term contracts, and to square individual liquidity imbalances (Hartmann *et al.*, 2001).

As the euro money market is strongly influenced by monetary policy, some details of the policy instruments of the ECB will first be outlined.

Monetary policy instruments

In addition to decisions concerning interest rates (see below), the ECB influences the euro money market through three monetary policy instruments:
- reserve requirements
- open-market operations
- standing facilities.

The ECB requires credit institutions to hold *required reserves*. All credit institutions established in the euro area have to keep 2 per cent of the total amount of overnight deposits, other deposits with maturity below two years, debt securities with maturity below two years, and money-market paper (excluding interbank liabilities) at reserve accounts with their national central banks. Reserve requirements have to be fulfilled on average over a one-month maintenance period (averaging).

The minimum-reserve system helps to stabilise money-market interest rates by the *averaging provision*, i.e., credit institutions' compliance with reserve requirements is judged on the basis of the average of the daily balances on their reserve accounts over a reserve maintenance period. As a consequence, credit institutions can smooth out daily liquidity fluctuations since transitory reserve imbalances can be offset by opposite reserve imbalances within the same maintenance period. The averaging provision also implies that if institutions believe that money-market rates are currently higher than in the remainder of the maintenance period, they can profit from lending in the market and run a reserve deficit. If they believe that money-market rates will go up, they can borrow in the market and run a reserve surplus. This mechanism stabilises the overnight interest rate during the maintenance period.

Open-market operations are the general instruments used to manage the liquidity situation and to steer interest rates. The *main refinancing operations* (MROs) are the most important instrument. These operations are conducted in the form of weekly tenders for repurchase agreements with a maturity of two weeks.[4] In this tender procedure, the ECB determines the overall quantity to be allotted on the basis of its assessment of the liquidity needed by the banking system. The rate applied in the MROs is set by the ECB's Governing Council (see chapter 2 for details on the governance structure of the ECB).

The *standing facilities* provide or absorb liquidity with an overnight maturity when unforeseen liquidity shocks occur. Therefore they provide a type of insurance mechanism for banks, but at penalty interest rates. The initiative in these transactions is on the side of the credit institution. The marginal lending facility can be used to obtain (against eligible collateral) overnight liquidity in case of an individual shortage, whereas the deposit facility may be used to make deposits in case of individual excess liquidity. As access to the standing facilities on a given day is not subject to rationing (provided adequate collateral is posted in the case of recourse to the marginal lending facility), the corresponding interest rates effectively bound the overnight-market interest rate, creating a 'corridor' (Hartmann *et al.*, 2001).

Interest rates

The key ECB interest rate is the minimum bid rate, which represents the floor for the price of central bank liquidity in the open-market operations. The two other key interest rates, on the marginal lending facility and the deposit facility, define the corridor within which the overnight interest rate can fluctuate. The Governing Council of the ECB sets the level of the minimum

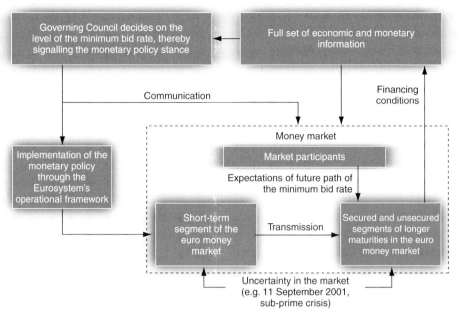

Figure 3.3   Monetary policy and the money market: a schematic view
Source: ECB (2008a)

bid rate in the Eurosystem's weekly MROs. In the MROs, the ECB aims to supply the liquidity necessary for the banking system to operate smoothly, in such a way that very short-term market interest rates (see below) remain appropriately aligned with the monetary policy stance of the ECB. Through the money-market yield curve, monetary policy is transmitted to financial instruments and credit conditions more generally, which in turn will influence saving and investment decisions and thus, in the end, affect price develop-ments in the euro area.

Sometimes, the money market is affected by turmoil in the financial markets, like that triggered in the second half of 2007 by the sub-prime crisis in the US. Under such circumstances, the ECB may need to provide additional liquidity in order to support market confidence (ECB, 2008a). Figure 3.3 summarises how the ECB affects the money market.

Apart from the ECB interest rates, there are three main market interest rates for the money market:

● EONIA (euro overnight index average). The *EONIA* is the effective over-night reference rate for the euro. It is computed daily as a volume-weighted average of unsecured euro overnight lending transactions in the interbank market, as reported by a representative panel of large banks.[5]

- EURIBOR (euro interbank offered rate). The *EURIBOR* is the benchmark rate of the large unsecured euro money market for maturities longer than overnight (one week to one year) that has emerged since 1999. It is based on information provided by the same panel of banks.
- EUREPO (the repo market reference rate for the euro) for different maturities. The *EUREPO* is the benchmark rate of the euro repo market and has been released since March 2002. It is the rate at which one prime bank offers funds in euros to another prime bank when the funds are secured by a repo transaction using general collateral (ECB, 2006).

Figure 3.4 shows the evolution of key ECB interest rates and short-term market interest rates since 10 March 2004. On most days, EONIA was slightly above, but very close to, the minimum bid rate. The small spread (about 6 to 7 basis points) reflects that the EONIA is an unsecured interbank rate and thus includes a small premium for credit risk and transaction costs. Larger spreads normally occur at the end of the reserve maintenance period when the need to fulfil the reserve requirement becomes more binding. Since October 2004 the ECB has more frequently conducted fine-tuning operations at the end of maintenance periods and this has reduced the size of spikes in the EONIA spread (ECB, 2008a).

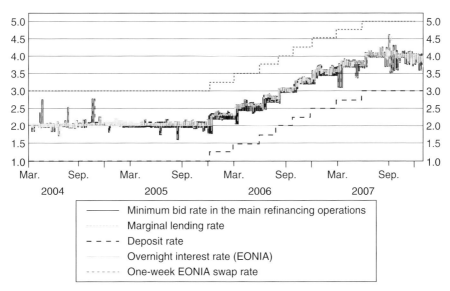

Figure 3.4   Key ECB interest rates and the shortest segment of money-market rates (%), 2004–2007
Source: ECB (2008a)

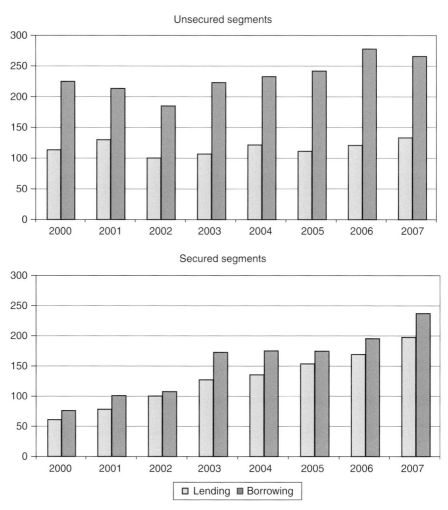

Figure 3.5   Average daily turnover in the money market (2002 Q2 = 100), 2000–2007
Source: ECB (2007d)

Developments in money-market segments

On the basis of data gathered via a survey among banks, the ECB (2007b, 2007d) provides detailed information about the euro money market. Unfortunately, these studies do not provide information on the size of the various segments of the market. Figure 3.5 shows the development of an index of daily turnover (turnover in the second quarter of 2002 is 100). The upper part of the figure refers to the unsecured segments, while the lower part shows the secured segments.

Apart from the ECB survey, another important source for information on the repos segment of the euro money market is the semi-annual survey by the European Repo Council (ERC). The total value of repo contracts outstanding on the books of the 74 institutions that participated in the survey was €6,430 billion in December 2006, compared with €5,883 billion in December 2005 (ICMA, 2007).

A breakdown by maturity shows that turnover is concentrated in short maturities. In the second quarter of 2006, overnight transactions accounted for 13 per cent of the overall secured market turnover, while transactions in the maturity band 'tomorrow/next (i.e., overnight contracts for the following day until the next day) to one month' amounted to 77 per cent, and maturities over one month to 10 per cent (ECB, 2007b).

As to concentration, in the second quarter of 2006 the largest five banks accounted for 37 per cent of the total turnover. Counterparty analysis on a geographical basis for secured activities shows that 29 per cent of counterparties were domestic, while 51 per cent of all deals were performed between counterparties from two different euro-area countries. The share of transactions in the secured market conducted via electronic trading platforms continued to be the highest among all market segments surveyed: 49 per cent was executed via electronic platforms, 26 per cent via a broker, and 25 per cent directly.

3.3 Bond markets

The re-denomination of debt from former national currencies into euros at the beginning of the monetary union paved the way for a European debt securities market. The increased role of the euro as an international investment currency has made the market in euro-denominated issues attractive for both investors and issuers. The bulk of euro-denominated debt securities is issued by euro-area issuers. However, for issuers outside the euro area it has also become attractive to borrow in euros. In the third quarter of 1999, 21 per cent of all foreign currency-denominated bonds was denominated in euros, while this figure stood at 31 per cent in the third quarter of 2006. The euro now accounts for about 27 per cent of all debt securities, the US dollar for roughly 43 per cent, and the yen for 14 per cent (ECB, 2007c).

The share of private-sector securities in all euro-denominated debt securities outstanding rose from 43 per cent in 1999 to 53 per cent in 2006 (ECB, 2007c). However, as Table 3.1 shows, debt securities issued by public

Table 3.1 Euro-denominated debt securities issued by euro area issuers (outstanding in € billion), 1999–2006

	Q1 1999	Q4 2000	Q4 2002	Q4 2004	Q4 2006	Increase (%)
Public issuers	3,283	3,436	3,835	4,274	4,596	40
MFIs	2,085	2,424	2,677	3,123	3,668	76
Non-MFI financial institutions	146	266	465	667	1,035	609
Non-financial corporations	286	373	473	518	561	96
Total	5,800	6,499	7,452	8,582	9,859	70

Source: ECB (2007c)

authorities still form the most important market segment, followed by debt securities issued by financial institutions (consisting of *monetary financial institutions* (MFIs) and non-MFI financial institutions), and those issued by non-financial corporations. Monetary financial institutions include all financial institutions whose business is (1) to receive deposits and/or close substitutes for deposits from entities other than MFIs and (2) to grant for their own account credit and/or invest in securities. *Non-MFI financial institutions* comprise insurance corporations, pension funds, and other financial institutions as, for example, financial vehicles set up for securitisation purposes (special-purpose vehicles, see section 3.5), investment funds and financing arms of non-financial corporations like industrial corporations, as well as financing arms of MFIs (ECB, 2007c).

Bonds are the main instrument of governments (mainly central governments, but also regional and local government authorities, and social securities funds) within the euro area to finance their budget deficits. Furthermore, government bonds often serve as a benchmark for pricing other assets and they are also frequently used as collateral in various financial transactions.

The non-government bond market is dominated by bank debt securities. This segment encompasses numerous different types of bonds, including unsecured bank debt securities and covered bonds. *Covered bonds* are claims of the bond holders against the issuing MFI that are secured by a pool of cover assets on the MFI's balance sheet, such as mortgage loans or loans to the public sector.

Around 90 per cent of euro debt securities, including securities issued by euro-area issuers and by non-euro area issuers, are at least A-rated (see Figure 3.6). The main reason is the high share of bonds issued by governmental issuers (all national euro-area governments are rated A or above). Moreover, covered bonds, accounting for around one third of all MFI issues,

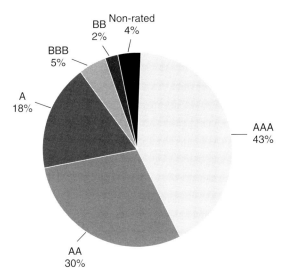

Figure 3.6   Rating of euro-denominated debt securities, September 2006
Source: ECB (2007c)

are typically A-rated. The share of A-rated and higher-rated debt securities has been fairly stable since 2001 (ECB, 2007c).

Government bonds

Issuance

In recent years, the euro-area government bond markets have changed substantially. The introduction of the euro in 1999 had a major impact on the operations of government-debt managers as the disappearance of exchange-rate risks within the euro area created the conditions for a pan-European capital market. As a result, debt managers have become small to medium-sized players in a larger European market, instead of being the dominant player in the national market. Investors now focus more on credit risk and liquidity, while bond portfolios have become increasingly internationally diversified, especially in the smaller euro-area countries. Consequently, competition among debt managers has increased, stimulating a more efficient primary market and a deeper, more liquid secondary market. Governments have put great effort into making their outstanding debt and new issues more attractive to international bond investors. To this end, they have adopted a number of supply-side innovations (see Box 3.2 for further details). These innovations were enabled by the rapid expansion of electronic trading

Box 3.2 Recent developments in government-debt management

The primary objective of debt-management agencies in the euro area is to ensure financing of the government's annual borrowing at the lowest possible (medium-term) cost with acceptable risks, although precise wordings and emphasis differ from country to country. The operational targets or guidelines for debt-management units differ more substantially. Often, these are based on asset-liability studies or cost-at-risk models, weighing interest costs against budgetary risks. Targets can take the form of a target (range) for the average maturity or the (modified) duration,[6] subject to certain restrictions such as quantitative limits on the use of interest-rate swaps.

Debt-management units were generally given more independence in the 1990s. A stronger focus on 'narrow' debt-management goals allowed for delegation to separate units. In addition, higher product complexity and competition among debt managers require a higher degree of operational independence and professionalism, which is easier to accomplish in a non-government unit. Cost considerations sometimes also played a role in the decision to delegate tasks to more independent units (Wolswijk and De Haan, 2005).

The increased competition has led to increasing liquidity of government securities and larger volumes of outstanding issues. While issues of around €2 billion were standard in smaller countries before the start of EMU, the minimum is now €5 billion, with large countries in the euro area having bond issuances of over €20 billion.[7] Governments sometimes focus on 'niches' targeting particular investor needs. For instance, Spain and France have introduced constant-maturity bonds, while France (followed by Greece and Italy) has taken the lead in the issuance of index-linked bonds (Baele *et al.*, 2004). In 2006, Germany issued an index-linked bond. Outside the euro area, the UK and the US are major issuers of index-linked bonds. In the segment of long-term debt securities, securities with a maturity of ten years or more play the major role as they have accounted for around 50 per cent of these instruments in the past four years (ECB, 2007c). The 3-, 5-, and 30-year segments also remained attractive, with about half of the debt managers issuing at least one security in those segments. More recently, debt managers have selected a somewhat wider spectrum of maturities, including some reversion to issuing short-term securities (Wolswijk and De Haan, 2005). Still, between 1999 and 2006 the outstanding amount of short-term public-debt securities increased by only 19 per cent, compared with an increase of 45 per cent for long-term public-debt securities. While in 1999 about 85 per cent of all long-term public-debt securities were fixed-rate bonds, the share of fixed-rate bonds had increased in 2006 to 90 per cent (ECB, 2007c).

Debt managers have also made issuance activity more regular and predictable by introducing pre-announced auction calendars, which has improved market transparency. Increased competition in the primary and secondary government-bond markets has also led to changes in distribution channels. Primary dealers and bank syndicates are now popular means to reach more non-domestic investors. Primary dealers mediate between the debt agency and buyers in both the primary and secondary markets. All euro-area countries (except Germany) now use primary dealers to distribute government bonds. Tasks for primary dealers usually include the obligation to bid at auctions or to buy a certain amount of newly issued bonds, promotion of government debt, and market making. In all countries concerned, many foreign financial institutions are included as primary dealers, reflecting the wish to spread ownership of government securities widely. Bank syndicates have also become increasingly popular as a way to distribute new government debt, particularly when approaching new market segments. Syndicate participants may select specific investors to whom the government security to be issued may be especially interesting. For smaller countries, a particular advantage is that a significant amount can be placed at once, thus immediately creating liquidity.

Eager to benefit from the improved diversification benefits and liquidity, investors have considerably increased their holdings of non-domestic bonds, leading to a reduction in the home bias of bond markets in the euro area. Domestic ownership of total government debt decreased from 75 per cent in 1997 to 54 per cent in 2003. A broadening of bond ownership has occurred in most countries, but in the smaller ones in particular. During 1997–2002, foreign ownership of long-term government debt in the Netherlands doubled to 56 per cent, while in Spain it increased from 18 to 41 per cent, and in France non-residents' share of marketable debt rose to 36 from 15 per cent (Wolswijk and De Haan, 2005).

systems. In addition to local systems, the European electronic platform for government securities, EuroMTS, was introduced in 1999, enabling quotation and trading of some European benchmark bonds (see chapter 5 for further details).

Table 3.2 provides an overview of public-debt securities by country of issuer in the period 2000–2006. The outstanding nominal amount of euro-denominated public-debt securities issued by euro-area public authorities increased on average by 4.9 per cent each year (ECB, 2007c). Countries with sharp increases either witnessed strong GDP growth (Ireland) or higher public-debt levels relative to GDP (Germany, Greece, France, and Portugal).

Government bond yields

Figure 3.7 shows the euro-area government-bond yields for three different maturities and the interest rate of the ECB's main refinancing operations. The

Table 3.2 Outstanding euro-denominated public-debt securities (€ billion), 2000–2006

	2000	2002	2004	2006	Average annual increase (%)
Austria	101.5	110.2	114.4	128.9	4.1
Belgium	242.8	256.0	254.2	256.3	0.9
Germany	779.9	867.3	1,006.6	1,123.1	6.3
Spain	303.0	319.0	330.9	336.9	1.8
Finland	53.9	51.0	54.8	53.4	−0.2
France	643.4	743.2	891.9	950.1	6.7
Greece[1]	11.4	123.3	158.8	185.5	10.7
Ireland	21.8	22.3	31.3	31.2	6.2
Italy	1,064.9	1,094.8	1,144.2	1,232.8	2.5
Luxembourg	0.7	0.6	0.4	0.1	−27.6
Netherlands	177.6	189.2	215.4	211.8	3.0
Portugal	47.2	59.8	72.9	89.8	11.3
Euro area	3,448.1	3,836.9	4,275.8	4,599.9	4.9
Rest of the world	105.3	108.0	123.8	127.1	3.2
Total	3,553.4	3,944.9	4,399.6	4,727.0	4.9

1) The sharp increase for Greece between 2000 and 2002 was the result of joining the euro area in January 2001. Before 2001, most Greek public-debt securities were denominated in drachma, and they were converted into euro as of 1 January 2001.
Source: ECB (2007c)

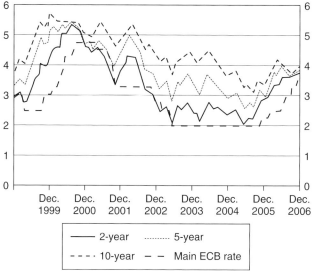

Figure 3.7   Euro-area government-bond yield (benchmark) (%), 1999–2006
Source: ECB (2007c)

yields are calculated as the weighted average of the 12 national euro-area yields for the respective maturity, using the nominal outstanding amounts of the related bonds as weights.

Yields of government bonds are influenced by expected short-term interest rates and the term premium. Risk-averse investors demand a risk premium (*term premium*) for investments in long-term bonds to compensate them for the risk of losses due to interest rate hikes; those losses increase with bond duration. The *term premium* leads to a positive *term spread*, i.e., the spread of yields for bonds with longer maturity over yields for bonds with shorter maturity, even when markets expect increasing and decreasing interest rates to be equally likely. The term spread in the euro area has been mostly positive since 1999, reflecting what is often called a 'normal' yield curve (ECB, 2007c). However, the term spread has been changing over time, with peaks in mid-1999 and mid-2004, while it was low in 2000 and again towards the end of 2006.

Apart from interest-rate expectations and the term premium, credit risk and liquidity also influence government bond yields. *Credit risk* is the risk of loss because of the failure of a counterparty to perform according to a contractual arrangement, for instance due to a default by a borrower. The spread between the yield of a particular bond and the yield of a bond with similar characteristics but without credit risk is the credit-risk premium. Rating agencies – like Moody's, Standard & Poor's, and Fitch – indicate issuers' credit risk by assigning them a rating. Table 3.3 shows the ratings of various euro-area countries since 1999.

Liquidity is the ease with which an investor can sell or buy a bond immediately at a price close to the mid-quote (i.e., the average of the bid–ask spread, as defined in section 3.1). The spread between the yield of a bond with liquidity and a similar bond with less liquidity is referred to as the liquidity premium.

Credit risk and liquidity premia of euro-denominated bonds are typically calculated as the spread of the bond yields over those of German government bonds. There are two reasons for this (ECB, 2007c). First, German government bonds have consistently received the highest ranking from the three main rating agencies (see Table 3.3), indicating that German government bonds are associated with zero or very low credit risk. Second, German government bonds are very actively traded, ensuring that they are very liquid. According to a recent study (Bearing Point, 2007), German government bonds – with a daily average trading volume of €25 billion (single-counting, i.e., only one side (the buy side) of a securities transaction is counted) in the secondary market – are the most important segment of the European bond market. In

Table 3.3 Rating of government debt since 1999

	Moody's	S&P	Fitch
Austria	Aaa	AAA	AAA
Belgium	Aa1	AA+	AA+ (since 05/2006)
			AA (06/2002 to 05/2006)
			AA− (until 06/2002)
Germany	Aaa	AAA	AAA
Spain	Aaa (since 12/2001)	AAA (since 12/2004)	AAA (since 12/2003)
	Aa2 (until 12/2001)	AA+ (03/1999 to 12/2004)	AA+ (09/1999 to 12/2003)
		AA (until 03/1999)	AA (until 09/1999)
Finland	Aaa	AAA (since 02/2002)	AAA (since 12/2003)
		AA+ (09/1999 to 02/2002)	AA+ (until 11/1999)
		AA (until 09/1999)	
France	Aaa	AAA	AAA
Greece	A1 (since 11/2002)	A (since 11/2004)	A (since 12/2004)
	A2 (until 11/2002)	A+ (06/2003 to 11/2004)	A+ (10/2003 to 12/2004)
		A (03/2001 to 06/2003)	A (06/2001 to 10/ 2003)
		A− (until 10/2001)	A− (until 06/2001)
Ireland	Aaa	AAA (since 10/2001)	AAA
		AA+ (until 10/2001)	
Italy	Aa2 (since 05/2002)	A+ (since 10/2001)	AA− (since 10/2006)
	Aa3 (until 05/2002)	AA− (07/2004 to 10/2006)	AA (06/2002 to 10/2006)
		AA (until 07/2004)	AA− (until 06/2002)
Netherlands	Aaa	AAA	AAA
Portugal	Aa2	AA− (since 06/2005)	AA
		AA (until 06/2005)	

Source: ECB (2007c)

addition to a liquid cash market, there is a very active derivatives market for German government bonds ('Bunds'). The Bund future is the most liquid futures contract (see section 3.5).

Figure 3.8 shows the yield spreads of ten-year euro-area government bonds over German government bonds. For most countries, spreads decreased between 1999 and 2003 and have been low (below 10 basis points) or even slightly negative since 2003. However, spreads for Italy, Greece, and Portugal have increased again somewhat in recent years. These countries were downgraded by the rating agencies (see Table 3.3).

Figure 3.8 shows that yield differentials vary considerably across countries, while for each country the yield differential varies considerably over time. Pagano and Von Thadden (2008) discuss studies that try to explain these yield

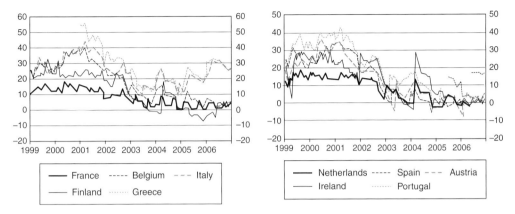

Figure 3.8   Ten-year spreads over German bonds (basis points), 1999–2006
Source: ECB (2007c)

differentials, arguing that they may arise from (1) intrinsic differences in country-specific default risk or different sensitivities of bonds' future payoffs to common shocks, or (2) market frictions, like trading costs, clearing and settlement fees, and taxes. As Pagano and Von Thadden (2008) point out, these factors may also interact. For instance, if an asset on which a transaction tax has to be paid becomes riskier, the effect on the price will be smaller the larger the tax, since the initial after-tax price is correspondingly lower. Pagano and Von Thadden (2008) conclude that credit risk explains a considerable portion of cross-country yield differences but explains very little of their variation over time.

Corporate bonds

In recent years the European corporate bond market has grown rapidly and the market's structure has undergone some important changes. Before 1998, the market was dominated by debt issued by highly rated financial corporations, whereas since that date industrial corporations have increasingly found their way to the corporate bond market (Baele *et al.*, 2004). Nevertheless, MFIs are still more important than non-financial firms, being the second largest group of issuers of debt securities in the euro-area economy. About 15 per cent of all MFI liabilities consist of debt securities; this share has remained stable since the start of the monetary union. MFIs issue both short-term and long-term debt securities. Short-term securities are in many cases certificates of deposits (CDs), which are closely related to bank deposits. The bulk of the

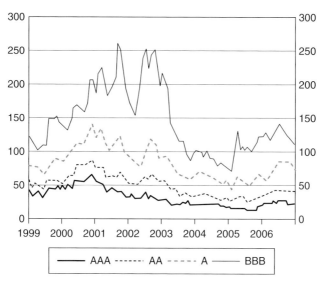

Figure 3.9 Spreads of corporate bonds over AAA-rated government bonds (basis points), 1999–2006
Source: ECB (2007c)

debt securities issued by MFIs – accounting for nearly 90 per cent of total outstanding – are, however, notes and bonds that have a long original maturity. MFIs are the largest issuers of floating-rate long-term debt securities. In 2006, 39 per cent of long-term debt securities of MFIs consisted of floating-rate issues (ECB, 2007c).

By issuing long-term debt securities at floating rate (rather than at a fixed rate), banks aim to match the characteristics of their assets. By aligning the fixing of the interest rate on the liability side with the fixing of the interest rate on the asset side, banks can reduce their exposure to interest-rate risk (ECB, 2007c).

Spreads of corporate bond yields over AAA-rated government bond yields as shown in Figure 3.9 mainly reflect the perceived credit risk that results from an investment in corporate bonds. When the corporate outlook deteriorates, these spreads increase. For example, spreads were high during the years 2001 and 2002 when economic growth was low, but decreased significantly in 2003. Corporate bond spreads are higher for bonds of lower-rated issuers than for bonds of higher-rated issuers (see Figure 3.9). Triple-B-rated euro-area bonds, for example, reached average spreads above 250 basis points during the economic downturn in 2002, while A-rated bonds remained below 150 basis points and triple-A-rated bonds below 65 basis points (ECB, 2007c). The ECB

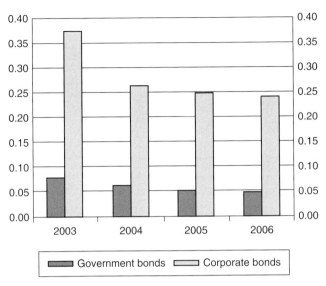

Figure 3.10   Average bid and ask spread (in % of mid-quote), 2003–2006
Source: ECB (2007c)

(2007c) identifies two possible explanations for this. First, the default probabilities of lower-rated corporate issuers may be more closely linked to the business cycle than the default probabilities of higher-rated corporations. Second, bond spreads widen when bonds become less liquid. During recessions, lower-rated corporate bonds may suffer and might be traded less actively, thus reducing their liquidity, leading to higher liquidity premia.

A liquid market allows market participants to trade at low trading costs. Kyle (1985) identifies three dimensions of liquidity:

- tightness: the cost of turning around a position during a short period. Tightness in essence refers to a low *bid–ask spread* (ECB, 2008b);
- depth: a market is deep if only large buy or sell orders can have an impact on prices;
- resiliency: a market is resilient if market prices reflect 'fundamental' values and, in particular, quickly return to 'fundamental' values after shocks.

The ECB (2007c) has examined the first dimension of liquidity analysing bid–ask spreads in the government- and corporate-bond markets. Figure 3.10 shows average (unweighted) spreads for the years 2003–2006. Bid–ask spreads were much higher for corporate bonds than for government bonds. According to the ECB (2007c), this is related to the number and the size of bonds in these markets.

There are fewer but much larger government bonds than corporate bonds, which translate into lower costs for market makers due to economies of scale and greater competition between market makers in government-bond markets. Furthermore, corporate-bond yields and prices are more volatile than government bond yields so that market makers are exposed to higher inventory risks on corporate-bond markets for which they require compensation in the form of higher spreads. (*Inventory risk* is the risk that bond prices will move while the market maker holds the bonds in inventory without perfectly hedging price risks.) Figure 3.10 shows also that bid–ask spreads in both market segments trend downwards over time until 2006. But since the start of the sub-prime mortgage crisis in 2007 (see Box 11.2), bid–ask spreads for government and corporate bonds have increased due to heightened uncertainty in financial markets.

An important type of MFI debt securities are covered bonds, making up about 33 per cent of all debt securities issued by euro-area MFIs (ECB, 2007c). As long as the issuing MFI is solvent, the covered bond generates cash flows to the bond holders that are independent of the performance of the assets. If, however, the issuing MFI becomes insolvent, the covered bond holders can claim the cover assets. Germany is by far the most important euro-area country for covered bonds (so-called *Pfandbriefe*), followed by Spain and France (see Table 3.4).

Table 3.4 Outstanding amounts of covered bonds (€ billion), 2001–2005

	2001	2002	2003	2004	2005
Austria	10.57	9.38	8.50	3.00	16.28
Belgium	0.00	0.00	0.00	0.00	0.00
Germany	1,104.83	1,088.00	1,056.69	1,010.11	975.93
Spain	13.51	25.27	82.50	100.51	163.23
Finland	0.05	0.05	0.07	0.07	1.50
France	64.01	70.91	87.20	100.67	124.77
Greece	0.00	0.00	0.00	0.00	0.00
Ireland	0.00	0.00	13.50	30.95	45.11
Italy	0.00	0.00	0.00	0.00	4.00
Luxembourg	11.01	13.10	16.67	19.48	24.97
Netherlands	0.99	0.88	0.69	12.75	2.00
Portugal	0.00	0.00	0.00	0.00	0.00
Euro area	1,204.97	1,207.58	1,265.82	1,277.53	1,357.79
Denmark	199.85	191.37	231.57	232.80	293.15
Sweden	65.45	70.91	60.51	82.49	92.81
United Kingdom	0.00	0.00	7.00	14.96	25.44

Source: ECB (2007c)

Maturities of covered bonds typically range from 2–10 years. The majority of covered bonds are rated AAA (ECB, 2007c).

According to the ECB (2007c), there are two objectives for the issuance of asset-backed securities, i.e., fund raising and credit-risk transfer. Both objectives can be achieved through a 'true sale' securitisation or through a funded synthetic securitisation. In a *'true sale' securitisation*, the originator (typically a bank) transfers the ownership of a pool of assets to a 'special purpose vehicle' (SPV), which issues securities backed by the pool of assets and transfers the funds raised through selling these securities to the originator. In a *funded synthetic securitisation* process, the ownership of the asset pool is not transferred to the SPV but remains on the balance sheet of the originator. The risks associated with the asset pool are transferred to the SPV by means of a credit derivative (see section 3.5 on derivatives).

Asset-backed securities can be classified according to the type of underlying collateral. *Mortgage-backed securities* (MBSs) are backed by mortgages loans. *Collateralised debt obligations* (CDOs) are backed by bonds or loans. All other securitisation products are called asset-backed securities in a narrow sense. These are typically backed by credit-card receivables, leasing receivables, trade receivables, and others. In November 2006, the amount of euro-denominated asset-backed securities outstanding stood at €832 billion (see Table 3.5). Around 47 per cent of all euro-denominated asset-backed securities issued in the euro area have been issued in Spain. Euro asset-backed securities issued

Table 3.5 Outstanding amounts of euro-denominated asset-backed securities (€ billion), November 2006

Spain	336.00	United Kingdom	58.39
Italy	148.59	United States	20.35
Netherlands	113.23	Jersey	19.51
Ireland	57.82	Cayman Islands	9.49
Luxembourg	24.95	Australia	6.58
France	19.40	Netherlands Antilles	2.56
Belgium	5.47	Virgin Islands, British	0.65
Portugal	2.43	Sweden	0.56
Austria	2.37	Guernsey C.I.	0.44
Germany	1.55	Czech Republic	0.42
Greece	0.11	Iceland	0.37
Finland	0.01	Denmark	0.36
		Others	0.73

Source: ECB (2007c)

Box 3.3 How much transparency is optimal?

Transparency refers to the absence or elimination of information asymmetries. In a fully transparent market, all relevant market information is common knowledge for all participants. The debate on bond-market transparency is a difficult one. According to Dunne *et al.* (2006), the very existence of most financial markets depends on striking a balance between transparency, thought to promote competition, fairness, and investor protection, and opacity, in the interest of encouraging ongoing participation of both end-customers and liquidity providers. If market participants do not obtain adequate fairness, protection, and incentives, they will not participate in sufficient numbers and the market will not function properly.

This can be illustrated by the so-called Winner's Curse, according to which the highest bidder has probably bid too much. If the highest bidder wants to resell the product immediately after the auction, the best price he will obtain is the underbidder's price. Because of incomplete information or subjective factors, bidders will form a range of estimates of the item's 'intrinsic value'. As a result, the largest overestimation of an item's value ends up winning the auction. With perfect information and fully rational participants skilled in valuation, no overpayments should occur. A number of dealers submit quotes and the highest-bidding dealer secures the bonds. Typically, the successful dealer enters the inter-dealer market to hedge his risk. The underbidders are aware of this and can benefit by taking up contrarian positions in the market, thereby making it difficult for the successful bidder to share his position. The more transparent the inter-dealer market, the more difficult it is for the successful bidder to hedge his risk. Consequently, an increase in market transparency makes dealers more cautious about participating.

Yet there are powerful arguments in favour of enhancing transparency. Transparency can facilitate 'best execution', i.e., it allows investors to verify whether dealers and others indeed execute orders at the best price available. Goldstein *et al.* (2007) observe a decrease in transaction costs which is consistent with investors' ability to negotiate better terms of trade with dealers once investors have access to broader bond-pricing data. Costs may also be lower for bonds with transparent prices (see Edwards *et al.*, 2007). Greater price transparency can enhance investor protection as price movements signal default probabilities. Strengthening overall transparency may also create a level playing field between large institutional and smaller investors. Large institutional investors may already be able to obtain all relevant information, while smaller investors are not able to exert the same pressure on dealers.

Finally, transparency may improve liquidity. As for municipal bond trades, Harris and Piwowar (2006) argue that ongoing regulatory initiatives to increase transparency in the municipal bond market will lead to liquidity improvements. These improvements should have the greatest impact on retail investors. Next to this, Goldstein *et al.* (2007) find that adding transparency to corporate-bond markets has either a neutral or a positive effect on liquidity. These findings seem contradictory to what has been argued by Dunne *et al.* (2006). However, Casey (2006) stresses that pre- and post-trade transparency may equally enhance or harm market liquidity and efficiency, depending on how they are applied, by whom, for what instruments, in which markets, and at which latency.

by SPVs located outside the euro area represented an outstanding amount of €120 billion in November 2006 (ECB, 2007c).

3.4 Equity markets

Equities grant the investor a residual right to receive income from the company's earnings. Equity can be issued either privately (unquoted shares) or publicly via shares that are listed on a stock exchange (quoted shares). The importance of equity finance in the EU is growing (see Figure 3.11), which is reflected in the relative size of European equity markets – an increase from 67 per cent of the US market in 2005 to 82 per cent in 2006 (EC, 2007). As Figure 3.12 shows, the market capitalisation of Euronext and the LSE are much higher than those of other exchanges in the EU.

Initial public offerings

Within the private equity market, venture capital is often provided by investors as 'start-up' money to finance new, high-risk companies in return for an equity position in the firm. When issuing public equity, a firm may obtain a listing on a stock exchange for the first time, the *initial public offering*. If a firm is already listed and issues additional shares, this is called *seasoned equity offering* (SEO) or *secondary public offering* (SPO). When a firm issues equity at a stock exchange, it may decide to substitute existing unquoted shares for quoted ones, or issue newly created shares. In the latter case, the funds raised accrue to the firm, while in the first case the proceeds are directed to the initial investors.

Public equity markets play a limited role as a source of new funds for listed corporations. The pecking-order theory (Myers and Majluf, 1984) suggests

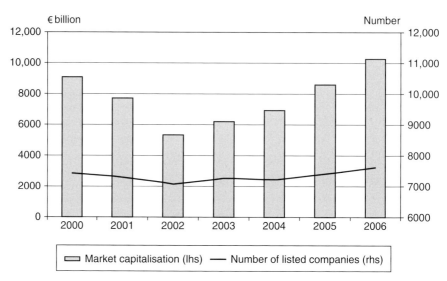

Figure 3.11 Market capitalisation and number of listed firms, 2000–2006
Source: EC (2007)

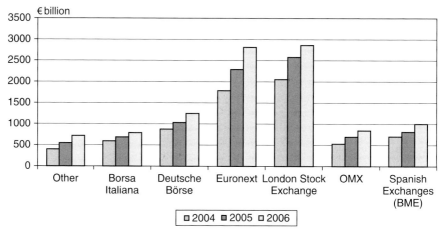

Figure 3.12 Market capitalisation of some exchanges in the EU, 2004–2006
Source: EC (2007)

that companies adopt a hierarchy of financial preferences. Due to asymmetric information, companies prefer internal financing (i.e., retained earnings) to external financing. If external financing is needed, companies first seek debt funding. Equity is issued only as a last resort. Figure 3.13 shows the different sources of financing (relative to gross value added, GVA) of non-financial

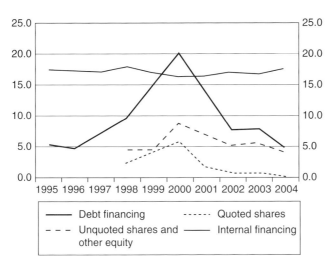

Figure 3.13   Net sources of funding of non-financial firms in the euro area (% of gross value added), 1995–2004
Source: ECB (2006)

corporations from 1995–2004. Corporations obtain funds via internal financing, defined as gross savings, which corresponds broadly to the sum of retained earnings and the depreciation allowance. As a percentage of GVA, internal financing is the largest financing source (about 18 per cent of GVA) and remains relatively stable over time. In line with the pecking-order theory, Figure 3.13 shows that debt financing via bank loans or bonds is the second most important financing source. The financing source of last resort is equity. Still, IPOs grew spectacularly from the mid-1990s (see below). Unfortunately, data on the net issuance of quoted shares are available only from 1997 onwards. As Figure 3.13 shows, this source of funding strongly increased between 1998 and 2000. It is likely that this increase was related to the spectacular growth in stock-market prices during this period (ECB, 2006). In contrast, from 2001–2004 the net issuance of public equity decreased.

There are various motives for IPOs. One of the main reasons, of course, is to obtain funds to finance investment. Moreover, the listing of a firm's shares on a stock exchange also increases its financial autonomy, as the firm becomes less dependent on a single financial provider (like a bank). Further, by issuing equity the firm's owners can diversify their investment risk by selling stakes in the company in a liquid market. Another advantage of public issuance is increased recognition of the company name. In addition, from the time of the IPO investors receive better information due to improved transparency and the disclosure requirements that are part of the listing conditions. At the same

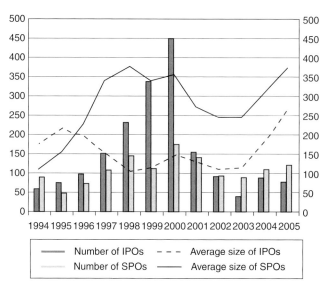

Figure 3.14   IPOs and SPOs in the euro area (numbers and € millions), 1994–2005
Source: ECB (2006)

time, the price of a company's stock acts as a measure of the company's value and as a disciplining mechanism for managers.

However, there are a number of disadvantages for a company inherent in listing its shares on a stock exchange. To start with, equity issuance is an expensive procedure, incurring costs such as underwriters' commission, legal fees, and other charges resulting primarily from the need to satisfy the additional disclosure requirements. From the perspective of investors, going public implies that the ownership of the company is likely to be shared more widely, resulting in a larger gap between external investors and managers. This separation of ownership and control could cause 'agency problems', where company insiders hold more accurate information on the prospects of the firm than external equity investors, resulting in a divergence of managers' and outside investors' interests. Lastly, by going public, a company exposes itself to scrutiny by shareholders, who may be excessively focused on short-term results.

As Figure 3.14 shows, the number of IPOs peaked in 2000. After that the number fell from the high of 447 in 2000 to 151 in 2001 and to 35 in 2003. A large number of the issues in the late 1990s were 'new economy' offerings, like the technology, media, and telecommunications (TMT) sector. The share of the TMT sector in total equity issuance increased from 26 per cent in the mid-1990s to 50 per cent from mid-1997 to mid-2001. Although it has declined since, it remained relatively high as a percentage of total issuance, at 42 per cent.

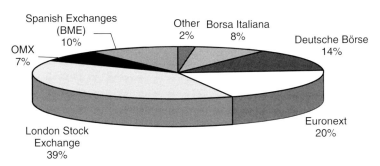

Figure 3.15 Market share (%) of EU stock exchanges (by stock turnover), 2006
Source: EC (2007)

While it is difficult to disentangle the different factors motivating a company's decision to issue public equity, the economic cycle is likely to play a significant role. This is mainly because equity is often used to finance demand for fixed investment, which fluctuates over the business cycle. Furthermore, significant increases in stock-market prices generally preceded increases in equity issuance. In the literature on behavioural finance (Shiller, 2003), a related factor explaining the timing of equity issuance is the effect of investor sentiment. Developments in investor optimism over time may have an impact on the cost of equity, thereby influencing the amount of equity issued. For example, excessive increases in risk aversion resulting in falling stock-market prices could raise the cost of equity, thereby dissuading companies from issuing equity. Although investor sentiment will inevitably change over time, it is difficult to measure risk aversion empirically, and/or investors' willingness to invest in the stock market. Companies also issue equity in order to finance the acquisition of other companies, either by using the cash proceeds of public offerings or by issuing shares, which are subsequently exchanged for the shares of a target company. Consequently, merger and acquisition (M&A) cycles can also be expected to correlate with equity-issuance activity.

Consolidation

The EU stock market is highly concentrated. Measured by trading activity, the market share of the five largest stock exchanges in Europe exceeded 90 per cent in 2006, with the LSE standing out with a 39 per cent share of total EU turnover (see Figure 3.15). The LSE and Euronext together account for nearly

60 per cent. The stock-market concentration level is almost identical in terms of market capitalisation, as the five largest stock exchanges have a market share of 85 per cent (EC, 2007). This high level of concentration may be explained by the fact that financial exchanges exhibit network externalities, as higher participation of traders on both sides of the market positively affects market liquidity and increases traders' utility.

Comparing Figures 3.12 and 3.15, it appears that the market capitalisation of the LSE and Euronext is similar in value, while the turnover of the LSE is twice that of Euronext. This suggests that shares listed on the LSE are more actively traded than shares listed on Euronext. The LSE thus provides for a deeper and more liquid market.

There has been an intensive regional cross-border consolidation. First, Euronext resulted from a merger of the Paris, Amsterdam, Brussels, and Lisbon stock exchanges during 2000–2002. Next, the stock exchanges of Copenhagen, Stockholm, Helsinki, Tallin, Riga, Vilnius, and Iceland merged between 2004 and 2006, creating the OMX Nordic Exchange. More recently, in June 2007 Italy's stock-exchange operator Borsa Italiana accepted a take-over from the LSE. In 2006, the first trans-Atlantic stock exchange merger took place between Euronext and the New York Stock Exchange (NYSE), strengthening its position as the largest securities trading venue in the world. In 2007, two other trans-Atlantic deals were announced: an acquisition of the New York-based International Securities Exchange by Deutsche Börse and a merger between Nasdaq and OMX (EC, 2007).

There is an advantage in consolidation. Bigger exchanges enjoy economies of scale that reduce trading costs, which in turn attracts more traders and listed companies (Wharton, 2006). Figure 3.12 confirms that the market capitalisation of Euronext and the LSE has grown faster than that of its smaller competitors. While consolidation allows an exchange to exploit economies of scale, it may also reduce competition and thus lower an exchange's incentive for financial innova-tion (in the form of developing new, cheaper, trading mechanisms). The impact of competition is interesting in equity trading. Competition may reduce trading fees, but fragmentation of the order flow between exchanges may reduce the liquidity of equity trading. Examining the competition between Euronext and the LSE in the Dutch equity market, Foucault and Menkveld (2008) find evidence of reduced fees and improved liquidity. Liquidity is improved as some brokers automate the routing decision between the two exchanges to obtain the best execution price. In that way, the order flow at the two exchanges is indirectly combined.

There are still some challenges. First, the clearing and settlement infra-structure in Europe has remained fragmented so far. As documented in chapter 5, post-trading costs per transaction in the EU are substantially higher than in the US. Next, cross-border exchanges like Euronext and OMX force national financial supervisors to co-operate. This challenge is discussed further in chapter 10.

3.5 Derivatives

Derivatives are financial instruments whose value is derived from the value of something else. They can be based on different types of assets (such as equities or commodities), prices (such as interest rates or exchange rates), or indexes (such as a stock-market index). Derivatives can be used as a source of revenue but are also important risk-management tools (see Batten *et al.*, 2004). As for the latter, the BIS (1994) stresses that derivatives allow parties to identify, isolate, and manage the market risk in financial instruments and commodities, i.e., changes in market prices of financial instruments and changes in interest and exchange rates. When used properly, derivatives can reduce risks through hedging. This is done by transferring the cost of bearing the risk from one party to the other; the former wants to reduce the exposure to risk, whereas the latter is willing to assume that exposure in the expectation of making a profit (Reilly, 2005). Financial innovation and increased market demand led to a rapid growth of derivatives trading in the last decade (see Figure 3.16).

The use of derivatives has a major impact on asset management and risk management. A portfolio manager can, for example, change its risk profile through derivative transactions at a very low cost. Without derivatives, the portfolio manager would have to conduct transactions in the underlying cash markets (i.e., money, bond, or equity markets) at a higher cost, including the costly transfer of securities (see chapter 5). Derivatives are thus a low-cost tool for risk management. Moreover, derivatives can be tailor-made in the over-the-counter market (see below). The spectacular growth of hedge funds can also be explained by the rise of low-cost derivatives markets. Hedge funds typically exploit small price differences of similar financial products, as explained in chapter 6. Only when the transaction cost is smaller than the price differential will hedge funds take a position.

There are two broad types of derivatives: forwards and options. A *forward contract* gives the holder the obligation to buy or sell a certain underlying instrument (like a bond) at a certain date in the future (i.e., the delivery or final settlement date), at a specified price (i.e., the settlement price). Forward

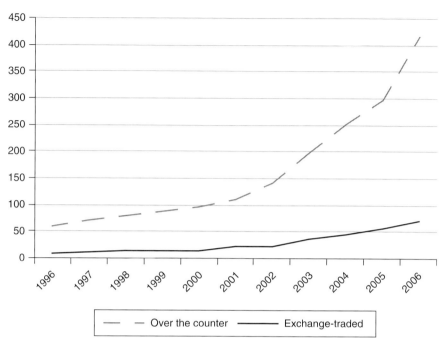

Figure 3.16 Global derivatives markets ($ trillion), notional amounts, 1996–2006
Source: International Financial Services London (2007)

contracts consist of futures and swaps. *Futures contracts* are forward contracts traded on organised exchanges. *Swaps* are forward contracts in which counterparties agree to exchange streams of cash flows according to predetermined rules. For example, an *interest-rate swap* is a derivative in which one party exchanges a stream of interest payments for another party's stream of cash flows. The most important difference with options is that *options* give the holder the right (but not the obligation) to buy or sell a certain underlying instrument at a certain date in the future at a specified price.

Derivatives are traded on organised exchanges or *over-the-counter*. The latter are contracts that are traded (and privately negotiated) directly between two parties. All contract terms, such as delivery quality, quantity, location, date, and price, are negotiable (Anderson and McKay, 2008). Figure 3.16 shows that the global notional amount[8] outstanding in OTC markets is substantially higher than the exchanges-traded amount. The notional outstanding value of OTC derivatives increased by 40 per cent from $ 298 trillion at end-2005 to $ 415 at end-2006. In 2007, the outstanding value even reached $ 516 trillion. As for the location of trading, Figure 3.17 shows that the United Kingdom is the leading OTC derivative market in the world with an average

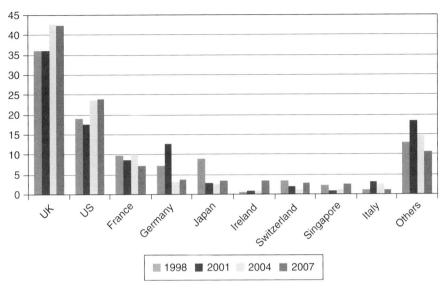

Figure 3.17 Location of OTC derivatives markets, percentage share of average daily turnover, 1998–2007
Source: International Financial Services London (2007)

daily share of total global turnover of 43 per cent. Derivatives such as swaps and forward-rate agreements are generally traded on OTC markets. Derivative contracts (such as futures contracts and options) that are transacted on an organised futures exchange are generally standardised. However, Anderson and McKay (2008) point out that the traditional distinction between exchange-based and OTC derivatives has become less clear. For instance, the International Swaps and Derivatives Association (ISDA) has provided a standard contract. This standardisation has made it easier for more participants to access the OTC markets. Furthermore, OTC trades are increasingly being cleared through clearinghouses in much the same way as exchange-based contracts.

Table 3.6 shows that the most important derivates are interest-rate derivatives, i.e., derivatives whose value is linked to interest rates. In June 2007 interest-rate derivatives accounted for 67 per cent of total amounts of outstanding OTC derivatives. Moving to exchange-traded derivatives, Figure 3.18 shows that the notional amounts of outstanding interest-rate derivatives traded on European exchanges increased rapidly between 1992 and 2006.

The oldest official derivatives market in Europe is the European Options Exchange (EOE) in Amsterdam, which started to trade options on stocks in 1978. EOE became part of the Amsterdam Exchanges and subsequently of Euronext. Next, the London International Financial Futures and Options

Table 3.6 Amounts of outstanding OTC derivatives ($ billion), 2003–2007

	Jun 03	Dec 03	Jun 04	Dec 04	Jun 05	Dec 05	Jun 06	Dec 06	Jun 07
Foreign-exchange derivatives	22.071	24.475	26.997	29.289	31.081	31.364	38.091	40.239	48.620
Interest-rate derivatives	121.799	141.991	164.626	190.502	204.795	211.970	261.960	291.115	346.937
Equity-linked derivatives	2.799	3.787	4.521	4.385	4.551	5.793	6.782	7.488	9.202
Commodity derivatives	1.040	1.406	1.270	1.443	2.940	5.434	6.394	7.115	7.567
Credit default swaps	n.a.	n.a.	n.a.	6.396	10.211	13.908	20.352	28.650	42.580
Other	21.949	25.508	22.644	25.879	27.915	29.199	35.928	39.682	61.501

Source: Bank for International Settlements

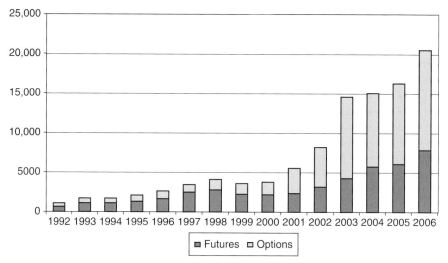

Figure 3.18   Notional amounts of outstanding interest-rate derivatives traded on European exchanges ($ billion), 1992–2006
Source: EC (2007b)

Exchange (LIFFE) began its operations in 1982. The major product lines of LIFFE are the short-term interest-rate and government-bond contracts that were its original strength, although one of the first futures contracts developed by LIFFE was the British government-debt contract based on the long-term US Treasury contracts (Batten *et al.*, 2004). LIFFE used a system of open-outcry floor trading. Later on, derivatives exchanges were opened in continental Europe. While some of these also adopted open-outcry floor trading, others (like the DTB, i.e., Deutsche Terminbörse) introduced electronic

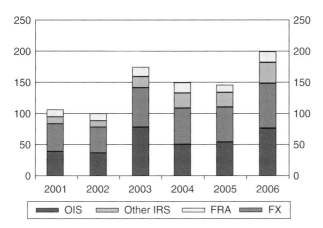

Figure 3.19   Market shares of various OTC derivatives markets in the euro area (index; 2002 Q2 = 100), 2001–2006
Source: ECB (2007b)

trading. DTB was founded in 1991. It introduced trading of futures on the Bund, i.e., German government bonds, in direct competition with a contract already trading at LIFFE. By 1998, the DTB had competed the Bund contract away from LIFFE (Anderson and McKay, 2008). Also LIFFE moved to electronic trading.

EUREX is a serious competitor to LIFFE in the area of bond and short-term interest-rate futures and options trading in Europe. This German–Swiss joint venture came about through the merger of the DTB and SOFFEX, the Swiss Options and Financial Futures Exchange, in 1998. Today it trades a wide range of bond and money-market derivative products. Access to the market is available in a number of major cities, including Chicago, New York, London, and Tokyo (Batten *et al.*, 2004).

Figure 3.19 provides figures on OTC market developments between 2001 and 2006 in the euro area. In addition to the forward-rate agreement (FRA) market and interest-rate swap (IRS) market – comprising overnight interest-rate swaps (OIS, also referred to as EONIA swaps) and other IRS – the figure shows the share of OTC derivatives linked to the foreign exchange market, comprising FX swaps and cross-currency swaps (Xccy swaps). The figure shows that measured by volume, the OIS and FX swap markets are by far the most important OTC derivatives market segments, followed by other IRS. According to the ECB (2007b), the unweighted maturity evolution of OIS transactions shows that half of the activity in the EONIA swap market took place in contracts expiring in one month or less.

Credit derivatives

As can be seen in Table 3.6, a very important development in the OTC derivatives markets during the last years has been the emergence of credit derivatives. The essence of a *credit derivative* is a contract in which a credit-protection seller promises a payment to a credit-protection buyer contingent upon the occurrence of a credit event (Anderson and McKay, 2008). The various types of contracts differ according to the terms and conditions that govern the promised payment, such as the definition of the 'credit event'. Various definitions are used, including formal bankruptcy and default. Increasingly diverse and complex products have appeared, but the most popular type of credit derivatives is the single-name credit default swap (CDS). Under this contract, the protection seller promises to buy at par from the protection buyer a specified bond (Anderson and McKay, 2008). A CDS requires fixed and regular premium payments from the protection buyer to the protection seller until a credit event occurs or the CDS matures. The premium is calculated as a percentage (called *credit spread*) of the nominal value of the reference obligation (the *notional amount*). Apart from single-name CDSs, the contract may refer to more (portfolio swaps and CDS indices) reference entities (i.e., the underlying names on which credit risk is exchanged). A CDS resembles an insurance contract, in that it protects the 'protection buyer' against predefined credit events, in particular the risk of default in return for a periodic fee paid to the protection seller. Following a credit event, contracts settle either physically (i.e., through the delivery to the protection buyer of defaulting bonds and/or loans for an amount equivalent to the notional value of the swap) or in cash, with the net amount owed by the protection seller determined after the credit event (IMF, 2005). CDSs are an attractive instrument for risk management. Protection buyers can transfer credit risks without transferring credit claims or debt securities, while protection sellers can assume credit risks without granting credit or buying debt securities. So, both sides can optimise credit-risk portfolios relatively efficiently (ECB, 2007c).

Data on notional amounts of CDSs on euro-denominated reference obligations are not available. Table 3.7, taken from ECB (2007c), describes the development in notional CDS amounts outstanding worldwide from two different sources, i.e., the ISDA and the BIS. The data from the two sources differ substantially. Nevertheless, they all indicate average annual growth rates in the CDS markets of 100 per cent or more. According to the ECB (2007c), the CDS market has grown far more rapidly than any other financial market segment over the past five years.

Table 3.7 Notional amounts of CDSs outstanding ($ billion), 2003–2006

	June 2003	June 2004	June 2005	June 2006
BIS	n.a.	n.a.	10,211	20,352
ISDA	2,688	5,442	12,430	26,006

Source: ECB (2007c)

The most common maturities of CDSs are three, five, seven, and ten years, with the five-year maturity serving as a benchmark. The most active market participants in CDS markets, both as protection buyers and sellers, have been banks, hedge funds, and insurance companies. The majority of reference obligations are bonds or loans that are rated A or better (ECB, 2007c).

3.6 Conclusions

Financial markets release information to aid the price-discovery process, they provide a platform to trade, and they provide an infrastructure to settle trades. The main trading mechanisms are quote-driven and order-driven markets.

The euro money market is the market for euro-denominated short-term funds and related derivative instruments. It consists of various segments, including unsecured deposit contracts with various maturities, ranging from overnight to one year, and repurchase agreements (repos, i.e., reverse transactions secured by securities) also ranging from overnight to one year. Credit institutions account for the largest share of the euro money market. The ECB has a major influence on the money market via its use of various monetary policy instruments (reserve requirements, standing facilities, and open-market operations). There are three main market interest rates for the money market: EONIA (euro overnight index average), EURIBOR (euro interbank offered rate), and EUREPO (the repo market reference rate for the euro).

The EU bond market has experienced spectacular growth since the introduction of the euro and is now matching the US bond market in size. The bulk of euro-denominated bonds (i.e., debt securities with a maturity of more than one year) is issued by euro area issuers. Although the share of corporate bonds in all euro-denominated bonds outstanding has risen, government bonds still form the most important market segment. Also after the introduction of the euro yield differentials vary considerably across countries, while for each country the yield differential varies considerably over time. The issuance of asset-backed securities has increased rapidly during the last decade.

The importance of equity finance in the EU is growing, although there are large differences across exchanges. The market capitalisation of Euronext and the London Stock Exchange, which are the biggest exchanges in terms of turnover, are much higher than those of other exchanges in the EU. Despite the increase in equity finance, public-equity markets play a limited role as a source of new funds for corporations that raise external financing generally via bank loans or debt securities. Still, the number and value of initial public offerings grew spectacularly from the mid-1990s.

Derivatives are financial instruments whose value is derived from the value of something else. They are traded on organised exchanges or over-the-counter. Derivatives can provide for a source of income but are also important risk-management tools. The most important derivatives are futures, forwards, options, and swaps. During recent years credit derivatives have become important. These are contracts in which a credit-protection seller promises a payment to a credit-protection buyer contingent upon the occurrence of a credit event.

NOTES

1. Insiders of a company may have more information than outsiders. Regulation typically forbids insider trading (see chapter 10).
2. The Financial Stability Forum (FSF) brings together senior representatives of national financial authorities (e.g., central banks, supervisory authorities, and treasury departments), international financial institutions, international regulatory and supervisory groupings, committees of central bank experts, and the European Central Bank.
3. In addition, the derivatives markets have become increasingly important over recent years. The derivative money-market segments can be grouped into exchange-traded instruments, such as short-term interest rate futures and options, and instruments that are typically traded over-the-counter. This section will focus on the unsecured deposit markets and the secured repo markets.
4. Since June 2000, MROs have been conducted as a multiple-rate (American) auction, i.e., bidders are served going down from the highest rates bid to the lowest ones at the rates they effectively bid in the auction until the quantity to be allotted is exhausted.
5. See http://www.euribor.org/html/content/panelbanks.html for an overview of the banks in the panel.
6. The modified duration measures the change in the current value of the debt portfolio when the yield of the portfolio changes by 1 basis point.
7. The lower limit for government securities to be eligible for trading on EuroMTS is €5 billion.
8. Hypothetical underlying quantity upon which payment obligations are based.

SUGGESTED READING

Harris, L. E. (2003), *Trading and Exchanges: Market Microstructure for Practitioners, An Introductory Textbook to the Economics of Market Microstructure*, Oxford University Press, Oxford.

Hull, J. C. (2005), *Options, Futures, and Other Derivatives*, 6th edition, Prentice Hall, Upper Saddle River (NJ).

Pagano, M. and E. Von Thadden (2008), The European Bond Markets under EMU, in: X. Freixas, P. Hartmann, and C. Mayer (eds.), *Handbook of European Financial Markets and Institutions*, Oxford University Press, Oxford, 488–518.

REFERENCES

Anderson, R. W. and K. McKay (2008), Derivatives Markets, in: X. Freixas, P. Hartmann, and C. Mayer (eds.), *Handbook of European Financial Markets and Institutions*, Oxford University Press, Oxford, 568–596.

Baele, L., A. Ferrando, P. Hördahl, E. Krylova, and C. Monnet (2004), Measuring Financial Integration in the Euro Area, ECB Occasional Paper 14.

Bailey, R. E. (2005) *The Economics of Financial Markets*, Cambridge University Press, Cambridge.

Bank for International Settlements (1994), Risk Management Guidelines for Derivatives, BIS, Basel.

Batten, J., T. Fetherson, and P. G. Szilagi (2004), *European Fixed Income Markets: Money, Bonds, and Interest Rate Derivatives*, John Wiley & Sons Ltd, Chichester.

Bearing Point (2007), The Electronic Bond Market – New Perspectives for Electronic Fixed Income Trading, May.

Casey, J. P. (2006), Bond Market Transparency: To Regulate or not to Regulate . . ., ECMI Policy Brief, Brussels.

Committee of European Securities Regulators (2008), The Role of Credit-Rating Agencies in Structured Finance, CESR, Paris.

Dunne, P., M. Moore, and R. Portes (2006), *European Government Bond Markets: Transparency, Liquidity, Efficiency*, CEPR, London.

European Central Bank (2004a), *The Monetary Policy of the ECB*, ECB, Frankfurt am Main.

European Central Bank (2004b), *The Euro Bond Market Study*, ECB, Frankfurt am Main, December.

European Central Bank (2006), Equity Issuance in the Euro Area, *Monthly Bulletin*, May, 89–99.

European Central Bank (2007a), *Financial Integration in Europe*, ECB, Frankfurt am Main.

European Central Bank (2007b), *Euro Money Market Study 2006*, ECB, Frankfurt am Main.

European Central Bank (2007c), *The Euro Bonds and Derivatives Markets*, ECB, Frankfurt am Main.

European Central Bank (2007d), *Euro Money Market Survey*, ECB, Frankfurt am Main.

European Central Bank (2008a), The Analysis of the Euro Money Market from a Monetary Policy Perspective, *ECB Monthly Bulletin*, February.

European Central Bank (2008b), *Bond Markets and Long-term Interest Rates in Non-euro Area Member States of the European Union – Statistical Tables*, ECB, Frankfurt am Main.

Edwards, A. K., L. E. Harris, and M. S. Piwowar (2007), Corporate Bond Market Transaction Costs and Transparency, *Journal of Finance*, 62(3), 1421–1454.

European Commission (2007), *European Financial Integration Report 2007*, EC, Brussels.

Financial Stability Forum (2008), *Report on Enhancing Market and Institutional Resilience*, FSF, Basel.

Foucault, T. and A. J. Menkveld (2008), Competition for Order Flow and Smart Order Routing Systems, *Journal of Finance*, 63, 119–158.

Goldstein, M. A., E. Hotchkiss, and E. Sirri (2007), Transparency and Liquidity: A Controlled Experiment on Corporate Bonds, *Review of Financial Studies*, 20(2), 235–273.

Harris, L. E. (2003), *Trading and Exchanges: Market Microstructure for Practitioners*, Oxford University Press, Oxford.

Harris L. E. and M. S. Piwowar (2006), Secondary Trading Costs in the Municipal Bond Market, *Journal of Finance*, 61(3), 1361–1397.

Hartmann, P., M. Manna, and A. Manzanares (2001), The Microstructure of the Euro Money Market, ECB Working Paper 80.

International Capital Market Association (2007), *European Repo Market Survey*, Number 12, conducted December 2006, Zürich, ICMA.

International Financial Services London (2007), *Derivatives 2007*, IFSL, London.

Kyle, A. S. (1985), Continuous Auctions and Insider Trading, *Econometrica*, 53, 1315–1336.

Myers, S. and N. Majluf (1984), Corporate Financing and Investment Decisions when Firms have Information that Investors do not Have, *Journal of Financial Economics*, 13, 187–221.

O'Hara, M. (2003), Presidential Address: Liquidity and Price Discovery, *Journal of Finance*, 58, 1335–1353.

Pagano, M. and E. Von Thadden (2008), The European Bond Markets under EMU, in: X. Freixas, P. Hartmann, and C. Mayer (eds.), *Handbook of European Financial Markets and Institutions*, Oxford University Press, Oxford, 488–518.

Reilly, A. (2005), Over-the-Counter Derivatives Markets in Ireland – An Overview, *CBFSAI Quarterly Bulletin*, Dublin, July.

Shiller, R. J. (2003), From Efficient Markets to Behavioral Finance, *Journal of Economic Perspectives*, 17, 83–104.

Wharton (2006), LSE, NYSE, OMX, Nasdaq, Euronext … Why Stock Exchanges Are Scrambling to Consolidate, Knowledge@Wharton, Wharton School, University of Pennsylvania.

Wolswijk, G. and J. de Haan (2005), Government Debt Management in the Euro Area: Recent Theoretical Developments and Changes in Practices, ECB Occasional Paper 25.

The Economics of Financial Integration

OVERVIEW

This chapter begins by defining financial integration and identifying its drivers. Financial integration may be defined as a situation without frictions that discriminate between economic agents in their access to – and their investment of – capital, particularly on the basis of their location. Not only market forces but also collective action and public action are shown to be driving financial integration.

The second part of the chapter deals with measuring financial integration. Three categories of measures have been used for this purpose. The first category consists of price-based indicators that measure discrepancies in prices or returns on assets caused by the geographic origin of the assets. The second category consists of news-based measures. The underlying idea is that in a financially integrated area, portfolios should be well diversified so that news (i.e., arrival of new economic information) of a regional character has little impact on prices, whereas common or global news is relatively more important. The third category of measures are quantity-based indicators that measure the effects of frictions faced by the demand for and supply of investment opportunities, like cross-border activities or listings, and statistics on the cross-border holdings of investors.

The third part of the chapter gives an overview of the extent to which various financial markets in the EU are integrated. An important reason why the European Union put the creation of a single financial market high on the policy agenda is that it widely believed that financial integration may stimulate economic growth. This growth effect and other consequences of financial integration are discussed at the end of the chapter.

LEARNING OBJECTIVES

After you have studied this chapter, you should be able to:
- define financial integration
- explain what drives financial integration
- describe the various ways of measuring financial integration, their shortcomings, and the reasoning underlying these various approaches
- assess the extent to which various financial markets in the EU are integrated
- discuss the consequences of financial integration.

4.1 Financial integration: definition and drivers

Definition of financial integration

While free capital mobility has been a reality in the EU since the late 1980s (see chapter 2), financial market segmentation due to exchange-rate risk persisted until the start of the monetary union in 1999. The introduction of the euro was a powerful catalyst for the creation of integrated financial markets by removing one of the most important obstacles to the cross-border provision of financial services. At the same time, it became clear that there are other impediments to truly integrated financial markets, such as different regulations and institutions across the Member States of the EU.

Following Baele *et al.* (2004, 2008), the following definition of an *integrated financial market* is adopted: the market for a given set of financial instruments and/or services is fully integrated if all potential market participants with the same relevant characteristics

(1) face a single set of rules when they decide to deal with those financial instruments and/or services;

(2) have equal access to the above-mentioned set of financial instruments and/or services; and

(3) are treated equally when they are active in the market.

Full integration requires the same access to banks or trading, clearing, and settlement platforms for both borrowers and lenders, regardless of their country of origin. In addition, full integration requires that there is no discrimination among comparable market participants based solely on their location of origin (Baele *et al.*, 2004).

This definition of financial integration is closely linked to the law of one price, which most empirical studies on financial integration take as the definition of financial integration (see section 4.2). According to the law of one price, assets with identical risks should be priced identically regardless of where they are transacted. As Baele *et al.* (2004) point out, the law of one price is very attractive since it allows for quantitative measures of financial integration, but it can be tested only on instruments that are listed or quoted. Hence, the analysis based on the law of one price cannot serve as a basis for measuring integration among unlisted instruments.

Drivers of financial integration

What drives financial integration? Following the ECB (2003), a differentiation can be made between (i) market forces, (ii) collective action, and (iii) public action.

Market forces

The first driver of financial integration is market forces. Firms benefit from the lower cost of capital that enhanced competition brings about, allowing a better allocation of capital. More productive investment opportunities will become available, and a reallocation of funds to the most productive investment opportunities will take place. Investors also benefit from access to a broader range of financial instruments and more opportunities to diversify their portfolios. The complete elimination of barriers to trading, clearing, and settlement platforms will allow firms to choose the most efficient trading, clearing, and/or settlement platforms. Also financial intermediaries may profit by exploiting the potential economies of scale and scope that a larger market offers. But financial intermediaries may also face pressure on their profit margins.

Figure 4.1 illustrates the impact of enhanced competition with an example. The starting position is a market rate of 4 per cent. In a segmented market with low competition, a bank lends to firms at 6 per cent and offers depositors a return of 2 per cent. The bank earns a margin of 4 per cent. As markets integrate, increased competition forces the bank to reduce its lending rate to 5 per cent and to increase its deposit rate to 3 per cent. The lending firms experience a lower cost of capital, while depositors receive a higher return. The margin for the bank is reduced to 2 per cent. The bank can (partly) offset the reduction of its profit margin by increasing its business in an integrated market.

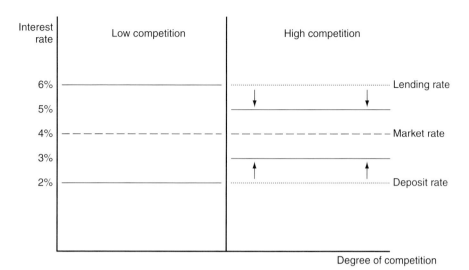

Figure 4.1   Impact of enhanced competition

Since investors and financial intermediaries may benefit from financial integration, market forces could lead to the elimination of market segmentation. For instance, issuance practices of government-bond issuers converged towards what was perceived as 'best' practice because they had to compete to attract investors (Wolswijk and De Haan, 2005). Likewise, mergers of stock exchanges, clearinghouses, and securities settlement systems are often motivated by efforts to exploit the economies of scale and scope potentially available within a broader market. Of course, market forces can foster integration only if there are no legislative or regulatory obstacles standing in the way.

Collective action

Sometimes market forces alone are not sufficient to remove obstacles to integration. This may happen, for instance, due to network externalities in the financial system. The more participants use a particular market, the more benefits it generally brings to its users. These benefits include greater depth and liquidity, reduced transaction costs, as well as easier and more effective opportunities for risk management (ECB, 2003). Individual market participants will not take these externalities into account. Through collective action, market participants can, for instance, agree on standard technical features of financial instruments, the definition of common practices and conventions, or the establishment of reference indices. However, the existence of powerful network externalities may also hamper integration as strong network effects are often associated with high switching costs, i.e., the cost of switching from one set of organisation, practices, conventions, rules, and infrastructure to another. A switch to a pan-European market entails costs – at least in the short term – for participants in national markets (ECB, 2003).

In 1998 a series of market conventions sponsored by several market organisations stimulated financial integration. A good example is the rules applicable to the basic market interest-reference rate, the EURIBOR (the rate at which euro interbank term deposits are offered by one prime bank to another at 11 am CET). A similar initiative permitted the establishment of the other basic interest reference rate for overnight unsecured interbank deposits, the EONIA. In 2002, another market convention added a new reference index, the EUREPO, i.e., the rate at which one prime bank offers funds in euros to another prime bank if in exchange the former receives eligible assets as collateral from the latter (see chapter 3 for further details).

Another good example of collective action is the creation of the Single Euro Payments Area (SEPA) that will allow customers to make non-cash euro payments to any beneficiary located anywhere in the euro area using a single bank account and a single set of payment instruments. In other words, there will no longer be any differentiation between national and cross-border retail payments within the euro area. This is a major step towards integration. Despite the introduction of the euro in 1999 and the development of TARGET (the EU-wide large-value payment system operated by the ESCB; see chapter 5), retail payments continued to be processed differently throughout the euro area. However, in 2002, the banking industry took the initiative to create the European Payments Council (EPC), which defined the new rules and procedures for euro payments. The goal of SEPA is an integrated, competitive, and innovative retail payments market for all non-cash euro payments which, in time, will be conducted entirely electronically.

Public action

While financial integration benefits first and foremost the market community, its effects are much more widespread (see section 4.4). The pervasive effects of financial integration on the whole economy justify the involvement of public authorities to support its development towards an optimal outcome, e.g., in situations where a public good cannot be supplied privately or where a market or co-ordination failure occurs (ECB, 2003). In both cases, neither market forces alone nor collective action within the private sector is sufficient to deliver the desirable level of integration. In this context, action by public authorities may come in many forms. It can be a catalyst or facilitator of collective action to help overcome co-ordination problems (for instance, the neutral role of the ECB in the fixing of the EONIA rate as a service to the banking sector). It can also extend to direct intervention, as in the case of the development of TARGET. An essential responsibility of public action is the establishment of an appropriate legislative and regulatory framework. The European Commission's FSAP, described in chapter 2, aims to create a single wholesale market and an open and secure retail market.

A good example of 'FSAP in action' is the regulation on cross-border euro payments (No 2560/2001) that gives EU consumers a guarantee that when they make a payment in euros to an account in another EU Member State, it will cost the same as it would to make a payment within their own Member State. As of 1 January 2006, the regulation applies to payments of up to €50,000. According to the European Commission (2006), prior to this regulation charges for cross-border euro payments were often excessive, with a €100 transfer costing the consumer on average €24. According to the Commission, charges for cross-border euro payments have reduced significantly since the introduction of the regulation, with a €100 transfer now costing on average less than €2.50.

4.2 Measuring financial integration

Following Baele *et al.* (2004, 2008), integration of financial markets can be assessed using three categories of measures. The first broad category consists of *price-based indicators*, which measure discrepancies in prices or returns on assets caused by the geographic origin of the assets. Most empirical research on financial market integration in Europe compares rates of return on assets. To properly test for integration, one should compare the prices of assets that have identical cash flows and risk characteristics but that are traded in different countries. The risk of an asset's return is composed of a systematic part and an idiosyncratic part; the latter can be diversified away, the former cannot. While this type of risk may be considered negligible in some cases, for example in the money market, it is crucial to control for it in the corporate bond and equity markets (Baele *et al.*, 2004).

The second category of measures consists of *news-based indicators*. The underlying idea is that in a financially integrated area, portfolios should be well diversified so that news (i.e., arrival of new economic information) of a regional character has little impact on prices, whereas common or global news is relatively more important. This presumes that the degree of systematic risk is identical across assets in different countries.

The third category consists of *quantity-based indicators*, which quantify the effects of frictions faced by the demand for and supply of investment opportunities. Examples are statistics giving information on the ease of market access, such as cross-border activities or listings, and cross-border holdings of securities. However, cross-border activity is an imperfect measure of integration. Increased cross-border traffic typically indicates an increase in integration. But there is no need for cross-border activity in a fully integrated market, as prices are the same everywhere.

The remainder of this section will provide further details on these measures of financial integration.

Price-based measures

The construction of price-based integration measures for the money and government-bond markets is facilitated by the fact that relatively homogeneous assets are available across countries. A widely used measure in research on integration of government-bond markets is the *difference between local yields and some benchmark*, which is often the German yield. In the market for ten-year government bonds, for instance, market participants consider German bonds to be the reference bond. Consequently, it seems reasonable to measure integration in this segment of the bond market by calculating the spread between the yield on a local asset and the German benchmark asset. In perfectly integrated markets the spread should be equal to zero. The time variation in the size of the spread serves as a good indicator of how integration is proceeding in a particular country and market.[1]

Another measure, proposed by Adam *et al.* (2002), is the *beta-convergence* measure. This concept has been developed in the economic growth literature but can be adapted for measuring financial-market integration. It measures the speed of adjustment of deviations of countries to the long-run benchmark value. It involves running the following panel regression:

$$\Delta R_{i,t} = \alpha_i + \beta R_{i,t} + \sum_{l=1}^{L} \gamma_l \Delta R_{i,t-l} + \varepsilon_{i,t} \tag{4.1}$$

where $R_{i,t}$ represents the yield spread on a ten-year government bond in country i at time t, relative to the German benchmark rate, Δ is the difference operator, and α_i is a country dummy. β is the coefficient with respect to the yield spread, and γ_l is the coefficient with respect to lagged yield differences. The error term on the right-hand side of the equation $\varepsilon_{i,t}$

denotes exogenous shocks that force interest-rate differentials between the considered countries.

A negative β coefficient signals convergence (if $\beta=0$ there is no convergence). In the case of a negative β, yields in countries with relatively high yield spreads decrease more rapidly towards the benchmark rate than yields in countries with relatively low yield spreads. Moreover, β is a direct measure of the speed of convergence in the overall market.

While beta-convergence measures the speed of convergence, it does not indicate to what extent markets are already integrated. Therefore, Adam *et al.* (2002) also use *the cross-sectional dispersion in yields* as a measure of the degree of integration, to which they refer as 'sigma convergence'.[2] Also this measure is borrowed from the empirical growth literature, where sigma convergence is said to occur if the cross-sectional distribution of a variable (in the economic growth literature this is typically income per capita) decreases over time. This indicator can be calculated at each point in time by taking the standard deviation of yields across countries. If the cross-sectional standard deviation $sd(i)_t$ is zero, the law of one price applies fully. The degree of financial integration increases when the cross-sectional standard deviation has a downward trend (moves towards zero). This measure is obtained from a regression of the cross-sectional dispersion on a time trend. It is also possible to differentiate between time periods. Adam *et al.* (2002) estimate, for instance, the following regression to check whether there is a systematic difference in convergence before and after the introduction of the euro:

$$sd(i)_t = (\alpha^{pre} + \sigma^{pre} trend) D^{pre} + (\alpha^{post} + \sigma^{post} trend) D^{post} + \varepsilon_t \qquad (4.2)$$

where $sd(i)_t$ is the cross-sectional standard deviation in period t and D^{pre} and D^{post} are dummy variables that take value 1 before and after January 1999, respectively (and zero otherwise). Perfect convergence is achieved when the slope (σ) and the intercept (α) coefficients are both zero. By comparing the intercepts and the slopes before and after the start of the currency union, it becomes possible to assess convergence before and after the adoption of the euro.

Baele *et al.* (2004) suggest measuring the degree of integration by examining whether discrepancies between interest rates in different countries are larger than within countries, arguing that in an integrated market the cross-country dispersion is not expected to be greater than the within-country dispersion. This analysis may be useful for particular markets, such as the unsecured overnight market (see chapter 3) where the dispersion of lending rates of individual banks across countries can be compared with the dispersion of bank rates within countries at each point in time. The ratio between these two measures of dispersion should be close to one if the market is fully integrated. If markets are not integrated, overnight lending rates may tend to be more dispersed across countries than within countries, raising the ratio above one.

In sum, the cross-sectional dispersion of interest-rate spreads or asset-return differentials can be used as an indicator of how far away the various market segments are from being fully integrated. Beta convergence is an indicator for the speed at which markets are integrating. Finally, the degree of cross-sectional variation of yields and (for some markets) the cross-border yield variation relative to the yield variability within individual countries may be informative with respect to the degree of integration.

News-based measures

To make news-based measures operational, one needs to provide a proxy for common news. Baele *et al.* (2004) argue that yield changes in the benchmark asset could be used to proxy all relevant common news. They suggest running the following regression:

$$\Delta R_{i,t} = \alpha_{i,t} + \beta_{i,t}\Delta R_{b,t} + \varepsilon_{i,t} \tag{4.3}$$

where $\Delta R_{i,t}$ is the change in the yield on an asset in country i at time t, $\Delta R_{b,t}$ is the yield change on a comparable asset in the benchmark country b, $\alpha_{i,t}$ is a time-varying intercept, $\beta_{i,t}$ is the time-dependent beta with respect to the benchmark asset, and $\varepsilon_{i,t}$ denotes a country-specific shock. If financial integration increases:

(i) the intercept $\alpha_{i,t}$ will converge to zero, since in integrated markets yield changes in one country should not be systematically larger or smaller than those in the benchmark market;

(ii) the coefficient $\beta_{i,t}$ will converge to one, so that *the average distance of the different country betas to unity* may serve as an integration measure for the overall market. The reason is that $\beta_{i,t}$ depends on both the correlation between local and benchmark yield changes and the ratio between local and benchmark yield volatilities. When integration increases, yield changes should increasingly be driven by common factors, and the correlation should increase towards one. For the same reason, the level of local volatility should converge towards that of the benchmark asset. As a result, increasing integration implies that $\beta_{i,t}$ should converge to one (Baele *et al.*, 2004);

(iii) the proportion of the variance in $\Delta R_{i,t}$ explained by the common factor $\Delta R_{b,t}$ will increase towards 1, so that *the proportion of local variance explained by the common factor* can be used as another measure of integration. The reason is that the country-specific error $\varepsilon_{i,t}$ in equation (4.3) should shrink as integration increases.

This method can be used to assess integration of the bond and credit markets. A variant of this approach can be used to assess integration of equity markets. The natural equivalent to the benchmarks for the equity market is to use returns on a euro area-wide equity-market portfolio. However, Baele *et al.* (2004) argue that available empirical evidence shows that equity returns are significantly affected by global factors, not just regional ones. Hence, for the purpose of examining integration in euro-area equity markets, they distinguish between global and euro area-wide effects on equity returns in the euro area. To this end, Baele *et al.* use the return on US stock markets as a proxy for world news, while the return on a euro area-wide stock-market index, corrected for US news, is used as the euro factor. While returns for all countries share the same two factors, they are allowed to have different sensitivities to these common factors. The portion of local returns not explained by common factors is due to local news.

Quantity-based measures

Baele *et al.* (2004) classify these measures into two groups. The first group includes measures dealing with cross-border activities in a specific market, and the second group refers to measures dealing with home bias.

Cross-border activity measures can be applied to the credit market and the money market. One way to assess the progress made towards integration is to consider whether the existing barriers to entry imposed on foreign economic agents willing to invest in a specific region have been reduced over time. An increase in the volumes of cross-border loans to non-banks and interbank loans would suggest that it has become easier for foreigners to access a regional credit market. In chapters 7 and 9 the cross-border activity of banks and insurers will be discussed.

For corporate and government bonds, Baele *et al.* (2004) regard an increase in the share of non-domestic bond holdings as a sign of further integration as it reflects that economic agents are able to access non-domestic financial products more easily. The extent of the *home bias*, i.e., the degree to which agents invest in domestic assets even though risk is shared more effectively if foreign assets are held, is a sign that financial integration is still not complete. In chapter 6 the home bias of the portfolios of institutional investors will be discussed.

4.3 Integration of European financial markets

This section summarises the main findings of empirical research on European financial integration. The available evidence suggests that the degree of integration varies depending on the market segment (ECB, 2007a) and is correlated with the degree of integration of the underlying financial infrastructure (see chapter 5 for further details). The markets have been described in more detail in chapter 3.

Box 4.1 Euro area vs. non-euro area member countries*

The information shown in section 4.3 refers only to countries in the euro area as our main source of information. The ECB provides information for the euro area only. In a somewhat older study, Adam *et al.* (2002) contrast samples consisting of euro-area countries and all (then) EU Member States. Table 4.1 is reproduced from this study. It shows estimates of equation (4.2) for both samples of countries. There is more evidence of convergence in the euro area than for the sample of EU countries, although convergence also occurred in the latter sample. In the interbank three-month rates the negative trend is more pronounced after 1999 for both groups of countries. The coefficients before and after 1999 are statistically different from each other, as indicated by the *F*-test. Across the euro area, perfect convergence is achieved after 1999. Most of the convergence in the ten-year government-bond market occurs before 1999 and among euro-area countries (also in this case the *F*-test rejects the hypothesis that the slope coefficients are equal).

   Hardouvelis *et al.* (2006) have examined to what extent the integration of equity markets in the EU is related to monetary integration. They assess the evolution of the relative influence of EU-wide risk factors over country-specific risk factors on required rates of return. The authors find that in the second half of the 1990s, the degree of integration gradually increased to the point where individual euro-area country stock markets appear to be fully integrated into the EU market. An important factor that drove the increase in the level of integration was the evolution of the probability of joining the single currency, that is proxied by each country's forward interest-rate differential with Germany. During the 1990s, this forward interest differential was widely used by market analysts as an indicator of the probability that an EU country would eventually manage to join the currency union. In contrast to the euro-area countries, the United Kingdom did not show any signs of increased stock-market integration. As pointed out in chapter 2, the UK has always been ambivalent about joining the euro area, having a so-called 'opt-out' clause. According to Hardouvelis *et al.* (2006, p. 367), 'the United Kingdom is the exception that proves the rule, indicating that the forces behind the formation of the Eurozone had a special role in stock market integration'.

Table 4.1 Sigma convergence (estimates of equation 4.2)

	Interbank 3-months rates		Benchmark 10-years yields	
	Euro and non euro-area	Euro-area	Euro and non Euro-area	Euro-area
$\sigma_{\text{pre-emu}}$	−0.0021 (0.0013)	−0.0182** (0.0019)	−0.0150** (0.0005)	−0.0185** (0.0006)
$\sigma_{\text{post-emu}}$	−0.0429** (0.0022)	Convergence achieved	−0.0012** (0.0009)	0.0005 (0.001)
$\alpha_{\text{pre-emu}}$	69.2651** (17.2878)	276.7812** (25.0592)	214.6554** (7.1433)	261.9454** (8.6341)
$\alpha_{\text{post-emu}}$	652.3706** (33.0800)	Convergence achieved	20.6913 (13.6687)	−5.3027 (16.5214)
Observations	81	81	81	81
R-squared	0.9895	0.9548	0.9812	0.9748
F-test	249.16		166.49	216.81
H_{0A}	(0.00001)		(0.00001)	(0.00001)
F-test	125.46		233.45	18.20
H_{0B}	(0.00001)		(0.00001)	(0.0001)

Source: Adam *et al.* (2002)

Money market

To assess the extent to which the various segments of the money-market rate are integrated, Figure 4.2 shows one of the price-based indicators explained in section 4.2, namely the (unweighted) standard deviation of the average daily interest rates prevailing in each euro-area country.

As the first panel of Figure 4.2 shows, the unsecured money market reached a stage of 'near-perfect' integration almost immediately after the introduction of the euro. The cross-sectional standard deviation of the EONIA lending rates and the 1-month and 12-month EURIBOR rates across euro-area countries fell sharply to close to zero following the introduction of the euro, and has remained stable thereafter.

The second panel of Figure 4.2 shows the standard deviation of the same interest rate, zooming in on the period after the start of the currency union. It becomes clear that even though the standard deviations are very low, they are not constant. For instance, at the end of 2006, the standard deviation for the EONIA increased.

The high level of integration suggested by price-based indicators for the euro-area money market coexists with a limited degree of cross-border activity in the euro-area short-term debt-securities market, as shown in Figure 4.3. According to the ECB (2007a), this may be due partly to the fact that short-term debt securities issued by euro-area governments have very similar risk characteristics and therefore offer little scope for international diversification.

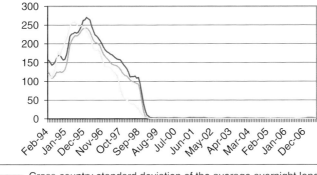

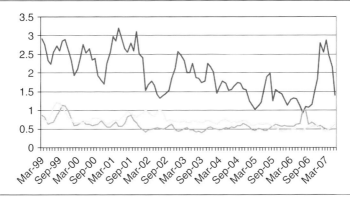

Figure 4.2   Integration of the money market: standard deviation of interest rates (basis points), 1994–2007
Note: The second figure magnifies the data in the previous figure by changing the scaling of the years
(x-axis) and the number of basis points (y-axis).
Source: ECB

Government bond market

Figure 4.4 shows the evolution of the standard deviations of the government
yield spreads over benchmark bonds. As explained in chapter 3, market participants in the market for ten-year government bonds in the euro area consider

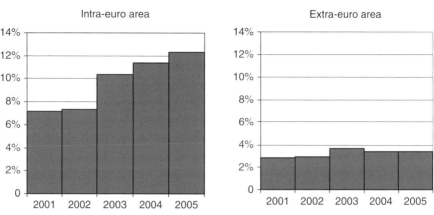

Figure 4.3   Cross-border holding (%) of short-term debt securities issued by euro-area residents, 2001–2005
Note: Intra-euro area is defined as the share of short-term debt securities issues by euro-area residents and held by residents in other euro-area countries. Extra euro-area is defined as the share of short-term debt securities issued by euro-area residents and held by non-residents of the euro area.
Source: ECB

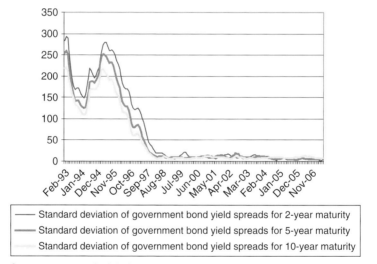

Figure 4.4   Cross-country standard deviation in government-bond yield spreads (basis points), 1993–2006
Source: ECB

German bonds to be the reference bond. In the two- and five-year segments, French government bonds are used as the benchmark. The cross-country standard deviations of government-bond yield spreads are calculated on the basis of daily data for the government-bond yield spreads relative to the benchmark. The figure shows that after the significant drop in the run-up to EMU, the dispersion of yield differentials remains close to zero; there is no further decrease after 1999. Overall, the cross-sectional dispersion for the two- and five-year maturities closely follows the pattern observed for the ten-year maturity bonds. However, before 1998 the dispersion in ten-year government bond yield spreads was systematically lower compared with the other segments.

As explained in section 4.2, in fully integrated markets bond yields should react only to common news, since purely local risk factors can be diversified away. This is the underlying idea of equation (4.3). Figure 4.5 shows the results. From the individual country regressions, the unweighted average $\alpha_{i,t}$ and $\beta_{i,t}$ values are calculated and measured in proportion to the values implied by complete market integration (0 and 1, respectively). The analysis is based on monthly averages of government-bond yields. The average distance in cross-country betas has come down significantly, from more than 1.0 in 1998 to close to 0 as of the end of 2000. The cross-sectional dispersion in the intercept has followed a similar pattern and stayed consistently below a level of around 1.5 basis points.

The measures of integration indicate that the degree of integration in the euro-area government-bond market has been very high since 1999. With the introduction of the euro, government-bond yields converged swiftly in all countries and yields became increasingly driven by common news. However, the results also indicate that yields of government bonds with similar, or in many cases identical, credit risk and maturity have not entirely converged. Differences in liquidity as well as in the availability of developed derivatives markets tied to the various individual bond markets may partly account for these spreads (Baele *et al.*, 2004). Overall, the evidence shows that euro government-bond markets now exhibit a high degree of integration, albeit not as high as in the euro-area money market.

Corporate bond market

In analysing corporate bond-market integration, yield differentials relative to a benchmark cannot be used, as corporate bonds are generally not sufficiently homogeneous to allow for easy comparison. The yield on a corporate bond typically depends on a number of factors, such as the bond's credit rating, time-to-maturity, liquidity, and cash-flow structure. Baele *et al.* (2004) introduce a model that investigates whether yields, once corrected for differences in systematic risk and other characteristics, still depend on the country where the bond was issued. In its most recent assessment of financial-market integration, the ECB (2007a) presents estimates of such a model, testing whether risk-adjusted yields have a systematic country component. In an

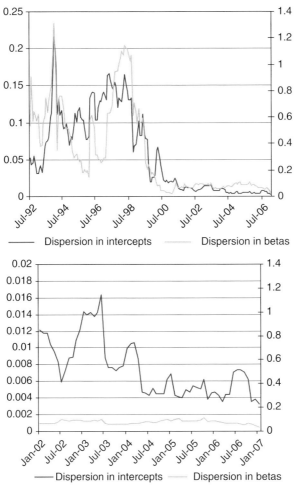

Figure 4.5   Average distance of intercepts/beta from the values implied by complete integration (10-year bond yields), 1992–2007

Note: The second figure magnifies the data in the previous figure by changing the scaling of the years (x-axis) and the number of basis points (y-axis).

Source: ECB

integrated market, the proportion of the total yield-spread variance that is explained by country effects should be close to zero. The indicators show that the euro-area corporate-bond market is quite well integrated: country effects explain only a very small and constant proportion of the cross-sectional variance of corporate bond-yield spreads (see Figure 4.6).

Further information on bond-market integration can be gained from data on the development of holdings of debt securities issued by governments and

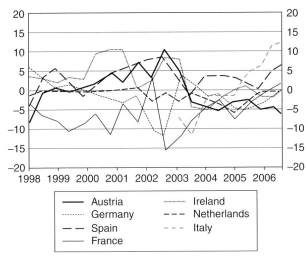

Figure 4.6   Estimated coefficients of country dummies
Source: ECB

non-financial corporations from other euro-area countries. The data available do not make a distinction between government and corporate bond holdings. The finding that bond markets are highly integrated is broadly confirmed by the strong rise in cross-border holdings (see Figure 4.7). According to the ECB (2007a), monetary financial institutions have strongly increased their cross-border holdings of debt securities since the end of the 1990s, from about 10 per cent to nearly 60 per cent. In particular, the holding of debt securities issued by non-financial corporations has increased remarkably from a very low basis, suggesting that investors are increasingly diversifying their portfolios across the euro area.

Equity market

If the equity markets in the euro area were integrated, prices should be mainly driven by common euro-area factors rather than country-specific ones. Assuming that equity returns in euro-area countries react to both a local and a global factor – proxied respectively by shocks in aggregate euro-area and US equity markets – it is possible to measure the proportion of the total domestic equity volatility that can be explained by local and global factors respectively. *Ceteris paribus*, a higher variance ratio associated with euro area-wide changes is an indication of a more integrated euro-area equity market,

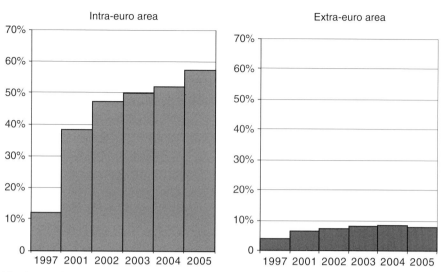

Figure 4.7   The degree of cross-border holdings of long-term debt securities issued by euro-area residents (%),
1997–2005
Source: ECB

Figure 4.8   Proportion of variance in local equity returns explained by euro-area and US shocks (%), 1973–2006
Source: ECB

signalling that national stock-market returns are increasingly driven by common news. Figure 4.8 shows that the variance ratios have increased over the
past 30 years with respect to both euro-area-wide and US shocks, although
the rise has been the strongest for the former. This suggests that regional euro-
area integration has proceeded more quickly than worldwide integration.

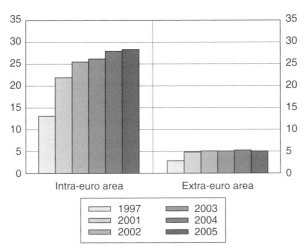

Figure 4.9   The degree of cross-border holdings of equity issued by euro-area residents (%), 1997–2005
Source: ECB (2007a)

At the same time, the level of the variance explained by common factors (about 38 per cent for euro-area shocks and 15 per cent for US shocks) reveals that local shocks are still important.

Also quantity-based measures of euro-area equity-market integration indicate a rising degree of integration in the equity markets (see Figure 4.9). Between 1997 and 2005 euro-area residents doubled their holdings of equity issued in another euro-area country (as a share of their total portfolio of shares issued in their own country and elsewhere in the euro area) to reach 29 per cent. The share of euro-area equity assets held outside the euro area remained much lower and increased only slightly. Since the introduction of the euro, euro-area investors have partially reallocated their equity portfolio from domestic holdings to holdings elsewhere within the euro area (see chapter 6 for further details).

So far, we have discussed financial integration in the EU-15. Box 4.2 reports on financial integration of the new EU Member States.

4.4 The consequences of financial integration

According to Baele *et al.* (2004), financial integration has three benefits: more opportunities for risk sharing and diversification, better allocation of capital, and the potential for higher growth. Financial integration may also have implications for financial stability and the structure of the EU financial system. These consequences of financial integration will be discussed in turn.

Box 4.2 Financial integration of the new EU Member States

The reports of the ECB on financial integration do not provide information regarding the new Member States of the EU (NMS). Cappiello *et al.* (2006) assess the degree of financial integration of Cyprus, the Czech Republic, Estonia, Hungary, Latvia, Poland, and Slovenia, amongst themselves and with the euro area. These authors examine integration between the NMS and the euro zone across two different periods: the pre-convergence and the convergence periods. They employ a factor model for market returns that distinguishes between common and local components. The intuition behind the model is similar to the news-based indicators discussed in section 4.2, i.e., the higher the amount of return variance explained by the common factor relative to the local components, the higher the degree of integration. The analysis is carried out on returns on equity market indices and ten-year government bonds.

The evidence suggests that the degree of integration of equity markets of the NMS with the euro zone has increased in their process towards EU accession. The three new EU member states with the largest economies and most developed financial markets (i.e., the Czech Republic, Hungary, and Poland) exhibit stronger return co-movements both between themselves and with the euro area. However, Capiello *et al.* (2006) find for the four smaller countries (i.e., Cyprus, Estonia, Latvia, and Slovenia) a very low degree of integration between themselves, although Estonia and, to a lesser extent, Cyprus show increased integration both with the euro zone and with the block of large accession economies. For the bond markets, Capiello *et al.* have reliable data for the largest countries only. They find that integration has increased only for the Czech Republic versus Germany (which is used as a benchmark for the euro area) and Poland.

In another recent study, Baltzer *et al.* (2008) apply various of the measures discussed in section 4.2 to the NMS. These authors find that financial markets in the NMS are significantly less integrated than those of the euro area. Nevertheless, Baltzer *et al.* conclude that there is strong evidence that the process of integration of the NMS has accelerated since their accession to the EU. This applies especially to money and banking markets that are becoming increasingly integrated both among themselves and vis-à-vis the euro area. Still, Baltzer *et al.* argue that the process of financial integration in the NMS is probably driven by different factors than those behind the euro area. The transition from planned to market economies has led to rapid financial developments, which has been further boosted by a strong foreign, mainly EU, banking presence (see chapter 8 for further details). In line with the results of Capiello *et al.* (2006), Baltzer *et al.* report that only the government-bond markets of the largest economies exhibit signs of integration. Indeed, Figure 4.10, which shows the spread between ten-year government bond yields of NMS and Germany, indicates that most NMS have been converging in recent years to the German benchmark. In particular, between the beginning of 2001 and mid-2003, government-bond yields and yield spreads relative to the German benchmark declined substantially. However, afterwards spreads remained mostly stable or decreased even further, with the exception of those of Cyprus, Hungary, and Poland.

Finally, the evidence of Baltzer *et al.* for equities suggests a relatively low level of integration, although there is evidence that stock markets are increasingly affected by euro-area shocks, especially after the accession date (May 2004).

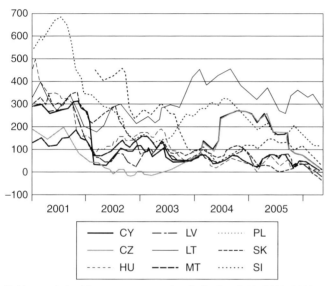

Figure 4.10   Yield spreads for 10-year government bonds (basis points), 2001–2006
Source: Baltzer et al. (2008)

Financial integration will provide additional possibilities to diversify portfolios and share idiosyncratic risk across regions. When agents in an area fully share risk, the consumption of agents in one region co-moves with that of agents located in other regions of that area, while consumption does not co-move with region-specific shocks. There is some evidence suggesting that in the euro area consumption in the various countries is still affected by country-specific shocks. For instance, Adjaouté and Danthine (2003) find that consumption growth rates in the euro area are less correlated than are GDP growth rates, suggesting that risk-sharing opportunities are far from fully exploited. Likewise, Adam *et al.* (2002) reject the hypothesis that consumption growth rates are unaffected by idiosyncratic changes in GDP growth rates.

Greater financial integration may also allow a better allocation of capital. Due to the elimination of barriers to trading, clearing, and settlement platforms, firms will be able to choose the most efficient trading, clearing, and/or settlement platforms. In addition, investors can invest their funds wherever they believe these funds will be allocated to the most productive uses (Baele *et al.*, 2004).

Financial integration may also affect economic growth, due to improved capital allocation and its contribution to financial development. As discussed in chapter 1, recent studies show that financial development is associated with higher economic growth. Why would integration spur financial development?

Integration will stimulate local financial markets and foster internal competition, as well as open these markets to competitive pressure from foreign intermediaries. Guiso *et al.* (2004) argue that financial integration should increase the supply of funds in the less financially developed countries of the integrating area. This may occur for two reasons. First, integration facilitates the entry of more efficient intermediaries to firms in backward areas. Second, integration enables these firms to access more distant financial markets. In both cases, firms in less financially developed countries will face easier and cheaper access to external finance and this should spur capital accumulation and economic growth. Another reason why financial integration may affect financial development runs via improved regulation (Guiso *et al.*, 2004). A 'level playing field' in regulation is an essential prerequisite of an integrated market, and this convergence in regulatory standards is likely to result in an improvement in the regulatory standards of less developed financial markets. All of this will contribute to further financial development, which in turn may affect economic growth. Therefore, financial integration can have a 'growth dividend' in Europe (see also Box 4.3).

Guiso *et al.* (2004) provide an estimate of this growth dividend, based on the empirical relationship between financial market development and growth in the manufacturing industry. These authors examine a scenario where EU countries raise their regulatory standards to the highest current EU standard. They estimate that the effect of achieving full financial integration on the growth of European manufacturing industry is around 0.7 percentage points per year. As EU manufacturing accounts for about one-fourth of EU total value added, this estimate translates into 0.2 percentage points of GDP growth. This overall growth effect results from markedly different country and sector effects, reflecting the heterogeneity of the EU in terms of sector composition and level of financial development. Especially smaller businesses are the main beneficiaries of integration as

---

Box 4.3 Financial integration and economic growth[3]

Theoretically, the economic growth effects of international financial integration are ambiguous. On the one hand, integration facilitates risk sharing and thereby enhances production specialisation, capital allocation, and economic growth. It also eases the flow of capital to capital-scarce countries with positive output effects. Finally, financial integration may enhance the functioning of domestic financial systems, through the intensification of competition and the importation of financial services, with positive growth effects. On the other hand, in the presence of pre-existing distortions, integration can actually retard growth. For instance, in countries with weak institutions − like weak financial and legal systems − integration may induce a capital outflow from capital-scarce countries to capital-abundant countries with better institutions. This line of reasoning suggests that financial integration will promote growth only in countries with sound institutions.

Empirical research on the impact of integration on growth is complicated by the difficulty in measuring integration across a wide array of countries that may impose a complex array of price and quantity controls on a broad assortment of financial transactions. Researchers have used (i) proxies for government restrictions on capital flows, (ii) measures of actual international capital flows, or (iii) the accumulated stock of foreign assets and/or liabilities.

The IMF's restriction measure is the most commonly used proxy of government restrictions on international financial transactions. It classifies countries on an annual basis by the presence or absence of restrictions, i.e., it is a zero-one dummy variable. The advantage of this variable is that it proxies directly for government impediments. Its disadvantage stems from the difficulty in accurately gauging the magnitude and effectiveness of government restrictions (Edison *et al.*, 2002).

Measures of actual international capital flows are also employed to proxy for international financial openness. These measures are based on the assumption that more capital flows indicate more integration. The advantage of these measures is that they are widely available and they are not subjective measures of capital restrictions, but a disadvantage is that many factors influence capital flows, including economic growth (Edison *et al.*, 2002).

Lane and Milesi-Ferretti (2001) have computed the accumulated stock of foreign assets and liabilities for an extensive sample of countries. These stock measures are less sensitive to short-run fluctuations in capital flows associated with factors that are unrelated to integration.

Empirical evidence yields conflicting conclusions about the growth effects of financial integration. While, for instance, Quinn (1997) finds that his measure of capital account openness is positively linked with growth, others report that this relationship is not robust (see Edison *et al.*, 2002 for a more detailed review). Edison *et al.* (2002) examine the growth impact of international financial integration, which they define as the degree to which an economy does not restrict cross-border transactions, using new data and new econometric techniques. The authors want not only to investigate the impact of international financial integration on economic growth but also to assess whether this relationship depends on the level of economic development, financial development, legal system development, government corruption, and macroeconomic policies. They use a wide array of measures of international financial integration for 57 countries, including (variants of) the IMF-restriction measure, various measures of capital flows (FDI, portfolio, and total capital flows), and the accumulated stock of liabilities (as a share of GDP) and the accumulated stock of liabilities and assets (as a share of GDP). Interestingly, the authors find that international financial integration does not accelerate economic growth even when controlling for particular economic, financial, institutional, and policy characteristics. However, in chapter 8 some recent research on the impact of financial integration in the NMS will be discussed that comes to more optimistic conclusions.

they get access to a larger and more developed financial market than that within their national borders. As will be discussed in chapter 8, there is also some recent evidence that financial integration has benefited the new EU Member States.

Financial integration may also have an impact on financial stability, although its direction is not clear. On the one hand, a larger and more diversified financial system will be better able to absorb economic shocks than financial systems in individual countries. According to the ECB (2007a), highly integrated financial markets also allow a more efficient sharing of financial risk that ultimately enhances the stability of the financial system itself. On the other hand, financial integration may also increase the risk of cross-border contagion (ECB, 2003). Economic shocks will spread more easily and rapidly in an integrated financial system (see chapter 11 for a further discussion).

Financial integration may also affect the structure of the financial system, which in turn may have implications for financial stability. Although financial integration will bring about an improvement in the supply of finance in the less financially developed markets and an increase in the size of local financial markets, financial integration does not imply that the financial structures of the countries concerned will converge. As pointed out by Guiso *et al.* (2004), it is possible that the most financially developed countries will share the services provided by their financial system with the other integrating countries. The economies of scale and scope may fuel the expansion of the established intermediaries and markets of the more developed markets. For instance, banks of more developed countries may provide cross-border loans to the firms of less advanced countries, so that the additional provision of credit will not show up in the private domestic credit of the latter countries. Likewise, firms of less financially developed countries can decide to get their shares listed on foreign stock exchanges. Pagano *et al.* (2001) identify a variety of reasons for doing so: overcoming equity rationing in the domestic market, reducing their cost of capital by accessing a more liquid market, and signalling their quality by accepting the scrutiny of more informed investors or the rules of a better corporate-governance system. Cross-border bank lending and listing at foreign stock exchanges implies that quantitative indicators of the financial structure remain different.

An important consequence of this discussion is that the size of the financial market of a given country may no longer be a good indicator of its degree of financial development (Guiso *et al.*, 2004). Distance and geographical segmentation become less important in financially integrated markets. In fact, in a fully integrated market, only the total size of the financial market of the integrating area matters as firms of a given country may have equal access to financial services of all other countries even if their domestic financial sector (scaled by GDP) differs from that in other countries. So differences in the size of local financial markets cannot be exploited to identify the link between financial development and economic growth if countries are perfectly financially integrated (Guiso *et al.*, 2004).

4.5 Conclusions

This chapter defines financial integration as a situation without frictions that discriminate between economic agents in their access to – and their investment of – capital on the basis of their country. Market forces are an important driver of financial integration. Competition can initiate the elimination of segmentation between national markets, resulting in lower prices. Collective action by trade associations is also driving integration. The setting of reference rates, such as the overnight rate (EONIA) and the interbank rate (EURIBOR), is an example of collective action. Finally, public authorities can foster integration. The establishment of an integrated large-value payment system (TARGET) by the ECB was crucial to create a single money market. Likewise, the European Commission's Financial

Services Action Plan contributes to completing the internal market for financial services.

There are different categories of financial-integration measures. Price-based measures are widely used to identify differences in returns caused by the geographic origin of the assets. While price-based indicators are the most direct measure of financial integration, they can be applied only to relatively homogeneous assets. Financial assets tend to differ in credit risk (corporate bonds) or business risk (equities). News-based measures assume that in an integrated market, only common or global news will move prices. Local news has little impact on a geographically diversified portfolio. Quantity-based measures examine cross-border activities. More cross-border business is an indicator of increased integration.

Examining the integration of Europe's financial markets, it is found that the money market and the government bond market are fully integrated. The corporate bond market also appears to be quite well integrated: country effects explain only a minor part of the differences in corporate bond yield spreads. Equity market integration is more difficult to assess. The empirical evidence suggests a rising degree of integration of equity markets. After the introduction of the euro, euro-area investors have partially reallocated their equity portfolio from domestic securities to securities elsewhere within the euro area.

Finally, financial integration enables better risk sharing and better allocation of capital. The result is a more efficient and competitive financial system that promotes economic growth. There is also a downside to financial integration. While a well-diversified financial system can better absorb economic shocks, these shocks can also spread more easily in an integrated financial system. It is therefore important that financial stability policies should stay in tune with advances in financial integration (see chapter 11).

NOTES

1. In analysing other segments of the bond market, like the corporate bond market, one cannot directly analyse yield differentials relative to a benchmark to assess integration. Corporate bonds are generally not homogeneous enough to allow easy comparison as they differ in their cash-flow structure, liquidity, sector, and, most importantly, credit rating. See Baele *et al.* (2004, 2008) for various price-based measures to assess the integration of the corporate-bond market.
2. As Adam *et al.* point out, beta and sigma-convergence indicators have different informational contents. The reason is that mean reversion (β convergence) does not imply that the cross-sectional variance decreases over time (σ convergence).
3. This box heavily draws on Edison *et al.* (2002).

SUGGESTED READING

Baele, L., A. Ferrando, P. Hördahl, E. Krylova, and C. Monnet (2008), Measuring European Financial Integration, in: X. Freixas, P. Hartmann, and C. Mayer (eds.), *Handbook of European Financial Markets and Institutions*, Oxford University Press, Oxford, 165–194.

Edison, H. J., R. Levine, L. Ricci, and T. Sløk (2002), International Financial Integration and Economic Growth, *Journal of International Money and Finance*, 21(6), 749–776.

Guiso, L., T. Jappelli, M. Padula, and M. Pagano (2004), Financial Market Integration and Economic Growth in the EU, *Economic Policy*, 524–577.

REFERENCES

Adam, K., T. Jappelli, A. M. Menichini, M. Padula, and M. Pagano (2002), Analyse, Compare, and Apply Alternative Indicators and Monitoring Methodologies to Measure the Evolution of Capital Market Integration in the European Union, Report to the European Commission, EC, Brussels.

Adjaouté, K. and J.-P. Danthine (2003), European Financial Integration and Equity Returns: A Theory-Based Assessment, in: V. Gaspar et al. (eds.), *The Transformation of the European Financial System*, ECB, Frankfurt.

Baele, L., A. Ferrando, P. Hördahl, E. Krylova, and C. Monnet (2004), Measuring Financial Integration in the Euro Area, ECB Occasional Paper 14.

Baele, L., A. Ferrando, P. Hördahl, E. Krylova, and C. Monnet (2008), Measuring European Financial Integration, in: X. Freixas, P. Hartmann, and C. Mayer (eds.), *Handbook of European Financial Markets and Institutions*, Oxford University Press, Oxford, 165–194.

Baltzer, M., L. Cappiello, R. A. De Santis, and S. Manganelli (2008), Measuring Financial Integration in New EU Member States, ECB Occasional Paper 81.

Cappiello, L., B. Gérard, A. Kadareja, and S. Manganelli (2006), Financial Integration of New EU Member States, ECB Working Paper 683.

European Central Bank (2003), The Integration of Europe's Financial Markets, *Monthly Bulletin*, October, 53–56.

European Central Bank (2007a), *Financial integration in Europe*, ECB, Frankfurt.

European Central Bank (2007b), *Euro Money Market Study 2006*, ECB, Frankfurt.

European Central Bank (2007c), *The Euro Bonds and Derivatives Markets*, ECB, Frankfurt.

Edison, H. J., R. Levine, L. Ricci, and T. Sløk (2002), International Financial Integration and Economic Growth, *Journal of International Money and Finance*, 21(6), 749–776.

European Commission (2006), Commission Staff Working Document Addressed to the European Parliament and to the Council on the Impact of Regulation (EC) No 2560/2001 on Bank Charges for National Payments, EC, Brussels.

Guiso, L., T. Jappelli, M. Padula, and M. Pagano (2004), Financial Market Integration and Economic Growth in the EU, *Economic Policy*, 524–577.

Hardouvelis, G. A., D. Malliaropulos, and R. Priestley (2006), EMU and European Stock Market Integration, *Journal of Business*, 79(1), 365–392.

Lane, P. R. and G. M. Milesi-Ferretti (2001), The External Wealth of Nations: Measures of Foreign Assets and Liabilities in Industrial and Developing Countries, *Journal of International Economics*, 55, 263–294.

Pagano, M., O. Randl, A. Roëll, and J. Zechne (2001). What Makes Stock Exchanges Succeed? Evidence from Cross-Listing Decisions, *European Economic Review*, 45, 770–82.

Quinn, D. (1997), The Correlates of Change in International Financial Regulation, *American Political Science Review*, 91, 531–51.

5

Financial Infrastructures

OVERVIEW

This chapter discusses the payment and post-trading (i.e., securities clearing and settlement) systems in the EU. Over the past decade, the volume and value of transactions that are processed via these systems have grown tremendously. Stable and efficient payment and post-trading systems have become of great importance for the operation of financial markets and the economy in general. At present, these infrastructures are very fragmented and competition is limited.

This chapter starts by examining the different elements of payment and post-trading systems. A distinction is made between retail and wholesale payment systems. Given the growing importance of card-based payment systems, the main focus will be on the set-up of the existing card schemes. Furthermore, the different steps of the post-trading process, which arranges the transfer of ownership and the payment between buyers and sellers in security markets, will be discussed. Finally, the role of central banks in the oversight of payment and settlement systems will be clarified.

The second part of the chapter gives an overview of the economic features of payment and security market infrastructures. These infrastructures are characterised by economies of scale and scope, and network externalities. Understanding these characteristics should enable the reader to better comprehend (future) developments within the EU payment and security market infrastructures.

The third part of this chapter describes: (i) the current situation in the payment and post-trading industry, (ii) the barriers to cross-border payment and security settlement services, and (iii) recent initiatives to promote further integration. Despite the Single Market and the common currency, the internal market for retail payments and post-trading services remains fragmented and could benefit from enhanced competition. Recent initiatives have the potential to take away some of the existing barriers for integration.

LEARNING OBJECTIVES

After you have studied this chapter, you should be able to:

- define what a payment system is
- explain the difference between wholesale and retail payment systems
- describe the various steps of the post-trading process
- understand the economic characteristics of payment and security market infrastructures, and explain how these characteristics influence the EU market structure
- assess the extent to which the different elements of the EU financial infrastructure are integrated
- discuss the barriers that need to be removed in order to strengthen integration of financial infrastructures.

5.1 Payment systems and post-trading services

Payment systems

A *payment* is a transfer of money between economic actors. This transfer can take place, for example, between a consumer and a merchant to pay for delivered goods or services using cash and non-cash money. Cash payments require no systems for settlement between economic actors. Settlement is immediately final when bank notes or coins are handed over. This is different for non-cash payments, such as a transfer from a bank account. In order to settle a transaction, one bank account has to be debited and another has to be credited. Different systems are in place to make sure that the non-cash transfer is completed in a safe and efficient manner. If the transaction takes place between accounts held at the same bank, the bank's internal administrative system can settle the transaction. In general, however, economic agents hold accounts at different banks and therefore non-cash payments require cooperation between banks. A *payment system* can be defined as a combination of technical, legal, and commercial instruments, rules, and procedures that ensure the transfer of money between banks. A distinction can be made between (i) retail payment systems and (ii) wholesale payment systems.

Retail payment systems

Retail payment systems are used for the transaction, clearing, and settlement of relatively low-value and non-time-critical payments initiated through payment instruments such as cheques, credit transfers, direct debits, and payment cards (BIS, 2001). Retail payments are generally made in large numbers (mass payments) by many economic actors and typically relate to the purchase of goods and services in both the consumer and business sectors (BIS, 2002a). Moreover, retail payments are made using a wide range of payment instruments and in varied contexts. Generally, private-sector systems are used for the transaction process and the clearing of retail payments.

Each retail payment system consists of:

- payment instruments used to initiate and direct the transfer of money between the accounts of the payer and the payee (see Box 5.1 for an overview of the main payment instruments available);

Box 5.1 Core payment instruments

Credit transfers: a payment initiated by the payer. The latter sends a payment instruction to his/her bank. The bank debits the payer's account and advises the receiver's bank to credit the beneficiary's account. This can happen through different channels and via intermediaries.

Direct debit: a payment initiated by the creditor, who sends the instructions to collect money via his/her bank or via a central processing entity (automated clearinghouse) to the debtor's bank(s). Direct debits are often used for recurring payments, like those for utilities. They require a pre-authorisation ('mandate') by the payer. Direct debits are also used for one-off payments in which case the payer authorises an individual payment.

Payment card: a differentiation can be made between two main types of card payment instruments: (i) *debit cards*, which allow the cardholder to charge purchases directly and individually to an account, and (ii) *credit cards*, which allow purchases within a certain credit limit. The balance is settled in full or partly by the end of a specified period. In the latter case the remaining balance is taken as extended credit on which the cardholder must pay interest.

Cash: in the euro area, only the ECB has the right to authorise the issue of banknotes. The national central banks in the euro area bring bank notes into circulation by providing them to the banking sector. Banknotes are mainly distributed to the public via ATMs (automated teller machines).

Source: European Central Bank

- payment infrastructures for transacting and clearing payment instruments, processing and communicating payment information, and transferring payment information between the paying and receiving institutions;
- financial institutions that provide payment accounts, instruments, and services to consumers, and organisations that operate payment transaction, clearing, and settlement service networks for those financial institutions;
- market arrangements (or payment schemes) such as conventions, regulations, and contracts for producing, pricing, delivering, and acquiring the various payment instruments and services in order to maintain a minimum level of efficiency and security between all payment service providers in a market. A *payment scheme* is the set of interbank rules, standards, and practices for the provision or operation of specific payment instruments. In a more practical sense, the scheme defines the characteristics of a specific payment instrument, e.g., the authorisation procedures, the fee structure, and the maximum time frame within which a payment is processed, thereby laying down the rules with which all participating payment service providers have to comply. These rules ensure predictability, security, and efficiency in the provision of the given payment instrument;
- laws, standards, rules, and procedures set by legislators, courts, and regulators that define and govern the mechanics of the payment process and the conduct of payment service markets in order to make payment service providers meet public policy goals (BIS, 2006).

A payment can start with a transaction initiated by the payer (*push transaction*) or initiated by the payee (*pull transaction*) and ends at the moment when the payee has received the agreed amount of money in good order. Depending on the actual payment instrument and the organisation of the banking sector, the payment instruction travels through one or more of the following: from an entry bank (paying/receiving bank or branch) to a settlement bank (bank head office or correspondent bank) and then to a clearinghouse or processing centre (see Figure 5.1). The latter is a central processing mechanism through which financial institutions agree to exchange payment instructions. Settlement takes place at a designated time based on the rules and procedures of the clearinghouse (see also the next section on wholesale payment systems). In most cases the actual settlement of the payment takes place at the central bank (or in some cases a private entity) where the respective settlement banks have their accounts. The distribution of the payment to the payee completes the payment process. *Payment finality*, i.e., the guarantee of a payment to the payee, is critical in this respect.

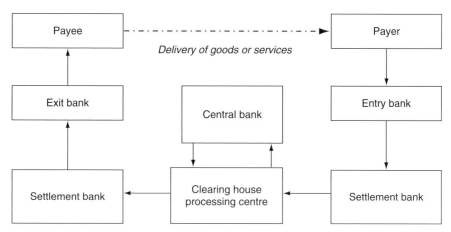

Figure 5.1   The process of initiating and receiving payments (push transaction)
Source: Khiaonarong (2003)

The efficiency of retail payment systems has been enhanced over time by
the transition from:

- cash payments to demand deposits and book money;
- paper-based payments to electronic payment systems; and
- manual processing of payments to automated end-to-end processing. The
  latter is also referred to as straight-through processing (STP).

Strengthening the efficiency of these systems is essential as the costs of retail
payments to society are substantial. Brits and Winder (2005) estimate that the
costs of point-of-sale (POS) payment instruments in the Netherlands amount
to €0.35 per transaction, making up 0.65 per cent of GDP. The authors find
that e-purses or electronic wallets are most cost efficient, irrespective of the
size of a transaction. Cash is most economical for purchases below €11.63,
while the debit card is to be preferred for larger purchases. In a similar study
conducted for Sweden, Bergman *et al.* (2007) report that the overall cost of
payments at a point of sale is approximately 0.4 per cent of GDP. Debit and
credit cards are socially less costly than cash for payments above €8 and €18,
respectively. The latter is interesting, as Brits and Winder (2005) argue that
from a cost perspective credit cards should not be used at all. Notwithstanding
these differences, it follows from both studies that a shift towards a more
cashless society is likely to improve economic welfare.

Despite its relatively high costs, cash is still most frequently used by
European citizens, as at least six out of seven payments are made in cash
(Capgemini, 2007). However, non-cash payments (like cheques, credit trans-
fers, direct debits, and payment cards) account for most of the value of

Table 5.1 Growth rate of non-cash payment instrument, 2001–2005

	Number of transactions per payment instrument (millions)			Share of the different instruments (%)	
	2001	2005	Compound annual growth rate (%)	2001	2005
Credit transfers	15,646	19,352	5	30	29
Direct debits	12,356	17,167	9	24	26
Cheques	8,494	7,040	−5	16	11
Cards	14,903	22,726	11	29	34
Total	51,542	66,638	7	100	100

Note: countries included are Austria, Belgium, Denmark, Finland, France, Germany, Greece, Ireland, Italy, Luxembourg, the Netherlands, Poland, Portugal, Slovenia, Spain, Sweden, and the UK.
Source: Capgemini (2007)

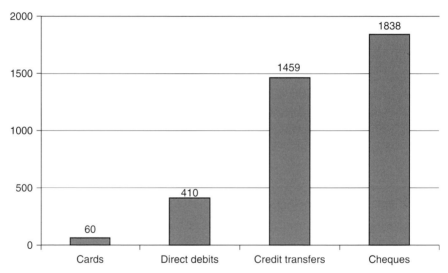

Figure 5.2   Average value of transactions per non-cash payment instrument (in €) in 2005
Note: countries included are Austria, Belgium, Denmark, Finland, France, Germany, Greece, Ireland, Italy, Luxembourg, the Netherlands, Poland, Portugal, Slovenia, Spain, Sweden, and the UK.
Source: Capgemini (2007)

payments in the EU, and the number of electronic payments (such as card transactions) has been growing rapidly (see Table 5.1). Figure 5.2 shows that the average value of an individual payment differs substantially between the various non-cash payment instruments, ranging from €60 for debit cards to €1838 for cheques. The average value of individual payments made by cards has decreased, indicating that consumers are using them more frequently as a substitute for cash. However, payment customs vary substantially across EU Member States. For example, countries like Greece, Italy, Poland, and Spain still have relatively low levels of non-cash usage.

Card-based payment systems

Card payments are the most popular non-cash payment instrument in Europe (as more than one third of all transactions are card transactions). Given the growing importance of card-based payment systems, this specific means of payment will be briefly explained. In principle, each debit or credit card payment involves the following four parties:

- the *cardholder*: the person who has received the payment card from the issuer;
- the *issuer*: the payment service provider that issues the payment card to the cardholder;
- the *merchant*: the person accepting the card payment in return for goods or services; and
- the *acquirer*: the payment service provider that provides payment services to the merchant.

Moreover, interbank payment arrangements are in place for executing funds transfers between the two intermediaries. There are different arrangements to organise the processing of a card payment. Figure 5.3 depicts a *four-party*

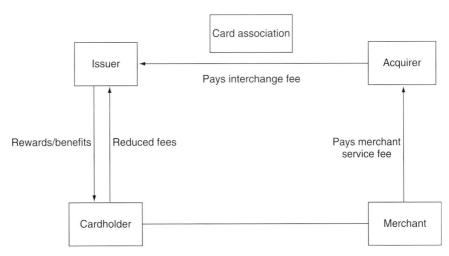

Figure 5.3   Four-party payment scheme
Source: Harper *et al.* (2006)

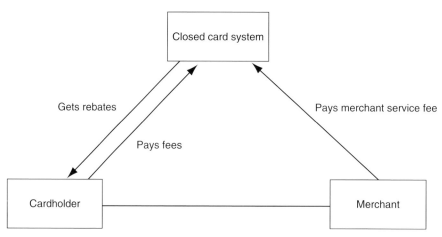

Figure 5.4   Three-party payment scheme
Source: Harper *et al.* (2006)

payment scheme (cardholder – issuer – acquirer – merchant). Such a scheme (such as Visa and Mastercard) is often referred to as 'open', as the issuer and acquirer can be any financial institution. A payment scheme where issuing and acquiring is performed by the same payment service provider (such as Diners Club or American Express) is referred to as a *three-party scheme* (cardholder – payment service provider – merchant). This is shown in Figure 5.4. As in a three-party scheme the issuer and acquirer are the same payment service provider, it is also referred to as a 'closed' system.

Card schemes operate under a rather controversial construction, which is also the subject of several regulatory and antitrust investigations, i.e., the interchange and merchant service fees. The *interchange fee* is a fee paid by an acquiring institution to an issuing institution for each payment card transaction at the point of sale of a merchant. The *merchant service fee* is the fee paid for each transaction by a merchant to an acquirer who processes the merchant's transaction through the network and obtains the funds from the cardholder's bank (European Commission, 2007). In a four-party card scheme, the merchant finally receives the amount of the transaction, minus the interchange fee and the merchant fee.

The usage of interchange or merchant service fees may raise several concerns. First, these fees may be seen as a collective agreement between competitors that distorts competition in the market for payment cards. Second, the non-transparent pricing of card payments (for example, as a result of a ban on surcharging[1]) creates hardly any incentive to make use of more efficient payment instruments. Third, as merchants adjust their prices for goods and services for these fees, cross-subsidisation occurs, i.e., consumers who make use of other (more efficient) means of payment subsidise the use of expensive (credit) cards.

Wholesale payment systems

Wholesale payment systems can be defined as those through which large-value and time-critical funds transfers are made between financial institutions within the system (for their own account or for their customers). Although no minimum value is set for these payments, the average value of payments passed through such systems is normally relatively high (BIS, 2001). In *real-time gross settlement (RTGS) systems*, each payment is immediately settled on a gross basis. The fact that each payment is processed on an individual basis at the time it is received (rather than at a later stage) enhances the stability of the system. TARGET (Trans-European Automated Real-time Gross Settlement Express Transfer System) is the most important interbank payment system for real-time processing of cross-border transfers throughout the EU. It has been developed to (i) provide a safe and reliable mechanism for the settlement of euro payments, (ii) increase the efficiency of cross-border payments in euros, and (iii) serve the needs of the monetary policy of the ECB and to promote the integration of the euro money market. According to the ECB (2007a), financial integration is more advanced in those market segments that are closer to the single monetary policy (see also chapter 4). The full integration of the large-value payment systems has been instrumental in achieving this result. At this moment, TARGET includes 16 national RTGS systems and the ECB payment mechanism (EPM). It is one of the two largest payment systems in the world (the other one being Fedwire). In 2006, it processed 83.2 million national and cross-border payments, with a total value of more than €533 trillion. It has a share of 89 per cent of the total value processed by all large-value euro payment systems.

In 2006 the daily average number of payments processed in TARGET as a whole, i.e., domestic and cross-border payments taken together, amounted to more than 326,196, with an average daily value of €2,092 billion. The average value of a cross-border interbank payment in 2006 was €19.6 million. However, during the last hour of the working day (when only interbank payments are possible) the average payment size reached €128.3 million. The average value of a customer payment in 2006 was €0.9 million.

Role of the Eurosystem

The smooth functioning of payment and security settlement systems is crucial for:

- a sound currency, i.e., stable and efficient payment systems are an essential condition for maintaining trust in the value of money;
- the conduct of monetary policy as these systems play an important role in monetary policy operations;
- the functioning of financial markets, i.e., in the absence of a stable and efficient payment infrastructure, financial markets would not be able to process the current volume and value of transactions;
- the maintenance of financial stability, i.e., problems in financial institutions can manifest themselves in payment or security settlement systems. Moreover, these systems can act as a channel for transmitting problems from one institution to another.

For all these reasons, central banks have an interest in the design and management of payment and security settlement systems. The Eurosystem has the statutory task of promoting the smooth operation of payment and settlement systems.[4] It fulfils this task by:

- providing payment and securities settlement facilities: the Eurosystem runs a settlement system for large-value payments in euros (TARGET2) and thereby functions as banker to the banks. The latter means that banks hold funds on their account at the central bank, and payments between banks are made by debiting and crediting central bank accounts. Moreover, the Eurosystem also provides a mechanism for the cross-border use of collateral in order to facilitate payments taking place when there is a deficit in the account of the paying bank;
- overseeing the euro payment and settlement systems: the Eurosystem applies internationally agreed standards to ensure the soundness and efficiency of systems handling euro transactions. It also assesses the continuous compliance of euro payment and settlement systems with these standards;
- overseeing compliance with the standards for securities clearing and settlement systems;
- ensuring an integrated regulatory and oversight framework for securities settlement systems;
- acting as a catalyst for change: the Eurosystem promotes efficiency in payment systems and securities markets by encouraging the removal of barriers towards integration.

5.2 Economic features of payment and securities market infrastructures

Payment and securities market infrastructures are characterised by economics of scale and scope and network externalities.

Economies of scale arise when the cost per unit falls as output increases. This effect occurs when it is possible to spread fixed costs over a higher output. Schmiedel and Schönenberg (2005) argue that economies of scale are usually a result of the need for service providers to create a 'critical mass' of customers in order to reap the benefit of sizeable investments in information technology and communication networks. If securities infrastructure providers are successful in attracting a significant number of issuers and participants, these set-up costs may be spread over a wider number of transactions. Similarly, there are strong economies of scale in the production of payment services. In a European cross-country study, Humphrey *et al.* (2003) find that costs increase by 2 per cent when volumes rise by 10 per cent. Bolt and Humphrey (2006) estimate payment scale economies using a panel of payment and banking data for 11 European countries over 18 years. Their results show that doubling of payment volume would increase total costs by only 27 per cent. Figure 5.6 shows how unit payment costs vary with the total number of payment transactions.[5] The figure clearly

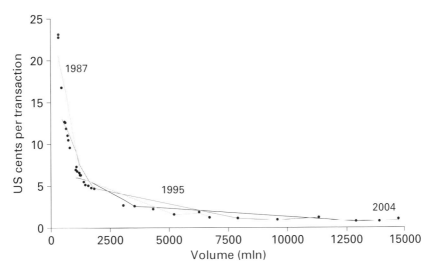

Figure 5.6   Economies of scale in the payment market
Source: Bolt (2007)

shows that the costs of payments decline as the volume of payments that are processed increases.

Economies of scope refer to the reduction of the per-unit costs resulting from the production of a wider variety of goods and services (i.e., when it is cheaper to produce good A and good B together rather than separately). So, integrated financial infrastructures can develop new products and services at a lower unit cost. A precondition for economies of scope is that it is possible to share (certain) input factors for the production of different goods and services.

Economies of scope for CSDs and CCPs can stem from extending the number of financial instruments or trading platforms for which they provide services. Moreover, there is a strong complementary relationship between the various components of securities settlement (Kazarian, 2006). This entails that economies of scope can be obtained by integration along the value chain of a securities transaction, i.e., by combining trading, clearing, and settlement into one firm. Such a supplier can offer its services at lower cost than different suppliers providing these services separately. A good example of such a vertically integrated entity (or 'silo') is Deutsche Börse. Serifsoy and Weiß (2007) argue that one of the adverse effects of vertical integration is the leverage of a (natural) monopoly from one stage of the value chain upstream or downstream to other stages. An integrated supplier may cross-subsidise its trading costs – and thereby attract customers from other platforms – through its monopoly profits on the clearing and settlement stage or vice versa. It may also foreclose the market for competitors as users can be forced to 'buy' another service from the same institution.

As for payment systems, economies of scope may exist when the system handles more than one type of payment instrument or service. This allows the operator of the system to spread out the fixed cost of the system over a wider range of payment instruments.

Generally, the demand for payment services is largely inelastic as payments in themselves do not generate value. A payment is made because of the purchase of a good or a service or to pay off a debt or a financial obligation. Payment services are therefore a convenience good rather than a primary good. However, payment service users may be (very) sensitive to relative payment prices (i.e., price differences between individual payment instruments).

Now we turn to network externalities. A *network* can be defined as a large system consisting of many similar (or complementary) parts that are connected to allow movement or communication between the parts or between the parts and a centre. The addition of a new participant in a network can increase the value of the network for all participants. This means that the value of the services and products offered to the participants depends on the

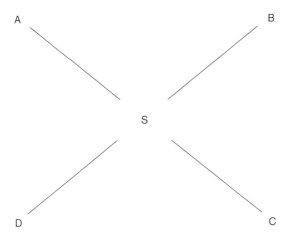

Figure 5.7   Simple network consisting of four side branches

number of other participants purchasing the same services and products (*network externalities*). As an example, consider a simple network consisting of a central junction S and side-branches A, B, C, and D, as shown in Figure 5.7 (based on Economides, 1993). The goods in this network are composite goods, each comprising two complementary components – for example, ASB is comprised of the complements AS and SB. Imagine that the network would consist of the three side-branches A, B, and C. In this case the network would create six products (i.e., ASB, ASC, BSA, BSC, CSA, and CSB). Economides (1993) shows that the addition of a new side-branch to a network composed of *n* side-branches, creates *2n* new products. So the addition of another side-branch, say D, creates six new products. This is an economy of scope in consumption that is called a *network externality*. Network externalities can be found in a variety of industries, such as telecommunications, airlines, railroads, etc. (Shy, 2001). The externality directly increases consumer utility through the provision of new goods, and it may also affect consumers indirectly through price decreases.

Financial markets exhibit positive size externalities as increasing the size of an exchange market increases the expected utility of all participants. Higher participation of traders on both sides of the market decreases the variance of the expected market price and increases the expected utility of risk-averse traders. *Ceteris paribus*, higher liquidity increases traders' utility. Thus, financial exchange markets exhibit network externalities (Economides, 1996).

Payment and securities market infrastructures also have characteristics of network industries, as the benefits to one market participant using a specific platform or system increase when another participant also chooses to do

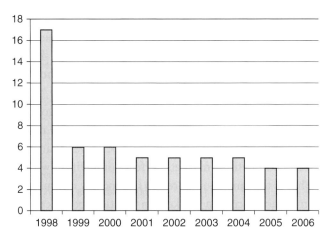

Figure 5.9   The number of large-value payment systems for euro transactions in the euro area, 1998–2006
Source: ECB (2007b)

providers) had individual arrangements under which one bank provided payment and other services to another bank (mostly on a cross-border basis), holding accounts at each other. These correspondent bank arrangements enabled financial institutions to operate cross-border payments without having a foreign branch or subsidiary.

This setting changed substantially in response to the launch of the euro, when the ESCB established TARGET, thereby connecting the existing domestic LVPSs and the ECB payment mechanism. Moreover, private banks introduced EURO1, a high-value payment system for cross-border and domestic transactions in euros between 70 participating banks operating in the European Union. Due to further consolidation, there are currently four LVPSs for euro transactions in the euro area (see Figure 5.9).[6] These multilateral payment systems have a market share of around 80 per cent. TARGET2 handles the largest value of payments.

Another important global LVPS is the Continuous Linked Settlement (CLS) system for foreign-exchange transactions. This specialised system, based in New York, provides global multi-currency settlement services for foreign-exchange transactions, using a payment-versus-payment (PvP) mechanism (i.e., a foreign-exchange operation is settled only if both counterparties simultaneously have a sufficient position in the currency they are selling). PvP has been introduced to prevent the Herstatt risk (or foreign-exchange settlement or cross-currency settlement risk). The term *Herstatt risk* refers to the failure of Bankhaus Herstatt in 1974 as a result of incomplete settlement of foreign-exchange transactions (see Box 5.2).

Box 5.2 The Herstatt crisis

On 26 June 1974, the German authorities closed Bankhaus Herstatt, a medium-sized bank that was very active in foreign-exchange markets. On that day, some of Herstatt's counterparties had irrevocably paid large amounts of D-Marks to the bank but not yet received dollars in exchange, as the US financial markets had just opened for the day. Herstatt's closure started a chain reaction that disrupted payment and settlement systems. Its New York correspondent bank suspended all US-dollar payments from the German bank's account. Banks that had paid D-Marks to Herstatt earlier that day therefore became fully exposed to the value of those transactions. Other banks in New York refused to make payments on their own account or for their customers until they had confirmation that their counter value had been received. These disruptions were propagated further through the multilateral net settlement system used in New York. Over the next three days, the amount of gross funds transferred by this system declined by an estimated 60 per cent. Bankhaus Herstatt's closure was the first and most dramatic case of a bank failure where incomplete settlement of foreign-exchange transactions caused severe problems in payment and settlement systems. Several other episodes occurred in the 1990s but they were less disruptive.

Source: BIS (2002b)

Retail payment systems

For retail payments, the EU still consists of 27 heterogeneous payment areas instead of one single payment market. According to Salo (2006), there are two important explanations for this. First, path dependence can explain the slow change of national payment habits. All national payment systems have their own membership criteria, standards, and practices. Second, critical mass or installed base of network facilities plays a crucial role in the start-up and growth of a network. Over time, national systems have been optimised to satisfy national-user preferences in the most efficient way. Since most payments take place nationally this is a very efficient outcome, but it prevents reaping European-scale benefits. Substituting the existing national systems with one European system does not only run the risk of not being able to satisfy all user requirements, it also means that substantial investments have to be made.

This characteristic of networks can present a barrier to entry for new payment-service providers. In fact, the start-up problem can be seen as a chicken-and-egg problem: consumers are not interested in purchasing the

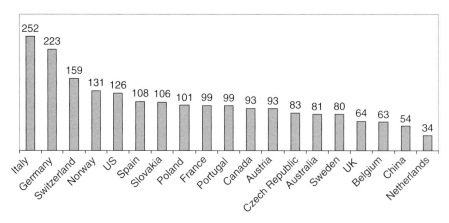

Figure 5.10   A comparison of prices for payment services (in €) in 2005
Source: Capgemini (2005)

good or service when the installed base is too small, and the installed base is too small because an insufficiently small number of consumers have purchased the good or service (Economides and Himmelberg, 1995).

For now, the way in which cross-border retail transactions are settled varies widely across countries and types of institutions (Freixas and Holthausen, 2008). The first pan-European clearinghouse (PE-ACH) for retail payments is the STEP 2 system, which the Euro Banking Association launched in 2003. Payments may be settled on a bilateral basis between national clearinghouses. In case the payee and payer have an account with the same cross-border financial group, the payment may also be settled in house.

The current fragmentation upholds the inefficiency of some payment systems within the EU. Figure 5.10 shows the substantial differences in direct prices for payment services between EU Member States. For example, on average a Dutch consumer annually pays €34 for these services, while an Italian consumer pays €252. According to the European Commission (2005), the estimated aggregated cost for the EU payment system ranges between 2–3 per cent of GDP. However, in some Member States (like Belgium, the Netherlands, and Sweden) these costs are substantially lower. Evidence suggests that the costs of payment services in these Member States are 0.3–0.5 per cent of GDP. The key determinant of the cost of payment systems is the use of cash, accounting for as much as 60–70 per cent of the total cost. The relatively low aggregated costs of payment services in, for example, the Benelux and Scandinavian countries are closely related to the relatively high usage of more efficient electronic payment instruments. At the national level, authorities have tried to minimise the cost of the payment system. This can be done by reducing the use of cash (the processing of which is very costly, particularly for banks) and by substituting paper-based payment instruments with electronic payments that can be automated from end to end.

According to the European Commission (2007), there are a number of competition concerns in the markets for payment cards and payment systems. Markets in many Member States are highly concentrated. Even though high concentration does not necessarily imply lack of competition, barriers to new entry exist especially in the market for payment cards where market parties charge high card fees (see Box 5.3).

There are large variations in merchant fees across the EU. For example, firms in Member States with high fees have to pay banks three or four times more of their revenue from card sales than those in Member States with low fees. There are also large variations in interchange fees between banks across the EU, which may not be passed on fully in lower fees for cardholders.

Box 5.3 Concentration in credit and debit card markets

According to the European Commission (2007), payment markets are still mostly fragmented, with little or no competition at the EU level. Market parties mostly compete domestically, with the rare exception of a few international network players, such as Visa, MasterCard, and AMEX, which compete at the European level. In some Member States, these international networks face strong competition from national debit networks, which sometimes account for up to 90 per cent of all card transactions. At the bank level, the picture is somewhat different. In most Member States, competition is strong among issuing banks while acquiring often remains a monopolistic or nearly monopolistic activity. The graphs in Figure 5.11 show the market structure in the EU markets for credit and debit cards using the so-called Herfindahl Index, which is defined as the sum of the squares of the market shares of all institutions in the sector ($HI = \sum_{i=1}^{n} s_i^2$, where s_i is the market share of institution i). The Herfindahl Index ranges between $1/n$ and 1, reaching its lowest value, the reciprocal of the number of institutions (n), when all institutions are of equal size, and reaching unity in the case of monopoly. The index as published by the European Commission has been rescaled and ranges between 0 (low concentration) and 10,000 (high concentration). As Figure 5.11 shows, the index in most Member States is (much) higher than 2,000, which is usually seen as an indication of a highly concentrated market.

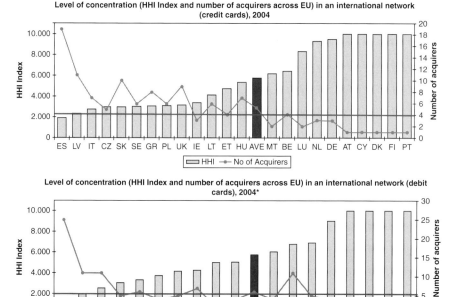

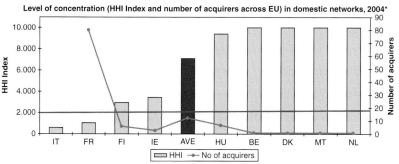

* Based only on the network's reported data

* Data source: Data from domestic (national) debit networks
** This is state of play until March 2004, when interpay (BeaNet) started the transfer of merchant contracts to banks

Figure 5.11 Concentration in payment systems

Note: The Herfindahl index (HHI) is defined as the sum of the squares of the market shares of each individual acquirer. The index ranges from 0 to 10,000, which reflects a move from a large number of acquirers with limited market shares to a monopolistic market situation.

Source: European Commission (2007)

High and sustained profitability (particularly in card issuing) suggests that banks in some Member States enjoy significant market power and can impose high card fees on firms and consumers. Furthermore, some rules and practices of market parties weaken competition at the retail level, for example by the blending of merchant fees and the prohibition of surcharging. Finally, the technical standards diverge across the EU, which may prevent many service providers from operating efficiently on a pan-EU scale.

These findings suggest that there is a need to address several barriers in order to strengthen competition in the EU retail payment market: technical, commercial, and legal barriers. It is crucial that common technical standards are developed and business models need to be aligned. As it is not clear to what extent market forces (see section 4.1) will initiate these changes, there may be a role for the European Commission to interfere and improve competition in the retail payment market through new legislative proposals. As for the commercial barriers, section 5.1 has shown that there are still substantial differences between user preferences and pricing structures in Europe. The adoption of the Directive on Payment Services (PSD) in 2007 created the legal foundation for an EU-wide single market for payments. The PSD aims to establish a modern and comprehensive set of rules applicable to all payment services in the EU.

Post-trading industry

As discussed in the previous section, CSDs/CCPs are characterised by economies of scale, economies of scope, and network effects. In principle, these characteristics are compatible with perfectly contestable markets (Schultze and Bauer, 2006). However, investments made by CSDs/CCPs, both in human and technical capital, are very specific and therefore not easily recoverable. Moreover, users face substantial switching costs when changing CSDs/CCPs. Consequently, the national markets for post-trading services are far from being perfectly contestable. The EU post-trading industry has evolved into nationally based systems that tend to be monopolistic, i.e., all trades in a given type of security are cleared and settled by a single national entity.

Several studies have compared the post-trading costs of domestic versus cross-border transactions, as well as the costs of a domestic transaction in the EU and those in the US. Table 5.2 shows that these studies generally conclude that cross-border prices and costs are considerably higher than the corresponding costs and prices for domestic transactions. The studies by NERA Economic Consulting (2004) and Deutsche Börse Group (2005) also conclude that the costs of domestic transactions differ significantly among Member States. Moreover, post-trading costs per transaction in the EU are substantially higher than in the US.

Table 5.2 Studies examining post-trading costs per transaction for users

	EU cross-border	US	Ratio	EU domestic	US	Ratio
Lannoo and Levin (2001)	3.10	0.40	7.75	1.74	0.40	4.35
LSE/OXERA (2002)	3.41	0.53	6.43	2.04	0.53	3.85
Giovannini Group (2001)	2.86	0.46	6.22	1.49	0.46	3.24
NERA (2004)	n.a.	n.a.	n.a.	0.10–0.65	0.10	1.00–6.50
DBG (2005)	n.a.	n.a.	n.a.	0.30–0.60	0.10	1.50–3.00

Source: Schultze and Bauer (2006)

The Giovannini Group (2001) concluded that fragmentation in the EU clearing and settlement infrastructure significantly complicates the post-trade processing of cross-border securities transactions relative to domestic transactions. Complications arise because of the need to access many national systems, whereby differences in technical requirements/market practices, tax regimes, and legal systems act as barriers to the efficient and safe delivery of post-trading services. The inefficiency that is created by these barriers is reflected in higher costs to pan-EU investors and is inconsistent with the objective of creating a truly integrated EU financial system. The Giovannini Group therefore called for the removal of a list of 15 barriers relating to (i) technical requirements/market practice, (ii) tax procedures, and (iii) legal certainty. However, government-led initiatives have been set aside in the EU, in favour of a coordinated strategy that involves commitments from both private market participants and government authorities (see Giovannini *et al.*, 2008).

Integration of national systems may bring about various benefits. Among other things, opportunities to exploit economies of scale and scope and increased competition have the potential to lower the cost of post-trading activities and lead to a more efficient allocation of capital, thereby furthering economic growth (see chapter 1). According to Schultze and Bauer (2006), a more efficient EU post-trading system, leading to a lowering of transaction costs of 7–18 per cent, could result in a higher level of GDP (on average between 0.2 and 0.6 per cent).

Initiatives to strengthen financial integration

Wholesale payments: TARGET2

Although integration of wholesale payment systems is almost complete, work is ongoing to strengthen the existing infrastructure. In November 2007, the Eurosystem launched TARGET2, the successor of TARGET, with the aim of strengthening integration of large-value euro payment systems. TARGET2 has replaced the decentralised technical structure of TARGET by a single shared platform (SSP). The SSP introduces a uniform wholesale payment infrastructure, where all banks are offered the same services, functionality, and interfaces, as well as a single price structure. This means that banks operate under similar conditions across Europe, thus promoting further efficiency and integration in the related financial markets (ECB, 2007c).

Retail payments: Single Euro Payments Area

As for retail payment systems, the introduction of the Single Euro Payments Area (SEPA) has the potential to remove a number of barriers discussed in the previous section. SEPA is a market-led initiative that aims to ensure that there are no longer any differences between national and cross-border payments within the euro area. It should give payment service providers the opportunity to benefit from economies of scale and scope.

SEPA is not merely aimed at improving the processing efficiency of the modest volumes of cross-border payments (EPC, 2006). It will lead to a major changeover of national payment markets in the euro area, as it will introduce new, common business rules and technical standards. Consequently, all electronic payments will be affected and existing national credit transfers, direct debits, and card payments will be phased out and gradually migrate to interoperable formats and processes. As of 2008, the new SEPA payment instruments (credit transfers, direct debits, and cards) will operate alongside existing national processes, with sufficient critical mass expected to be achieved within a few years, making SEPA irreversible. After the full transition, purely national payment instruments will no longer exist. Next to this, the European banking community has defined a framework for the clearing and settlement of payments in SEPA. The framework defines the principles that infrastructure providers must comply with to ensure that they can process SEPA credit transfers and direct debits.

The ECB and the European Commission support the continued self-regulation by the industry. However, given the importance and size of the social and economic benefits of SEPA, the European Commission has indicated that it reserves the right to introduce or propose necessary legislation to achieve it.

Post-trading process: Code of Conduct and TARGET2-Securities

After calls from the European Commission to resolve the problems of EU cross-border clearings and settlement, the trading and post-trading infrastructure providers presented a Code of Conduct on Clearing and Settlement in 2006. The Code aims to enhance transparency and increase competition in the post-trading sector. For that, the Code includes measures aimed at ensuring price transparency, access and interoperability, unbundling and accounting separation, and an independent monitoring process.

Next to this, the ESCB is working on an initiative to establish TARGET2-Securities, i.e., a platform for the cross-border and domestic settlement of securities against central bank money. According to ECB (2006), the objective of TARGET2-Securities is to maximise safety and efficiency in the settlement of euro-denominated securities transactions. Safety is achieved by making use of delivery versus payment mechanism, while efficiency is strengthened by settling cash and securities on the same IT platform. It is unclear how this initiative will relate to other initiatives in the market.

5.4 Conclusions

Payment systems are composed of instruments, procedures, and transfer systems that ensure the transfer of money from one economic actor to the other. Relatively low-value and non-urgent mass payments are processed through retail payment systems, while wholesale payment systems process large-value and high-priority payments between financial institutions.

In securities markets, the clearing and settlement (or post-trading) process provides for the transfer of ownership and payment between buyers and sellers of securities. This process can be divided into four main activities: (i) the confirmation of terms of the trade as agreed by the buyer and the seller, (ii) clearance, by which the respective obligations of the buyer and seller are established, (iii) the transfer of the securities from the seller to the buyer, and (iv) the transfer of funds from the buyer to the seller.

Payment and securities market infrastructures are characterised by economics of scale and scope, and network externalities. This means that the average costs of payment and post-trading services may fall considerably when the current fragmentation of EU financial infrastructures is overcome. In this respect, the introduction of SEPA in 2008 may allow providers of payment services to benefit from economies of scale and scope, thereby increasing overall economic efficiency.

The integration of EU large-value payment systems has been quite remarkable, while retail payment systems and post-trading processes remain fragmented thus far. The latter has resulted in large variations in fees and higher costs and risks for cross-border transactions. Different initiatives have been launched to remove existing barriers for integration in these markets. In this respect, the ECB has played a prominent role that goes beyond mere oversight, as the ECB has positioned itself as (joint) proprietor of many different integration initiatives in the domain of financial infrastructures.

NOTES

1. *Surcharging* refers to the situation in which a merchant passes on the costs of a payment by charging a fee for the use of the card. However, in most card networks the merchants are prohibited from applying higher prices to card transactions.
2. Examples of ICSDs are Euroclear and Clearstream International.
3. Netting can be carried out on either a bilateral or a multilateral basis. While bilateral netting is an arrangement between only two parties to net their bilateral obligations, multilateral netting is arithmetically achieved by summing each participant's bilateral net positions with those of the other participants to arrive at a multilateral net position vis-à-vis all other participants (Kazarian, 2006).
4. See article 105.2 of the Treaty establishing the European Community and Article 3 of the Statute of the European System of Central Banks and of the European Central Bank.
5. Although the curves in Figure 5.6 are not average costs curves, they give a fair reflection of how payment unit costs change with payment volume. The curves refer to estimates for three different years.
6. The other two LVPSs are the French Paris Net Settlement (PNS) and the Finnish Pankkien On-line Pikasiirrot ja Sekit-järjestelmä (POPS).

SUGGESTED READING

Freixas, X. and C. Holthausen (2008), European Integration of Payment Systems, in: X. Freixas, P. Hartmann, and C. Mayer (eds.), *Handbook of European Financial Markets and Institutions*, Oxford University Press, Oxford, 436–450.

Giovannini, A., J. Berrigan, and D. Russo (2008), Post-trading Services and European Securities Markets, in: X. Freixas, P. Hartmann, and C. Mayer (eds.), *Handbook of European Financial Markets and Institutions*, Oxford University Press, Oxford, 540–567.

Kazarian, E. G. (2006), Integration of the Securities Market Infrastructure in the European Union: Policy and Regulatory Issues, IMF Working Paper 06/241.

Serifsoy, B. and M. Weiß (2007), Settling for Efficiency – A Framework for the European Securities Transaction Industry, *Journal of Banking and Finance*, 31, 3034–3057.

REFERENCES

Bergman, M., G. Guibourg, and B. Segendorf (2007), The Costs of Paying – Private and Social Costs of Cash and Card Payments, Sveriges Riksbank Working Paper 212.

Bank for International Settlements (1992), *Delivery Versus Payment in Securities Settlement Systems*, BIS, Basel.

Bank for International Settlements (2001), *BIS Glossary Nr. 7*, BIS, Basel.

Bank for International Settlements (2002a), *Policy Issues for Central Banks in Retail Payments*, BIS, Basel.

Bank for International Settlements (2002b), *BIS Quarterly Review December 2002 – International Banking and Financial Market Developments*, BIS, Basel.

Bank for International Settlements (2006), *General Guidance for National Payment System Development*, BIS, Basel.

Bolt, W. (2007), Retail Payments and Card Use in the Netherlands: Pricing, Scale, and Antitrust, *Competition Policy International*, 3(1), 257–270.

Bolt, W. and D. Humphrey (2006), Payment Scale Economies and the Replacement of Cash and Stored Value Cards, De Nederlandsche Bank Working Paper 122.

Brits, H. and C. Winder (2005), Payments Are No Free Lunch, De Nederlandsche Bank Occasional Studies, 3, Nr. 2.

Capgemini (2005), *World Retail Banking Report*.

Capgemini (2007), *World Payments Report*.

Deutsche Börse Group (2005), The European Post-Trade Market – An Introduction, White Paper.

European Central Bank (2006), Speech by J-M Godeffroy: 'Ten Frequently Asked Questions About Target2 Securities' on 20 September 2006 at the British Bankers Association, London. Available at: http://www.ecb.int/paym/t2s/defining/outgoing/html/10faq.en.html

European Central Bank (2007a), *Financial Stability Review*, ECB, Frankfurt am Main.

European Central Bank (2007b), *Financial Integration in Europe*, ECB, Frankfurt am Main.

European Central Bank (2007c), *A Single Currency – An Integrated Market Infrastructure*, ECB, Frankfurt am Main.

Economides, N. (1993), Network Economics with Application to Finance, *Financial Markets, Institutions & Instruments*, 2(5), 89–97.

Economides, N. (1996), The Economics of Networks, *International Journal of Industrial Organization*, 16(4), 673–699.

Economides, N. and C. Himmelberg (1995), Critical Mass and Network Evolution in Telecommunications, in: G. Brock (ed.), *Toward a Comprehensive Telecommunications Industry: Selected Papers from the 1994 Telecommunications Policy Research Conference*, Lawrence Erlbaum Associates, New Jersey.

European Commission (2005), Annex to the Proposal for a Directive of the European Parliament and of the Council on Payment Services in the Internal Market – Impact Assessment, EC, Brussels.

European Commission (2007), *Report on the Retail Sector Inquiry*, EC, Brussels.

European Payment Council (2006), *Making SEPA a Reality – Implementing the Single Euro Payments Area*, EPC, Brussels.

Freixas, X. and C. Holthausen (2008), European Integration of Payment Systems, in: X. Freixas, P. Hartmann, and C. Mayer (eds.), *Handbook of European Financial Markets and Institutions*, Oxford University Press, Oxford, 436–450.

Giovannini Group (2001), *Cross-Border Clearing and Settlement Arrangements in the European Union*, Brussels, November.

Giovannini, A., J. Berrigan, and D. Russo (2008), Post-trading Services and European Securities Markets, in: X. Freixas, P. Hartmann, and C. Mayer (eds.), *Handbook of European Financial Markets and Institutions*, Oxford University Press, Oxford, 540–567.

Harper, I., S. Rimes, and C. Malam (2006), The Development of Electronic Payment Systems, in: R. Cooper, G. Madden, A. Lloyd, and M. Schipp (eds.), *The Economics of Online Markets and ICT Networks*, Springer, New York, 25–40.

Humphrey, D.B., M. Willesson, T. Lindblom, and G. Bergendahl (2003), What Does It Cost to Make a Payment?, *Review of Network Economics*, June, 159–174.

Kazarian, E.G. (2006), Integration of the Securities Market Infrastructure in the European Union: Policy and Regulatory Issues, IMF Working Paper 06/241.

Khiaonarong, T. (2003), Payment Systems Efficiency, Policy Approaches, and the Role of the Central Bank, Bank of Finland Discussion Paper 1.

Lannoo, K. and M. Levin (2001), The Securities Settlement Industry in the EU – Structure, Costs and the Way Forward, CEPS Research Report.

London Stock Exchange/Oxera (2002), Clearing and Settlement in Europe – Response to the first report of the Giovannini Group.

NERA Economic Consulting (2004), The Direct Costs of Clearing and Settlement: An EU–US Comparison, City Research Series 1.

Rochet, J.-C. and J. Tirole (2006), Two-Sided Markets: A Progress Report, *The RAND Journal of Economics*, 35(3), 645–667.

Salo, S. (2006), Promoting Integration of European Retail Payment Systems: Role of Competition, Cooperation and Regulation, paper presented at the SUERF Seminar The Adoption of the Euro in New Member States: Challenges and Vulnerabilities on the Last Stretch, Malta, 4. May

Schmiedel, H. and A. Schönenberg (2005), Integration of Securities Market Infrastructure in the Euro Area, European Central Bank Occasional Paper 33.

Schultze, N. and D. Bauer (2006), Annex II of Economic Impact Study on Clearing and Settlement, EC, Brussels. Available at: http://ec.europa.eu/internal_market/financial-markets/docs/clearing/draft/annex_2_en.pdf

Serifsoy, B. and M. Weiß (2007), Settling for Efficiency – A Framework for the European Securities Transaction Industry, *Journal of Banking and Finance*, 31, 3034–3057.

Shy, O. (2001), *The Economics of Network Industries*, Cambridge University Press, New York.

Part III

Financial Institutions

6

The Role of Institutional Investors

OVERVIEW

Over the last decades, the intermediation of financial assets has gradually shifted from banks towards institutional investors, such as pension funds, life insurance companies, and mutual funds. In this process of re-intermediation, the assets of institutional investors of the EU-15 countries tripled from 44 per cent of GDP in 1985 to 122 per cent in 2004.

This chapter starts off with an overview of the growth of institutional investors over the last two decades. The development of the main types of institutional investors is documented. There is a small group of countries with large-scale funded pensions (Denmark, Finland, Ireland, the Netherlands, and the United Kingdom). Other countries rely more on life insurance and mutual funds. New types of institutional investment, such as hedge funds and private equity, are also discussed.

Both the demand side (growing investments by pension funds to cater for ageing, and by mutual funds to accommodate wealth accumulation of households) and the supply side (shift from bank-financing to market-financing) point to further growth of institutional investment. There is no substantial institutional investment yet in the new EU Member States, but institutional investors in these countries are expected to grow in line with economic development.

This chapter also analyses the impact of institutional investors on the functioning of the financial system. Institutional investors are pooling funds and transferring economic resources over different asset classes and countries. They also transfer resources over time. Moreover, they increase the efficiency of the financial system.

One would expect institutional investors to invest according to the principles of finance theory as implied by the international version of the Capital Asset Pricing Model (CAPM). This theory shows the gains of international diversification. However, there is a home bias in investments of institutional investors. Still, this bias declined from 1997 to 2004, especially in the countries in the euro area, a trend which can be attributed to the introduction of the euro. With the elimination of exchange-rate risk, investors based in the euro area have re-allocated part of their portfolio from their home country to the wider euro area.

LEARNING OBJECTIVES

After you have studied this chapter, you should be able to:
● describe the different types of institutional investors and their functions
● understand the growth of institutional investment and the factors that explain this growth
● explain the theory of international diversification
● assess the home bias of institutional investments and the change in the home bias following the introduction of the euro.

6.1 Different types of institutional investors

This section describes the main types of institutional investors in the EU and their role in the EU financial system. *Institutional investors* are specialised financial institutions that manage collectively savings of small investors (Davis and Steil, 2001). The size of institutional investors differs across countries. Most countries in southern Europe are characterised by low institutional saving, while the role of institutional investors in north-western Europe is more important. The three most important categories of institutional investors are pension funds, life insurance companies, and mutual funds. Table 6.1 illustrates the role of these institutional investors in the EU-15. For comparative purposes, Switzerland and the US are also included in this and following tables.

Pension funds

Pension funds collect, pool, and invest funds contributed by sponsors (employers) and beneficiaries (employees and their family members) to provide for the future pension entitlements of beneficiaries.

In the EU, pay-as-you-go (PAYG) pensions are common to provide for some basic pension level (first tier). This system is not funded but based upon solidarity between generations, as the working generation has to pay for the pensions of the retired generation. Some countries have

Table 6.1 Assets of different types of institutional investors (% of GDP), 2004

	Pension funds	Life insurance companies	Mutual funds	Total
Austria	4	30	53	88
Belgium	4	52	34	90
Denmark	27	71	39	137
Finland	41	22	20	83
France	5	66	67	139
Germany	3	38	39	80
Greece	–	5	20	25
Ireland	39	n.a.	294	333
Italy	2	31	29	62
Luxembourg	–	111	4089	4200
Netherlands	110	65	18	193
Portugal	10	27	22	59
Spain	8	24	28	60
Sweden	11	65	29	106
United Kingdom	50	88	28	166
EU-15	19	52	52	123
Switzerland	91	100	29	220
United States	63	32	63	158

Notes: EU-15 is calculated as a weighted average; – means nil or negligible; n.a. means not available.
Source: European Fund and Asset Management Association (EFAMA), Investment Company Institute (ICI), OECD, Federal Reserve

accumulated major pension assets, which provide beneficiaries with an additional pension (second tier). These funded pensions can be based on defined benefit or defined contribution (Davis and Steil, 2001 and Feldstein and Siebert, 2002). *Defined benefit (DB) funds* offer employees a guaranteed rate of return (the risk is borne by the employer) while the returns of *defined contribution (DC) funds* are solely determined by the market (the risk is borne by the employees). DC plans have gained popularity in recent years, as employers have sought to minimise the risk of their obligations, while employees desire funds that are readily transferable if they move from one job to another. A hybrid is the *collective defined contribution* (CDC) pension. This does not guarantee a certain return by the company, but employees are able to save collectively for their pension via their employer and to pool risks.

The role of pension funds in the financial system differs across countries. In countries with large pension assets (relative to GDP), such as the Netherlands, Switzerland, the UK, and the US, pension funds are an important vehicle for collective saving for retirement purposes (see Table 6.2). Pension funds in these countries are among the largest investors, with assets under management worth billions of euros (for example, the Dutch civil servants' pension fund ABP; see Box 6.1). Historically, some large EU countries (like Germany, France, and Italy) have relied on other forms of retirement funding. The lack of a funded pension system in these countries directed households towards life insurances and mutual funds.

Since early withdrawal of funds is usually restricted or forbidden, a pension fund has long-term liabilities resulting in a long-term oriented investment strategy. This allows a pension fund to hold high-risk/return instruments (for example, investments in commodities, hedge funds, and private equity).

Table 6.2 Assets of pension funds (in € billion and % of GDP), 1985–2004

	1985		1990		1995		2000		2004	
	euro	%	euro	%	euro	%	euro	%	euro	%
Austria	–	–	–	–	1.7	0.9	7.8	3.7	9.8	4.1
Belgium	2.6	2.4	2.8	1.8	7.78	3.5	14.5	5.8	10.5	3.7
Denmark	–	–	15.4	14.4	27.9	20.0	42.5	24.5	53.7	27.2
Finland	–	–	–	–	–	–	4.9	3.7	61.9	40.7
France	–	–	–	–	–	–	–	–	90.5	5.5
Germany	25.2	2.6	37.8	3.0	49.6	2.6	66.8	3.2	76.5	3.5
Greece	–	–	–	–	–	–	–	–	–	–
Ireland	n.a.	n.a.	n.a.	n.a.	n.a.	n.a.	51.9	49.6	56.8	38.5
Italy	n.a.	n.a.	28.3	3.0	29.7	3.4	52.4	4.4	32.6	2.3
Luxembourg	–	–	–	–	–	–	–	–	–	–
Netherlands	117.9	67.5	168.5	72.6	267.9	83.6	457.8	109.5	538.7	110.0
Portugal	–	–	0.9	1.5	6.8	7.8	13.1	10.7	13.9	9.7
Spain	n.a.	n.a.	n.a.	n.a.	22.7	5.0	51.3	8.1	68.8	8.2
Sweden	–	–	2.8	1.5	4.2	2.2	7.4	2.8	32.2	11.4
United Kingdom	252.9	41.9	393.6	50.3	578.1	66.6	1,199.7	76.7	862.9	49.8
EU-15	398.6	13.2	650.0	15.9	996.2	16.1	1,970.1	22.6	1,908.5	19.2
Switzerland	n.a.	n.a.	101.0	54.3	n.a.	n.a.	280.1	105.0	264.8	91.4
United States	1,831.9	33.1	1,786.2	39.2	3,619.6	64.0	8,000.9	75.3	5,898.3	62.6

Notes: EU-15 is calculated as a weighted average; – means nil or negligible; n.a. means not available.
Source: European data from OECD, US data from Federal Reserve

Box 6.1 ABP

The ABP (Algemeen Burgerlijk Pensioenfonds) is the Dutch pension fund for employers and employees of the government and the educational sector. It was founded by the government in 1922 and privatised in 1996. ABP provides its 2.4 million customers (employees, former employees, pensioners) with income security against pension, disability, and death.

ABP is the third largest pension fund in the world with around €210 billion of assets at the end of 2006. Given its objective to guarantee an adequate pension at all times at the lowest possible premiums, ABP's investment policy is geared towards a long-term risk-return profile. Diversification is a key element of that policy. The investment mix consists of 55 per cent in equities and alternative investments, such as real estate, private equity, and commodities, and 45 per cent in bonds. Over time, the share of equities has increased (see Figure 6.1). The geographical mix consists of 12 per cent of assets in the Netherlands, 41 per cent in the rest of Europe, and 47 per cent in the rest of the world (Annual Report 2006, ABP).

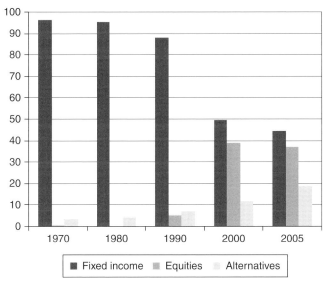

Figure 6.1   Portfolio of ABP (% share), 1970–2005
Source: ABP

Clients of a pension fund have no (direct) influence on the investment process of the fund but are protected by regulation, since pension funds have to comply with the 'prudent person' rule (they should, for example, diversify their portfolios). Moreover, pension funds are under the scrutiny of financial supervisors (see chapter 10).

Life insurance companies

Life insurance companies offer a mix of long-term saving and insurance products. Historically, life insurance companies provided insurance for dependants against the risk of death, but life insurers increasingly also offer long-term saving products. Pension funds and life insurance companies therefore often have close ties. Life insurance companies offer annuities for guaranteeing pension benefits as well as guaranteed investment contracts that may be purchased by pension funds.

All EU-15 countries (except for Greece) have significant life insurance assets relative to GDP. Table 6.3 indicates that life insurance assets in the EU-15 are concentrated in the UK, France, and Germany. The Netherlands and Italy also have a large life insurance industry. Life insurance companies function as retirement saving vehicles in countries with a weak pension sector (such as Belgium, France, Germany, and Italy). As life insurance companies offer a diverse range of products, they have different kinds of liabilities, which

Table 6.3 Assets of life-insurance companies (in € billion and % of GDP), 1985–2004

	1985		1990		1995		2000		2004	
	euro	%	euro	%	euro	%	euro	%	euro	%
Austria	9.9	10.9	18.0	13.8	35.8	19.5	50.4	23.9	71.6	30.4
Belgium	22.8	20.8	40.7	26.2	62.2	28.6	105.7	42.0	150.6	52.3
Denmark	n.a.	n.a.	39.0	36.4	63.3	45.5	103.1	59.4	139.3	70.6
Finland	–	–	6.4	5.8	14.6	14.7	38.0	28.7	32.9	21.6
France	92.0	12.7	192.6	19.7	498.9	41.5	981.1	68.1	1,103.0	66.5
Germany	175.5	18.4	293.6	23.0	516.5	26.8	783.2	38.0	840.0	38.1
Greece	–	–	–	–	2.8	3.1	6.5	5.2	9.1	5.4
Ireland	n.a.	n.a.	n.a.	n.a.	n.a.	n.a.	n.a.	n.a.	n.a.	n.a.
Italy	n.a.	n.a.	48.5	5.4	91.5	10.6	242.6	20.4	424.8	30.6
Luxembourg	–	–	–	–	5.9	37.0	23.9	108.6	30.0	110.9
Netherlands	52.0	29.8	85.4	36.8	164.2	51.3	263.9	63.1	316.0	64.5
Portugal	–	–	1.4	2.5	8.9	10.2	25.2	20.7	38.4	26.8
Spain	n.a.	n.a.	n.a.	n.a.	59.3	13.0	137.4	21.8	199.2	23.7
Sweden	n.a.	n.a.	58.3	30.9	91.9	48.0	195.1	74.3	183.9	65.2
United Kingdom	214.6	35.6	333.3	42.6	621.7	71.6	1,568.7	100.3	1,528.4	88.2
EU-15	566.8	20.2	1,117.2	22.4	2.237.6	33.6	4,524.7	52.6	5,067.1	51.6
Switzerland	n.a.	n.a.	84.7	45.6	147.2	61.1	222.1	83.3	290.0	100.1
United States	896.6	16.2	991.3	21.8	1,570.2	27.8	3.369.9	31.7	3,032.3	32.2

Notes: EU-15 is calculated as a weighted average; – means nil or negligible; n.a. means not available.
Source: European data from OECD, US data from Federal Reserve

allows them a certain degree of diversification. Life insurance companies sell their products in a competitive market and compete both with each other and with pension funds and mutual funds. As a result, life companies may have a strong incentive for risk taking on the asset side.

From a customer point of view, the economic function of life insurance companies is (next to insurance for dependants) the provision of customised saving schemes. Saving and investing via life insurance is aimed not only at retirement but also at other long-term saving objectives (like the education of siblings), which makes them not only a substitute but also a supplement to pensions. While pension schemes are more standardised, life insurance products can be tailored towards the needs of an individual. But this advantage comes at a price. The transaction and marketing costs of life policies are far higher than the costs of pension contracts.

Mutual funds

The mutual fund industry is among the most successful financial innovations (Khorana, *et al.*, 2005). *Mutual funds* are investment vehicles whose underlying assets are identifiable and are marked-to-market on a regular (usually daily) basis. Moreover, the specific assets of the fund can be created or redeemed upon demand. Mutual funds contractually link investors' claims to the underlying asset. Investors can easily enter and exit the fund and pay or receive current market prices for their investments. Investors in mutual funds are residual claimants and bear all the risk of the fund.

The primary role of mutual funds is the pooling of funds. In contrast to pension funds, they do not necessarily transfer these funds over time. Many investors in mutual funds have a relatively short investment horizon, so the mutual fund is not specifically intended for retirement saving. The size of mutual funds differs sharply, ranging from small, specialised funds to major players like Fidelity and Vanguard (having €1,000 billion and €800 billion of assets under management at the end of 2005, respectively). These larger funds also have important stakes in companies, which makes them prominent players in corporate governance.

Investors choose a fund with a specific investment objective (for instance, a bond fund, an equity fund, or an emerging-market fund). The asset allocation of the fund is generally fixed by the prospectus, while the security selection process is either active or passive. Active asset managers try to 'beat the market' by picking stocks that they consider good investments. Passive funds 'track' the index and do not deviate from the market benchmark. They generally incur lower transaction costs and have lower investment fees.

Table 6.4 Assets of mutual funds (in € billion and % of GDP), 1985–2004

	1985		1990		1995		2000		2004	
	euro	%	euro	%	euro	%	euro	%	euro	%
Austria	1.3	1.5	10.5	8.1	26.1	14.2	91.8	43.6	125.3	53.1
Belgium	3.2	2.9	19.0	12.2	18.9	8.7	89.4	35.5	98.8	34.3
Denmark	–	–	2.7	2.5	5.1	3.7	34.0	19.6	77.2	39.1
Finland	–	–	0.1	0.1	0.9	0.9	13.9	10.5	30.8	20.3
France	101.5	14.0	288.3	29.5	410.3	34.2	854.1	59.3	1,110.3	66.9
Germany	44.2	4.6	108.0	8.5	304.6	15.8	813.9	39.5	855.0	38.7
Greece	–	–	0.7	1.0	8.1	9.0	33.8	26.8	33.0	19.6
Ireland	n.a.	n.a.	n.a.	n.a.	27.4	53.4	208.3	199.3	434.6	294.5
Italy	n.a.	n.a.	30.8	3.5	103.9	12.1	460.6	38.7	396.9	28.6
Luxembourg	14.1	269.5	69.0	790.5	313.1	1980.2	874.6	3975.3	1,106.2	4088.7
Netherlands	13.2	7.6	23.5	10.1	50.7	15.8	108.0	25.9	89.1	18.2
Portugal	–	–	2.2	3.9	14.9	17.1	25.2	20.6	31.5	22.0
Spain	n.a.	n.a.	n.a.	n.a.	114.5	25.1	184.2	29.2	237.5	28.3
Sweden	n.a.	n.a.	28.4	15.0	28.3	14.8	83.6	31.8	81.4	28.9
United Kingdom	62.7	10.4	92.3	11.8	250.8	28.9	563.5	36.0	486.6	28.1
EU-15	240.3	8.3	675.4	13.6	1,677.5	25.0	4,438.7	50.9	5,194.1	52.2
Switzerland	8.7	6.7	13.6	7.3	43.5	18.1	95.1	35.6	83.3	28.8
United States	559.3	10.1	846.9	18.6	2,139.1	37.8	7,484.9	70.4	5,951.7	63.2

Notes: Mutual fund data includes both UCITS (equity, bonds, balanced, money market, funds of funds, and other UCITS funds) and non-UCITS (real estate funds, special funds, and other non-UCITS). UCITS are collective investment schemes, which can operate freely throughout the EU on the basis of a single authorisation (see chapter 10). EU-15 is calculated as a weighted average; – means nil or negligible; n.a. means not available.
Source: European Fund and Asset Management Association (EFAMA), Investment Company Institute (ICI), OECD

Table 6.4 illustrates the growth of mutual funds between 1985 and 2004. Luxembourg and Ireland are outliers due to a favourable tax treatment of these funds. Remarkable is the large size of mutual fund investment in France. The Netherlands, in which pensions and life insurance policies are the prime long-term saving vehicles, has the smallest mutual fund market size relative to GDP. Also in Greece and Finland this market is small.

Special types of institutional investors

In addition to the three main types of institutional investors described above, two other important institutional asset managers are hedge funds and private equity investors. During the last decade, they have gained popularity as they offer opportunities to diversify risk and increase expected returns.

Originally, *hedge funds* were eclectic investment pools, typically organised as private partnerships and often located offshore for tax and regulatory reasons. Since they operate through private placements and restrict share ownership to wealthy individuals and institutions, most disclosure and regulation requirements that apply to mutual funds and banks do not apply to hedge funds. Funds legally domiciled outside the main financial market countries are generally subject to even fewer regulations. Hedge-fund managers, who are paid on a fee-for-performance basis, are free to use a variety of investment techniques, including short positions and leverage, to raise returns and limit the investment risks. In contrast to investment funds, hedge funds concentrate more on absolute than on relative returns. The primary aim of most hedge funds used to be to reduce volatility and risk while attempting to deliver positive returns under all market conditions ('hedging'). However, the investment strategy of many funds has become more risky over the last decade, including the use of leverage. The aggressive investment style of some hedge funds can land them in financial trouble, as the bail-out of the hedge fund LTCM in 1998 illustrates (see Box 6.2).

Box 6.2 The LTCM crisis

The hedge fund Long-Term Capital Management (LTCM) was founded in 1994. Its Board of Directors included Nobel Prize winners Myron Scholes and Robert Merton. The core strategy of LTCM was convergence trades, trying to take advantage of small differences in prices among closely related securities (Jorion, 2000). Compare, for example, a less liquid (called off-the-run) Treasury bond yielding 6.1 per cent versus 6.0 per cent for the more recently issued (called on-the-run) Treasury bond. The yield spread represents some compensation for the liquidity risk. Over a year, a trade that is long off-the-run and short on-the-run would generate a return of 10 basis points. The key is that eventually the two bonds converge to the same value at maturity. LTCM used this strategy in a variety of markets, such as spreads on different government bonds, mortgage-backed versus government securities, high-yielding versus low-yielding European bonds, equity pairs (stocks with different share classes), and so on. Most of the time, these trades should be profitable except for default or market disruption.

Such strategies generate tiny profits, so that leverage has to be used to create attractive returns. At the time of the crisis in 1998, LTCM had borrowed $125 billion compared with equity of $5 billion. This led to a *leverage ratio L*, defined as debt to equity, of 25. The following equation illustrates the impact of leverage: $r_{equity} = r_{assets} + L \cdot (r_{assets} - r_{debt})$. When the return on assets r_{assets} is higher than the return on debt r_{debt}, a large leverage would generate a high return on equity r_{equity}. But when the return on assets drops below that on debt, a large leverage would generate sizeable losses.

Initially, this strategy was very productive, with annual profits of almost 40 per cent. But losses occurred due to the Russian financial crisis in August 1998 when the Russian government defaulted on its bonds. Panicking investors sold Japanese and European bonds to buy US Treasury bonds. The profits that were supposed to occur as the value of these bonds converged became huge losses as the value of the bonds diverged. LTCM's equity capital dropped to around $600 million. The Federal Reserve Bank of New York organised a bail-out of $3.6 billion by major creditors (14 leading investment banks) to avoid more collapses, without committing its own money. In return, the participating banks got a 90 per cent share in the fund. The fear was that there would be a chain reaction as LTCM liquidated its securities to cover its debt, leading to a drop in prices, which would force other companies to liquidate their own debt, creating a vicious cycle. The total losses amounted to $4.6 billion. After the bail-out, the panic abated and the positions formerly held by LTCM were eventually even liquidated at a small profit to the bailers (Jorion, 2000). LTCM closed its books in 2000.

Critics have pointed out that this bail-out increased moral-hazard problems as financial institutions could take more risks because they suffer less in case of failure (Kho *et al.*, 2000). While central bankers typically argue that a bail-out is necessary to prevent contagion and systemic threats, academics stress moral hazard. Furfine (2006) has estimated the potential costs of the Fed's intervention by examining the rates for interbank borrowing of large banks. The spreads on interbank borrowing go down if the market believes that these banks are 'too big to fail'.

Figure 6.2 illustrates the enormous growth of the hedge-fund industry. It is estimated that hedge funds in total managed around €1,100 billion in 2006. Total investment positions of hedge funds are even bigger as they can leverage their assets through borrowing money and through the use of derivatives, short positions, and structured securities. The growth of the hedge-fund industry was initially driven by investments by wealthy individuals and institutions looking for higher returns. However, during the last decade small investors have been able to invest via *funds of hedge funds*, which are investment funds that invest solely in hedge funds. Also pension funds invest in hedge funds and funds of funds, as illustrated in Figure 6.3.

The distinctions between hedge funds and other types of funds are blurring. Hedge funds are characterised as unregulated private funds that can take on significant leverage and employ complex trading strategies using derivatives

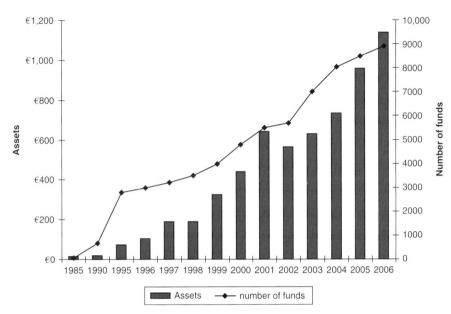

Figure 6.2   Global hedge funds market (number of funds and assets in € billion), 1985–2006
Source: International Financial Services London (2007a)

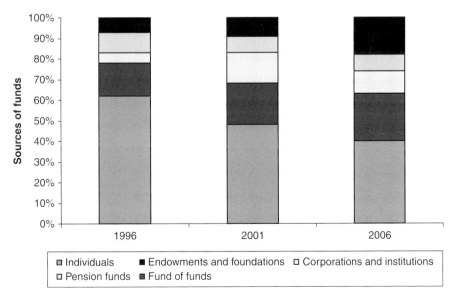

Figure 6.3   Hedge funds' sources of capital (% of total funds), 1996–2006
Source: International Financial Services London (2007a)

or other new financial instruments. Although private equity funds are usually not considered hedge funds, they are also typically unregulated and often use leverage for their investments (see Box 6.3 for a further discussion of the regulation of these funds). Traditional asset managers also increasingly use

---

Box 6.3 Regulating hedge funds and private equity

The spectacular rise in hedge funds and private equity investments has led to calls for regulation of these alternative investment categories. The first question is, why should they be regulated? The second question is, can they be regulated?

Chapter 10 reviews the different forms of regulation. Financial stability concerns arise when the failure of a financial institution affects the stability of the financial system. As the size of hedge funds and private equity investors grows, some transparency on their investments and investment strategies may be helpful for central banks to detect potential vulnerabilities in the financial system. But that is no reason for direct regulation, as these players do not belong to the core of the financial system.

Another concern for regulators is asymmetric information between financial institutions and their customers (i.e., depositors, insurance policy holders, and pension holders). Prudential supervision aims to protect these retail customers by ensuring the soundness of financial institutions. However, investors in hedge funds and private equity funds are predominantly professional parties, who can take care of themselves. An indirect approach has also been advocated (Financial Stability Forum, 2007). Insofar as banks, insurance companies, and pension funds grant loans to or invest in hedge funds and private equity, these regulated financial institutions should manage the counterparty risk of these invest-ments. Prudential supervisors are checking the risk-management policies towards alter-native investments of banks, insurers, and pension funds.

Some retail investors have invested in hedge funds. The standard conduct-of-business rules for mutual funds on information disclosure to retail investors can be applied to hedge funds that deal with retail investors. So, no new rules are needed.

Turning to the second question, direct regulation of hedge funds and private equity is very difficult. Hedge funds and private equity managers can choose the jurisdiction from which they operate (often off-shore jurisdictions). If a country would issue overly strong regulations, these funds will probably move to less-regulated countries. Addressing public concerns about the impact of hedge funds and private equity, the industry has chosen the path of self-regulation. The Hedge Fund Standards Board (2008) in London has issued a voluntary code of best-practice standards for hedge funds to promote transparency. The best-practice standards state that hedge funds should disclose i) their investment strate-gies, ii) general details of their investments and instruments, and iii) their leverage profile.

derivatives or invest in structured securities that allow them to take leveraged or short positions.

In general, hedge funds provide liquidity and absorb risk. Moreover, due to their innovative trading strategies, they also play a role in financial innovation. Hedge funds thus improve the efficiency of the financial system. At the same time, they have the potential to amplify market price fluctuations if their investment behaviour becomes one-sided or if they concentrate on specific markets, in particular small-sized and low-liquidity markets.

Private equity investors invest in non-public companies and often finance these investments with a significant amount of debt, up to 90 per cent in the case of a leveraged buy-out. By means of investment funds, which are open to certain institutions and wealthy individuals, they invest in companies and aim at annual returns of 20–25 per cent. This makes them attractive for institutional investors also. Some institutional investors invest in private equity by means of their own private equity branch. An example is AlpInvest, a private equity company owned by two Dutch pension funds (ABP and PGGM, the Dutch pension fund for the healthcare and social work sector).

Table 6.5 illustrates that the US and the UK have the biggest private equity markets. Relative to GDP, private equity markets are small. Still, these markets are growing rapidly, driven by the demand for risky assets and exposure to the non-public market. Private equity funds have become an important source of funds for start-up firms, private middle-market firms, firms in financial distress, and public firms seeking buyout financing (Smit, 2003).

Table 6.5 Ten most important countries with private equity investments (€ billion and %) in 2006

	Total investment value	Market share	As % of GDP
United States	175.5	60.5	1.7
United Kingdom	40.9	14.1	2.3
France	10.6	3.7	0.6
Sweden	4.5	1.6	1.5
Germany	3.7	1.3	0.2
Spain	2.9	1.0	0.3
Netherlands	2.5	0.9	0.5
Others	49.4	17.0	–
Total	290.0	100.0	–

Source: International Financial Services London (2007b)

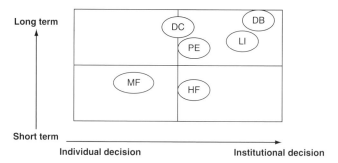

Figure 6.4   Investment horizon and decision power about asset allocation
Note: MF = mutual fund; DC = defined contribution pension scheme; DB = defined benefit pension scheme; LI = life insurance company; PE = private equity; HF = hedge fund.
Source: Bosch and Schoenmaker (2006)

Differences among institutional investors

Institutional investors differ from each other along three dimensions. First, the client base of the investor can be captive or can be determined via the market. In continental Europe, defined benefit pension funds often have a captive client base, as most employers use only one fund. In contrast, mutual funds must compete for clientele by means of low fees and/or an excellent track record.

Second, the investment horizon of institutional investors differs sharply. While pension funds have a very long investment horizon, mutual funds can have short-term investment objectives.

Third, the asset-allocation process differs across institutional investors. Mutual funds mainly focus on security selection or 'stock picking' and individual investors select the mutual fund that best matches with their risk preferences. Pension funds and life insurance companies take investment decisions concerning the percentage of equity and bonds in their portfolios, and diversify the risks within these asset classes. Figure 6.4 illustrates these differences.

6.2 The growth of institutional investors

Re-intermediation

Institutional investors have made banks less important as intermediaries of financial assets, a development which Rajan (2007) calls *'re-intermediation'* (see Table 6.6). Also in countries with a bank-dominated financial system, like

Table 6.6 Bank and institutional intermediation ratios (in % of intermediated claims), 1970–2000

		1970	1980	1990	2000	Δ 1970–2000
France	Bank	94	68	82	65	**−29**
	Institutional	5	4	19	27	**22**
Germany	Bank	84	86	83	73	**−11**
	Institutional	10	12	17	23	**13**
Italy	Bank	98	98	95	64	**−34**
	Institutional	6	5	11	31	**25**
United Kingdom	Bank	58	64	55	44	**−14**
	Institutional	28	26	32	38	**10**
Canada	Bank	45	55	44	38	**−7**
	Institutional	23	19	25	35	**12**
Japan	Bank	45	36	38	24	**−21**
	Institutional	10	10	16	17	**7**
United States	Bank	58	58	42	21	**−37**
	Institutional	31	31	40	44	**13**
G7	**Bank**	**69**	**66**	**63**	**47**	**−22**
	Institutional	**16**	**15**	**23**	**31**	**15**

Notes: The intermediation ratio measures the share of the financial claims of banks and institutional investors as a percentage of total intermediated claims. The sum of bank and institutional ratios can be below 100, due to financial claims of other financial institutions, or over 100, due to double counting. Data for other EU Member States and time periods are not available, but the objective of this table is to show the shift from bank to institutional intermediation.

Source: Davis (2003)

France and Italy, the role of institutional investors has increased. This is mainly due to the growth of the mutual fund industry. However, Germany is still mainly bank-oriented. In the Anglo-Saxon countries, institutional investors are the most important financial intermediaries. The US is the prime example, where institutional claims are twice as large as bank claims. As Box 6.4 explains, re-intermediation is less important in the new EU Member States, as the role of institutional investors in those countries is currently rather limited.

Table 6.7 illustrates that the total claims of institutional investors in the EU-15 have increased enormously over the last two decades. The weighted average of assets to GDP rose from 44 per cent in 1985 to 122 per cent in 2004. In the US, institutional investment shows a similar trend, with an increase from 59 per cent of GDP in 1985 to 158 per cent in 2004. When the global stock markets tumbled after the Internet bubble in 2000, the assets of institutional investors declined sharply. Since 2003, however, stock prices

Box 6.4 Institutional investment in the new EU Member States

Institutional investment can be seen as a luxury good. The most basic financial needs of households are the use of currency (coins and banknotes) and bank services (depositing and lending). Only when their income is increasing do households start to buy insurance and to save for retirement. This relationship is presented in Figure 6.5. Institutional investment starts to develop at a GDP per capita of around €5,000 and becomes meaningful beyond levels of €15,000. Greece and Portugal had a relatively low GDP per capita when they entered the EU in the 1980s. Figure 6.5 illustrates that their GDP per capita has gradually caught up with the EU average and that their institutional sector has also gradually developed. Currently, the new EU Member States have a very small institutional sector, but institutional investment in these countries is expected to grow in line with economic development.

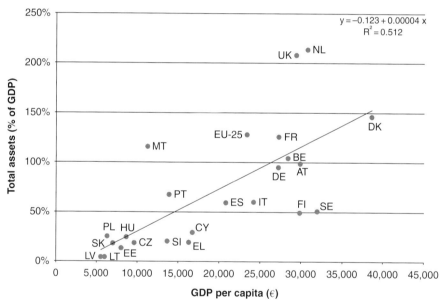

Figure 6.5   Institutional investment and economic development, 2005
Note: Total assets of institutional investment are defined as the assets of pension funds, insurance companies and mutual funds. Ireland and Luxembourg are excluded, as they attract mutual funds from other countries due to a favourable tax regime.
Source: Own calculations based on ECB (2006)

Table 6.7 Assets of institutional investors (% of GDP), 1985–2004

	1985	1990	1995	2000	2001	2002	2003	2004
Austria	12	22	35	71	74	76	81	88
Belgium	26	40	41	83	82	76	83	90
Denmark	n.a.	53	69	103	107	104	116	137
Finland	n.a.	6	16	43	38	38	42	83
France	27	49	76	127	127	122	130	139
Germany	26	34	45	81	82	73	79	80
Greece	0	1	12	32	27	24	25	25
Ireland	n.a.	n.a.	53	199	288	265	295	333
Italy	n.a.	12	26	63	60	56	60	62
Luxembourg	269	790	2017	4084	4227	3623	3821	4200
Netherlands	105	120	151	199	185	172	182	193
Portugal	n.a.	8	35	52	53	52	56	59
Spain	n.a.	n.a.	43	59	54	53	57	60
Sweden	n.a.	47	65	109	108	91	100	106
United Kingdom	88	105	167	213	204	170	173	166
EU-15	44	49	73	125	123	111	117	122
Switzerland	n.a.	107	141	224	227	202	222	220
United States	59	80	122	177	172	137	151	158

Notes: EU-15 is calculated as a weighted average; n.a. means not available.
Source: European Fund and Asset Management Association (EFAMA), Investment Company Institute (ICI), OECD, Federal Reserve

have recovered and institutional assets are returning to their previous levels. The turmoil on the global financial markets at the beginning of this century reveals the vulnerability of institutional investors (with equity investments of up to 50 per cent of their portfolio) to such downward market pressures.

Drivers of growth of institutional investment

The growth of institutional investment can be explained by supply and demand factors. Institutional investors have become more efficient in their function as a financial intermediary, while households have an enhanced need for services provided by institutional investors. Institutional investors are well placed to perform the key functions of the financial system as identified in chapter 1, i.e., trade, manage, and diversify risk, and reduce information and trading costs.

Supply-side factors

Institutional investors are pooling funds from individual households. Due to economies of scale, they are able to invest these funds more efficiently than individuals. Moreover, institutional investors are able to invest in assets that are indivisible (such as property) and therefore often not available to small investors. So, institutional investors provide diversified portfolios at low cost to households. For instance, a mutual fund requires a low level of minimum investment and offers households the possibility to invest in a diversified way. Costs of asset management are low as they are shared among many households, so that institutional investors offer an attractive risk-return profile.

Because of their policy to hedge exposure and to diversify their investments, institutional investors are increasingly using derivatives. Many of the new risk-management tools have been developed especially for institutional investors, increasing the efficiency of the financial system. Furthermore, when institutional investors adopt more active trading policies, they enhance the liquidity of markets, leading to higher efficiency and lower transaction costs. Davis (2003, p. 21) states that 'by demanding liquidity, institutional investors help to generate it'.

With respect to corporate governance, institutional investors have more 'bargaining power' than individual investors as they are often important shareholders in companies. However, the different types of institutional investors are not equally active in corporate governance. Gillan and Starks (2003) distinguish between pressure-sensitive and insensitive institutional investors. Pressure-sensitive investors are bankers and insurers who care about current or potential business relations with corporations in which they invest. They are more passive institutions. Pension funds and mutual funds are not sensitive to pressure and therefore are more active institutions. In particular, public pension funds are the pioneers in active corporate governance. Well-known examples are Hermes (the UK postal pension fund), CALPERS (California Public Employees Retirement Scheme), and ABP (see Box 6.1). More recently, hedge funds have become aggressive players in corporate governance.

Also deregulation has spurred the development of institutional investors. For example, commissions have been reduced and institutional investors have more freedom to investment internationally and to distribute their products to a wider public. Deregulation has also stimulated competition among asset-management institutions, which has lowered costs for the end-user, i.e., households. The European Commission plays a crucial role in regulatory issues concerning institutional investors. Because of the ageing problems that the EU Member States face (see below), the Commission urged countries to reform their pension schemes. At the same time, the Commission proposed a number of directives that would impose severe restrictions on pension funds and life insurance companies ('quantitative portfolio regulations'). After lengthy negotiations between the Commission, the Member States, and the pension funds, a new Pension Directive has been adopted to stimulate the single European market for pension funds. This directive promotes prudential investing of pension funds applied to the portfolio as a whole rather than to individual investments (the 'prudent person' principle). No quantitative restrictions have been imposed on the portfolio composition of EU pension funds. EU pension funds are thus able to optimise their risk-return profile (see section 6.3 on international diversification).[1]

In contrast, insurance companies still face certain regulatory restrictions. The percentage of equity as well as the percentage of foreign assets in their portfolio is restricted. The new regulatory framework for the insurance industry, Solvency II, is supposed to remove most of these restrictions, which would be advantageous for the proper development of institutional investments in the EU. Chapter 10 explains the regulatory framework for financial institutions in Europe.

The final supply-side factor furthering the development of institutional investors consists of fiscal advantages. Pension funds benefit from deferred taxation (contributions and investment returns are not taxed, but payouts are taxed). Life insurance contributions also often benefit from deferred taxation, while mutual funds enjoy a favourable tax regime in some EU countries (such as Luxembourg and Ireland).

Demand-side factors

Demand-side factors also play an important role in explaining the vast growth of institutional investment. The need for saving via institutional investors is linked to the level of social security benefits to which households are entitled. Institutional investment is stimulated when social security provides only a minimum level of income after retirement. In that case, the remaining part of income is provided via some kind of institutional saving.

The demand for institutional savings is mainly fuelled by demographic developments. Table 6.8 shows that the EU population is ageing. The need to save for retirement is thus increasing. Saving for retirement is done primarily via institutional investors. Which institutions benefit most from these demographic developments depends on the country-specific situation. In countries where pension funds are well established, like the Netherlands and the UK, retirement saving primarily takes place via pension funds. Employees in

Table 6.8 Dependency ratio: actual figures and forecasts, 2000–2050

	2000	2005	2010 (f)	2020 (f)	2030 (f)	2040 (f)	2050 (f)
Austria	22.9	23.6	26.3	30.3	40.8	50.4	53.2
Belgium	25.5	26.3	26.4	32.2	41.3	47.2	48.1
Denmark	22.2	22.6	24.8	31.2	37.1	42.1	40.0
Finland	22.2	23.7	25.4	37.0	45.0	46.1	46.7
France	24.6	25.3	25.9	33.2	40.7	46.9	47.9
Germany	23.9	27.8	31.0	35.1	46.0	54.6	55.8
Greece	24.2	26.8	28.0	32.5	39.1	49.8	58.8
Ireland	16.8	16.5	17.5	22.5	28.3	35.9	45.3
Italy	26.8	29.4	31.3	36.6	45.2	59.8	66.0
Luxembourg	21.4	21.2	21.6	24.7	31.5	36.7	36.1
Netherlands	20.0	20.7	22.2	29.0	36.7	41.6	38.6
Portugal	23.7	25.2	26.5	31.5	39.0	48.9	58.1
Spain	24.5	24.5	25.4	30.0	38.9	54.3	67.5
Sweden	26.9	26.4	28.0	34.4	38.5	41.5	40.9
United Kingdom	23.9	24.4	25.1	30.3	37.4	43.8	45.3
EU-15	**24.3**	**25.9**	**27.5**	**32.8**	**41.2**	**50.0**	**53.2**

Notes: The figure for the EU-15 is a weighted average in which the GDP of the EU-15 countries is used as weights; (f) means forecast.
Source: Eurostat

France, where pension funds are practically non-existent, save for their retirement via life insurance companies and mutual funds.

Demographic projections for the EU indicate that by 2050 the dependency ratio will be double that of today, moving from 26 in 2005 to 53 in 2050. The *dependency ratio* is equal to the number of individuals aged below 15 or above 64 divided by the number of individuals aged 15 to 64, expressed as a percentage. This can be explained by the expected fertility rates and life expectations in the EU. Total fertility rates have declined dramatically over the past decades, falling from an average of 2.7 children per woman of child-bearing age in 1970 to 1.6 in 2004. At the same time, life expectancy in the EU-15 increased from 71 years in 1970 to 79 years in 2003. It is expected to increase further.

Finally, over the last two decades European households have become wealthier, which has resulted in an increase in their investment horizon. These household investors bother less about the liquidity of their investments, as they are better positioned to absorb liquidity shocks. Less liquid investments offer a higher return. So wealthier households will search for the highest risk-return profile in the medium to long run. This means a shift from the traditional savings account (which can often be withdrawn on demand) towards long-term investments. However, most retail investors are risk averse and do not feel very comfortable with making investment decisions. So investing via institutional investors instead of direct investment will be more convenient.

6.3 Portfolio theory and international diversification

Portfolio theory

According to the international version of the CAPM, investors should hold an internationally diversified portfolio since such a portfolio maximises returns given a certain risk profile. This can be explained by Figure 6.6 which plots the mean and standard deviation of annualised monthly returns from January 1980 to December 2005 for two different equity portfolios. The first is the MSCI (Morgan Stanley Capital International) USA index, which is a proxy for the American stock market. The second is based on the MSCI Europe index, which is a proxy for the European stock market. Moving along the curve from 100 per cent US stocks to 100 per cent European stocks, the line plots

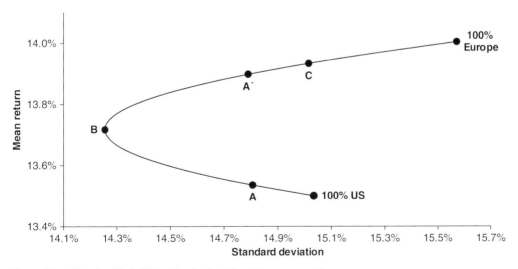

Figure 6.6   The simplified efficient frontier for US and European equities
Note: This graph is based on returns from the MSCI USA Index and MSCI Europe Index over the period 1980–2005.
Source: Bosch and Schoenmaker (2006)

the mean returns and standard deviations. This is a simplified version of the so-called *efficient frontier*, i.e., the portfolio with the minimum standard deviation for a given return.

The mean of the MSCI USA is lower than portfolio C, which has the same standard deviation but includes a fraction of European stocks. In fact, as long as investors prefer higher returns and lower variance, the minimum-variance portfolio at point B (with 40 per cent European equity) is preferable to a portfolio consisting of US shares only. However, as will be explained in more detail in the next section, American investors hold only 7 per cent of European stocks in their equity portfolio, which is indicated by point A.

Figure 6.6 illustrates that it is beneficial for investors to diversify geographically. The formal international CAPM model can be derived from the standard mean-variance framework modified to include foreign securities (Lewis, 1999). In the mean-variance framework, investors optimise their portfolio by increasing their return (i.e., the mean of their wealth) and decreasing their risk (i.e., the variance of their wealth). By introducing foreign stocks, investors have to choose the optimal mix of domestic and foreign stocks in their portfolio. Box 6.5 presents the international CAPM model derived by Lewis.

Box 6.5 The international CAPM model*

Suppose that domestic investors have access to two risky assets, a domestic and a foreign stock. The domestic investor chooses the proportion of his wealth portfolio held in foreign stocks, x (with $0 < x < 1$). The investor's objective is to increase mean wealth, $E(W_1)$, and decrease the variability of wealth, $\text{var}(W_1)$. His objective function is given by:

$$\text{max} \qquad V = V(E(W_1), \text{var}(W_1)) \tag{6.1}$$

$$\text{subject to} \quad V_1 > 0, \ V_2 < 0 \tag{6.2}$$

Where W_1 = next-period wealth, and E = the expected value conditional upon information known at time 0. V_1 is the partial derivative of V with respect to the first term, and V_2 with respect to the second term. The one-period return is a combination of the foreign return earned on the fraction of foreign stocks, denoted by x, and the domestic return earned on the fraction of domestic stocks, denoted by $(1-x)$, and is given by:

$$\begin{aligned} W_1 &= W_0(1 + x \cdot r^f + (1 - x) \cdot r^h) \\ &= W_0(1 + x \cdot (r^f - r^h) + r^h) \end{aligned} \tag{6.3}$$

Where W_0 = current wealth, r^f = foreign return, and r^h = domestic return. The variance of the one-period return is given by:

$$
\begin{aligned}
\text{var}(W_1) &= \text{var}(W_0(1 + x \cdot (r^f - r^h) + r^h)) \\
&= W_0^2 \ \text{var}(1 + x \cdot (r^f - r^h) + r^h) \\
&= W_0^2 (x^2 \ \text{var}(r^f - r^h) + 2 \cdot x \cdot (\rho_{fh} \cdot \sigma_f \cdot \sigma_h - \sigma_h^2) + \sigma_h^2)
\end{aligned}
\tag{6.4}
$$

Where $\sigma_h^2 = \text{var}(r^h) = $ the variance of the domestic stock return, $\sigma_f^2 = \text{var}(r^f) = $ the variance of the foreign stock return to the domestic investor, and $\sigma_{fh} = \rho_{fh} \cdot \sigma_f \cdot \sigma_h = \text{cov}(r^f, r^h) = $ the covariance between the domestic and foreign returns. The optimal fraction of foreign stock x^* can be calculated by deriving the first-order condition of the objective function V. The first-order condition is given by:

$$
\begin{aligned}
\frac{\delta V}{\delta x} &= V_1 \cdot W_0 \cdot (r^f - r^h) \\
&\quad + V_2 \cdot W_0^2 \cdot (2 \cdot x \cdot \text{var}(r^f - r^h) + 2 \cdot \sigma_{fh} - 2 \cdot \sigma_h^2) = 0
\end{aligned}
\tag{6.5}
$$

Dividing by W_0 and arranging terms leads directly to:

$$
\begin{aligned}
x^* &= \frac{r^f - r^h}{\text{var}(r^f - r^h)} \cdot \frac{-V_1}{2 \cdot V_2 \cdot W_0} + \frac{\sigma_h^2 - \sigma_{fh}}{\text{var}(r^f - r^h)} \\[2mm]
&= \frac{(r^f - r^h)/\gamma}{\text{var}(r^f - r^h)} + \frac{\sigma_h^2 - \sigma_{fh}}{\text{var}(r^f - r^h)}
\end{aligned}
\tag{6.6}
$$

where γ is the parameter of risk aversion $\frac{-2 \cdot V_2 \cdot W_0}{V_1}$. The interpretation of the demand function for foreign stock is straightforward. The first term on the right-hand side of equation 6.6 represents the demand arising from higher-potential returns from the foreign stock. The lower the risk aversion, γ, the greater the response of demand to higher expected returns. However, as γ increases, the importance of relative returns across countries declines. In the limiting case when γ equals infinity, i.e., investors are infinitely risk averse, the first term disappears. The demand for foreign stock then reduces to the second term, i.e., the portfolio share that minimises the variance of the wealth portfolio. This portfolio is illustrated by point B in Figure 6.6. Thus, in general, the demand for foreign stock depends on a combination of the risky portfolio share given by the first term and the minimum-variance portfolio given by the second term.

Source: Lewis (1999)

in which *Foreign Equity*$_i$ = share of country i's holdings of foreign equity in country i's total equity portfolio (1 – share of domestic equity); *Foreign Equity to Total Market*$_i$ = the share of foreign equity in the world portfolio available to country i (1 – share of country i in the total market capitalisation). The country portfolio is calculated as the domestic market capitalisation plus foreign equity holdings minus foreign owners of domestic equity.

Equation 6.7 measures to what extent domestic equity is overweighed compared with foreign equity in the investment portfolio. *EHB* will be equal to 0 if investors show no preference for equity issued domestically. If domestic investors have a preference for domestic equity, the ratio will be between 0 and 1. The home-bias formula can be illustrated as follows. Country i investors allocate 15 per cent of their portfolio to foreign equity, while the total world-market portfolio comprises 75 per cent of foreign equity and 25 per cent of domestic equity. Country i investors thus exploit international diversification to only one-fifth (15/75) and thus have a home bias of 0.8. *EHB*$_i$ is 1.0 if domestic investors invest 100 per cent of their equity portfolio domestically. In a similar vein, the preference of investors for domestic-debt securities can be measured. This home-bias measure for bonds is *BHB*$_i$.

Finally, the *regional bias* can be measured. The question is whether European investors show a preference for European securities in their foreign securities portfolio in comparison with US securities. Within the part of the investment portfolio that is invested in foreign equity and bonds, EU investors should, according to the international CAPM, show no preference for either European or US equities and bonds.

Similar to the analysis of the domestic home bias, it can be tested whether European investors have a bias towards European equities and bonds. The regional bias for European investors is measured as one minus the US asset acceptance ratio. This ratio measures the extent to which the share of US assets in the foreign equity portfolio of country i diverges from the relative share of US assets in the total foreign-market portfolio. The regional bias for equities is given by:

$$REB_i = 1 - \frac{US\,Equity_i}{US\,Equity\,to\,Foreign\,Market\,Portfolio_i} \qquad (6.8)$$

in which *US Equity*$_i$ = share of country i's holdings of US equity in country i's total foreign-equity portfolio (1 – share of EU equity in foreign portfolio); *US Equity to Foreign Market Portfolio*$_i$ = share of US equity in the foreign-equity portfolio which is available for country i. The available foreign portfolio for country *i* is total domestic market capitalisation of EU and US minus domestic market capitalisation of country *i*.

The foreign-market portfolio differs per country. For example, as the UK comprises a large part of total EU equity, the foreign-equity portfolio for the UK is smaller than that of other countries. The same applies to the foreign-bond portfolio. It is expected that the regional bond bias (RBB) is higher than the regional equity bias (REB) for the countries in the euro area, because there is no exchange rate (and interest-rate risk) involved, and international diversification of bonds primarily focuses on credit-risk diversification.

Evidence on the home bias

Some recent empirical studies measure the development of the home bias in the EU-15 (De Santis and Gérard, 2006; Bosch and Schoenmaker, 2006). Table 6.9 gives an overview of the equity and bond home bias in 1997, 2001, and 2004.[2] All countries experienced a sharp decline of the equity home bias

Table 6.9 Equity and bond home bias, 1997–2004

	Equity home bias					Bond home bias				
	1997	2001	2004	Δ97–01	Δ97–04	1997	2001	2004	Δ97–01	Δ97–04
Austria	0.82	0.49	0.68	−0.33	−0.14	0.80	0.53	0.35	−0.27	−0.44
Belgium	0.86	0.73	0.69	−0.13	−0.17	0.84	0.63	0.56	−0.21	−0.28
Denmark	0.83	0.65	0.74	−0.18	−0.09	0.93	0.88	0.83	−0.05	−0.10
Finland	0.96	0.86	0.75	−0.10	−0.21	0.91	0.56	0.45	−0.35	−0.45
France	0.90	0.85	0.79	−0.05	−0.11	0.88	0.70	0.59	−0.18	−0.28
Germany	n/a	0.77	0.77	n/a	n/a	n/a	0.75	0.62	n/a	n/a
Greece	n/a	0.99	0.97	n/a	n/a	n/a	0.91	0.76	n/a	n/a
Italy	0.89	0.80	0.85	−0.09	−0.04	0.95	0.83	0.81	−0.12	−0.14
Netherlands	0.77	0.56	0.43	−0.21	−0.33	0.71	0.31	0.17	−0.40	−0.54
Portugal	0.94	0.89	0.85	−0.06	−0.10	0.84	0.62	0.58	−0.22	−0.27
Spain	0.95	0.89	0.93	−0.06	−0.02	0.96	0.76	0.63	−0.20	−0.33
Sweden	0.86	0.70	0.73	−0.16	−0.13	0.93	0.77	0.74	−0.17	−0.19
United Kingdom	0.84	0.80	0.80	−0.04	−0.04	0.61	0.49	0.38	−0.12	−0.23
United States	0.83	0.82	0.81	−0.01	−0.02	0.97	0.97	0.96	−0.00	−0.01
EU-13	0.86	0.78	0.78	−0.07	−0.08	0.84	0.69	0.60	−0.15	−0.24
euro area	0.87	0.79	0.77	−0.08	−0.10	0.88	0.71	0.61	−0.17	−0.27
non-euro area	0.84	0.78	0.79	−0.06	−0.05	0.72	0.60	0.53	−0.12	−0.19

Note: EU-13, euro, and non-euro area are calculated as a weighted average; n.a. means not available.
Source: Bosch and Schoenmaker (2006)

from 1997 to 2001. In most countries the home bias decreased further after 2001, but in some countries (such as Austria, Denmark, Italy, and Spain) the home bias increased after 2001. The Netherlands has the lowest home bias (0.43 in 2004); it also had the largest decline from 1997 to 2004. The southern European countries have a bias around 0.90. The equity home bias in the UK and the US decreased slightly from 1997 to 2004 but was still relatively high (0.80 and 0.81, respectively).

The weighted average bias for the EU-13 (EU-15 except for Ireland and Luxembourg) declined by 0.08 from 1997 to 2001, after which the bias remained stable at 0.78. It is interesting that the EU bias has decreased after the introduction of the euro, without a significant change of the US bias over this period. While the weighted-average bias for the countries in the euro area was higher in 1997 than the bias of the non-euro countries, the bias for the countries in the euro area decreased by 0.10 from 1997 to 2004 compared with 0.05 for the non-euro countries.

Table 6.9 also illustrates that the BHB has declined in all countries in the sample, and this reduction is in general larger than that of the EHB. In 2004, the BHB is the lowest for the Netherlands (0.17), followed by Austria and the UK. Denmark, Sweden, Greece, and Italy still exhibit a large BHB relative to the other EU Member States.

Compared with the EHB, the BHB is on average lower for the EU-13 countries. The weighted average BHB for the EU-13 was 0.60 in 2004, a reduction of 0.24 since 1997. The differences between the EU countries are larger for the BHB than for the EHB. The US has an exceptionally high BHB at 0.96. It can be concluded that US investors are very domestically focused within their long-term debt portfolios, and allocate only a small percentage of their bond portfolio to EU bonds. This is partly in line with theory. As the US economy is very large, there is more scope for US investors to diversify credit risk domestically without incurring exchange-rate risk.

For the EU, the largest decline has taken place in the period 1997 to 2001, which is related to the introduction of the euro. The decrease of the home bias for bonds from 1997 to 2004 is larger for the countries in the euro area (0.27) than for those outside the monetary union (0.19). The fact that the non-euro countries still have a lower BHB is fully driven by the UK. The reported results for the EHB and BHB are largely in line with the findings of De Santis and Gérard (2006). They also find a decline in the home bias from 1997–2001 for the countries in the sample.

As illustrated above, all countries in the sample exhibit a home bias towards domestic equities and bonds. Within the portfolio of foreign securities of the

Table 6.10 Regional equity and bond bias of European investors, 1997–2004

	Regional bias towards EU-13 equities					Regional bias towards EU-13 bonds				
	1997	2001	2004	Δ97–01	Δ97–04	1997	2001	2004	Δ97–01	Δ97–04
Austria	0.53	0.50	0.56	−0.03	0.03	0.68	0.82	0.86	0.14	0.18
Belgium	0.70	0.71	0.76	0.01	0.06	0.69	0.81	0.91	0.12	0.21
Denmark	0.58	0.42	0.39	−0.16	−0.19	0.75	0.71	0.65	−0.04	−0.10
Finland	0.69	0.61	0.73	−0.08	0.04	0.76	0.86	0.90	0.10	0.15
France	0.48	0.59	0.74	0.11	0.25	0.74	0.77	0.80	0.02	0.06
Germany	n/a	0.59	0.62	n/a	n/a	n/a	0.85	0.87	n/a	n/a
Greece	n/a	0.44	0.23	n/a	n/a	n/a	0.62	0.81	n/a	n/a
Italy	0.53	0.48	0.52	−0.05	−0.01	0.62	0.75	0.75	0.13	0.13
Netherlands	0.25	0.26	0.11	0.01	−0.14	0.81	0.70	0.74	−0.11	−0.07
Portugal	0.33	0.65	0.80	0.32	0.47	0.59	0.84	0.85	0.25	0.26
Spain	0.33	0.72	0.73	0.39	0.39	0.85	0.87	0.83	0.01	−0.02
Sweden	0.26	0.23	0.23	−0.03	−0.03	0.51	0.52	0.58	0.01	0.07
United Kingdom	0.47	0.53	0.38	0.07	−0.09	0.48	0.47	0.38	0.00	−0.10
EU-13	0.43	0.50	0.47	0.07	0.04	0.62	0.72	0.74	0.09	0.11
euro area	0.41	0.52	0.53	0.11	0.12	0.73	0.79	0.82	0.06	0.09
non-euro area	0.45	0.48	0.36	0.03	−0.09	0.43	0.49	0.41	0.06	−0.02

Notes: EU-13, euro, and non-euro area are calculated as a weighted average; n.a. means not available.
Source: Bosch and Schoenmaker (2006)

14 countries in the sample, a distinction can be made between investments in European and US securities. If the home-bias puzzle is mainly a geographical phenomenon, this implies that within their foreign portfolio European investors give too much importance to European securities.

Table 6.10 reports the output concerning the regional bias for equities and bonds. Investors in all European countries in the sample overweigh European relative to US equities. This means that the home bias also persists on a regional level. The weighted average REB for the EU-13 increased from 1997 to 2004. The split between countries inside and outside the euro area identifies an interesting pattern. The REB increased by 0.12 for the euro countries, while the bias declined by 0.09 for the non-euro countries.

The Netherlands has the lowest REB of the EU-13 countries (0.11 in 2004), followed by Sweden and Greece (both 0.23). Denmark noticed the largest absolute decline (0.19) from 1997 to 2004. Portugal, Spain, Belgium, and France show a high preference for European equities in their foreign-investment portfolios. It is remarkable that the bias of Portugal, Spain, and France increased strongly from 1997 to 2004. Investors in these countries evidently moved to a euro-area investment strategy and thereby reduced their foreign (US) equity holdings.

Table 6.10 also reports the RBB of European investors. The weighted average for the EU-13 countries increased from 1997 to 2004. The increase in the RBB was driven by the euro countries. The RBB increased by 0.09 for the countries in the euro area and declined by 0.02 for those outside. The absolute value of the bias in 2004 was twice as large for the euro countries (0.82 vs. 0.41). The UK has the lowest RBB, followed by Sweden and Denmark (which are all non-euro countries). While the Netherlands had the lowest bias in all previous tables, its RBB is equal to the EU-13 weighted average, at 0.74. Countries in the euro area, such as Austria, Belgium, and Finland, saw their RBB increase to around 0.90 in 2004. It can be concluded that for these countries the decline in the BHB is caused by a shift from domestic towards EU-13 bonds, and not to US bonds. These countries diversify the credit risk of the bond portfolio to a significant extent, but within the EU. The interest-rate risk is hedged by investing primarily in EU bonds, which have interest rates which are almost identical (euro area) or linked (non-euro area) to domestic rates. Moreover, exchange-rate risk is largely eliminated.

The international diversification strategy of institutional investors is graphically illustrated in Figures 6.7–6.10. Data for 1997 and 2004 are compared for four regions: the US, the EU-13, the ten euro countries within the EU-13, and the three non-euro countries within the EU-13. Figures 6.7 and 6.8 illustrate that the decline in the home bias is larger for the EU than for the US.

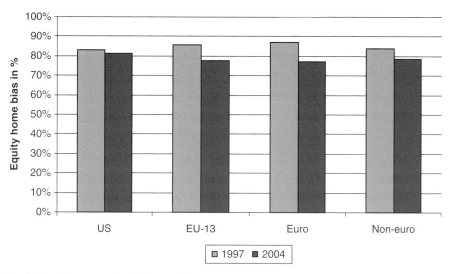

Figure 6.7   Equity home bias per region, 1997 vs. 2004

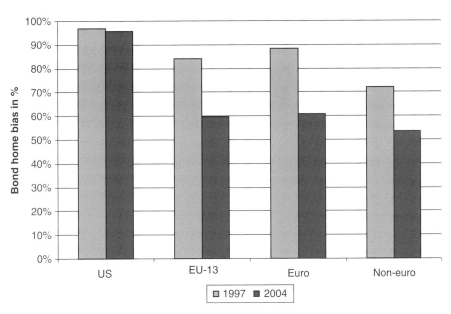

Figure 6.8   Bond home bias per region, 1997 vs. 2004

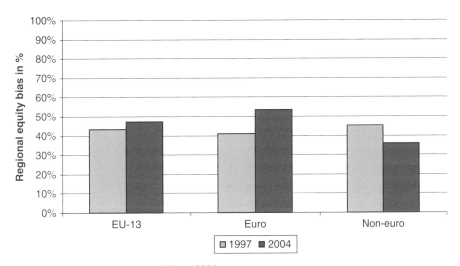

Figure 6.9   Regional equity bias per region, 1997 vs. 2004

Within the EU-13 countries, the ten euro countries show a larger decline in the home bias than the three non-euro countries.

While the equity and bond home bias in the euro area has declined faster than in the non-euro countries (Figures 6.7 and 6.8), the reverse is true for the regional bias (Figures 6.9 and 6.10). In fact, this bias has increased

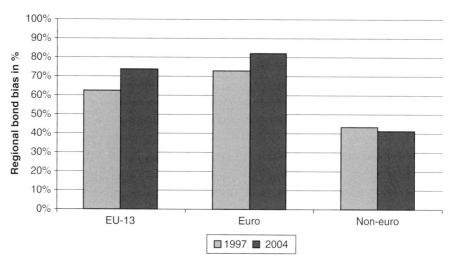

Figure 6.10   Regional bond bias per region, 1997 vs. 2004

for both equity and bonds in the euro area, but has decreased on average for the three non-euro countries. These results are consistent with the theory of economic integration. Since the introduction of the euro in 1999, investors in the euro countries have allocated a larger part of their portfolio to foreign assets than have non-euro countries and the US. At the same time, the regional bias of the euro area has increased, as investors in euro countries have invested their foreign assets mainly in their own region. Investors based in the euro area have thus shifted from a country-based investing strategy towards a sector-based strategy. So there is a 'euro effect' as the euro has caused a decrease of the home bias but an increase of the regional bias. The regional bias decreased for the non-euro countries, which means that they partly shifted their foreign assets towards US assets compared with EU assets.

Explaining the home bias

If the gains of international diversification are positive and significant, why do (institutional) investors not hold the theoretically optimal portfolio? Table 6.11 explains which factors influence the size of the equity home bias.

The first factor is the ratio of total exports to GDP. This is a proxy for 'trade'. Investors in countries with a large export-to-GDP ratio have a lower need for international diversification, as the companies in these countries are already

Table 6.11 Determinants of the equity home bias (OLS regression)

Independent variables	Expected sign	Coefficient	t-value
Constant		0.915***	17.3
Export	+/−	−0.324***	3.9
Institutional	−	−0.146**	2.4
Insider	+	0.127	1.3
Market cap	+	0.159*	2.0
N		42	
Adj. R^2		0.69	
F-statistic		16.25	

Notes: OLS panel regression using EHB_i as the dependent variable. Data for 1997, 2002, and 2004 for the EU-13 and the US are used for this analysis. Period-specific fixed effects are included in the regression. (***), (**), and (*) indicate statistical significance at the 1 per cent, 5 per cent, and 10 per cent levels, respectively.
Source: Bosch and Schoenmaker (2006)

diversifying via their international business. However, this ratio could also be a proxy for the mindset of investors in a country indicating the openness of that country. If companies tend to do business abroad and diversify their business geographically, investors could act in the same manner.

Table 6.11 reports that export to GDP has a significant negative effect on the home bias. This supports the theory that countries with relatively large trade volumes can be considered as more 'open' and have a lower bias due to the *openness effect*. The domestic companies in these countries have significant exposure to the world market due to their level of international trade. However, investors in these countries are subject to a lower EHB, as they also tend to 'trade' (invest) internationally.

The second factor is the size of the institutional sector. Table 6.11 shows that the relative size of the institutional sector has a negative and significant effect on the home bias. Countries in which institutions manage a larger part of the financial assets exhibit larger international diversification. Indeed, this finding indicates that institutional investors, as professional asset managers, are subject to a lower home bias than non-financial corporations or households. This is the *professionalism effect*.

The third factor is the percentage of shares held by corporate insiders. Insider ownership is expected to increase the home bias in two ways. First, domestic investors hold shares that foreign investors cannot own. Second, domestic investors allocate a lower amount to foreign equity, as they have locked up a part of their portfolio in domestic assets. It should be noted, however, that the theory concerning insider ownership is developed to explain the bias towards a country (Stulz, 2005), but not necessarily the home bias of a country itself. The share of corporate insiders is the only variable that is not significant in Table 6.11, although it has the expected positive sign.

The fourth factor is the size of the domestic stock market to GDP. Table 6.11 illustrates that the relative size of the domestic stock market has a positive and significant effect on the home bias. Thus, investors are more domestically oriented if their domestic stock market is well developed. This indicates that investors are subject to the *availability effect*, which means that investors are more eager to invest in domestic assets when these domestic assets are relatively better available.

Finally, behavourial approaches may also explain the home bias. Behavioural finance draws upon psychological effects of individual behaviour. Huberman (2001), for example, argues that familiarity with domestic companies makes it easier for investors to invest in domestic equity. Campbell and Kräussl (2007) find that investors concerned with downside risk tend to hold a larger proportion of their portfolio in domestic equity, due to the greater downside risk from investing abroad.

6.5 Conclusions

The institutionalisation of the investment process, where professional market investors manage private savings, is a global trend. This chapter distinguishes three main types of institutional investors: pension funds, life insurance companies, and mutual funds. Both the demand side (growing investments by pension funds to cater for ageing and by mutual funds to accommodate wealth accumulation of households) and the supply side (shift from bank-financed companies to market-financed companies via equity and bonds) point to future growth of institutional investment.

As in many other financial sectors, distinctions between types of institutional investors are blurring. Mutual funds, in particular, are being used as a vehicle for retirement saving and are a specific asset class for pension funds. Private equity and hedge funds are alternative investments, which are increasingly added to the portfolio of pension funds. Insurance companies launch their own investment funds and are widely involved in pension provision, provision of annuities, and guaranteed investment contracts for pension funds, while also performing asset management for pension funds.

Institutional investors play an important role in monitoring companies in which they invest. This promotes good corporate governance. As dominant investors, institutions have the clout to influence the management of companies.

Finance theory suggests that investors should aim for international diversification of their investment portfolio to maximise returns given a certain risk profile. Nevertheless, there is a strong home bias in equity and bond portfolios. This chapter shows that the increasing professionalism of institutional investors (compared with individual investors) has led to a decline in the home bias in Europe. The elimination of exchange-rate risk following the introduction of the euro has led to a further decline of the home bias in the euro area.

NOTES

1. Davis and Steil (2001) discuss the two main approaches, namely '*prudent person rules*', which enjoin portfolio diversification and broad asset-liability matching, and '*quantitative portfolio regulations*', which limit holdings of certain types of asset within the portfolio. Both seek to ensure adequate portfolio diversification and liquidity of the asset portfolio, but in different ways.
2. Data concerning foreign equity and bond holdings are extracted from a country-level dataset of the IMF, the Coordinated Portfolio Investment Survey (CPIS). Luxembourg and Ireland are excluded from the EU-15 as they attract large amounts of foreign investment due to favourable tax policies, while the US is added to the dataset. This results in a sample of 14 countries. A proxy for the world-market portfolio is the domestic market capitalisation of the EU-13 and the US. In this way, we analyse to what extent the EU-13 countries and the US overweight domestic equity in their portfolio compared with foreign equity.

SUGGESTED READING

Davis, E. P. and B. Steil (2001), *Institutional Investors*, MIT Press, Cambridge (MA).

Elton, E. J., M. J. Gruber, S. J. Brown, and W. M. Goetzmann (2007), *Modern Portfolio Theory and Investment Analysis*, 7th edition, John Wiley & Sons, New York.

Feldstein, M. S. and H. Siebert (eds.) (2002), *Social Security Pension Reform in Europe*, University of Chicago Press, Chicago.

Gillan, S. L. and L. T. Starks (2003), Corporate Governance, Corporate Ownership, and the Role of Institutional Investors: A Global Perspective, *Journal of Applied Finance*, 13, 4–22.

Lewis, K. K. (1999), Trying to Explain Home Bias in Equities and Consumption, *Journal of Economic Literature*, 37, 571–608.

REFERENCES

Ahearne, A. B., W. Griever, and F. Warnock (2004), Information Costs and the Home Bias, *Journal of International Economics*, 62, 313–336.

Algemeen Burgerlijk Pensioenfonds (2007), *Annual Report 2006*, ABP, Heerlen.

Bosch, T. and D. Schoenmaker (2006), The Role and Importance of Institutional Investors in Europe, *Financial and Monetary Studies*, 24(3/4), SDU, The Hague.

Campbell, R. A. and R. Kräussl (2007), Revisiting the Home Bias Puzzle: Downside Equity Risk, *Journal of International Money and Finance*, 26, 1239–1260.

Chan, K., M. V. Covrig, and L. K. Ng (2005), What Determines the Domestic Bias and Foreign Bias? Evidence from Mutual Fund Equity Allocations Worldwide, *Journal of Finance*, 60, 1495–1534.

Davis, E. P. and B. Steil (2001), *Institutional Investors*, MIT Press, Cambridge (MA).

Davis, E. P. (2003), Institutional Investors, Financial Market Efficiency and Stability, The Pensions Institute (London) Working Paper PI-0303.

De Santis, R. A. and B. Gérard (2006), Financial Integration, International Portfolio Choice and the European Monetary Union, ECB Working Paper 626.

Elton, E. J., M. J. Gruber, S. J. Brown, and W. M. Goetzmann (2007), *Modern Portfolio Theory and Investment Analysis*, 7th edition, John Wiley & Sons, New York.

European Central Bank (2006), *EU Banking Structures*, ECB, Frankfurt am Main.

European Fund and Asset Management Association (2005), *Trends in European Investment Funds*, EFAMA, Brussels.

Feldstein, M. S. and H. Siebert (eds.) (2002), *Social Security Pension Reform in Europe*, University of Chicago Press, Chicago.

Financial Stability Forum (2007), *Update of the FSF Report on Highly Leveraged Institutions*, FSF, Basel.

Furfine, C. (2006), The Costs and Benefits of Moral Suasion: Evidence from the Rescue of Long-Term Capital Management, *Journal of Business*, 79, 593–622.

Gillan, S. L. and L. T. Starks (2003), Corporate Governance, Corporate Ownership, and the Role of Institutional Investors: A Global Perspective, *Journal of Applied Finance*, 13, 4–22.

Hedge Fund Standards Board (2008), *Best Practice Standards*, HFSB, London.

Huberman, G. (2001), Familiarity Breeds Investment, *Review of Financial Studies*, 14, 659–680.

International Financial Services London (2007a), *City Business Series: Hedge Funds*, IFSL, London.

International Financial Services London (2007b), *City Business Series: Private Equity*, IFSL, London.

Jorion, P. (2000), Risk Management Lessons from Long-Term Capital Management, *European Financial Management*, 6, 277–300.

Karolyi, G. A. and R. M. Stulz (2003), Are Financial Assets Priced Locally or Globally?, in: G. M. Constantinides, M. Harris, and R. M. Stulz (eds.), *The Handbook of the Economics of Finance*, Elsevier, Amsterdam, 975–1020.

Kho, B. C., D. Lee, and R. M. Stulz (2000), US Banks, Crises, and Bailouts: From Mexico to LTCM, *American Economic Review*, 90, 28–31.

Khorana, A., H. Servaes, and P. Tufano (2005), Explaining the Size of the Mutual Fund Industry Around the World, *Journal of Financial Economics*, 78, 145–185.

Lewis, K. K. (1999), Trying to Explain Home Bias in Equities and Consumption, *Journal of Economic Literature*, 37, 571–608.

Organisation for Economic Co-operation and Development (2003), *Institutional Investors Statistical Yearbook*, OECD, Paris.

Rajan, R. G. (2007), Benign Financial Conditions, Asset Management, and Political Risks: Trying to Make Sense of our Times, in: D. D. Evanoff, G. G. Kaufman, and J. R. LaBrosse (eds.), *International Financial Stability: Global Banking and National Regulation*, World Scientific Publishing, Singapore, 19–28.

Schröder, M. (2003), Benefits of Diversification and Integration for International Equity and Bond Portfolios, ZEW Economic Studies 19, Heidelberg.

Smit, H. T. J. (2003), The Economics of Private Equity, ERIM (Erasmus University, Rotterdam) Report Series EIA-2002-13.

Stulz, R. M. (1999), Globalisation of Equity Markets and the Cost of Capital, NBER Working Paper 7021.

Stulz, R. M. (2005), The Limits of Financial Globalisation, *Journal of Finance*, 60, 1595–1638.

7

European Banks

OVERVIEW

The traditional business of banking is the provision of long-term loans that are funded by short-term deposits. Banks have a comparative advantage against other financial institutions in providing liquidity. They have also developed technologies to screen and monitor borrowers in order to reduce asymmetric information between the lender and the borrower. These liquidity-providing and monitoring functions give banks also a key position in modern capital-market transactions, such as underwriting, trading, and derivatives transactions.

Risk is fundamental to the business of banking. Progress in information technology in combination with demands by supervisors has spurred the development of advanced risk-management models. This, in turn, has prompted the centralisation and integration of some management functions such as risk management, treasury operations, compliance, and auditing. This integrated approach to risk management aims to ensure a comprehensive and systematic approach to risk-related decisions throughout the banking group. Moreover, banks with an integrated risk-management unit can exploit diversification opportunities at the group level.

The European banking market is made up of 27 national banking systems. Each national banking system has its own characteristics, such as the number of banks, the level of concentration, and the intensity of competition. Some banking systems are highly concentrated, but this does not necessarily lead to a lack of competition. An important condition for competitive pressure is that the market is open to new entry (contestability). The European Commission therefore promotes the removal of remaining obstacles to cross-border mergers and acquisitions.

Domestic banking mergers used to be very common, while more recently the frequency of cross-border mergers has increased. While it is not possible yet to speak of an integrated banking market, the level of cross-border penetration has gradually increased.

LEARNING OBJECTIVES

After you have studied this chapter, you should be able to:

- explain the role of banks as liquidity providers to the economy
- explain the role of banks in screening and monitoring (potential) borrowers
- explain the use of risk-management models by modern banks and the centralisation of the risk-management function
- explain the dynamics of domestic and cross-border mergers and acquisitions in banking.

7.1 Theory of banking

Drivers of bank profitability

Banks perform multiple functions. The traditional business of banks is lending. Before a bank grants a loan, it screens the creditworthiness of a potential borrower. After the loan is granted, a bank monitors whether the borrower takes excessive risks. The lending business generates income for banks. As loans are funded with deposits, the difference (or spread) between the lending and borrowing rate determines a bank's profitability. Banks also make profits through various fee-earning activities, like capital-market transactions, such as underwriting and trading, and derivatives transactions. Banks use modern risk-management models to measure and control the risks arising from these transactions. These risk-management models are built on the monitoring technology that banks use in their lending business.

Lending business

Banks take deposits from the public and grant loans on their own account. These loans are typically held to maturity (the 'originate and hold' model). Banks are thus engaged in the transformation of liquid deposits into illiquid loans. The intermediation function of banks can be explained using a simple balance sheet (see Figure 7.1). On the liability side, banks fund themselves with many small deposits D from the public. The effective deposit rate r_D includes both the explicit interest paid and the cost of free services (for example, free access to ATMs). While deposits are redeemable on demand, depositors usually do not ask for their money back at the same time. Banks therefore hold only a fraction of these deposits in the form of liquid reserves

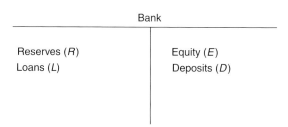

Figure 7.1   Simplified balance sheet of a bank

R that consist of balances with the central bank or readily tradable assets, such as Treasury securities, that pay the risk-free rate r_F.

Banks grant loans L on their own account. The expected loan rate r_L is different from the contracted rate on loans, as some borrowers default on their loan. Assuming a risk-neutral bank, the difference between the contracted or promised loan rate r_P and the expected loan rate r_L is given by:

$$E(1 + r_P) = (1 + r_P) \cdot (1 - p) + (1 + r_P) \cdot p \cdot \gamma = 1 + r_L \qquad (7.1)$$

where p is the probability of default and γ the recovery rate (the fraction of the principal and interest recovered in case of default). Equation 7.1 can be illustrated with a simple example. Assume a promised loan rate of 9 per cent, a probability of default of 5 per cent and a recovery rate of 80 per cent. The expected loan rate is 7.91 per cent, calculated as (1.09 * 0.95) + (1.09 * .05 * 0.8) = 1.0791.

The bank's profit π is the interest margin net of cost (C) and is given by:

$$\pi = L \cdot r_L + R \cdot r_F - D \cdot r_D - C \qquad (7.2)$$

An important determinant of bank profitability is the risk premium RP, i.e., the difference between the promised loan rate and the risk-free rate $(r_P - r_F)$. The risk premium covers the expected loan losses (that are a function of p and γ), the cost of the loan business, and the reward for risk taking on the loans.

Fee-based business

Banks also make profits from fee-earning activities. These off-balance-sheet activities are related to the traditional loan business and include securitisation of assets, credit lines, and guarantees, such as letters of credit. Off-balance-sheet activities also encompass derivative transactions, such as forwards, options, and swaps. Nowadays, large banks are the key players in the derivatives markets.

> **Box 7.1** Securitisation techniques
>
> Securitisation is often arranged via a special purpose vehicle which buys the assets from the originator and issues securities against these assets. The SPV is a separate legal entity and the originator is generally not liable for the SPV's possible bankruptcy.
>
> Individual securities are often split into tranches, each with a different level of risk exposure. The higher tranche has priority (seniority) over the lower tranches on the cash that the SPV receives. This permits the highest tranche to achieve a much better credit rating than the average of the assets backing all the tranches together. The lower tranches have a correspondingly lower credit rating.
>
> Deals may include a third-party guarantor, which provides (partial) guarantees for a fee. Specialised financial institutions, called 'monolines', guarantee the timely repayment of the principal and interest.
>
> The 'originate and distribute' model can reduce information at the level of the originator (Buiter, 2007). Under the traditional 'originate and hold' model the loan officer collects information on the creditworthiness of the borrower. This information is also useful for the monitoring of the borrower until the loan matures. When the loans are sold, the incentive to gather information at the origination stage is diluted. Reputation considerations of the originating bank mitigate this problem, but do not eliminate it. Moreover, the information collected by the originator is often not effectively transmitted to the SPV. The holders of the securities issued by the SPV can, of course, collect their own information. Holders of residential mortgage-backed securities (RMBS), for example, can send staff to specific addresses to assess and value the individual residential properties. However, this is very costly and implies that the benefits of securitisation are wiped out.

Asset securitisation involves the sale of income-generating financial assets (such as mortgages, car loans, trade receivables, credit card receivables, and leases) by a bank, the originator of the financial assets, to a *special purpose vehicle* (SPV). The SPV finances the purchase of these financial assets by the issue of bonds, which are secured by those assets (see Box 7.1). Banks can thus liquefy their illiquid loans. The resulting 'originate and distribute' model separates the functions of granting loans and funding loans. When loans on their balance sheet are securitised, banks can provide new loans.

Finally, banks are increasingly involved in fee-earning capital-market and asset-management activities. European banks deliver services like underwriting securities, advising on mergers and acquisitions (M&As), and managing assets. In this way, they have recovered part of the business lost due to disintermediation (see chapter 6). Currently, non-interest income of banks in the EU amounts to 44 per cent of total income (ECB, 2006).

Banks as liquidity providers

Banks have an advantage compared with other financial institutions in providing liquidity. This advantage is rooted in the structure of the banking system (Garber and Weisbrod, 1990). First, there is an active and deep interbank market in which banks trade their liquidity surpluses and deficits (see chapter 3). Under normal circumstances, liquidity shocks at individual banks can easily be offset. A bank with a surplus lends to a bank with a deficit, and vice versa. As shown in chapter 4, the euro interbank market has worked smoothly from the first day of EMU. Money-market rates quickly converged to a single euro-wide money-market rate. TARGET (the wholesale payment system of the national central banks and the European Central Bank) provided the infrastructure for transferring funds in real time (see chapter 5).

Second, aggregate liquidity shocks are smoothed by the central bank. A central bank conducts open-market operations to inject (withdraw) liquidity in the money market if there is an aggregate shortage (surplus). Banks are the usual counterparties of the central bank in these open-market operations. In case an individual bank cannot square its position at the end of the day, it can use facilities offered by the central bank. To stimulate banks to do their business as much as possible on the money market, the rates for these standing facilities are slightly off-market. The ECB's deposit rate is, for example, 1 per cent below the official refinancing rate for open market operations and the marginal lending rate is 1 per cent above the official refinancing rate.

These features of the banking system enable banks to provide liquidity to other financial institutions if and when needed. More importantly, they are also the main provider of liquidity to households and firms. The liquidity pyramid in Figure 7.2 illustrates these relationships. The central bank is at the top of the pyramid, as it can create liquidity without limit by expanding its balance sheet (granting loans and taking deposits). As explained above, the central bank only provides liquidity to banks that in turn provide liquidity to the rest of the financial system and to households and firms. Especially during crises it is important that central banks act swiftly to provide liquidity. However, banks also play a crucial role under these circumstances, as the examples presented in Box 7.2 illustrate.

Banks as delegated monitor

Asymmetric information lies at the core of banking. A borrower has private information on the cash flow of an investment project, which is unobservable

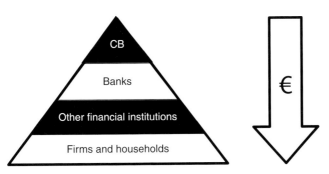

Figure 7.2   Liquidity pyramid of the economy
Note: CB = central bank. In this liquidity pyramid, the central bank provides liquidity to the banking system. Banks in turn provide liquidity to other financial institutions. Banks also provide liquidity to firms and households.

to outside lenders. Banks therefore monitor (potential) clients. *Monitoring* is defined here in a broad sense (Freixas and Rochet, 2008) as:

- screening projects ex ante (adverse selection);
- preventing opportunistic behaviour of the borrower during the project (moral hazard);
- auditing a borrower who fails to meet its contractual obligation (costly state verification).

Banks have a comparative advantage in monitoring (potential) borrowers if the following conditions are met (Diamond, 1984). First, a bank can develop economies of scale in monitoring by financing many investment projects. Second, the capacity of individual lenders is small compared to the size of many investment projects so that each project needs several lenders who would then need to monitor the borrowers. Finally, the costs of delegating this monitoring to a bank are small. Box 7.3 presents the Diamond model of delegated monitoring that shows that under these conditions it is efficient to delegate monitoring to a bank.

When the number of borrowers is large, it is efficient to delegate monitoring to one party. In the model shown in Box 7.3, a bank emerges as the delegated monitor for all lenders. Another party to whom lenders may delegate monitoring is a credit-rating agency. A *credit rating agency* assigns credit ratings to firms and governments that issue debt obligations, such as bonds (see chapter 3).[1] A credit rating measures the creditworthiness of a firm. It basically looks at the firm's ability to pay back a loan, which can be derived from observing the firm's cash flows. The resulting credit rating affects the interest rate charged for the bonds.

What determines the choice between direct and intermediated lending? In practice, direct lending in the form of issuing bonds at the capital market is less expensive than bank lending. So only those firms that cannot issue direct

---

Box 7.2 Liquidity management during crises

On 19 October 1987 the US stock market crashed, with the S&P 500 stock market index falling about 20 per cent. The crash showed the vulnerability of the trading systems as they were not capable of processing so many transactions at once. Uncertainty about information contributed to a pull-back by investors from the market. Another factor contributing to the crash were *margin calls* to securities traders that accompanied the large price changes. When securities traders buy securities with borrowed money, they have to deposit a margin with the clearinghouse to cover the credit risk of the clearinghouse. As the value of securities declined, the clearinghouse called for extra margin. While necessary to protect the solvency of the clearinghouse processing the trades, the size of the margin calls reduced market liquidity as securities traders had drawn on their working capital to meet these margin calls and subsequently had difficulties in continuing trading. The Federal Reserve stepped in by providing highly visible liquidity support through massive open-market operations. More importantly, the Federal Reserve also encouraged banks to extend liquidity support to securities traders (brokers and dealers). The extension of credit by banks to securities firms was key to their ability to meet their clearing and settlement obligations and to continue to operate in these markets.

Another example was the sub-prime mortgage market crisis in the summer of 2007. Many banks, including various large banks like Goldman Sachs, City Group, and Merrill Lynch, announced large losses due to this crisis. As it was unclear to what extent banks were exposed to these risks, banks were reluctant to provide short-term loans to each other. The ECB and the Federal Reserve therefore stepped in and provided massive liquidity support. The Bank of England (BoE), however, initially remained on the sidelines. On 12 September 2007 BoE governor Mervyn King said the Bank of England would be prepared to provide emergency loans to any bank that ran into short-term difficulties as a result of temporary market conditions. But he appeared to rule out following the lead of the ECB and US Federal Reserve in pumping huge sums into the banking system to ease the liquidity drought. On 13 September, British bank Northern Rock, the country's fifth largest mortgage lender, applied to the BoE for emergency funds caused by liquidity problems. Concerned customers withdrew an estimated £2 billion in just three days; this was the first run on a British bank in more than a century. On 17 September, Chancellor Alistair Darling intervened to try to end the crisis by agreeing to guarantee all deposits held by Northern Rock.

---

debt on financial markets will request bank lending (Freixas and Rochet, 2008). When the uncertainty about the firm's cash flows is relatively small (i.e., the asymmetric information between the firm and the lenders is limited), the firm can borrow on the market. As the uncertainty increases, banks come into play as they have more possibilities than credit rating agencies to ask

---

Box 7.3 When is it optimal to delegate monitoring to banks?*

Consider n identical borrowers who need funds for their investment projects. Each investment requires one unit of account and the returns of the investment are identically independently distributed. The cash flow $\tilde{y}$ that a borrower obtains from his investment is unobservable for lenders. The asymmetric information regarding the cash flow gives rise to moral hazard, which can be solved either by monitoring the firm at a cost K or by signing a debt contract with a cost C (in case of insufficient cash flow). It is assumed that monitoring is more efficient than using the debt contract: $K < C$. The next assumption is that each lender has only $\frac{1}{m}$ available for investment (i.e., lenders have a small capacity to lend). So each project needs m lenders. If small lenders provide the funds needed for the investment (direct lending), the total costs of monitoring all projects by all borrowers would amount to $n \cdot m \cdot K$.

Next, a bank is introduced. Facing the same trade-off between monitoring or signing debt contracts, the bank will also choose to monitor borrowers since $K < C$. The bank emerges as a delegated monitor, which monitors the borrowers on behalf of lenders. But who will monitor the bank? It is very costly for all lenders to monitor the bank. The solution is that the bank offers a debt contract (deposit). The lender is promised a nominal amount $\frac{r_D}{m}$ in return for a deposit $\frac{1}{m}$. The bank is liquidated if its announced cash flow $\tilde{z}$ falls below the total sum promised to depositors $n \cdot r_D$. Now, a mechanism is needed to ensure that a bank will truthfully reveal the realised cash flow $\tilde{z} = \sum_{i=1}^{n} \tilde{y}_i - n.K$. The threat of an audit in case of failure at a cost is used to make the contract incentive compatible.

Suppose that depositors are risk neutral and have access to outside investments with a return of r. The equilibrium repayment on deposits r_D is then determined by:

$$E\left[\min\left(\sum_{i=1}^{n} \tilde{y}_i - n \cdot K, n \cdot r_D\right)\right] = n \cdot r \qquad (7.3)$$

Equation 7.3 shows that the return r is equal to the minimum of the expected cash flow of the project minus monitoring costs and the expected unit return on deposits. In equilibrium, the expected unit return on deposits r_D equals r. Next, the total cost of delegation C_n is equal to the expectation of a costly audit in case of failure:

$$C_n = E\left[\max\left(n \cdot r_D + n \cdot K - \sum_{i=1}^{n} \tilde{y}_i, 0\right)\right] \qquad (7.4)$$

Delegated monitoring is more efficient than direct lending if the combined cost of monitoring by the bank and delegation is lower than the cost of monitoring by all lenders:

$$n \cdot K + C_n < n \cdot m \cdot K \tag{7.5}$$

Dividing by n gives:

$$K + \frac{C_n}{n} < m \cdot K \tag{7.6}$$

Since $m > 1$, monitoring by bank is less costly than monitoring by all lenders if $\frac{C_n}{n}$ goes to zero when n goes to infinity. Dividing equations (7.3) and (7.4) by n produces:

$$E\left[\min\left(\frac{1}{n}\sum_{i=1}^{n}\tilde{y}_i - K, r_D\right)\right] = r \tag{7.7}$$

and

$$\frac{C_n}{n} = E\left[\max\left(r_D + K - \frac{1}{n}\sum_{i=1}^{n}\tilde{y}_i, 0\right)\right] \tag{7.8}$$

According to the law of large numbers, $\frac{1}{n}\sum_{i=1}^{n}\tilde{y}_i$ converges to $E(\tilde{y})$. Since $E(\tilde{y}) > K + r$, equation (7.7) shows that $r_D = r$ when n goes to infinity. Substituting these results into equation (7.8) yields:

$$\lim_{n}\frac{C_n}{n} = \max(r + K - E(\tilde{y}), 0) = 0 \tag{7.9}$$

So, the cost of delegation goes to zero when n goes to infinity.

Source: Freixas and Rochet (2008)

for information and to intervene when necessary. When the uncertainty becomes too large, a firm cannot obtain finance. The resulting equilibrium is that large, well-capitalised firms with a track record of published annual reports finance themselves directly, while smaller, new firms have to turn to banks.

7.2 The use of risk-management models

Risk taking is fundamental to the business of banking. Only by taking calculated financial risks can a bank earn a rate above the risk-free rate of return. Banks unbundle and bundle financial risks. First, risks are decomposed so that they can be managed one by one. For example, the risk on a bank loan with a fixed interest rate can be separated into interest-rate risk (i.e., the risk of loss because of rising interest rates) and credit risk (i.e., the risk of loss because of a default by a borrower). The bank can separately manage the interest-rate risk (e.g., by buying an interest-rate derivative with the same maturity as the bank loan) and the credit risk (e.g., by requiring collateral from the borrower). Next, risks are aggregated to reap the benefits of diversification. An example is a diversified portfolio of loans to companies from different sectors and/or geographic regions. The traditional role of banks in monitoring credit risk has evolved towards the use of advanced models to measure and manage risk. Risk management has been broadened from credit risk to market risk (i.e., the risk of loss because of unfavourable movements in market prices) and operational risk (i.e., the risk of loss from inadequate or failed internal processes, people or systems, or from external events). Progress in information technology has facilitated the development of risk-management models, which rely on statistical methods to process financial data. The financial-services sector is one of the most IT-intensive industries (Berger, 2003).

Modern risk management

The main risk types for a bank are credit risk, market risk, and operational risk. The concept of economic capital can be used for measuring different risks in a comparable way. *Economic capital* is defined as the amount of capital a bank needs in order to be able to absorb losses over a certain time interval with a certain confidence level. Banks usually choose a time horizon of one year. The confidence interval depends on the bank's objectives. A common objective for a large international bank is to maintain an AA credit rating (Hull, 2007). Companies rated AA have a one-year probability of default of 0.03 per cent. This results in a confidence level of 99.97 per cent. Figure 7.3 illustrates the calculation of economic capital.

Economic capital can be used to calculate the *risk adjusted return on capital* (RAROC) that is given by:

$$RAROC = \frac{\text{Revenues} - \text{Costs} - \text{Expected Losses}}{\text{Economic Capital}} = \frac{\pi}{E} \qquad (7.10)$$

Both the numerator and the denominator are adjusted for risk in the RAROC formula. This is an improvement compared with the widely used standard *return on equity measure* (ROE), defined as earned profit divided by available equity. An example can illustrate the working of RAROC. An AA-rated bank estimates its expected losses as 1 per cent of outstanding loans per year

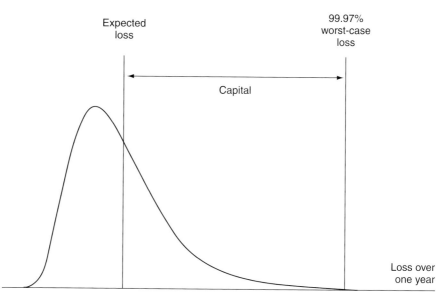

Figure 7.3   Economic capital of an AA-rated bank
Source: Hull (2007)

on average. The worst-case loss at 99.97 per cent confidence is 4 per cent of outstanding loans. So the economic capital for €100 of loans is €3 (the difference between worst-case loss and expected loss). The numerator starts with the revenues: the spread between the promised loan rate and the risk-free rate is 2.20 per cent. The costs of the bank amount to 0.75 per cent of the loan. So RAROC is $\dfrac{2.20 - 0.75 - 1.00}{3.00} = 15$ per cent.

RAROC is emerging as the leading methodology for large banks (as well as other financial institutions, such as insurance companies) to measure and manage risk. The use of internal risk models has been stimulated by supervisors allowing banks to use their internal models to calculate capital requirements (see chapter 10 for the new Basel II capital adequacy rules). Within the RAROC framework, banks first calculate the risk for credit, market, and operational risk and then aggregate the different risk types for the whole bank. To assess the overall risk profile of the bank, correlations across risk types have to be taken into account. But such a full approach that incorporates diversification effects between risk types is still in the early stages of development (Van Lelyveld, 2006).

The first type of risk is credit risk. *Credit risk* is defined as the risk of loss because of the failure of a counterparty to perform according to the

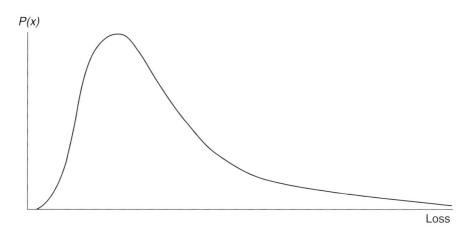

P(x)

Loss

Figure 7.4 Loss distribution for credit risk

contractual arrangement, for instance due to a default by a borrower.[2] In a modern bank, counterparties include not only the traditional counterparties on loans (borrowers) but also counterparties in derivatives transactions and in payment and settlement systems. Diversification is an important tool to manage credit risk. By lending to companies from different sectors, banks can diversify away the sectoral exposures in their loan portfolio. Similarly, international expansion would reduce the business cycle risk. As long as business cycles across euro-area countries are not fully synchronised, there is scope for diversification within Europe. Clearly, geographic (and sectoral) diversification would not protect a bank against a worldwide economic downturn. A second tool to manage credit risk is monitoring counterparties.

The typical time horizon for credit risk is one year. This type of risk thus fits nicely into economic capital models that also use the one-year horizon. Figure 7.4 gives the loss distribution for credit risk. Its shape is quite skewed, as the vast majority of counterparties will repay (almost) in full and only a minority default (partly) on their payment obligation.

The second type of risk is market risk. *Market risk* is the risk of loss because of unfavourable movements in market prices like interest rates, foreign exchange rates, equity prices, and commodity prices. Market risk relates primarily to a bank's trading portfolio and focuses on changes in market value. Losses due to market risk materialise when an adverse price movement causes the mark-to-market valuation of a trading position to decline. Banks typically manage their trading portfolio within a Value-at-Risk framework (VaR) with a ten-day time horizon (see Box 7.4). The rationale is that a bank can close its position (e.g., selling a security or taking an opposite position in a new

---

Box 7.4 Value-at-Risk

A primary tool for measuring market risk is the *Value-at-Risk methodology*. The VaR measure summarises the expected maximum loss (i.e., Value at Risk) over a target horizon of N days within a given confidence interval of X per cent. As will be discussed in chapter 10, the Basel capital framework calculates capital for a bank's trading book using the VaR measure with $N = 10$ and $X = 99\%$. This means that the bank is 99 per cent certain that the loss level over 10 days will not exceed the VaR measure. So only in 1 out of 100 trading days is the bank's loss expected to exceed the VaR measure.

The main advantage is that the risk of a portfolio comprising various financial assets is contained in a single measure, the VaR measure. Figure 7.6 illustrates VaR for the situation where the change in the value of a portfolio is approximately normally distributed. The basic VaR methodology assumes a normal (bell-shaped) distribution of returns. However, the returns on financial assets are non-normal with heavy tails (Danielsson and De Vries, 2000). So VaR underestimates the market risk of a portfolio. Extreme value theory, which uses extreme values (e.g., one-day losses of 5 per cent or larger) to measure the tails of a distribution more accurately, is typically applied to get a better estimation of the downside risk of a portfolio of assets. Alternatively, banks can complement the VaR methodology with stress-test scenarios to get a better picture of potential losses.

Source: Hull (2007)

---

derivative transaction) within ten business days. Under certain assumptions, the standard deviation of ten-day losses can be translated to the one-year horizon of economic capital models.[3]

A specific market risk occurs when assets and liabilities in the balance sheet are not matched. This risk is labelled *asset and liability management (ALM) risk*. The ALM risk of banks refers to the interest-rate risk in the banking book, where long-term assets (loans) are funded by short-term liabilities (deposits). Insurance companies face the opposite problem: their liabilities have typically a longer maturity than assets (see chapter 9).

The loss distribution for market risk is very different from that for credit risk. Figure 7.5 shows that the loss distribution for market risk is symmetrical. A good example is the price of equity. According to the efficient market hypothesis, all available information (including information on the future prospects of a company) is reflected in the equity price of a company. So today's stock price is the best predictor of tomorrow's stock price. The stock price will move only with the arrival of new information, which appears randomly. The stock price follows a random walk with equal likelihood of upward and downward movements.

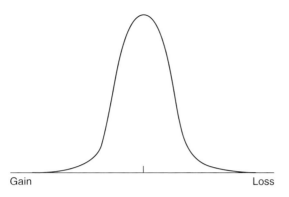

Gain   Loss

Figure 7.5   Loss distribution for market risk

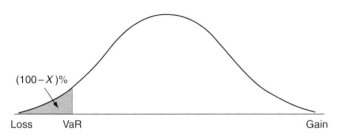

$(100-X)\%$

Loss   VaR   Gain

Figure 7.6   Calculation of VaR with a confidence level of X%
Source: Hull (2007)

More recently, operational risk has become part of risk management. *Operational risk* is defined as the risk of loss from inadequate or failed internal processes, people or systems, or from external events. A famous example of operational risk is the failure of Barings Bank in 1995. Nick Leeson, a trader for Barings in Singapore, made money by arbitraging between the Nikkei 225 futures on the Singapore and the Osaka exchanges. Barings had no effective risk limits in place and Nick Leeson could build up large positions. When the market moved against Leeson, Barings' total loss was close to $1 billion (Hull, 2007). A more recent example was the rogue trader scandal at Société Générale (SocGen) that cost the bank €4.9 billion. Jérôme Kerviel, a junior trader at SocGen, secretly built up huge and risky positions in the derivatives market. He was taking greater and greater risks over a period dating back to March 2007 for large amounts and to 2005 for smaller amounts. SocGen only discovered the fraud between 18 and 20 January 2008. Unwinding the positions over the subsequent three days cost the bank billions. The variety of concealment techniques used, a lack of systematic checks by staff when

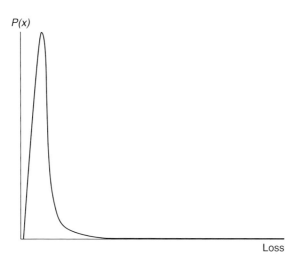

Figure 7.7   Loss distribution for operational risk

warning flags were raised, and shortcomings in the control systems all contributed to the late discovery of Kerviel's activities.

Other examples of operational risk are IT failures or terrorist attacks. The
Barings and SocGen examples illustrate that operational risk can interact with
credit and market risk. When a trader exceeds limits, losses result only if
the market moves against the trader. Figure 7.7 provides the loss distribution
for operational risk. The loss distribution is very skewed, even more skewed
than the credit-risk loss distribution. Most of the time, operational losses are
modest, but occasionally they are very large.

While credit, market, and operational risk can threaten their solvency (and
are therefore incorporated in the economic capital calculation), banks also
incur liquidity risk. *Liquidity risk* arises when a bank has insufficient liquid
resources to meet a surge in liquidity demand. (In chapter 3, *market liquidity*
is discussed and defined as the ease with which an investor can sell or buy a
security immediately at a price close to the fair price.) The classical case of a
surge in liquidity demand for a bank is the sudden withdrawal of deposits. Banks
manage their liquid resources in two ways. The first way is maintaining a pool of
liquid assets. Reserves at the central bank are the most liquid assets but generate
a relatively low return. Other liquid assets are government bonds, which can
be easily sold. But a bank typically holds only a fraction of its demand deposits
in liquid assets. The remainder is invested in illiquid, but high-return, assets
such as loans. These assets can be liquidated immediately only at low prices.

The second way banks can manage liquidity risk is by preserving a diversified
funding base (also referred to as *funding liquidity*). As explained in section 7.1,

banks can fund themselves in the interbank market. As long as banks have sufficient confidence in each other, a bank is able to borrow from other banks. Trust is therefore the most important 'asset' for a bank. When a bank loses the trust of other banks, it will face liquidity problems and possibly even failure. A case in point is the failure of Continental Illinois Bank in May 1984. This bank experienced funding difficulties in domestic markets and Continental therefore had to turn to more expensive Eurodollar deposits in London. Rumours that Continental was on the verge of bankruptcy resulted in a run on Continental's wholesale deposits by both domestic and foreign banks.

Centralisation of risk management

The organisational structure of international banks is moving from the traditional country model to a business-line model with integration and centralisation of key management functions (Schoenmaker and Oosterloo, 2007). These management functions comprise risk management, internal controls, treasury operations (including liquidity management and funding), compliance, and auditing. One of the most notable advances in risk management is the growing emphasis on developing a firm-wide assessment of risk. Such an integrated approach to risk management aims to ensure a comprehensive and systematic approach to risk-related decisions throughout the financial group. It allows senior management to have a full picture of the group's overall risk profile. RAROC provides the methodology to compare and aggregate different risks.

Moreover, financial groups with a centralised risk management unit in place could reap economies of scale in risk management. Nevertheless, these centralised systems still rely on local branches and subsidiaries for local market data. The potential capital reductions that can be achieved by applying the advanced approaches of the new Basel II framework (see chapter 10) encourage banking groups to organise their risk management more centrally. A well-constructed risk and capital management framework can deliver significant benefits and substantially strengthen the competitive position of financial groups. The emergence of so-called chief risk officers (CROs) at the headquarters of large financial groups illustrates this trend towards centralisation.

The dominant approach among large international financial institutions is to adopt a 'hub and spoke' organisational model (Kuritzkes et al., 2003). The spokes are responsible for risk management within business lines, while the hub provides centralised oversight of risk and capital at the group level. Activities at the spoke include the credit function within a bank, as local managers are familiar with the local conditions, such as the business cycle relevant for credit risk in a country. Moreover, aggregation across risk factors within a business line also typically takes place in the spokes.

While the hub is dependent on risk reporting from the spokes, in many cases it is also responsible for overseeing the development of an integrated economic capital framework (such as RAROC) that is then implemented within the spokes. The specific roles of the hub vary, but tend to include assuming responsibility for group-level risk reporting, participating in decisions about group capital structure, funding practices, and target debt rating, acting as liaison with regulators and rating agencies, and advising on major risk transfer transactions, such as collateralised loan obligations and securitisations.

7.3 The European banking system

Banking markets across Europe

The banking markets of most EU Member States are dominated by domestic banks. One way to assess the presence of foreign banks is *cross-border penetration*. This measure is defined as the assets of banks from other EU Member States as a percentage of the country's total banking assets. Average cross-border penetration in the EU gradually increased from 11 per cent in 1995 to 19 per cent in 2006 (Figure 7.8). However, the degree of cross-border penetration is very uneven across the EU Member States, as Table 7.1 shows.

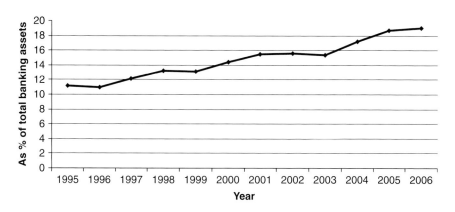

Figure 7.8   Cross-border penetration in European banking (%), 1995–2006
Note: Share of assets from other EU countries measured as a percentage of total banking assets. The share is calculated for the EU-25.
Source: Authors' calculations based on ECB (2004) and ECB (2007)

Table 7.1 Cross-border penetration in EU Member States, 2005

	(1) Number of banks	(2) Total banking assets (in € billion)	(3) Assets of domestic banks (in % of (2))	(4) Assets of banks from other EU countries (in % of (2))	(5) Assets of banks from third countries (in % of (2))
Austria	880	721	80	19	1
Belgium	100	1,055	77	21	2
Cyprus	391	60	72	22	5
Czech Republic	56	105	7	89	5
Denmark	197	722	79	19	2
Estonia	11	12	1	99	0
Finland	363	235	42	58	0
France	854	5,090	88	10	1
Germany	2,089	6,827	89	9	1
Greece	62	281	72	28	0
Hungary	215	75	41	56	3
Ireland	78	942	57	35	8
Italy	792	2,509	91	9	0
Latvia	23	16	47	50	3
Lithuania	78	13	25	75	0
Luxembourg	155	792	5	87	7
Malta	18	27	68	32	0
Netherlands	401	1,698	98	1	1
Poland	739	152	33	59	8
Portugal	186	360	77	22	1
Slovakia	23	36	3	97	0
Slovenia	25	30	78	22	0
Spain	348	2,151	89	11	0
Sweden	200	653	91	9	0
United Kingdom	400	8,320	48	26	26
EU-15	7,105	32,356	75	17	8
NMS-10	1,579	526	35	60	5
EU-25	8,684	32,882	74	18	8

Notes: Share of business from domestic banks, share of business of banks from other EU countries, and share of business of banks from third countries are measured as a percentage of the total banking assets in a country. The shares add up to 100 per cent. Figures are for 2005. EU-15, NMS-10, and EU-25 are calculated as a weighted average (weighted according to assets).
Source: ECB (2006)

While the banking systems of the new Member States are dominated by foreign banks (see also chapter 8), average cross-border penetration in the EU-15 is only 17 per cent. With 87 per cent Luxembourg has the highest cross-border penetration (reflecting the country's favourable tax-regime), while the corresponding figures for France, Germany, Italy, the Netherlands, and Sweden are less than 10 per cent.

Table 7.1 also shows that the penetration by banks from third countries is well below 10 per cent for all EU Member States, except for the UK where it stands at 26 per cent, illustrating London's position as a major international financial centre. Most banking business in London is focused on large firms (i.e., wholesale). There is much evidence suggesting that EU wholesale banking markets are highly integrated, in contrast to retail banking, i.e., banking services delivered to consumers and SMEs. Most small customers receive their financial services from domestic suppliers, and the range and terms under which products are available differ substantially across the EU Member States. Box 7.5 identifies some reasons why integration of retail banking markets is so difficult.

Box 7.5 Retail banking market integration

According to Dermine (2006), the 'law of one price', which represents the theoretical benchmark for integrated markets, is unlikely to hold in retail banking markets for various reasons. First, trust and confidence are important in these markets. Customers want to be sure that their money is in safe hands. Knowledge of the respective bank, the national legal system, language, cultural preferences, and geographical proximity may lead to a preference for a domestic bank, i.e., there are differentiated products. Second, retail customers generally buy a package of financial services from the same bank, rather than individual services. Therefore, the 'law of one price' may hold for the bundle of services, but not necessarily for each individual service. Third, asymmetric information in lending is quite important, and local knowledge can help to reduce this information asymmetry. Local banks may therefore be in a better position to lend to SMEs than foreign banks. Fourth, the 'law of one price' assumes the absence of transportation costs and regulatory barriers. But differences in legislation, like tax and consumer-protection rules, may create substantial barriers for foreign bank entry.

Still, there is evidence that EU retail banking markets also have become more integrated. Figure 7.9 shows that differences in EU retail banking interest rates have diminished substantially, but integration is still far from being perfect. In 2006 variation ranged from 20 per cent for loans to enterprises to 28.4 per cent for mortgage loans to households. Furthermore, using the beta- and sigma-convergence measures as explained in chapter 4, Vajanne (2007) finds evidence for increased convergence in retail banking credit interest rates for households and non-financial corporations in the euro-area between January 2003 and May 2006.

Nevertheless, Kleimeier and Sander (2007) argue that integration in EU retail banking markets is still far from perfect, while integration has been strong in wholesale markets. In particular, they find that price stickiness is a major feature of European retail banking (i.e., banks are slow with lowering lending interest rates when the ECB reduces its interest rate). As a way forward, Kleimeier and Sander (2007) propose to foster integration of wholesale markets in conjunction with developing and preserving competitive banking markets. Competition can speed up the transmission of monetary impulses onto retail bank lending interest rates. As the pass-through becomes faster and more homogeneous across countries, it will create a de facto integrated retail-banking market.

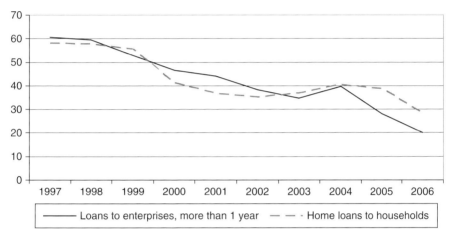

Figure 7.9   Convergence of retail banking interest rates (coefficient of variation, %), 1997–2006
Source: European Commission (2007)

In 2005, there were nearly 9,000 banks in the EU. These banks can be segmented into three groups. The first, very large, group of banks consists of small banks operating in a region of a country. In particular Germany and Austria have many small savings and co-operative banks, most of which have assets of less than €500 million. About 20 per cent of German banks belong to public savings groups and about 60 per cent to the co-operative banking sector (Hackethal, 2004). The second group consists of medium-sized banks with assets ranging from €500 million to €50 billion. These banks often operate on a country-wide scale. The third group are the large banks having assets up to €1,400 billion; they usually do a significant part of their business abroad.

Table 7.2 shows the biggest 30 banks in Europe, representing nearly half of the assets of the European banking system assets. Schoenmaker and Oosterloo

Table 7.2 Biggest 30 banks in Europe in 2005

Banking groups	(1) Capital strength[a] (in € billion)	(2) Total assets (in € billion)	(3) Business in home country (as % of (2))	(4) Business in rest of EU (as % of (2))	(5) Business in rest of world (as % of (2))
Global banks[b]					
1. HSBC (UK)	63	1,273	25	9	65
2. Barclays (UK)	28	1,349	50	16	34
3. BBVA (Spain)	16	392	40	3	57
European banks[c]					
1. Santander (Spain)	33	809	40	26	34
2. UniCredit (Italy)	29	787	24	72	4
3. ABN AMRO (Netherlands)	27	881	34	30	36
4. UBS (Switzerland)	26	1,328	25	28	47
5. ING (Netherlands)	23	834	23	29	48
6. Deutsche Bank (Germany)	22	992	28	36	36
7. Groupe Caisse d'Epargne (France)	19	594	40	47	13
8. Credit Suisse (Switzerland)	17	863	32	34	34
9. Fortis (Belgium)	16	639	48	47	6
10. Nordea (Sweden)	11	325	25	75	0
11. KBC (Belgium)	11	326	50	29	21
Domestic banks[d]					
1. Crédit Agricole (France)	51	1,170	83	9	8
2. Royal Bank of Scotland (UK)	41	1,133	77	7	16
3. HBOS (UK)	30	789	90	5	5
4. Rabobank (Netherlands)	25	506	73	14	13
5. BNP Paribas (France)	21	1,258	55	21	21
6. Crédit Mutuel (France)	20	437	100	0	0
7. Société Générale (France)	19	848	57	21	21
8. Lloyds TSB (UK)	17	452	95	3	3
9. Banca Intesa (Italy)	15	273	76	15	9
10. Groupe Banques Populaires (France)	15	289	92	4	3
11. Commerzbank (Germany)	12	460	71	25	5
12. Dexia (Belgium)	12	509	51	37	12
13. Dresdner Bank (Germany)	11	462	69	22	9

Table 7.2 (cont.)

Banking groups	(1) Capital strength[a] (in € billion)	(2) Total assets (in € billion)	(3) Business in home country (as % of (2))	(4) Business in rest of EU (as % of (2))	(5) Business in rest of world (as % of (2))
14. SanPaolo IMI (Italy)	11	263	92	7	2
15. Landesbank Baden-Württemberg (Germany)	11	405	93	5	2
16. Bayerische Landesbank (Germany)	10	333	78	14	7

Notes:
[a] Top 30 banks are selected on the basis of capital strength (Tier 1 capital (see chapter 10) as published in *The Banker*).
[b] Global banks: less than 50 per cent of assets in the home country and less than 25 per cent in the rest of Europe.
[c] European banks: less than 50 per cent of assets in the home country and more than 25 per cent in the rest of Europe.
[d] Domestic banks: more than 50 per cent of assets in the home country.
Source: Schoenmaker and Van Laecke (2006)

(2005) split large banks in three categories, depending on the composition of their assets. A global bank has less than 50 per cent of its assets in the home country and less than 25 per cent in the rest of Europe. These banks include HSBC and Barclays from the UK and BBVA from Spain.

A European bank has less than 50 per cent of its assets in the home country and more than 25 per cent in the rest of Europe. Some European banks focus on a specific region in the EU. Fortis, for example, primarily operates in Belgium and the Netherlands. Similarly, the Nordea Group primarily operates in the Nordic countries. Other European banks operate Europe-wide; examples include Deutsche Bank and UniCredit.

Finally, a domestic bank has more than 50 per cent of its assets in the home country. Examples include the Rabobank (Netherlands) and the Royal Bank of Scotland (UK). The latter took over ABN-AMRO in 2007, together with Fortis and Santander.

Figure 7.10 shows that the number of European banks has increased from 7 in 2000 to 11 in 2005, while the number of domestic and global banks has declined. The increased number of European banks is in line with the rising cross-border penetration shown in Figure 7.8.

Domestic and cross-border mergers and acquisitions

Mergers and acquisitions (M&As) have changed and will continue to change the European banking markets. It was widely expected that the Single Market initiative (see chapter 2) would ease the path for cross-border M&As. Instead, banks prepared themselves for the Single Market by merging with other domestic banks. Cross-border mergers increased only after the start of EMU (see Figure 7.11).

Boot (1999) argues that domestic banks in Europe were often protected as they were regarded as national flagships. A fundamental belief that national financial institutions should not be controlled by foreigners prevented almost any cross-border merger up to the late 1990s. The recent shift towards cross-border deals was caused by two factors. First, some national banking systems have become so concentrated that further domestic mergers would be blocked by the competition authorities. In principle, the European Commission (DG Competition) permits mergers up to the threshold of 2,000 for the Herfindahl Index (see below). Several countries are close to, or even above, this threshold.

Second, the European Commission (2005) reviewed obstacles to cross-border mergers and suggested remedies to remove them. The abuse of supervisory powers to block cross-border mergers was identified as a possible obstacle to cross-border mergers. New legislation has subsequently been passed to clarify and limit the criteria to assess possible M&As.

As the potential for domestic mergers is increasingly exhausted, the number of cross-border bank mergers has increased. Figure 7.11 illustrates that the cross-border share in total M&A deals has risen, accounting for 20 per cent of the value of all deals in recent years, up from about 10 per cent in the 1990s. While early cross-border mergers in the 1990s created regional banks, such as Fortis in the Benelux countries and Nordea in Scandinavia, recent mergers are more widely spread across Europe. Examples are the takeover of Abbey National (UK) by Santander (Spain) in 2004 and the takeover of HypoVereinsbank (Germany) by UniCredit (Italy) in 2005.

Important drivers of cross-border mergers are geographic diversification and a potential efficiency improvement (see Box 7.6 for further details). A good example was the takeover of Abbey National by Santander. The former had strategic problems as it was venturing into corporate banking without success and used outdated IT systems. The inefficiency of Abbey National was illustrated by a high cost-to-income ratio of 83 per cent and a negative return on equity of 10 per cent. In contrast, Santander had

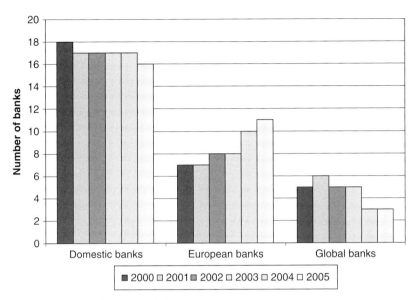

Figure 7.10   Biggest 30 banks in Europe, 2000–2005
Note: See Table 7.2 for definitions.
Source: Schoenmaker and Van Laecke (2006)

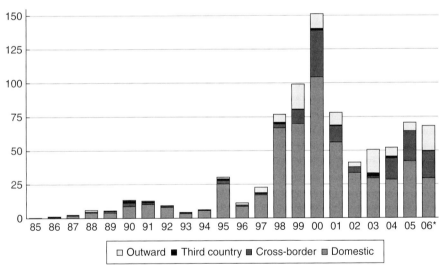

Figure 7.11   Banking M&As in Europe (value of completed deals, € billion), 1985–2006
Note: M&As exclude buyback, recapitalisation and exchange offers. 'Cross-border' refers to intra-EU
M&As; 'third country' denotes M&As by non-EU resident banks in the EU; and 'outward' stands for
M&A activity of EU banks outside the EU.
* First half of 2006.
Source: Dierick *et al.* (2008)

> **Box 7.6** The economics and performance of M&As
>
> The classical motive for M&As in financial services is market extension (Walter, 2004). By merging with or acquiring another bank, it becomes possible to expand geographically into markets in which the acquiring bank has been absent or weak. The risk profile of the bank may be improved to the extent that business is spread across different macroeconomic environments. Or the bank wants to broaden its product range or client coverage because it sees profit opportunities that may be complementary to what it is already doing (see chapter 9 for the expansion of banks into insurance activities).
>
> A key issue is whether economies of scale exist in banking. In an information- and distribution-intensive industry with high fixed costs such as financial services, there may be potential for scale economies. In particular, domestic mergers offer scope for cost synergies, as overlapping branch networks can be rationalised. But there is also potential for diseconomies of scale attributable to disproportionate increases in administrative overheads or management of complexity. Recent empirical evidence finds economies of scale only in banks up to $25 billion in size (Saunders and Cornett, 2002).
>
> Campa and Hernando (2006) examine the performance record of mergers and acquisitions in the European financial industry. Merger announcements imply positive excess returns to shareholders of the target company (the takeover premium), while the returns to shareholders of the acquiring firms are essentially zero around announcement. One year after the announcement, excess returns are not significantly different from zero for both targets and acquirers. Campa and Hernando (2006) also provide evidence on the operating performance. M&As usually involve target banks with lower operating performance than the average bank. The M&A transactions result in significant improvements in the target banks performance beginning on average two years after the transaction is completed.

developed a new payment technology and had a cost-to-income ratio of 63 per cent. After the takeover, Santander successfully introduced this technology with new management at Abbey National to improve efficiency; in 2006, Abbey's cost-to-income ratio was 56 per cent.

Market structure and competition

Table 7.3 shows some indicators about the structure of the EU banking sector. Between 1997 and 2005 the total number of banks in the EU decreased from 12,138 to 8,684, i.e., a reduction of nearly 40 per cent.[4]

Due to the decline in the number of credit institutions the concentration in the national banking markets has increased. Table 7.3 presents two concentration measures: the market share of the biggest five banks (CR5) and the Herfindahl Index, which is defined as the sum of the squares of the market shares of all banks in the sector ($HI = \sum_{i=1}^{n} s_i^2$, where s_i is the market share of bank i). While the CR5 ratio is easily measurable, it does not take into account the remaining banks in the industry in contrast to the Herfindahl Index. The latter ranges between $1/n$ and 1, reaching its lowest value, the reciprocal of the number of banks (n), when all banks in a market are of equal size, and reaching unity in the case of monopoly. The index as published by the ECB has been rescaled and ranges between 0 and 10,000.

Table 7.3 shows that there are substantial concentration differences across the EU. In Austria, France, Germany, Ireland, Italy, Luxemburg, Spain, and the United Kingdom the concentration ratios in the banking markets are relatively low. The highest concentration ratios can be found in Belgium, Estonia, Finland, Lithuania, and the Netherlands.[5]

Another important feature of markets is the degree of competition. Panzar and Rosse (1977) have constructed a measure of competition, the so-called *H-statistic*, that is defined as the sum of the factor price elasticities of interest revenue with respect to borrowed capital, labour and physical capital. The value of H can be interpreted as follows. In case of a monopoly, H is lower than or equal to zero. This also applies to an oligopolistic market with cartels or complete imitation of each other's behaviour. A value of H between zero and one indicates monopolistic competition. A value equivalent to one points to perfect competition, as each change in input prices leads to a comparable change in output prices. The results of Bikker *et al.* (2006) as shown in Table 7.3 suggest that there is strong competition (i.e., values of H above 0.75) in the banking sectors of the Czech Republic, Ireland, the Netherlands, Spain, and the United Kingdom. France and Germany have an intermediate level of competition (H around 0.60), while banking competition in Italy is low.

The *structure-conduct-performance (SCP) paradigm* postulates a connection between market structure, banking behaviour, and profitability. The reasoning is as follows: in markets with a high degree of concentration, firms have more market power, which allows them to set prices above marginal costs and achieve higher profits. While earlier studies find a relationship between concentration and profitability, more recent studies suggest that there is no connection between the two (Claessens and Laeven, 2004; Jansen and De Haan, 2006).

Table 7.3 Market structure indicators, 1997 and 2005

	Size		Concentration				Competition
	Number of banks		CR5 (in %)[a]		Herfindahl Index[b]		H-statistic
	1997	2005	1997	2005	1997	2005	1990–2005
Austria	928	880	44	45	515	560	0.07
Belgium	131	100	54	85	699	2,108	0.54
Cyprus	623	391	92	60	2,747	1,029	−0.11
Czech Republic	50	56	67	66	2,533	1,155	0.77
Denmark	213	197	70	66	1,431	1,115	0.30
Estonia	12	11	83	98	4,312	4,039	0.47
Finland	348	363	88	83	2,150	2,730	−0.24
France	1,258	854	40	54	449	758	0.58
Germany	3,420	2,089	17	22	114	174	0.65
Greece	55	62	56	66	885	1,096	0.47
Hungary	286	215	53	53	2,101	795	0.16
Ireland	71	78	41	46	500	600	1.11
Italy	909	792	25	27	201	230	0.08
Latvia	37	23	51	67	1,450	1,176	0.57
Lithuania	37	78	84	81	2,972	1,838	0.45
Luxembourg	215	155	23	31	210	312	0.31
Malta	29	18	98	75	4,411	1,330	0.72
Netherlands	648	401	79	85	1,654	1,796	0.80
Poland	1,378	739	46	49	859	650	0.10
Portugal	238	186	46	69	577	1,154	−0.14
Slovakia	29	23	63	68	2,643	1,076	0.26
Slovenia	34	25	62	63	2,314	1,369	0.38
Spain	416	348	32	42	285	487	0.87
Sweden	237	200	58	57	830	845	0.48
United Kingdom	537	400	24	36	208	399	0.76
EU-25[c]	12,138	8,684	34	42	429	601	0.60

Notes:
[a] CR5 is the share of the five largest banks, measured as a percentage of total assets.
[b] The Herfindahl Index is calculated as the sum of the squares of all the banks' market shares according to total assets, and rescaled from 0 to 10,000.
[c] EU-25 is calculated as a weighted average (weighted according to assets).
Source: Number of banks and concentration from European Central Bank (2004, 2006) and Allen *et al.* (2006); competition from Bikker *et al.* (2006)

Two alternative theories suggest that concentration does not necessarily reduce market competition. According to the *contestability theory*, a concentrated banking market can still be competitive as long as the entry barriers for potential newcomers are low. According to the *efficiency hypothesis*, the most efficient banks gain market share at the cost of less efficient banks. In other words, high concentration can be a result of fierce competition in a market (Bikker *et al.*, 2006).

Claessens and Laeven (2004) examine the competitiveness of a banking market in a large cross-section of countries and find no evidence that banking system concentration is negatively associated with competitiveness. In fact, they sometimes find evidence that more concentrated banking systems are more competitive.

Concentration is loosely related to bank size. Markets become more concentrated when the number of banks decreases or when the skewness of the size distribution of banks increases (i.e., the number of large banks increases). But the markets in some countries (e.g., Germany and France) have low levels of concentration and large banks. As Bikker *et al.* point out (2006), large banks may have market power as they are probably in a better position to collude with other banks and may benefit from a more established reputation. Furthermore, they are in a better position than small banks to create new banking products due to economies of scale. Indeed, Bikker *et al.* (2006) report that market power increases with bank size. Their research covers 18,467 banks in 101 countries over a period of 16 years.

A final characteristic of the market structure is the performance and efficiency of banks. As indicated in section 7.2, the ideal performance indicator should be risk adjusted. However, data on risk-adjusted indicators like RAROC is not (yet) widely available for European banks. We therefore use the standard return on equity measure (ROE). A widely used efficiency indicator is the *cost-to-income ratio*, which measures costs as a percentage of income. But this indicator should also be treated with care. The cost-to-income ratio can improve because of lower costs (indicating more efficiency) or higher income (indicating less competition). Figure 7.12 provides some

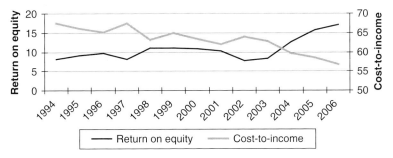

Figure 7.12   Performance of banks in the EU-15 (in %), 1994–2006
Source: Deutsche Bank Research (2008)

figures on the performance and efficiency of banks for banks in the EU-15. The ROE is on the left-hand side and the cost-to-income ratio on the right-hand side of the graph. Both the performance (increasing ROE) and the efficiency (decreasing cost-to-income) improved significantly between 1994 and 2006.

7.4 Conclusions

Banks are key players in the financial system, providing liquidity to other financial institutions and to firms and households. They have also developed technologies to monitor borrowers. Banks have expanded their business from traditional lending to modern capital-market transactions, thereby preserving their role in the financial system.

Banks use advanced models to measure, manage, and price market risk. The use of these advanced models has spurred the centralisation of risk management. While the business is done by the local bank managers who are familiar with the economic environment in which the local business units have to operate, the influence of the head office on the pricing of bank products is increasing.

Cross-border banking has gradually increased to almost 20 per cent in 2006. This chapter has documented the emergence of banks that operate Europe-wide. Nevertheless, retail banking markets are still segmented. Customers have a preference to do business with banks they 'know' and thus have a bias towards domestic banks. Cultural differences appear to be more important than regulatory differences. The policy of the European Commission is shifting from harmonising rules (chapter 10) to ensuring effective competition (chapter 12) in turn.

New evidence suggests that concentration does not necessarily reduce market competition. The contestability theory indicates that a banking market is competitive as long as the barriers for potential newcomers are low. Competition policy is important to open national markets: both to promote new entrants within a country and to promote foreign entry through cross-border mergers.

NOTES

1. There is, however, an important conflict of interest. Credit-rating agencies are paid by the firms and governments whose securities they rate. This conflict is unavoidable due

to the free-riding problem, i.e., ratings are valuable only if everybody knows them, but lenders (investors) have no reason to pay for information that is available to everyone else too.

2. A *counterparty* is a legal and financial term. It means a party to a contract.

3. Assuming a normal distribution, the time horizon of the standard deviation can be expanded by multiplying with $\sqrt{t}$. Given that there are 252 business days in the year, the standard deviation of the one-year loss distribution equals the standard deviation of the ten-day loss distribution multiplied by $\sqrt{25.2}$ (Hull, 2007).

4. The trend in the US is comparable, though less pronounced. The number of US banks dropped from 10,923 in 1997 to 8,832 in 2005, i.e., a decline of around 25 per cent.

5. The European Commission investigates a proposed merger when the (rescaled) Herfindahl Index would pass the threshold of 2,000 after the merger (see chapter 12).

SUGGESTED READING

Claessens, S. and L. Laeven (2004), What Drives Bank Competition? Some International Evidence, *Journal of Money, Credit, and Banking*, 36, 563–583.

Freixas, X. and J. C. Rochet (2008), *Microeconomics of Banking*, Second edition, MIT Press, Cambridge (MA).

Hull, J. C. (2007), *Risk Management and Financial Institutions*, Pearson Education, Upper Saddle River (NJ).

Schoenmaker, D. and C. van Laecke (2006), Current State of Cross-Border Banking, FMG Special Papers 168, London School of Economics, London.

REFERENCES

Allen, F., L. Bartiloro, and O. Kowalewski (2006), The Financial System of EU 25, in: K. Liebscher, J. Christl, P. Mooslechner, and D. Ritzberger-Grünwald (eds.), *Financial Development, Integration and Stability in Central, Eastern and South-Eastern Europe*, Edward Elgar, Cheltenham, 80–104.

Berger, A. N. (2003), The Economic Effects of Technological Progress: Evidence from the Banking Industry, *Journal of Money, Credit, and Banking*, 35, 141–176.

Bikker, J. A., L. Spierdijk, and P. Finnie (2006), The Impact of Bank Size on Market Power, DNB Working Papers 120, De Nederlandsche Bank, Amsterdam.

Boot, A. W. A. (1999), European Lessons on Consolidation in Banking, *Journal of Banking and Finance*, 23, 609–613.

Buiter, W. H. (2007), Lessons from the 2007 Financial Crisis, CEPR Policy Insight 18.

Campa, J. M. and I. Hernando (2006), M&As Performance in the European Financial Industry, *Journal of Banking and Finance*, 30, 3367–3392.

Claessens, S. and L. Laeven (2004), What Drives Bank Competition? Some International Evidence, *Journal of Money, Credit, and Banking*, 36, 563–583.

Danielsson, J. and C. De Vries (2000), Value-at-Risk and Extreme Returns. *Annale d'Economie et de Statistique*, 60, 239–269.

Dermine, J. (2006), European Banking Integration: Don't Put the Cart before the Horse, *Financial Markets, Institutions & Instruments*, 15(2), 57–106.

Deutsche Bank Research (2008), *European Banks: The Silent (R)evolution*, Deutsche Bank, Frankfurt am Main.

Diamond, D. W. (1984), Financial Intermediation and Delegated Monitoring, *Review of Economic Studies*, 51, 393–414.

Dierick, F., C. Freund, and N. Valckx (2008), Cross-Border Banking in the European Union: Developments and Policy Implications, ECB Occasional Paper, forthcoming.

European Central Bank (2004), *Report on EU Banking Structures*, ECB, Frankfurt am Main.

European Central Bank (2006), *EU Banking Structures*, ECB, Frankfurt am Main.

European Central Bank (2007), *EU Banking Structures*, ECB, Frankfurt am Main.

European Commission (2005), *Cross-Border Consolidation in the EU Financial Sector*, SEC 1398, EC, Brussels.

European Commission (2007), *European Financial Integration Report*, EC, Brussels.

Freixas, X. and J. C. Rochet (2008), *Microeconomics of Banking*, 2nd edition, MIT Press, Cambridge (MA).

Garber, P. M. and S. R. Weisbrod (1990), Banks in the Market for Liquidity, NBER Working Paper 3381.

Hackethal, A. (2004), German Banks and Banking Structure, in: J. P. Krahnen and R. H. Schmidt (eds.), *The German Financial System*, Oxford University Press, Oxford, 71–106.

Hull, J. C. (2007), *Risk Management and Financial Institutions*, Pearson Education, Upper Saddle River (NJ).

Jansen, D. J. and J. De Haan (2006), European Banking Consolidation: Effects on Competition, Profitability, and Efficiency, *Journal of Financial Transformation*, 17, 61–72.

Kleimeier, S. and H. Sander (2007), Integrating Europe's Retail Banking Markets: Where Do We Stand?, Research Report in Finance and Banking, Centre for European Policy Studies, Brussels.

Kuritzkes, A., T. Schuermann, and S. Weiner (2003), Risk Measurement, Risk Management, and Capital Adequacy in Financial Conglomerates, in: R. Herring and R. Litan (eds.), *Brookings-Wharton Papers on Financial Services: 2003*, Brookings Institution, Washington DC, 141–193.

Panzar J. C. and J. N. Rosse (1977), Chamberlin vs Robinson: An Empirical Study for Monopoly Rents, Studies in Industry Economics, Research Paper 77, Stanford University, Stanford.

Saunders, A. and M. M. Cornett (2002), *Financial Institutions Management: A Risk Management Approach*, McGraw-Hill, Boston.

Schoenmaker, D. and C. Van Laecke (2006), Current State of Cross-Border Banking, FMG Special Papers 168, London School of Economics, London.

Schoenmaker, D. and S. Oosterloo (2005), Financial Supervision in an Integrating Europe: Measuring Cross-Border Externalities, *International Finance*, 8, 1–27.

Schoenmaker, D. and S. Oosterloo (2007), Cross-Border Issues in European Financial Supervision, in: D. Mayes and G. Wood (eds.), *The Structure of Financial Regulation*, Routledge, London, 264–291.

Vajanne, L. (2007), Integration in Euro Area Retail Banking Markets – Convergence of Credit Interest Rates, Discussion Paper 27/2007, Bank of Finland, Helsinki.

Van Lelyveld, I. (ed.) (2006), *Economic Capital Modelling: Concepts, Measurement and Implementation*, Risk Books, London.

Walter, I. (2004), *Mergers and Acquisitions in Banking and Finance: What Works, What Fails, and Why*, Oxford University Press, Oxford.

8

The Financial System of the New Member States

OVERVIEW

This chapter discusses the financial structure of the new Member States of the European Union. It starts by analysing the importance of financial markets and financial institutions in financing investment in the NMS. Stock-market capitalisation in various NMS has increased, but its level in the NMS is still far below that in the EU-15. By far the most important category of financial institutions in the NMS are banks; the role of insurance companies, investment funds, and pension funds in the NMS is still underdeveloped in comparison with the EU-15. The chapter describes the banking sector in the NMS in some detail. This sector is generally highly concentrated. Foreign bank presence is very large in most NMS, mainly in the form of subsidiaries of foreign banks.

Since the banking sector in the NMS is strongly dominated by foreign banks, this chapter also examines the determinants of foreign bank entry. Next to this, the considerations for a particular way of foreign bank entry (greenfield investment or acquisition) as well as the organisational form of representation (representative office, agency, branch, or subsidiary) are discussed.

The final part of the chapter analyses how beneficial financial integration has been for the economic development of the NMS. Some recent studies conclude that the ongoing global financial integration may have had little or no value in advancing economic growth, especially in less developed countries. Capital is often found to flow 'uphill', i.e., from less developed to industrial countries. And when it does flow into less developed economies, it is often found to be negatively correlated with growth, calling into question the desirability of foreign capital. There is, however, evidence that the NMS are different in this regard and that financial integration has stimulated their economic growth.

LEARNING OBJECTIVES

After you have studied this chapter, you should be able to:

- outline the main features of the financial system of the new EU Member States
- explain the motives for foreign banks entering these countries
- explain the considerations for the various ways of foreign bank entry and the organisational form of representation of a foreign bank
- discuss the contribution of financial integration to the economic performance of the new EU Member States.

8.1 The financial system

The new Member States of the EU, with the exception of Cyprus and Malta, have been engaged in a transition process from former planned economies into market economies. As their entry into the EU illustrates, they have made huge progress in this regard. GDP growth in the NMS has outstripped that of the EU-15, whereas average inflation fell from double-digit figures in 1998 to euro-area levels in 2003 (although more recently some NMS saw their inflation increase again). However, there are still significant economic differences between the NMS and the EU-15. Despite continuing convergence, GDP per capita levels of the NMS still lag far behind, accounting for only 51 per cent of the EU-15 average in 2003 in PPP terms (ECB, 2005).

As part of their entry into the EU, the NMS had to liberalise their financial sector. Table 8.1 presents some indicators of financial sector reform for the NMS as published by the European Bank for Reconstruction and Development (EBRD) and the Fraser Institute. In its annual *Transition Report*, the EBRD assesses progress in transition through a set of transition indicators that have been used to track reform. The measurement scale for the indicators ranges from 1 to 4+, where 1 represents little or no change from a rigid, centrally planned economy and 4+ represents the standards of an industrialised market economy. Two of these indicators refer to the financial sector: banking reform and interest rate liberalisation, and securities markets and non-bank financial institutions. In its annual report *Economic Freedom of the World*, the Fraser Institute provides indicators of international capital-market controls and credit-market regulations, ranging between 0 and 10 (no restrictions).

Table 8.1 Indicators of financial-sector liberalisation, 2000–2007

Country	EBRD banking sector reform		EBRD securities markets reform		Fraser Institute international capital market controls		Fraser Institute credit market regulations	
	2000	2007	2000	2007	2000	2005	2000	2005
Bulgaria	3.00	3.67	2.00	2.67	5.00	4.90	5.90	9.20
Cyprus	n.a.	n.a.	n.a.	n.a.	0.00	6.80	8.90	8.30
Czech Republic	3.00	4.00	3.33	3.67	7.00	6.10	5.80	9.30
Estonia	3.67	4.00	3.00	3.67	7.80	7.50	7.80	9.70
Hungary	4.00	4.00	3.67	4.00	4.50	5.90	8.10	9.50
Latvia	3.00	4.00	2.33	3.00	7.60	6.90	7.90	9.10
Lithuania	3.00	3.67	3.00	3.33	7.80	6.10	6.40	9.70
Malta	n.a.	n.a.	n.a.	n.a.	0.80	8.00	6.60	8.80
Poland	3.33	3.67	3.67	3.67	3.80	3.60	7.10	8.30
Romania	2.67	3.33	2.00	2.67	4.50	6.60	4.60	6.50
Slovakia	3.00	3.67	2.33	3.00	5.50	7.10	7.40	9.10
Slovenia	3.33	3.33	2.67	2.67	5.30	5.70	6.50	7.80
NMS-12 (unweighted)	3.20	3.73	2.80	3.24	4.97	6.26	6.92	8.78

Note: The EBRD indicators range from 1 to 4+, while the Fraser Institute indicators range from 0 to 10.
n.a. means not available.
Source: EBRD and Fraser Institute

As Table 8.1 shows, the NMS have made significant progress in reforming their financial sectors. But with respect to restrictions on international capital market transactions, the indicator of the Fraser Institute suggests that further steps are needed.

As was shown in chapter 1 (see Figure 1.2), the financial development in most NMS is substantially below that of the EU-15. Several factors can explain the relatively low financial depth in the former transition NMS (ECB, 2005). First, these countries have moved from centrally planned economies to market economies in a very short period of time. Hence, they all started with low levels of intermediation, given the absence of know-how and experience in their early years of capitalism. Second, initially enforcement of creditor rights was inadequate and there was often regulation in place prohibiting foreign borrowing, imposing ceilings on interest rates, or limiting the amount of financial services that banks could offer. Third, due to the large presence of multinational companies, foreign bank lending and inter-company loans play a significant role in the financing of non-financial enterprises in most NMS.

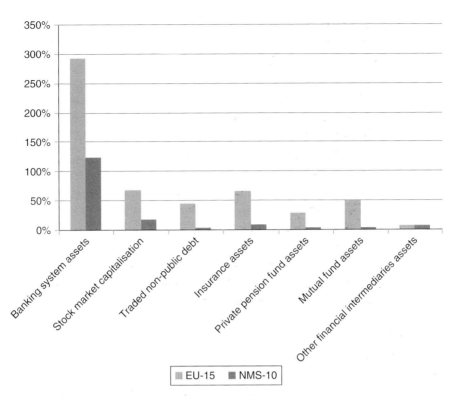

Figure 8.1   The financial system in the NMS-10 and the EU-15 (% of GDP), 2002
Source: Allen *et al.* (2006)

Figure 8.1 shows that NMS rely more heavily on bank finance than on direct market finance, as is the case in the EU-15. However, as Figure 8.1 also shows, banking assets are much lower in the NMS than in the EU-15. A distinction should be made here between Cyprus and Malta and the other NMS, i.e., the Central and Eastern European Countries (CEEC) and the Baltic States. Cyprus and Malta have a level of domestic credit to the private sector that is comparable to that of the EU-15 (ECB, 2005).

Also the stock-market capitalisation is substantially lower in the NMS than in the EU-15 even though stock-market capitalisation increased substantially between 1995 and 2004 in some NMS. As Allen *et al.* point out (2006), the privatisation of former state-owned companies has induced the development of equity markets. A strategy of mass-privatisation schemes was employed in the Czech Republic, Slovakia, and Lithuania and as a consequence stock markets quickly comprised a large number of companies. However, low liquidity and limited transparency implied that only a few companies were actively traded, and most companies were later delisted. For example, in the Czech Republic the number of listed companies declined from 1,716 in 1995 to 55 in 2004 (Allen *et al.*, 2006). Estonia, Hungary, Latvia, Poland, and Slovenia adopted a different privatisation strategy as only financially sound and recognised companies were privatised via the stock market. In addition, minority stakes in these companies were often sold prior to the initial public offering to a foreign investor. As a result, the equity markets in those countries have been growing gradually. For instance, in Poland the number of listed companies increased from 9 at the end of 1991 to 250 in 2004 (Allen *et al.*, 2006). However, stock exchanges are still not very well developed in most NMS. In 2003, the ratio of stock market to GDP for the EU-15 countries was 68 per cent, against 24 (19) per cent for the (former transition) NMS (ECB, 2005).

As Figure 8.1 shows, banks are by far the most important part of the financial system of the NMS. The following section will therefore focus on the banking sector in the NMS.

8.2 The banking sector

Table 8.2 provides a number of indicators of the banking system in the NMS. The largest part of the NMS banking sector comprises commercial banks that accounted for 86 per cent of the whole banking sector in 2003. In some countries (like Hungary and Poland), there is also a significant number of small co-operative banks (ECB, 2005).

The number of banks fell in almost all NMS. Some banks failed, but by far the biggest part of the decline reflects mergers and acquisitions. Especially foreign banks were very active in this regard and as a consequence on average 70 per cent of NMS total banking assets were controlled by foreign institutions in 2004, against only 19 per cent in the EU-15 (Allen *et al.*, 2006). In some of the NMS, over 90 per cent of the banking assets are foreign-owned. The following section will discuss foreign-bank entry in these countries in more detail. Box 8.1 discusses the impact of foreign-bank entry on the efficiency of the banking system of the NMS.

Concentration of banking markets is relatively high in most NMS due to foreign entry and a decrease of market share of former state-owned banks. In general, the aggregated market share of the five largest banks (CR5 ratio) varies between 50 and 99 per cent. Moreover, in some Member States the Herfindahl Index exceeds the 2,000-point threshold (see chapter 7 for an

Table 8.2 Structure of the banking sector in the NMS, 1997–2005

Country	Number of banks 1997	Number of banks 2005	Asset share of foreign banks 1997	Asset share of foreign banks 2005	CR5 (in %)[a] 1997	CR5 (in %)[a] 2005	Herfindahl Index[b] 1997	Herfindahl Index[b] 2005	H-statistic 1990–2005
Cyprus	623	391	10.2	30.1	92	60	2,747	1,029	−0.11
Czech Republic	50	56	24.0	91.8	67	66	2,533	1,155	0.77
Estonia	12	11	29.0	98.0	83	98	4,312	4,039	0.47
Hungary	286	215	53.0	77.0	53	53	2,101	795	0.16
Latvia	37	23	55.0	57.8	51	67	1,450	1,176	0.57
Lithuania	37	78	41.0	93.0	84	81	2,972	1,838	0.45
Malta	29	18	47.1	39.1	98	75	4,411	1,330	0.72
Poland	1,378	739	15.3	67.6	46	49	859	650	0.10
Slovakia	29	23	30.0	97.0	63	68	2,643	1,076	0.26
Slovenia	34	25	5.0	38.0	62	63	2,314	1,369	0.38
NMS-10[c]	2,515	1,579	26.0	69.0	63	60	2,123	1,042	0.31

Notes:
[a] CR5 is the share of the five largest banks, measured as a percentage of total assets.
[b] The Herfindahl Index is calculated as the sum of the squares of all the banks' market shares according to total assets, and rescaled from 0 to 10,000.
[c] NMS-10 is calculated as a weighted average (weighted according to assets).
Source: Allen *et al.* (2006) and Bikker *et al.* (2006)

Box 8.1 The impact of foreign ownership on bank performance

Various studies using micro data have examined whether foreign banks are more efficient than domestic banks. Why would the efficiency of a foreign bank differ from the efficiency of a domestic bank? Foreign banks may use better risk management and more advanced technologies and may have access to an educated labour force that is able to adapt new technologies. However, domestic banks may have better information about their country's economy, language, laws, and politics. The existing literature does not give an unambiguous answer as to which effect dominates. However, in their review of previous studies, Lensink *et al.* (2008) conclude that foreign banks in transition and developing markets show higher efficiency than their domestically owned counterparts. However, foreign banks in developed countries exhibit lower efficiency in comparison with domestic banks.

A good example of this literature is the study by Bonin *et al.* (2005), who have used data from 1996 to 2000 for 11 transition countries to investigate the effect of foreign ownership on the banking sectors in general and bank efficiency in particular. Using stochastic frontier estimation procedures, they compute profit and cost-efficiency scores. Their results indicate that majority foreign ownership generates higher efficiency. Similar results are reported by Fries and Taci (2005), who examine banks in 15 European transition nations between 1994–2001. They conclude that privatised banks with majority foreign ownership are the most efficient and those with domestic ownership are the least.

However, Zajc (2006), who examines banks in CEEC for the period 1995–2000, concludes that foreign banks are less cost efficient than domestic banks. Also Lensink *et al.* (2008), using stochastic frontier analysis for a broad sample of 2,095 commercial banks in 105 countries (including some NMS), conclude that, on average, foreign ownership has a negative effect on bank efficiency. They also argue that in countries with a good regulatory environment and good governance, the efficiency-reducing effects of a rise in foreign ownership are considerably lower. Their estimation results also suggest that if the institutional distance between the host and the home-country governance becomes smaller, foreign bank inefficiency will decrease as well.

explanation of this index). Countries with a smaller market size generally have the highest concentration, but even in countries with the lowest CR5 ratios (Hungary and Poland) market concentration is only around the average level of the EU-15 (ECB, 2005). However, given the small size of the NMS, it may be more relevant to benchmark them against the smaller EU-15 countries. In this comparison, the average CR5 in the NMS is only 7 percentage points higher than the average of smaller EU-15 countries (ECB, 2005).

Given the high concentration in most of the NMS, concerns may arise as regards the degree of competition. According to the structure-conduct-performance (SCP) hypothesis, high concentration enables banks to collude, which may in turn provide for the possibility of realising extra profits. However, the ECB (2005) reports that concentration and profit margins in 2003 were negatively related, i.e., margins were among the lowest in highly concentrated markets and were the highest in markets with lower concentration, suggesting that concentration ratios do not necessarily reflect competitive conditions within the region. The final column of Table 8.2 shows the so-called H-statistic proxy for competition as estimated by Bikker *et al.* (2006). It follows that there is strong competition (i.e., values of H above 0.70) in the banking sectors of the Czech Republic and Malta. Countries such as Estonia, Latvia, and Lithuania have an intermediate level of competition (H around 0.60), while banking competition in Cyprus and Poland is low.

Table 8.3 presents some indicators of the performance of the banking sector in the NMS. The average ratio of overhead costs to total assets in the NMS was double that of the EU-15, at 3.16 per cent in 2003, yet it had decreased by 4 per cent since 1995. The deterioration of interest margins and high overhead

Table 8.3 Performance of the banking sector (%), 1995–2003

Country	Net interest margin		Overhead costs		Cost/income		ROA	
	1995	2003	1995	2003	1995	2003	1995	2003
Cyprus	2.24	2.51	2.13	2.29	63.37	67.39	0.75	−0.06
Czech Republic	3.61	2.54	2.66	2.52	53.37	61.48	0.44	1.28
Estonia	6.14	4.03	3.92	2.80	53.12	52.86	3.64	2.17
Hungary	5.05	4.62	4.23	4.01	65.81	63.15	1.75	1.73
Latvia	6.34	3.10	5.57	3.18	65.32	60.68	3.17	1.41
Lithuania	7.16	3.42	6.14	3.39	80.07	79.98	−0.22	1.27
Malta	2.45	2.00	1.67	1.49	53.22	47.11	0.93	1.08
Poland	5.61	3.38	3.35	3.84	55.04	68.36	1.97	0.43
Slovakia	2.63	3.58	3.52	3.28	79.08	70.73	−1.26	1.34
Slovenia	4.48	3.29	3.61	3.06	59.15	64.12	1.11	0.88
NMS-10[a]	4.38	3.23	3.29	3.16	59.88	64.67	1.19	0.94

Note:
[a] NMS-10 is calculated as a weighted average (weighted according to assets).
Source: Allen *et al.* (2006)

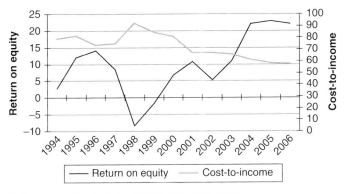

Figure 8.2   Performance of banks in the NMS (in %), 1994–2006
Note: The figures for the return on equity and the cost-to-income ratio are based on the three largest NMS: Czech Republic, Hungary and Poland.
Source: Deutsche Bank Research (2008)

costs was responsible for the fact that the average cost-to-income ratio in the NMS, at 64.67 per cent, exceeded that of the EU-15 (60.69 per cent in 2003). Figure 8.2 provides some figures on the performance and efficiency of banks over a longer period. The return on equity is on the left-hand side and the cost-to-income ratio on the right-hand side of the graph. Both the performance (increasing ROE) and the efficiency (decreasing cost-to-income)

Table 8.4 Quality of the balance sheet of the banking sector, 2003

Country	Non-performing loans (as % of total loans)	Provisions (as % of total loans)	Capital adequacy ratio
Cyprus	12.7	6.8	10.6
Czech Republic	6.4	2.4	14.5
Estonia	0.7	0.7	14.3
Hungary	3.5	1.8	11.9
Latvia	1.7	1.0	10.3
Lithuania	2.6	0.6	13.2
Malta	7.5	1.8	20.9
Poland	16.2	7.1	13.8
Slovakia	18.5	7.2	21.6
Slovenia	21.9	8.4	11.6
NMS-10[a]	11.0	4.7	14.0

Note:
[a] NMS-10 is calculated as a weighted average (weighted according to assets).
Source: ECB (2005)

significantly improved between 1994 and 2006. Performance increased from 2004, while there were some setbacks in the wake of the Asian crisis in 1997–1998 and the bursting of the Internet bubble in 2002.

Table 8.4 shows some indicators of the quality of the balance sheet of the banking sector in the NMS. For the NMS as a whole, the ratio of non-performing and other doubtful loans as a percentage of total loans stood at 10.4 per cent in 2004, while the corresponding figure for the EU-15 was 3.1 per cent (ECB, 2005). Still, there is quite some diversity across the NMS as regards asset quality. The banking sectors in the Baltic States recorded an average ratio of non-performing and other doubtful loans of only 1.5 per cent, as opposed to 11.1 per cent in the CEEC. In the latter group the ratio of non-performing and other doubtful loans ranged from 3.5 per cent to 21.9 per cent. According to the ECB (2005), the non-performing loans ratio of foreign banks in the NMS was 1.9 percentage points lower than that of domestic banks.

8.3 What attracts foreign banks?

As shown in the previous section, foreign bank presence is very large in most NMS. With few exceptions, the four or five largest banks are all foreign. A foreign bank is usually defined as a bank of which more than 50 per cent

Table 8.5 Number of foreign banks in 11 former communist countries, 1995–2004

	1995	1996	1997	1998	1999	2000	2001	2002	2003	2004
Bulgaria	3	3	7	17	22	25	26	26	25	24
Croatia	1	5	7	10	13	21	24	23	19	15
Czech Rep.	23	23	24	25	27	26	26	26	26	26
Estonia	5	4	4	3	3	4	4	4	4	6
Hungary	21	24	30	28	29	33	31	27	29	27
Latvia	1	14	15	15	12	12	10	9	10	9
Lithuania	0	3	4	5	4	6	6	7	7	6
Poland	18	25	29	31	39	46	46	45	43	44
Romania	8	10	13	16	19	21	24	24	21	23
Slovakia	18	14	13	11	10	13	12	15	16	16
Slovenia	6	4	4	3	5	6	5	6	6	7
Total	104	129	150	164	183	213	214	212	206	203

Source: Naaborg (2007)

of the shares are owned by non-domestic residents. This implies that a bank may be a domestic bank in one country but a foreign bank everywhere else. Most of the banks involved in the NMS are viewed as strategic investors with a strong commitment to the local economy, rather than financial investors (ECB, 2005). Strategic ownership has the advantage of providing both stability and expertise in retail banking and risk management. This section discusses in some detail foreign bank entry in the previous transition countries.

Foreign bank presence

Table 8.5 shows the development of the number of foreign banks between 1995 and 2004 in Bulgaria, Croatia, the Czech Republic, Estonia, Hungary, Latvia, Lithuania, Poland, Romania, Slovakia, and Slovenia.

In the second part of the 1990s, the relative number of foreign banks grew strongly, especially in Bulgaria, Croatia, Hungary, Lithuania, Poland, and Romania. In 2000, the number of foreign banks reached a peak and since then it has decreased slightly as some foreign banks left Croatia and Hungary.

Table 8.6 shows the share of foreign banks in total bank assets for the same countries. The share of state-owned banks evaporated from 51 per cent in 1995 to 3 per cent in 2004. Only in Poland and Slovenia are governments still

Table 8.6 Share of foreign banks in total bank assets in 11 former communist countries (in %), 1995–2004

	1995	1996	1997	1998	1999	2000	2001	2002	2003	2004
Bulgaria	1	2	18	25	42	72	71	72	82	82
Croatia	0	1	4	8	39	84	89	90	91	91
Czech Rep.	17	20	24	27	40	66	89	86	86	85
Estonia	n.a.	2	2	90	90	97	98	98	98	98
Hungary	19	46	62	63	62	67	67	85	84	63
Latvia	n.a.	53	72	81	74	74	65	43	53	49
Lithuania	0	28	41	52	37	55	78	96	96	91
Poland	4	14	15	17	49	73	72	71	72	71
Romania	n.a.	n.a.	n.a.	36	44	47	51	53	55	59
Slovakia	19	23	30	33	24	43	78	84	96	97
Slovenia	5	5	5	5	5	15	15	17	19	20
Median	4	17	21	33	42	67	72	84	82	82

Source: Naaborg (2007)

important shareholders of banks (Naaborg, 2007). After several banking crises had hit most transition countries in the mid-1990s, bank privatisation furthered foreign participation.

Table 8.6 shows that countries differed with regard to the timing of foreign bank entry. Hungary and Latvia were frontrunners. Already in 1997, more than 60 per cent of total bank assets in these countries was owned by foreign banks. Although the share of foreign banks in total bank assets in Slovenia has also increased, it is still far below that of most other former communist countries.

In general, the presence of non-EU banks in the region is rather limited. Banks from Austria, Belgium, Italy, and the Netherlands especially entered the CEEC. The banking sectors of the Baltic states are dominated by Nordic banks.

Motives for foreign-bank entry

The literature documents several motives for cross-border bank expansion. Following Naaborg (2007), three groups of motives can be identified. The first entry motive is related to foreign activities of non-financial firms. According to the *defensive expansion theory* (Grubel, 1977), banks follow foreign direct investments (FDI) by the non-financial sector to defend their relationships with clients. The defensive expansion theory is also often referred to as the *'follow the customer'* motive. Apart from FDI, other cross-border activities of non-financial firms, like exporting goods and services, may induce banks to follow their customers abroad. Banks that follow their customers focus on preventing losses in pre-existing activities, rather than on generating profits in the new location.

A second set of entry motives is associated with the potential to increase profitability. Expected high rates of economic growth may offer profitable business opportunities, which may be attractive especially in case of strong competitive pressure in the home banking market. Investing in the foreign country may also be profitable for other reasons, like expected exchange-rate developments or an attractive tax regime. Furthermore, foreign banks may apply ownership-specific factors, such as superior entrepreneurial skills or superior technology and management expertise, to foreign banking markets at low marginal costs.

The final set of foreign-entry determinants refers to the institutional context of the host market. Institutional parameters include financial regulation, the quality of the financial supervisor, the quality of law enforcement, the openness of the host-country authorities towards foreign-bank entry, and the role of information costs. Information costs mainly depend on the distance between the home and the host country, and the cultural similarity of both countries.

Surveying the literature, Naaborg (2007) concludes that the majority of studies on foreign bank entry confirm the 'follow the customer' view. There are, however, some studies reporting evidence that does not support this motive for foreign-bank entry. For instance, Berger *et al.* (2003) find that nearly 66 per cent of the non-domestic multinationals firms in Europe do business with a bank headquartered in the host nation, while less than 20 per cent selected a bank from their home nation. The importance of profitability in foreign bank entry is less controversial. High rates of expected economic growth have attracted foreign banks to the NMS (ECB, 2005). However, the results of Vander Vennet and Lanine (2007) do not confirm that European banks acquired poorly managed banks in the NMS in order to upgrade their performance. Finally, there are various studies suggesting the importance of the institutional context. For instance, Berger *et al.* (2004) and Buch and DeLong (2004) find that cross-border bank-merger activity increases when home and host country are geographically close, share a common language and legal system, and have similar economies in terms of size and level of GDP per capita.

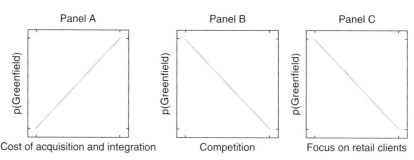

Figure 8.3   What drives greenfield investments?
Source: Naaborg (2007)

Entry mode and organisation form of representation

A large part of the foreign ownership of banks in the NMS stems from privatisation of former state-owned banks. Usually, foreign banks initially bought a small equity share in the bank and over time increased their shareholding. In addition, a number of banks entered these markets via greenfield operations (in a *greenfield investment*, a foreign firm starts operations on its own in a host country), thereby avoiding inheriting bad loans from the past. Greenfields also avoid post-acquisition integration failures rooted in cross-cultural differences and technological mismatches (Dikova, 2005).

Naaborg (2007) points out that the choice between acquisition and greenfield is influenced by many time-varying factors, such as the number and attractiveness of banks available for possible acquisition. Figure 8.3 summarises them.

Panel A relates the probability of the choice for a greenfield to the relative price of an acquisition. The costs of an acquisition are the sum of the direct purchasing costs and the post-acquisition expenses. The former depends on (i) the price quoted, and (ii) potential competitive biddings by other banks. Post-acquisition expenses are related to (i) reviewing the loan portfolio and costs due to mistakes in estimating the quality of the loan portfolio, and (ii) the restructuring and integration of the subsidiary into the parent bank. Post-acquisition expenses of a greenfield are generally lower than those of an acquisition as one can start with a clean loan book, a homemade structure, and experienced screening staff. Post-acquisition costs include integrating the subsidiary in the structure of the parent bank, like the implementation of a similar IT system and the need to implement best practices in the newly acquired bank (e.g., risk-management techniques). Foreign banks regard the operational risks of greenfields higher than the operational risks of acquisitions.

A second determinant of the choice for a greenfield or an acquisition is the degree of competition in the local banking sector (panel B in Figure 8.3). Fierce competition makes it hard for a greenfield investment to become successful. A good example is the 1996 greenfield of Dutch Rabobank in Hungary that aggressively tried to get business but was not able to gain enough market share and had to cease banking business in 2002.

Finally, Naaborg (2007) finds evidence that the choice between greenfield and acquisition is related to the customer focus of the banks (Panel C, Figure 8.3). The stronger the focus is on retail, the less likely a greenfield investment becomes.

Another component of foreign bank entry is the organisational form of representation. Foreign representation can be materialised by a small-scale office, such as a representative office or an agency, or by a large-scale office, such as a branch or a subsidiary. A representative office is the most limited but most easily established organisational form. It does not engage in attracting deposits and extending loans, but is generally established to test the possibility of further involvement. An agency is a more costly form of foreign banking operation than a representative office and may be warranted if banks engage in substantial export servicing and subsequent heavy involvement in the foreign-exchange market. Representation with an agency also allows a bank to make commercial loans, although business related to consumer loans or deposits is not permitted. A foreign branch constitutes a higher level of commitment than a representative office or agency. The crucial difference between a foreign branch and a foreign subsidiary is that, legally, a branch forms a unit with its parent and a subsidiary is an independent legal entity. Other differences between branch and subsidiary regard supervision, risk, and performance. While home-country supervisors supervise branches, local supervisory authorities supervise subsidiaries. Subsidiaries are subject to local lending limits associated with the level of their capital, while for branches no local lending limits are involved as from a consolidated point of view, they rely on the capital of the foreign parent.

Naaborg (2007) concludes that the choice between branch or subsidiary was largely driven by local regulations in place. For instance, the Polish authorities did not permit foreign branches for quite a while. In Hungary, banks were also obliged to take the form of a subsidiary. In other countries branches were allowed, but sometimes the authorities insisted that the branch should be capitalised. Table 8.7 shows that most foreign presence is now in the form of subsidiaries of foreign banks (see chapter 10 for a further discussion of the problems this may create for supervision).

Table 8.7 Foreign branches and foreign subsidiaries in the banking system of the NMS, 2003

	CY	CZ	EE	HU	LT	LV	MT	PL	SI	SK	**Total**
Number of foreign branches	2	9	1	0	3	1	2	1	1	3	23
Total assets (€ million)	408	7,610	537	0	555	405	4,753	693	205	3,034	18,200
% of total banking assets	2	10	9	0	9	5	27	1	1	13	6
Number of foreign subsidiaries	4	18	3	28	5	7	8	45	5	16	139
Total assets (€ million)	2,921	62,315	5,622	33,708	4,876	3,701	6,662	74,716	3,879	19,834	218,234
% of total banking assets	11	79	97	62	76	44	38	67	18	84	62

Source: ECB (2005)

8.4 Financial integration and convergence

The availability of sufficient credit to the private sector is important for economic development. As Figure 8.4 shows, the ratio of domestic credit to the private sector as a percentage of GDP in the former transition NMS increased on average from 29 per cent in 1995 to 35 per cent in 2003 (ECB, 2005). This increase coincided with a rapid increase in economic and financial development. However, in some countries (the Czech Republic and Slovakia), the ratio of domestic credit to GDP has shown a decreasing trend that mainly reflects the protracted restructuring of bad loans accumulated earlier (ECB, 2005).

An important issue here is the role of foreign banks. It is widely believed that allowing foreign bank entry as part of a liberalisation process will enhance the efficiency of the banking system. Foreign banks may help improve the quality, pricing, and availability of financial services, both directly as providers of these services and indirectly through increased competition. Foreign banks are often argued to improve the allocation of credit since they have more sophisticated systems for evaluating and pricing of risks. They are also more experienced in the use of derivative products. Also the likely improvement of human capital due to foreign-bank presence will be beneficial, because the skills required for the banking business were scarce during the first years of transition. Finally, foreign-bank presence may also lead to improvements of bank regulation and supervision, since these banks may demand improved

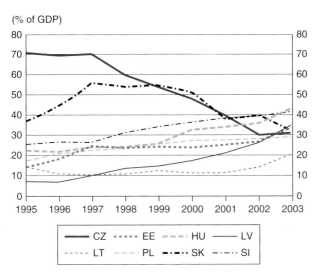

(% of GDP)

Legend: CZ, EE, HU, LV, LT, PL, SK, SI

Figure 8.4   Credit to the private sector (% GDP), 1995–2003
Source: ECB (2005)

systems of regulation and supervision from the regulatory authorities in the recipient countries. This may contribute to improving the quality of banking operations of domestic banks. All these spill-over effects may contribute to more efficient domestic banking practices, which, in turn, may enhance economic growth in transition countries (De Haan and Naaborg, 2004).

However, some worries – notably with respect to the intermediation role of foreign banks – have also been aired. In particular, foreign banks were initially believed to focus their activities on large enterprises and not on the retail and SME segments as large enterprises are easier to monitor or are more profitable, allowing foreign banks to 'cherry pick' the most profitable activities in the economy. Alternatively, foreign banks often follow their customers abroad and hence when the latter set up operations in the NMS, foreign banks also establish a local presence. Once established abroad, foreign banks may focus their activities mainly on these large enterprises. Furthermore, foreign-bank credit may turn out to be less stable than domestic credit, especially during adverse economic times. Foreign banks may easily withdraw funds in case of a worldwide recession or an economic downturn in the home country (see Box 8.2 for a further discussion of this issue).

Some empirical literature has documented the effect of foreign ownership on aggregate lending growth and on the extension of credit to specific market segments in transition countries. There is counterevidence to indicate that foreign banks in fact lend more to local customers through co-financing with

Box 8.2 Foreign banks and credit stability

One of the potential concerns related to high foreign ownership is that foreign banks may react differently than domestic banks to adverse changes in business-cycle conditions – either at home or in a host country – or in the case of a host-country banking crisis. There may be various explanations for such destabilising behaviour (ECB, 2005). Parent banks may reallocate their capital across regions or countries on the basis of expected risks and returns. Owing to differences in business-cycle conditions, activities of subsidiaries in low-growth countries may be scaled down substantially in favour of other countries. Similarly, deteriorating economic conditions in the home country may force parent banks to downsize their operations abroad. However, Buch *et al.* (2003) argue that one might expect that FDI in banking has stabilising features for two reasons. First, FDI flows are typically less volatile than other forms of capital flows such as international portfolio investments and international bank lending. Second, because FDI provides banks with superior information on host markets and because it requires a stronger commitment to servicing the foreign market, it may be less destabilising than other forms of entry.

De Haas and Van Lelyveld (2006) analyse for some NMS whether aggregate foreign-bank credit declined during periods of economic and/or financial downturn, and if so, whether such declines were steeper than those of domestic banks. They explicitly pay attention to both cross-border credit flows and activities of foreign subsidiaries within these countries. Their data refer to more than 100 banks in the Czech Republic, Estonia, Hungary, Poland, and Slovenia. Table 8.8 shows the changes in foreign subsidiaries' credit as well as cross-border credit during each period in which domestic banks on aggregate contracted their credit. It is striking that in all but one of these periods, foreign bank subsidiaries increased credit. The results for cross-border credit are more mixed.

So the results of De Haas and Van Lelyveld (2006) show no evidence of 'cut and run' behaviour by foreign banks. Temporary reductions in cross-border credit into Estonia, Hungary, and the Czech Republic were met by increases in local subsidiaries' credit. Foreign banks' local affiliates have been rather stable credit sources, even when domestic banks reduced their credit supply.

Table 8.8 Behaviour of foreign banks during periods of domestic credit contraction

	Period	Credit by foreign subsidiaries	Cross-border credit
Estonia	1999–2000	+	–
Hungary	1996–2000	+	+
Poland	2000	+	–
Slovenia	1999	–	+
Czech Republic (I)	1997	+	+
Czech Republic (II)	1999–2000	+	–

Source: De Haas and Van Lelyveld (2006)

local banks because of the latter's strength in seizing enterprise assets of firms in liquidation (ECB, 2005).

Finally, some recent work on the benefits of international financial integration for growth will be discussed. As shown in chapter 1, there is substantive evidence that financial development is positively related to economic growth. At the same time, recent research on the benefits of global financial integration – as surveyed by Kose *et al.* (2006) – finds little robust evidence for long-run growth benefits from global financial integration. In fact, Prasad *et al.* (2006, p. 10) report that capital has been flowing 'uphill' from less developed to industrial countries. Within developing economies, high-growth countries have received smaller net capital from abroad than those growing more slowly. Their provocative conclusion is that '... while developing countries grow faster by relying less on foreign savings, it is just the opposite for industrial countries. Put another way, neither China nor the United States, both fast growing countries for their stage of development, are running perverse current account balances relative to the norm. They are just extreme examples of their respective class of country!'

Abiad *et al.* (2007) argue that the recent enlargement of the EU provides fertile ground for testing the relationship between financial integration and income convergence. A particular implication of financial integration in the EU has been the flow of foreign capital to the NMS. In the past decade, various NMS have run large current-account deficits, which contrasts with the experience of many other emerging markets. For instance, East Asian economies have run substantial surpluses in recent years.

A country's current-account balance is, by definition, the difference between its savings and investment rates. In assessing the determinants of this balance researchers have therefore been guided by the underlying determinants of savings and investment. In their study, Abiad *et al.* estimate various models for the current-account balance-to-GDP ratio using five-year, non-overlapping observations over 1975–1979, 1980–1984, 1985–1989, 1990–1994, 1995–1999, and 2000–2004. As explanatory variables they include the government budget balance (as a ratio to GDP), the growth rate of real PPP-adjusted GDP per capita, the log of PPP-adjusted GDP per capita, the lagged net foreign assets-to-GDP ratio (NFA/GDP), the elderly and youth dependency ratios, and trade integration (i.e., the ratio of imports and exports to GDP).

To test for the role of financial integration, Abiad *et al.* also include a measure of financial integration and its interaction with the level of per-capita income. If financial integration facilitates the flow of capital from rich to poor countries the coefficient on the interaction term should be positive, implying

Table 8.9 Regressions for the current account, 1975–2004

	Dependent variable: five-year average CA/GDP					
	Global			Europe		
Log of GDP per capita	0.0187	0.0176	0.0178	0.058	0.0225	−0.0081
	[3.08]**	[2.88]***	[2.87]***	[2.82]***	[0.92]	[0.29]
Contemporaneous growth	−0.005	−0.005	−0.005	0.002	0.001	0.004
in GDP per capita	[2.54]**	[2.53]**	[2.53]**	[0.35]	[0.30]	[1.10]
Contemporaneous fiscal	0.389	0.387	0.388	0.040	−0.015	−0.119
balance/GDP	[3.55]***	[3.54]***	[3.59]***	[0.31]	[0.11]	[0.76]
NFA/GDP	0.032	0.033	0.033	−0.020	−0.023	−0.028
	[4.95]***	[5.04]***	[4.42]***	[1.31]	[1.34]	[1.88]*
Old dependency ratio	−0.335	−0.342	−0.340	−0.142	−0.380	−0.292
	[3.93]***	[3.86]***	[3.84]***	[0.67]	[1.56]	[1.39]
Young dependency ratio	−0.061	−0. 066	−0.066	0.270	0.002	−0.018
	[1.84]*	[1.90]*	[1.89]*	[1.51]	[0.01]	[0.12]
Trade openness/GDP	−0.015	−0.018	−0.018	−0.007	−0.026	−0.014
	[1.67]*	[1.74]*	[1.75]*	[0.47]	[1.53]	[1.04]
Financial integration/GDP		0.002	0.005		0.018	−0.430
		[0.80]	[0.23]		[2.13]**	[2.64]***
Log of GDP per capita*			−0.004			0.045
(Financial integration/			[0.15]			[2.70]***
GDP)						
Observations	488	488	488	87	87	87
Number of countries	115	115	115	23	23	23
R-squared	0.38	0.38	0.38	0.20	0.31	0.39

Notes: Robust t statistics in brackets. * significant at 10%; ** significant at 5%; *** significant at 1%.
Source: Abiad *et al.* (2007)

that poorer countries are able to run larger deficits the more financially integrated they are. Abiad *et al.* measure financial integration as the ratio of gross stocks of foreign assets plus liabilities to GDP. The European sample consists of 23 members of the EU, excluding Luxembourg and Ireland from the analysis given their unusually high degree of financial integration. Table 8.9 is reproduced from their study. For the global sample, the relationship between initial per-capita income and the current account balance is positive and statistically significant; in other words, capital flows from less developed to industrial countries. However, the size of the effect is small. Higher GDP growth and lower budget deficits are associated with a smaller balance (or larger deficit), and higher dependency ratios are associated with a lower current account balance, presumably because higher dependency reduces the savings rate.

As to the financial integration variable, the expectation is that the sign would be negative since countries with large external liabilities will need to run larger balances, while those that have accumulated assets should be able to run deficits. However, in the global sample, there is no relationship between the degree of a country's financial integration and its current account – either directly or indirectly through making it easier for poorer countries to gain access to capital. But the results for the European sample are sharply different. Now there is no statistically significant relationship between the current account balance and several 'conventional' determinants, like contemporaneous growth and the dependency ratios. Furthermore, a higher level of financial integration is associated with a lower current account balance in the European sample. The negative coefficient is even significant at the 10 per cent level in column 6. In Europe, financial integration has a strong relationship with the current-account deficit, and the direction of that relationship depends on a country's income. While poorer countries that are more financially integrated run larger deficits, richer countries that are more financially integrated run larger surpluses. In other words, financial integration leads countries to borrow more from abroad if they are poorer, and rich countries to lend more abroad if they are richer. The results suggest that an increase in financial integration by 100 per cent of GDP would increase Lithuania's current account deficit by 3.5 per cent of GDP, and would raise the Netherlands' surplus by 2.1 per cent of GDP. Abiad *et al.* conclude that the general increase in financial integration in Europe is an important force in explaining the increased dispersion of current accounts. In subsequent regressions, they find that in the global sample the current-account deficit has no bearing on growth. In Europe, the effects are important. A larger current-account deficit raises growth and this is all the more so the lower a country's per-capita income. In other words, a larger current-account deficit contributes to speeding up the convergence process.

8.5 Conclusions

Stock-market capitalisation in various new EU Member States has increased, but its level in the NMS is still far below that in the EU-15. By far the most important category of financial institutions in the NMS are banks. The banking sector is generally highly concentrated. Foreign bank presence is very large in most NMS, mainly in the form of subsidiaries of foreign banks. The choice between entering a country via a branch or a subsidiary was largely driven by local regulations in place. Most evidence suggests that foreign banks in transition markets show higher efficiency than their domestically owned counterparts. Scant available evidence also suggests that foreign banks increased credit during periods of domestic credit contraction.

The evidence on the determinants of foreign bank entry is mixed. Many, but not all, studies confirm the 'follow the customer' view. The importance of profitability in foreign bank entry is less controversial. Various studies suggest that the institutional context matters: cross-border bank-merger activity increases when home and host country are geographically close, share a common language and legal system, and have similar economies in terms of size and level of GDP per capita.

The final part of the chapter analysed how beneficial financial integration has been for the economic development of the NMS, suggesting that financial integration has stimulated their economic growth.

SUGGESTED READING

Allen, F., L. Bartiloro, and O. Kowalewski (2006), The Financial System of EU 25, in: K. Liebscher, J. Christl, P. Mooslechner, and D. Ritzberger-Grünwald (eds.), *Financial Development, Integration and Stability in Central, Eastern and South-Eastern Europe*, Edward Elgar, Cheltenham, 80–104.

De Haan, J. and I. Naaborg (2004), Financial Intermediation in Accession Countries: The Role of Foreign Banks, in: D. Masciandaro (ed.), *Financial Intermediation in the New Europe*, Edward Elgar, Cheltenham, 181–207.

European Central Bank (2005), *Banking Structures in the New EU Member States*, ECB, Frankfurt am Main.

REFERENCES

Abiad, A., D. Leigh, and A. Mody (2007), International Finance and Income Convergence: Europe is Different, IMF Working Paper 07/64.

Allen, F., L. Bartiloro, and O. Kowalewski (2006), The Financial System of EU 25, in: K. Liebscher, J. Christl, P. Mooslechner, and D. Ritzberger-Grünwald (eds.), *Financial*

Development, Integration and Stability in Central, Eastern and South-Eastern Europe, Edward Elgar, Cheltenham, 80–104.

Berger, A. N., Q. Dai, S. Ongena, and D. C. Smith (2003), To What Extent Will the Banking Industry Be Globalised? A Study of Bank Nationality and Reach in 20 European Nations, *Journal of Banking and Finance*, 27, 383–415.

Berger, A. N., C. M. Buch, G. DeLong, and R. DeYoung (2004), Exporting Financial Institutions Management via Foreign Direct Investment Mergers and Acquisitions, *Journal of International Money and Finance*, 23, 333–366.

Bikker, J. A., L. Spierdijk, and P. Finnie (2006), The Impact of Bank Size on Market Power, DNB Working Paper 120, De Nederlandsche Bank, Amsterdam.

Bonin, J. P., I. Hasan, and P. Wachtel (2005), Bank Performance, Efficiency and Ownership in Transition Countries, *Journal of Banking and Finance*, 29, 31–53.

Buch, C. M. and G. DeLong (2004), Cross-border Bank Mergers: What Lures the Rare Animal?, *Journal of Banking and Finance*, 28, 2077–2102.

Buch, C. M., J. Kleinert, and P. Zajc (2003), Foreign Bank Ownership: A Bonus or Threat for Financial Stability?, in: Securing Financial Stability: Problems and Prospects for New EU Members, SUERF Study 2003/4, available at www.suerf.org/download/studies/study20034.pdf

De Haan, J. and I. Naaborg (2004), Financial Intermediation in Accession Countries: The Role of Foreign Banks, in: D. Masciandaro (ed.), *Financial Intermediation in the New Europe*, Edward Elgar, Cheltenham, 181–207.

De Haas, R. and I. van Lelyveld (2006), Foreign Banks and Credit Stability in Central and Eastern Europe. A Panel Data Analysis, *Journal of Banking and Finance*, 30, 1927–1952.

Deutsche Bank Research (2008), *European Banks: The Silent (R)evolution*, Deutsche Bank, Frankfurt am Main.

Dikova, D. (2005), *Studies on Foreign Direct Investments in Central and Eastern Europe*, PhD thesis, University of Groningen.

European Central Bank (2005), *Banking Structures in the New EU Member States*, ECB, Frankfurt am Main.

Fries, S. and A. Taci (2005), Cost Efficiency of Banks in Transition: Evidence from 289 Banks in 15 Post-communist Countries, *Journal of Banking and Finance*, 29, 55–81.

Grubel, H. (1977), A Theory of Multinational Banking, *Banca Nazionale del Lavozo Quarterly Review*, 123, 349–363.

Kose, M. A., E. Prasad, K. Rogoff, and S. Wei (2006), Financial Globalization: A Reappraisal, IMF Working Paper 06/189.

Lensink, R., A. Meesters, and I. J. Naaborg (2008), Bank Efficiency and Foreign Ownership: Do Good Institutions Matter?, *Journal of Banking and Finance*, 32, 834–844.

Naaborg, I. J. (2007), *Foreign Bank Entry and Performance with a Focus on Central and Eastern Europe*, PhD thesis, University of Groningen.

Prasad, E., R. Rajan, and A. Subramanian (2006), Patterns of International Capital Flows and their Implications for Economic Development, presented at the symposium The New Economic Geography: Effects and Policy Implications, The Federal Reserve Bank of Kansas City, Jackson Hole, Wyoming, August 24–26, available at www.kc.frb.org/PUBLICAT/SYMPOS/2006/sym06prg.htm

Vander Vennet, R. and G. Lanine (2007), Microeconomic determinants of acquisitions of Eastern European Banks by Western European Banks, *Economics of Transition*, 15(2), 285–308.

Zajc, P. (2006), A Comparative Study of Bank Efficiency in Central and Eastern Europe: The Role of Foreign Ownership, *International Finance Review*, 6, 117–156.

9

European Insurers and Financial Conglomerates

OVERVIEW

The function of insurance is to protect individuals and firms from adverse events through the pooling of risks. Life insurance protects against premature death, disability, and retirement. Non-life insurance protects against risks such as accidents, illness, theft, and fire. Insurance is a risky business, as insurance companies collect premiums and provide cover for adverse events that may or may not arise somewhere in the future. The pattern of small claims, such as fire or car accidents, is fairly predictable. However, larger accidents or catastrophes (like hurricanes) involve high claims with low probability.

The insurance business is plagued by asymmetric information problems. There is a moral hazard problem when the behaviour of the insured, which can be only partly observed by the insurer, may increase the likelihood that the insurer has to pay. After signing the contract, the insured may behave less cautiously because of the insurance. Another problem is adverse selection. High-risk individuals (for instance, ill people) may seek out more (health) insurance than low-risk persons. The insurer may therefore end up with a pool of relatively high risks. Mechanisms to separate high from low risks are explained in this chapter.

Insurance companies tend to centralise risk management, using internal risk-management models at their headquarters. But there is still a role for local business units to capture factors that are location-specific. The same is true for asset management. As insurance companies are large asset managers, they can profit from economies of scale through the pooling of assets.

Insurance systems vary considerably across Europe. Life insurance is quite prominent in the EU-15, but far less so in the new EU Member States. Non-life insurance is more evenly spread across the EU. With the creation of the European single insurance market, insurers used mergers and acquisitions – at both the national and the European level – to become large enough to act at the European level. While it is still not possible to speak of an integrated insurance market, the level of cross-border insurance has gradually increased.

Finally, the chapter analyses financial conglomerates that combine banking and insurance. These conglomerates have the possibility of cross-selling insurance products through the bank and they may also gain from increased diversification possibilities. Yet it is difficult to manage a complex financial group that runs fairly different lines of business.

LEARNING OBJECTIVES

After you have studied this chapter, you should be able to:
● explain the nature of insurance business
● explain the economics of insurance risk
● explain the use of risk-management models by insurers and the centralisation of the risk-management function
● describe the structure of the European insurance market
● identify the characteristics of financial conglomerates and the role they play in the financial system.

9.1 Theory of insurance

Small vs. large claims insurance

The function of *insurance* is to protect individuals and firms against adverse events. Insurance companies are able to provide this protection through the pooling of individual risks. By combining the risks of various clients in a pool, insurance companies can spread the risks over this (large) group of clients. There are different types of insurance. *Life insurance* protects against premature death, disability, and retirement. While it is difficult to predict the death of an individual, death rates for large populations are fairly stable and therefore easier to predict. Other types of insurance are grouped under the name of *non-life insurance*, which protects against risks such as accidents, theft, and fire. Non-life insurance is sometimes also called property and casualty (P&C) or property and liability (P&L) insurance.

The risk dynamics of non-life insurance are more diverse than those of life insurance. Relatively small accidents (like car accidents) are fairly

Insurance company

| Assets (*A*) | Equity (*E*) |
| | Technical provisions (*TP*) |

Figure 9.1   Simplified balance sheet of an insurance company

predictable and can easily be pooled by an insurance company. But larger accidents or catastrophes follow a different pattern: they are low-probability but high-impact events. A good example is hurricane Katrina in New Orleans in 2005. The risk of such a catastrophe is too big for one insurance company and is therefore divided among different insurance and re-insurance companies.

The intermediation function of insurers can be illustrated with a simple balance sheet (see Figure 9.1). Insurers collect premiums *P* from clients and make payouts on claims *C* by these clients when the risk materialises. On the asset side, insurers invest the collected premiums in assets *A*, which earn a return R_A. On the liability side, insurers make technical provisions *TP* to cover expected future claims. In addition, insurers maintain a capital buffer *E* to cover unexpected claims.

Insurers evaluate the risk of prospective clients. If a client is accepted, the insurers have to decide how much coverage a client should receive and how much he should pay for it. The function of an underwriter is to acquire – or to 'write' – business that will bring the insurance company profits. The insurance business is viable only when the collected premiums exceed the payout on claims. When a claim is made, the insurer must determine the extent of the loss. Many insurers employ 'adjusters' who determine the liability of the insurer and the settlement to be made. The *claim ratio* measures the adjusted claims as a ratio to premiums earned, i.e., *C/P*. A claim ratio of less than 100 per cent means that premiums earned are sufficient to cover claims.

The insurance company also has to cover its expenses *Exp*. The biggest expenses are commissions paid to insurance agents for the acquisition of business. These acquisition costs are very high. To reduce their acquisition costs, insurers are increasingly selling insurance to the public directly (*direct writing*). The insurer must also gather information about potential clients to assess the underwriting risk and avoid adverse selection (see below). Finally, insurers incur administrative expenses. The *expense ratio* expresses total expenses relative to premiums earned, i.e., *Exp/P*.

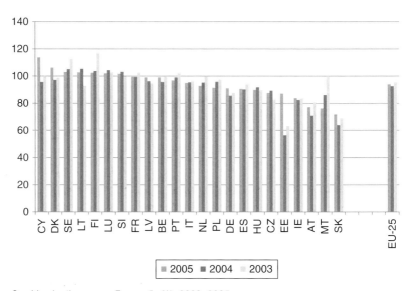

Figure 9.2   Combined ratios across Europe (in %), 2003–2005
Note: Claims and expenses in percentage of premiums. Data are not available for Greece and the
United Kingdom.
Source: CEIOPS (2006)

A common economic measure to assess the profitability of non-life insurers
is the combined ratio *CR*, which expresses claims and expenses relative to
premiums earned:

$$CR = C/P + Exp/P = \frac{C + Exp}{P} \qquad (9.1)$$

Figure 9.2 shows the combined ratio for various EU Member States. The
combined ratios for Cyprus and Denmark are well above 100 per cent,
indicating that the non-life insurance sector in these countries makes a loss.
However, investment returns are not included (see below). In Austria, Malta,
and Slovakia the combined ratio ranges between 70 per cent and 80 per cent,
indicating a healthy profit. The combined ratio of the EU-25 average is 94 per
cent. This results in a margin of 6 per cent.

The combined ratio provides an incomplete view of a non-life insurer's
profitability. Premiums are invested before payouts are made. Investment
returns are therefore an important source of income for insurers. The *profitability* π, as a percentage of premium earned, is equal to the results on claims
and expenses (100 – *CR*) and the investment returns:

$$\pi = 100 - CR + R_A/P = 100 + \frac{R_A - C - Exp}{P} \qquad (9.2)$$

Equation 9.2 illustrates that the successful management of an insurance company depends on making adequate investment returns and properly calculating underwriting risks while keeping a lid on acquisition and administrative expenses. This equation can be illustrated with a simple example. Assume a claim ratio of 65 per cent of earned premiums, an expense ratio of 32 per cent, and allocated investment income of 9 per cent. The profit is 12 per cent of earned premiums (100 + 9 – 65 – 32 = 12).

The stochastic properties of large claims are very different from those of small claims. Small claims have a distribution with light tails (e.g., the normal distribution). In a large portfolio, the expected claim size approaches the average claim size according to the law of large numbers. Box 9.1 sets out the mathematics of calculating small-claim risks in more detail.

In contrast, large claims are characterised by distributions with heavy tails. Insurance portfolios with heavy-tailed claim sizes are dangerous. Figure 9.4 shows the log-normal distribution, an example of a heavy-tailed distribution. In the tail on the right are events with a low probability but a large impact on the overall claim amount. We need extreme-value statistics to model these large claims. The distribution needs to be fitted from a relatively small number of observations (the excesses over high thresholds). Embrechts *et al.* (1997) provide an overview of modelling extreme events.

Large losses are caused not only by nature (natural catastrophes) but also by men (man-made disasters). Table 9.1 provides an overview of the largest catastrophes over the last 30 years. Hurricane Katrina in New Orleans caused an insured loss of €50 billion, while the total loss (insured and uninsured) mounted to over €100 billion. The terrorist attack on the Twin Towers and the Pentagon in 2001 led to an insured loss of €16 billion. Another man-made disaster was the explosion in 1988 on the oil platform Piper Alpha in the North Sea, causing an insured loss of €2.6 billion. The highest insured losses are suffered in the US, Europe, and Japan due to the higher insurance density in the industrialised countries. Emerging markets generally have a lower insurance density, so that only a small proportion of victims benefits from insurance cover. An example was the tsunami in the Indian Ocean in 2004, which had a death toll of 220,000. Yet this extreme event is not taken up in Table 9.1 as only insured losses are counted.

Re-insurance

Individual insurers cannot bear these large losses on their own – their equity would be wiped out when an extreme event occurs. The risks (and premiums)

Box 9.1 The mathematics of small claims insurance*

This box abstracts from expenses, investment returns, and dividend payouts and focuses on the premium setting P and the claim process C. The premium setting follows the dynamics of the claim process. The pattern of small claims is different from that of large claims.

The stochastic properties of the small claim-size model can be derived formally following Mikosch (2004). The total size of the claims $C(t)$ is the product of the number of claims $N(t)$ over period t and the size of the claims X_i. The total claim amount is given by:

$$C(t) = \sum_{i=1}^{N(t)} X_i, \quad t \geq 0 \tag{9.3}$$

where N is independent of the claim size. Both the number of claims and the size of claims are random variables. The claim numbers can often be described as a Poisson process. A *Poisson process* is a stochastic process, which is used for modelling random events that occur independently of one another. A variable following a homogeneous Poisson process has the property that the mean and variance of the distribution are the same. So for N it is possible to write: $\lambda = E(N) = \text{var}(N)$ where λ is the frequency of claims.

Equation (9.3) specifies the realised claims at time t. But an insurer needs to estimate the expected claims at the time of selling an insurance, i.e., $T = 0$. Exploiting the independence of the claim size sequence X_i and the claim number process $N(t)$, the expected total claim amount is given by:

$$E[C(t)] = E\left[E\left(\sum_{i=1}^{N(t)} X_i | N(t)\right)\right] = E[N(t) \cdot E(X_1)] = \lambda \cdot t \cdot E(X_1) \tag{9.4}$$

Equation 9.4 shows that the expected total claim amount grows linearly with t. Using the properties of the Poisson distribution, i.e., $\lambda \cdot t = E[N(t)] = \text{var}\,(N(t))$, the variance is denoted by:

$$\text{var}\,(C(t)) = \lambda \cdot t\left[\text{var}(X_1) + (E(X_1))^2\right] = \lambda \cdot t \cdot E(X_1^2) \tag{9.5}$$

An insurer with a large portfolio is interested in the asymptotic behaviour of the total claim amount. Applying the law of large numbers, the mathematical foundation of insurance, the total claim amount is given by:

$$\lim_{t} \frac{C(t)}{t} = \lambda \cdot E(X_1) \tag{9.6}$$

The law of large numbers thus says that the total claim amount is the expected claim amount. Put differently, the number of claims is the average number of claims λ and the claim size is the average claim size $E(X_i)$. But the total claim amount may vary in practice. The risk of insurance is determined by the variance of the claims. The claim amount for a large population follows a normal distribution (i.e., a symmetric, bell-shaped curve).

Figure 9.3 visualises the law of large numbers for a portfolio of Danish fire insurance claims (Mikosch, 2004). The data cover the period 1980–1992 and include about 2,500 observations. Because the sample of fire insurance claims contains very large values, the ratio C_n/n converges to $E(X_1)$ very slowly in Figure 9.3.

Next, an insurer needs to set a premium $P(t)$ to cover the claims. As the total claim amount varies, it is necessary to choose a premium by loading the expected claim amount by certain positive number ρ. The premium is given by:

$$P(t) = (1 + \rho) \cdot E[C(t)] \tag{9.7}$$

for some positive number ρ, called the safety loading. It is evident that the insurance business is more on the safe side the larger ρ. The safety loading can thus absorb fluctuations in the claim amount. But an overly large safety loading would make the insurance business less competitive.

The final step is to define the surplus or risk process of the portfolio. Following Mikosch (2004), $E(t)$ is the insurer's capital or equity balance at given time t (see also Figure 9.1) and is given by:

$$E(t) = E(0) + P(t) - C(t), \quad t \geq 0 \tag{9.8}$$

where $E(0)$ is initial capital. A large initial capital is needed and reinforced by supervisors (see chapter 10). When starting an insurance company, the supervisor requires a sufficiently large initial capital buffer to prevent the business from bankruptcy due to many small or a few large claims in the first period, before the premium income can balance the losses and the gains.

What is the risk for an insurer with a sufficient capital balance $E(0)$ and a sufficiently prudent premium rate $((\rho > 0)$? First, there may be an upward drift $\delta > 0$ in the claim amount which was not expected by the insurer at the time when setting the premium. The realised claim amount is thus larger than expected: $C(t) = (1 + \delta) \cdot E[C(t)]$. Examples of such a drift are a shorter life expectancy due to a new illness or more car accidents due to an unexpected shift in weather conditions (e.g., strong winters with frozen roads). The insurer will incur losses when $\delta > \rho$ and potentially bankruptcy when cumulative losses wipe out the capital balance $(\delta - \rho) \cdot E[C(t)] > E(0)$.

Second, the principle of independence may be violated. A case in point is the accumulation of payouts on life policies by ING in the aftermath of the terrorist attack at the Twin Towers in New York at September 11 2001. While it thought to have an adequate geographical spread of its life portfolio in the New York and New Jersey area, ING appeared to have a large concentration among people working in the Twin Towers.

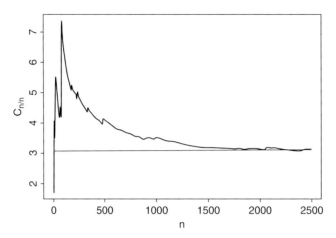

Figure 9.3   The law of large numbers and fire insurance claims
Source: Mikosch (2004)

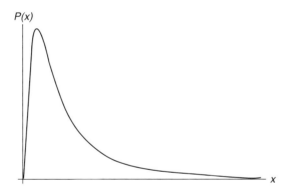

Figure 9.4   Heavy-tailed distribution

of catastrophe insurance are therefore shared among insurers (Rejda, 2005). A common mechanism to share insurance risk is *re-insurance*, which is shifting part or all of the insurance originally written by one insurer to another insurer.[1] The insurer that originally writes the business is called the ceding company. The insurer that accepts part or all of the insurance risk from the ceding company is the re-insurer. Finally, the re-insurer may in turn re-insure part or all of the risk with another insurer.

The insurance risk of extreme events is thus sliced in different layers and divided between different insurers. Re-insurance can be designed in different ways. One format is *proportional re-insurance*. The insurer cedes a proportion of the premiums and the risks to a re-insurer. The remainder of the premiums and risks is retained by the ceding insurer (the retention amount).

Table 9.1 Catastrophes: the 25 most costly insurance losses, 1970–2006

Insured loss (in € billion, 2006 figures)	Victims (dead and missing)	Date (year)	Event	Country
50.4	1,836	2005	Hurricane Katrina: floods	US, Mexico
17.5	43	1992	Hurricane Andrew: floods	US, Bahamas
16.2	2,982	2001	Terror attack on WTC, Pentagon	US
14.5	61	1994	Northridge earthquake (M 6.6)	US
10.4	124	2004	Hurricane Ivan: damage to oil rigs	US, Caribbean
9.8	35	2005	Hurricane Wilma: torrential rain, floods	US, Mexico
7.9	34	2005	Hurricane Rita: floods	US, Mexico
6.5	24	2004	Hurricane Charley	US, Cuba
6.3	51	1991	Typhoon Mireille	Japan
5.6	71	1989	Hurricane Hugo	US, Puerto Rico
5.5	95	1990	Winter storm Daria	France, UK, Benelux
5.3	110	1999	Winter storm Lothar	Switzerland, UK, France
4.2	22	1987	Storm and floods in Europe	France, UK, Netherlands
4.2	38	2004	Hurricane Frances	US, Bahamas
3.7	64	1990	Winter storm Vivian	Europe
3.7	26	1999	Typhoon Bart	Japan
3.3	600	1998	Hurricane Georges: flooding	US, Caribbean
3.1	41	2001	Tropical storm Allison: heavy rain, floods	US
3.1	3,034	2004	Hurricane Jeanne: floods, landslides	US, Caribbean
2.9	45	2004	Typhoon Songda	Japan, South Korea
2.7	45	2003	Thunderstorms, tornadoes, hail	US
2.6	70	1999	Hurricane Floyd: heavy rain, floods	US, Bahamas
2.6	167	1988	Explosion on oil platform Piper Alpha	UK
2.5	59	1995	Hurricane Opal: floods	US, Mexico
2.5	6,425	1995	Kobe earthquake (M 7.2)	Japan

Notes: The losses include property and business interruption, but exclude liability and life-insurance losses. The losses are indexed to 2006.
Source: Sigma No.2, Swiss Re (2007a)

Another format, in particular used for catastrophe insurance, is *excess-of-loss re-insurance*. Losses in excess of a certain limit (i.e., the retention limit) are paid by the re-insurer up to some maximum limit. These amounts are expressed in money amounts. Excess-of-loss contracts allow for tailor-made slicing of the insurance risk. The terrorist attacks on September 11 2001 show the importance of re-insurance. Re-insurers paid out at least half of the insured losses (Rejda, 2005).

In case of large catastrophes, traditional insurance and re-insurance may not suffice. The financial losses due to, for instance, a large flood can super-sede the absorption capacity of individual insurers and re-insurers. Therefore, many countries have a government programme that covers part of the risk (see Box 9.2). However, government involvement gives rise to moral hazard, as private parties may seek to shift the risk to government (Loubergé, 2000; Kessler, 2008). There are several ways to mitigate this undesired effect. First, governments could provide cover for only the top layer of the risk. Private (re) insurers are then taking the first layers of risk of the catastrophe and have an

---

Box 9.2 Flood insurance

While flooding affects many people worldwide and often causes serious damage (see Table 9.1), insurance cover for the risk of flooding is not widespread. This box reviews (lack of) insurance solutions in some selected countries.

The oldest insurance scheme is found in the US. The National Flood Insurance Program (NFIP) that was set up in 1968 covers losses through river flooding. The maximum cover for residential buildings/contents is $250,000/100,000. Premiums are high and vary in line with the flood hazard. Prior to the Mississippi floods of 1993, 15–20 per cent of property in exposed areas was insured under NFIP. After the most recent floods, these figures went up markedly. There is no cap on insured losses, as NFIP is government funded.

In France, the insurance market is based on private insurers, but is statutorily regulated. The Caisse Centrale de Réassurance (CCR) is the main re-insurer and is guaranteed by the state. Insurance penetration is practically 100 per cent.

The United Kingdom has only private insurers and no state insurance. Insurance cover is generally included in homeowners' and household contents policies in conjunction with storm cover. Premium rates are often high for storm/flood and are broken down to individual postcodes. Insurance penetration is 95 per cent.

The Netherlands has an enormous loss potential. Some 70 per cent of property is at risk as vast areas lie below sea level (storm surge) and/or can be flooded by the Rhine or the Maas rivers. The Dutch insurers concluded a market agreement in 1965 to exclude flood cover. The result is that the state is expected to pay (partial) compensation in the event of a disaster. An example is the flooding of the Rhine and the Maas in 1995 with an economic loss of €900 million, of which €180 million was paid by the government.

Source: Swiss Re (1998)

incentive to take appropriate precautionary measures, thereby reducing moral hazard. Second, governments should charge sufficiently high premiums, thereby pushing the insurance coverage back to the market as much as possible. Private (re)insurers have a competitive motive to underbid the premium charged by the government. Only when the risk is too high in relation to the premium will private (re)insurers drop out. In that case the government ends up providing residual coverage for catastrophes.

An alternative to traditional re-insurance and government insurance is securitisation of the risk. A recent example is the catastrophe bond (also known as cat bond). *Cat bonds* are corporate bonds that permit the issuer of the bond to skip or defer scheduled payments if a catastrophic loss beyond a certain threshold occurs. If insurers have built up a portfolio of risks by insuring properties in a region that may be hit by a catastrophe, they could create a special-purpose entity that issues the cat bond. Investors who buy the bond make a healthy return on their investment, unless a catastrophe (like a hurricane or an earthquake) hits the region; in that case, the principal initially paid by the investors is forgiven and is used by the sponsor to pay the claims of policy holders. The bonds pay relatively high interest rates and help institutional investors to diversify their portfolio, because natural disasters occur randomly and are not correlated with the stock market or other common factors (Rejda, 2005).

Asymmetric information

Under the assumption of full information complete insurance is possible at actuarially fair premium rates. But complete coverage is not always available in insurance markets due to asymmetric information (Loubergé, 2000). Insurance is subject to moral hazard when the contract outcome is partly influenced by the behaviour of the insured and the insurer cannot observe, without costs, to which extent reported losses can be attributed to the behaviour of the insured. Complete coverage may not be attainable under moral hazard. This is due to the trade-off between the goal of efficient risk sharing, which is met by allocating the risk to the insurer, and the goal of efficient incentives, which requires leaving the consequences of decisions about care with the decision maker, i.e., the insured.

Insurance is also subject to adverse selection. The ex-ante information asymmetry arises because the insured generally knows more about his risk profile than the insurer. The risk type of the insured cannot be determined ex ante by the insurer; the insurer can only charge the same premium rate based

---

Box 9.3 Some numerical examples with high- and low-risk individuals

The working of the Rothschild–Stiglitz model can be easily illustrated with some numerical examples. The first example is with a relatively small proportion of high-risk individuals, so the insurer is still able to offer a single contract to all insured (high- and low-risk). The case where everybody can be charged the same premium is called a *pooling equilibrium*. Assume two types: healthy people with a low risk of illness at 1/1000 ($p^L = 0.001$) and unhealthy people with a high risk of illness 1/100 ($p^H = 0.01$). The cost of illness is €100,000 per episode. The population comprises 90 per cent healthy people and 10 per cent unhealthy people. Table 9.2 provides the details. The cost of insurance for the healthy is €100 (= 100,000 * 1/1000) and for the unhealthy €1,000 (= 100,000 * 1/100). The average cost is €190 (= 0.90 * 100 + 0.10 * 1,000). If insurance is offered at an actuarially fair premium of €190 for the whole population, both types will buy full insurance as the premium is below their reservation prices of €200, respectively €1,500.

In the second example, the proportion of healthy people is changed to 80 per cent (see Table 9.3). This has an impact on the average cost, which becomes €280 (= 0.80 * 100 + 0.20 * 1,000). Now, healthy people are unwilling to buy insurance at this premium as it is above their reservation price of €200. The pooling equilibrium breaks down; only the unhealthy people will buy insurance. Since the insurer knows that, it will charge a premium of €1,000. The result is that the 80 per cent healthy people are not insured.

In the third example, we assume that the insurer has enough market power to charge premiums above the actuarially fair premium. The figures are shown in Table 9.4. The average premium is €150 (= 0.50 * 100 + 0.50 * 200). Since healthy people are not willing to pay €150, there is again no pooling equilibrium. We now try to set up a separating equilibrium with two policies. The general policy is available for €240. In addition, the insurer offers an insurance policy for €100 to anyone who can pass a medical test, which costs €40. The healthy people will pick up the second contract. They pay €100 for the insurance and €40 for the medical test. Unhealthy people can pass the test only when they bribe the doctor, which is costly (€110). So unhealthy people will take the general policy at a premium of €240 rather than the second policy at a cost of €250 (€100 for the insurance and €150 for the test). This equilibrium with two different contracts and premiums is a separating equilibrium.

insurer. A typical example of such compulsory insurance is health insurance. As part of its social policy, a government may find it desirable that all citizens are fully insured in case of illness at an affordable premium. Without compulsion, low-risk individuals would have partial insurance and high-risk individuals would pay a high premium (the separating equilibrium).

Table 9.2 Pooling equilibrium

Type	% of population	risk of illness	cost to insure	willingness to pay
Healthy people	90	1/1000	€100	€200
Unhealthy people	10	1/100	€1,000	€1,500

Table 9.3 No equilibrium

Type	% of population	risk of illness	cost to insure	willingness to pay
Healthy people	80	1/1000	€100	€200
Unhealthy people	20	1/100	€1,000	€1,500

Table 9.4 Separating equilibrium

Type	% of population	risk of illness	cost to insure	willingness to pay	cost of medical test
Healthy people	50	1/1000	€100	€140	€40
Unhealthy people	50	1/500	€200	€250	€150

9.2 The use of risk-management models

While the underwriting of risk is one of their core competencies, insurers are similar to banks when it comes to risk-management systems and practices (Von Bomhard, 2005). In fact, the banking industry imported risk-management skills from the insurance sector and developed them further. Several banking crises, like the Scandinavian banking crisis in the 1990s (see chapter 11), have underlined the importance of good risk and capital management for banks. Another reason are the similarities between traditional actuarial thinking that prevails in insurance companies and financial economic thinking that prevails in banks.

Modern risk management

The main risk types for an insurer are underwriting risk, market risk, credit risk, and operational risk. As explained in chapter 7, economic capital has emerged as a 'common currency' for risk taking within financial institutions. *Economic capital* is defined as the amount of capital a financial institution needs to absorb losses over a certain time interval with a certain confidence level. Financial institutions usually choose a time horizon of one year.

The risk-adjusted return on capital for an insurer is given by

$$\text{RAROC} = \frac{\text{Revenues} - \text{Costs} - \text{Expected Claims}}{\text{Economic Capital}} = \frac{\pi}{E} \tag{9.9}$$

The revenues consist of premiums P and investment returns R_A (see equation 9.2). Both the numerator and the denominator are adjusted for risk in the RAROC formula. RAROC divides profit by economic capital. RAROC can be used to assess past performance, but also to forecast future performance. It can thus be applied to determine whether activities should be discontinued or expanded.

RAROC is emerging as the leading methodology for large financial institutions to measure and manage risk. The use of internal risk models has been stimulated by supervisors, who allow insurers to use their internal models to calculate capital requirements (see chapter 10 on the new Solvency II capital adequacy rules). Within the RAROC framework, insurers first calculate the risk for each risk type (underwriting, market, credit, and operational risk) and then aggregate these.[2]

The first type of risk is *underwriting risk*. Insurers make provisions for future claims. An unforeseen increase in the size and frequency of claims is a key risk factor for insurers. In life insurance, *longevity risk* is the risk that future trends in survival rates prove to be higher than projected. The payout period on annuities or pension contracts may thus be longer than expected. Insurance premiums to cover underwriting risk tend to follow a cyclical pattern. Several studies (e.g., Niehaus and Terry, 1993) identify the existence of an underwriting cycle in insurance markets. Box 9.4 explores different theories explaining the underwriting cycle.

The second type of risk is market risk. A specific market risk occurs when assets and liabilities in the balance sheet are not matched. This risk is labelled *asset and liability management risk*. In insurance companies, ALM risk is very important (Van Lelyveld, 2006). ALM risk increases when there is a significant mismatch between assets and liabilities. For life business, asset durations are generally shorter than liability durations. *Duration* is the effective maturity of an asset or liability. This duration mismatch will primarily cause an interest-rate risk, as most assets consist of bonds.[3] Insurers also invest in equities and other investments to increase returns (see chapter 6 on investment strategies of insurers). While equities tend to generate a higher return than bonds in the long run (Dimson *et al.*, 2002), they also generate a considerably higher

---

Box 9.4 The underwriting cycle

The *underwriting or insurance cycle* is a distinct pattern of upward and downward movements in insurance premiums and their subsequent impact on underwriting profitability. Cyclical patterns, typically running over a period of six to nine years, tend to be particularly pronounced in insurance markets. While both demand and supply of insurance varies over time, variations in supply are the more important. New financial capital can come into a market quickly to increase supply when premiums are high, and also can be withdrawn quickly when returns on insurance are low.

There are several theories explaining the underwriting cycle (see Niehaus and Terry, 1993). The first one is based on fluctuations in profits and assumes a competitive market. If profits are high, some insurers may reduce insurance premiums to attract more clients in expectation of these higher profits. Other insurers, not wishing to lose market share, may then also reduce premiums.

The second theory is founded on the availability and cost of equity capital. There are two main effects when stock markets rise markedly. First, the cost of capital falls for existing and new insurers. Second, rising share prices increase the value of an insurer's asset holdings and thereby also the value of equity. The increased availability and reduced cost of capital increases supply and hence exerts downward pressure on premiums.

The third theory holds that claims rather than capital-market effects are the key cause of underwriting cycles. It supposes that insurers tend to underestimate the potential for large claims when there are no large individual losses or accumulation of losses. However, when a very large loss occurs, premiums rise sharply. A case in point is car insurance. After a few 'soft' winters without frozen roads, the frequency of car accidents seems to be relatively low and premiums may decrease. But after a 'strong' winter with multiple car accidents, premiums tend to rise again. This theory assumes that insurers have a short memory. This theory also supposes that following a major loss, insurers will try to recover some of their losses. Of course, exceptionally large losses or accumulations of loss are likely to be more or less random in their timing, but their effects may appear to be cyclical.

ALM risk. Insurers use advanced models to optimise their risk-return profile. The ability to invest in equities rather than in bonds depends on the size of an insurer's capital buffer. The larger the capital buffer, the more risk (and thus equity investments) the insurer is allowed to take (see chapter 10 for further details).

The third type of risk is credit risk. While banks grant loans, insurers typically invest in traded assets such as bonds. Credit risk is present because the value of bonds may decline as a result of an increase in the perceived

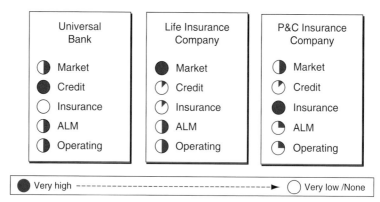

Figure 9.6   The relative role of risk types in banking and insurance
Source: Oliver, Wyman and Company (2001)

likelihood that the issuer will not be able to meet scheduled payments in the future. For most banks, lending activities are typically the main source of credit risk. But a typical insurer attributes only 5–10 per cent of total risk capital to credit risk (Van Lelyveld, 2006).

The fourth type of risk is operational risk. This is the risk of loss from inadequate internal processes, people or systems, or from external events. While developments in the insurance industry generally follow those in banking, most insurers model external-event risk separately as an underwriting risk.

The impact of the various types of risk differs across banking and insurance. The main business of banks is granting loans. Credit risk is the most important risk driver in banking, followed by market and ALM risk. ALM risk is caused by long-term assets funded by short-term deposits. The main risk in life insurance is market risk related to the large asset portfolios. Life insurers collect premiums on life policies, which are invested over a long period. The next type of risk is ALM risk, which is opposite to banking ALM risk. Life insurers typically invest the premiums on their long-term policies in shorter-lived assets. Insurance or underwriting risk is the main risk driver for P&C insurers. Figure 9.6 illustrates the relative importance of the different types of risk.

Centralisation of risk management

The organisational structure of international financial firms is moving from the traditional country model to a business-line model with integration of key management functions. One of the most notable advances in risk management is the growing emphasis on developing a firm-wide assessment of risk. These integrated approaches to risk management aim to ensure a comprehensive and systematic approach to risk-related decisions throughout the financial firm. Once firms have a centralised risk-management unit in place, they may benefit from economies of scale in risk management. Nevertheless, these centralised systems still rely on local branches and subsidiaries for local market data. The potential capital reductions that can be achieved by applying the advanced approaches of the new Basel II framework encourage banking groups to organise their risk management more centrally (see chapter 7). The same is true for the future Solvency II framework for the European insurance industry (Drzik, 2005). Firms that implement a well-constructed risk- and capital-management framework can derive significant near-term business benefits, and substantially strengthen their medium-term competitive position.

Kuritzkes *et al.* (2003) provide evidence that internationally active financial conglomerates are putting in place centralised risk and capital-management units. The dominant approach is to adopt a so-called 'hub and spoke' organisational model. The spokes are responsible for risk management within business lines, while the hub provides centralised oversight of risk and capital at the group level. Activities at the spoke include the credit function within a bank, or the actuarial function within an insurance subsidiary or group, each of which serves the front-line managers for most trading decision making.

Schoenmaker *et al.* (2008) confirm the shift to a more holistic approach in the European insurance industry. Recent developments in the field of accounting (for instance the introduction of International Financial Reporting Standards (IFRS) and the Sarbanes Oxley Act in the US) and in supervision (Solvency II) contribute to the centralisation of risk- and capital-management processes. Moreover, as insurance groups operate in various countries, the need for a coherent policy regarding risk and capital management is increasing. This, in turn, has led to the adoption of chief risk officers in large insurance groups.

Hub functions

Applying the hub-and-spoke model to a sample of large European insurance companies, Schoenmaker *et al.* (2008) identify which functions are executed at the centre (hub) and which functions are performed at the local business units (spokes). The hub accommodates decisions and responsibilities for the group as a whole at a central level in the organisation. Although large insurance groups have a distinct central risk-management framework in place, there are great differences between the responsibilities and actual implementation of these frameworks. In some groups central risk- and capital-management processes are still in their infancy, while in other groups these processes are much more advanced and commonly accepted in the organisation.

All groups use their risk-management framework to get an overview and to monitor the group-wide risk exposure. The majority of the groups also use their risk framework for specifying their risk profile and setting risk management, control, and business-conduct standards for the group's worldwide operations (i.e., 'the rules of the game'). This group-wide risk profile specifies some risk-tolerance levels. Within these boundaries, the local units can act more or less independently. Furthermore, group-wide policies regarding risk management enable a broadly consistent approach to the management of risks at the business-unit level.

The risk-management framework encompasses several bodies with their own specific tasks. On top of the central risk-management framework is the group risk committee at the executive level, with the chief executive officer (CEO) or chief financial officer (CFO) bearing the ultimate responsibility. This committee is often responsible for setting the strategic guidelines and policies for risk management, for monitoring consolidated risk reports at group level, and for allocating economic capital to various entities of the group. Sometimes groups also have risk committees below the executive level. This may be the case in a financial group with both banking and insurance activities. The group risk committee is then responsible for the group as a whole, while banking and insurance risk committees reporting to the group risk committee are responsible for the risk management in banking and insurance, respectively.

Furthermore, many groups also have central or group risk-management teams. These teams are responsible for the development and implementation of the risk-management framework, for supporting the work of the risk committees, for reporting and reviewing risks, and for recommendations concerning risk methodologies. Many times, these central/group risk-management teams are headed by a CRO who oversees all aspects of the group's risk management and often reports to the CEO or CFO of the group and is present at meetings of the executive board.

Spoke functions

In the spokes, decisions are being taken on the level of the business/country unit. Insurance is very much a local business, with significant differences between the operational environment of the host countries in which the insurance group is active. Specific local knowledge is often required with respect to national rules and regulations (such as fiscal legislation, contracts, social security, consumer protection, or local risks), complicating the steering process at a central level. So a great number of decisions still have to be made by the local business units. In general, the actuary determines the specific risk at the local level. At the group level, these local models are subsequently monitored and assessed. Although the general conditions for determining local risk models are set at the central level, the local units carry the ultimate responsibility for their risk management.

So, despite the emergence of centralised risk management, the risk-management practices of the largest insurance groups are still to a large extent influenced by the risk-management policies of the local business units. Therefore, in general one could say that the 'rules of the game' are being determined at central level in the hub and that the local managers in the spokes determine 'how the game is actually being played' within the margins of these rules. This general principle is summarised in Figure 9.7 which gives an overview of the roles and responsibilities for each level of the organisation, whereby the spokes are placed within a field of jurisdiction-specific parameters in order to capture the location-specific factors that influence the business decisions.

9.3 The European insurance system

Insurance markets across Europe

The insurance markets vary significantly across Europe. This is illustrated by differences in the *insurance penetration*, i.e., insurance premiums as a percentage of GDP, which ranges from 0.1 per cent in Latvia to 9.3 per cent in the United Kingdom (see Table 9.5).[4] There is a large difference between the new Member States of the EU and the EU-15. Whereas the prevalence of life insurance is 5.6 per cent in the EU-15, it amounts to only 1.3 per cent in the NMS. Life insurance is basically a savings product for the future, where the payout is linked to somebody's life. Life insurance may be considered as a 'luxury' good: only at high income levels do households start to save for retirement (Focarelli and Pozzolo, 2008).

Non-life insurance is less diverse across Europe. It looks more like a 'necessary' good offering basic protection against accidents, such as car accidents, fire, or illness. Non-life penetration is 3.3 per cent in the EU-15 and 1.8 per cent in the NMS. Also at the country level the differences are

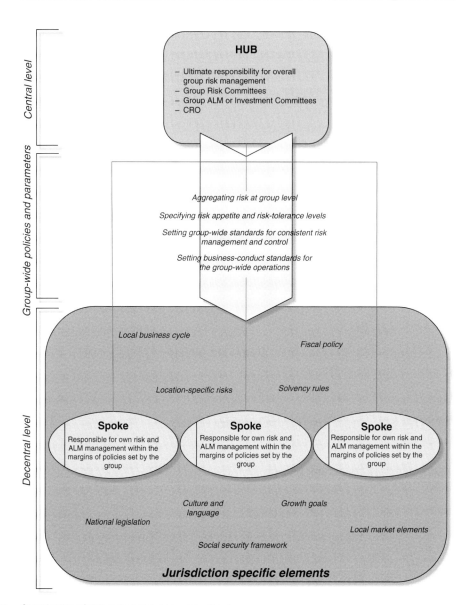

Central level

HUB
- Ultimate responsibility for overall group risk management
- Group Risk Committees
- Group ALM or Investment Committees
- CRO

Group-wide policies and parameters

Aggregating risk at group level

Specifying risk appetite and risk-tolerance levels

Setting group-wide standards for consistent risk management and control

Setting business-conduct standards for the group-wide operations

Decentral level

Local business cycle

Fiscal policy

Location-specific risks

Solvency rules

Spoke
Responsible for own risk and ALM management within the margins of policies set by the group

Spoke
Responsible for own risk and ALM management within the margins of policies set by the group

Spoke
Responsible for own risk and ALM management within the margins of policies set by the group

Culture and language

Growth goals

National legislation

Local market elements

Social security framework

Jurisdiction specific elements

Figure 9.7   Organisation of risk and capital management in insurance groups

less pronounced than for life insurance. The insurance penetration ranges from 0.8 per cent in Romania to 4.7 per cent in Luxembourg.

Table 9.6 illustrates the major business lines of non-life insurers. Motor insurance is the largest class of non-life business, but health and accident insurance are catching up. The strong increase of health insurance reflects the privatisation of the health-care sector in the Netherlands in 2006. Another

Table 9.5 Insurance penetration in the EU, 2005

	Number of insurers	Total premium income (in € billion)	Insurance penetration (in % of GDP)		
			Total	Life	Non-life
Austria	73	15.3	6.2	2.9	3.3
Belgium	171	33.8	11.3	8.4	2.9
Bulgaria	30	0.5	2.3	0.3	1.9
Cyprus	33	0.6	4.4	2.0	2.4
Czech Republic	45	3.9	3.9	1.5	2.4
Denmark	206	17.0	8.2	5.3	2.9
Estonia	12	0.3	2.7	0.7	2.0
Finland	67	14.3	9.1	7.2	1.9
France	486	175.9	10.3	7.1	3.2
Germany	663	158.0	7.1	3.2	3.8
Greece	95	3.9	2.2	1.1	1.1
Hungary	28	2.8	3.2	1.4	1.8
Ireland	226	13.6	8.4	6.0	2.4
Italy	239	109.8	7.7	5.2	2.6
Latvia	20	0.2	1.5	0.1	1.4
Lithuania	27	0.3	1.5	0.4	1.0
Luxembourg	95	11.2	38.1	33.4	4.7
Malta	25	0.3	6.5	3.0	3.5
Netherlands	300	47.3	9.4	4.9	4.5
Poland	74	7.7	3.2	1.6	1.6
Portugal	69	13.4	9.0	6.1	2.9
Romania	37	0.9	1.1	0.3	0.8
Slovakia	26	1.3	3.4	1.5	1.9
Slovenia	18	1.5	5.4	1.7	3.8
Spain	362	48.8	5.4	2.3	3.1
Sweden	415	22.5	7.8	5.2	2.6
United Kingdom	1,170	236.8	13.2	9.3	3.9
EU-15	4,637	921.6	9.0	5.6	3.3
NMS	375	20.3	3.1	1.3	1.8
EU-27	5,012	941.9	8.6	5.4	3.2

Notes: Insurance penetration is measured as premium as a percentage of GDP. EU-15, NMS, and EU-27 is calculated as a weighted average (weighted according to total premium income). *Source:* CEA (2007)

notable development is the doubling of premiums for general liability between 1995 and 2006.

In 2005, 5,000 insurance companies operated in the EU. Their number has declined since the creation of the European single market, due to mergers

Table 9.6 Non-life premium income in the EU (in € billion), 1995–2006

	1995	2000	2005	2006
Motor insurance	78.1	98.2	118.9	119.8
Health and accident	51.0	65.8	87.7	108.8
Property insurance	47.3	54.0	74.0	76.8
General liability	16.8	19.8	31.3	32.3
Marine, aviation, and transport	12.1	11.1	12.3	11.7
Legal expenses	3.7	4.1	5.7	6.3
Other non-life	14.9	15.8	22.7	24.7
Total non-life	224.1	268.5	352.9	380.7

Source: CEA (2007)

and acquisitions at both the national and the European level. Insurance companies aim for sufficient critical mass to be able to compete effectively at the European level.

The insurance market has a large number of small and medium-sized insurers with a very low market share and a small number of insurance groups with a high market share. The small insurers, with premium income below €10 million, are found in the non-life insurance sector in particular. Some 30 per cent of the smaller insurers are mutual companies (CEA, 2007). Large insurance groups have a premium income ranging from around €5 billion up to €100 billion. Table 9.7 shows the largest 25 insurers in Europe, amounting to over half of the premium income of the European insurance market.

Within the group of large insurance groups, Schoenmaker *et al.* (2008) define insurers as 'domestic' if they receive more than 50 per cent of their premiums in the home country. An example is the RBS Group in the UK. If 50 per cent or less of their premiums are collected in the home country and more than 25 per cent in other EU countries, the insurers are considered 'European'. Some European insurers focus on a specific region within Europe. Fortis, for example, primarily operates in Belgium and the Netherlands. Others, like Allianz, AXA, and Generali, operate Europe-wide. The remaining international insurers are 'global' insurers operating on a worldwide scale. This group includes ING and Aegon from the Netherlands, and Prudential from the UK.

Figure 9.8 shows that the number of European insurers fluctuates around eight between 2000–2006, while the number of global insurers remains small at three.

In order to operate successfully in a foreign market, an insurer needs to know the legislation (e.g., on liability), fiscal treatment, and accident statistics

Table 9.7 Biggest 25 insurance groups in Europe in 2006

Insurance groups	(1) Premium income[a] (in € billion)	(2) Total assets (in € billion)	(5) Premium income in home country (as % of (1))	(4) Premium income in rest of Europe (as % of (1))	(5) Premium income rest of world (as % of (1))
Global insurers[b]					
1. ING (Netherlands)	47	333.771	23	15	62
2. Aegon[e] (Netherlands)	25	314.813	18	31	51
3. Prudential (UK)	24	322.442	36	0	64
European insurers[c]					
1. Allianz (Germany)	91	1,053.226	35	46	20
2. AXA (France)	72	727.555	26	44	30
3. Generali (Italy)	63	377.641	38	58	5
4. Zurich Financial Services (Switzerland)	37	283.869	11	54	35
5. Old Mutual (UK)	21	191.474	20	28	52
6. Fortis (Belgium)	14	114.927	43	49	8
7. Swiss Life (Switzerland)	14	116.342	44	56	0
8. Royal & Sun Alliance (UK)	9	33.727	46	35	19
Domestic insurers[d]					
1. Aviva (UK)	50	435.923	51	38	11
2. CNP (France)	32	263.272	83	9	8
3. Crédit Agricole (France)	26	n.a.	90	5	5
4. Talanx (Germany)	19	92.926	53	26	21
5. HBOS (UK)	18	123.092	90	5	5
6. Ergo (Germany)	16	124.440	84	16	0
7. BNP Paribas (France)	16	97.164	51	30	19
8. Eureko (Netherlands)	14	86.448	89	11	0
9. Groupama (France)	14	84.998	83	16	1
10. Fondiaria-Sai (Italy)	10	41.223	99	1	0
11. RBS Group (UK)	9	18.837	79	6	15
12. Unipol (Italy)	9	41.650	95	3	2
13. Lloyds TSB (UK)	7	269.921	90	5	5
14. Legal & General (UK)	6	324.445	86	8	6

Notes:
[a] Top 25 insurance groups are selected on the basis of gross written premium in 2006.
[b] Global insurers: less than 50 per cent of premium in the home country and less than 25 per cent in the rest of Europe.
[c] European insurers: less than 50 per cent of premium in the home country and more than 25 per cent in the rest of Europe.
[d] Domestic insurers: more than 50 per cent of premium in the home country.
[e] Since more than half of its activities are consistently collected in the rest of the world, Aegon is marked as a global insurance group.
n.a. means not available.
Source: Schoenmaker *et al.* (2008)

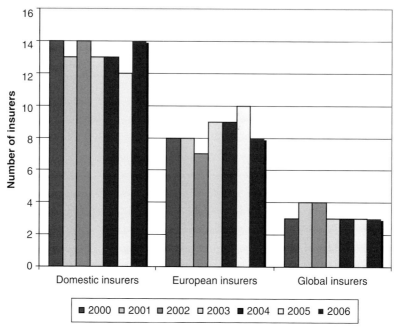

Figure 9.8   Biggest 25 insurers in Europe, 2000–2006
Note: See Table 9.7 for definitions.
Source: Schoenmaker *et al.* (2008)

(e.g., the number of car accidents) of that country. As these differ across EU countries, a major effort is required before entry of a foreign market. Cross-border insurance is therefore typically done by large insurance groups. The preferred method of entering a foreign market is through a subsidiary, usually by the acquisition of a local insurer. Figure 9.9 illustrates the cross-border penetration of the top 25 insurers in Europe. The cross-border penetration rose from 30 per cent to 32 per cent between 2000 and 2006. The corresponding figure for the largest 30 banks in Europe was an increase from 20 per cent to 23 per cent (see chapter 7). Large insurance groups are thus more internationally oriented than their counterparts in banking.

Market structure and performance

Between 1994 and 2005 the total number of insurers in the EU decreased from 5,201 to 5,012 (see Table 9.8). This consolidation mainly reflects mergers or acquisitions of small and medium-sized domestic insurers. At the same time, some of the large insurers expanded domestically as well as cross-border.

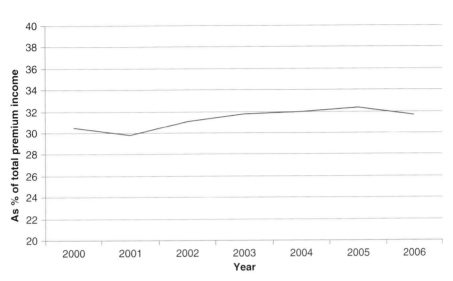

Figure 9.9   Cross-border penetration of top 25 EU insurers (%), 2000–2006
Note: Share of premium income from EU countries measured as a percentage of total premium income. The share is calculated for the top 25 insurance groups in Europe, which represent more than half of total premium income for the EU-27.
Source: Schoenmaker *et al.* (2008)

There are different types of insurance companies. The main model is the limited-liability (or joint-stock) insurance company owned by shareholders, whose liability for losses is restricted to the share capital. The model of mutual insurer, owned by the policy holders, still counts for about 20 per cent of the European market (ACME, 2003). The significance of mutuals is large in some markets, such as France and Germany (about 30 per cent), and small in other markets, like the United Kingdom (about 10 per cent). There is a trend towards 'demutualisation', meaning that mutuals are converted into limited-liability insurance companies.

Again, there are substantial differences between the EU-15 and the NMS. First, the number of insurers in the EU-15 is substantially higher than in the NMS. This is largely due to the significant number of small insurers in countries like France, Germany, and in particular the United Kingdom.

Second, the trend in the number of insurers is different. On average, the number of insurers in the EU-15 declined by about 5 per cent over the 1994–2005 period, while in the NMS the corresponding figure increased by nearly 15 per cent. The change in the number of insurers influences the degree of concentration in the different national insurance markets. Table 9.8 presents the CR5 ratio, which measures the market share of the top five insurers

Table 9.8 Market structure indicators, 1994/95 and 2005

	Size		CR5 (in %)[a]				Competition
	Number of insurers		Life		Non-life		Combined ratio[b]
	1994	2005	1995	2005	1995	2005	2005
Austria	74	73	46.0	59.4	53.6	75.2	77
Belgium	252	171	64.4	78.1	52.1	61.6	99
Bulgaria	30	30	n.a.	81.1	n.a.	68.4	n.a.
Cyprus	46	33	88.6	85.5	35.8	49.4	114
Czech Republic	27	45	96.9	73.5	93.1	85.1	88
Denmark	250	206	56.8	60.1	62.8	69.0	106
Estonia	15	12	99.9	100.0	64.5	96.6	87
Finland	57	67	99.4	89.1	87.7	91.5	102
France	577	486	50.0	55.6	40.8	51.7	99
Germany	742	663	30.7	45.3	23.1	38.0	91
Greece	149	95	67.8	67.8	38.7	37.2	n.a.
Hungary	13	28	92.5	85.5	95.5	81.5	90
Ireland	122	226	61.3	71.8	50.1	64.0	84
Italy	265	239	45.0	61.8	34.1	67.9	95
Latvia	42	20	n.a.	100.0	n.a.	71.8	99
Lithuania	35	27	n.a.	90.1	n.a.	79.2	103
Luxembourg	76	95	67.1	n.a.	82.0	n.a.	102
Malta	24	25	n.a.	100.0	n.a.	74.9	76
Netherlands	492	300	68.0	73.0	35.0	52.8	93
Poland	34	74	99.5	73.3	90.0	76.7	91
Portugal	87	69	59.4	83.3	52.7	67.8	97
Romania	39	37	n.a.	n.a.	n.a.	n.a.	n.a.
Slovakia	11	26	98.2	72.8	97.7	89.7	72
Slovenia	10	18	90.0	82.7	94.8	96.1	102
Spain	417	362	29.4	39.0	20.4	40.2	91
Sweden	494	415	73.8	67.2	77.4	86.6	103
United Kingdom	821	1,170	29.4	43.1	27.2	51.8	n.a.
EU-15[c]	4,875	4,637	43.3	54.4	32.8	51.6	94
NMS[c]	326	375	96.1	76.4	90.5	81.9	91
EU-27[c]	5,201	5,012	43.6	54.7	33.6	52.5	94

Notes:

[a] CR5 is the share of the five largest life (non-life) insurers, measured as a percentage of total life (non-life) premium.

[b] Combined ratio is measured as claims and expenses in % of premium.

[c] EU-15, NMS, and EU-27 are calculated as a weighted average (weighted according to premium).

n.a. means not available.

Source: CEA (2007) and CEIOPS (2006)

in the insurance industry. The table illustrates that the insurance markets in the NMS are generally more concentrated than the markets in the EU-15. However, there is convergence. The concentration ratios in the EU-15 are increasing, while concentration in the NMS is decreasing.

Overall, life insurance markets are more concentrated than non-life markets. That can be explained by the nature of the product. Life-insurance companies carry closely related (savings) products dependent on life expectancy. By contrast, non-life insurance is an industry with very different business lines (see Table 9.6). Among non-life insurers, there are many mono-liners that underwrite one type of insurance only. These specialised insurers are by definition smaller than multi-liner insurers that combine different business lines.

Measurement of competition in the insurance industry is still underdeveloped. There are no adequate indices of insurance prices that would allow comparison. An alternative approach is to rely on indirect measures, such as profitability (European Commission, 2007). A common economic measure to assess the profitability of non-life insurers is the combined ratio (see section 9.1). However, the use of the combined ratio has two major drawbacks. First, when claims are more likely to arise in the future, the matching principle of accounting is not satisfied. Clients pay, for example, their premium for their insurance in year 1, while the payout on claims may arise only in year 2 or 3. Second, investment returns are not included in the combined ratio. This is an important source of income, as premiums are invested in financial assets that are held until claims are paid.

The combined ratios are reported in the last column of Table 9.8. The figures indicate that the non-life insurance industry is competitive in Europe with a combined ratio of 94 per cent (EU-27) yielding a margin of 6 per cent. The margin is slightly higher in the NMS with a margin of 9 per cent. At the country level, the picture is more diverse. The majority of EU Member States has a combined ratio between 90 per cent and 100 per cent. Some countries (Cyprus, Denmark, Finland, Lithuania, Luxembourg, Slovenia, and Sweden) have combined ratios above 100 per cent and make a loss. Finally, a group of countries (Austria, the Czech Republic, Estonia, Ireland, Malta, and Slovakia) have combined ratios between 70 per cent and 90 per cent. These ratios suggest a lack of competition, but the results should be interpreted with care and provide only an indication of lack of competition.

Insurance is sold through a variety of distribution channels. Only a minor share of insurance products is sold directly by employees of an insurance company. Insurance companies increasingly sell their products directly via the Internet channel, but that is not yet reflected in the data. Internet sales are expected to grow fast, particularly for simple non-life insurance products. Historically, insurance intermediaries in the form of brokers and agents play a dominant role. Brokers are fully independent, specialist insurance intermediaries. They are not tied to any specific insurance company. Insurance agents are typically less independent than insurance brokers. Agents can work exclusively for one insurance company, but may also offer competing products from a wide range of insurers. A final distribution channel is a network of banks or post offices, through which insurance products are sold.

Distribution channels vary significantly across European countries. The distribution of life insurance is mainly driven by bancassurance networks (banking combined with assurance), with the exception of the United Kingdom and Ireland where brokers dominate the distribution of life products (see Figure 9.10). Poland, Slovakia, and Slovenia also show a weaker role for banks. In non-life insurance, insurance products are principally distributed via agents in a large number of countries (Spain, France, Italy, Poland, Portugal, Slovakia, and Slovenia). The broker channel dominates in some other countries (the United Kingdom, Ireland, the Netherlands, and Belgium). The predominance of brokers and agents on almost every market finds its origin in the preference of the insured to benefit from proximity at the time of the contract and, above all, in the case of a claim. The insurance companies' employee channel is used more for non-life than for life products.

9.4 Financial conglomerates

Financial conglomerates combine banking and insurance activities. There are various arguments in favour of financial conglomerates: commercial integration, financial integration, and operational integration. First, commercial integration is related to cross-selling of multiple financial services to clients. The most important form of cross-selling is the provision of insurance services to the bank's customer base. This is called *bancassurance*. Cross-selling can also happen the other way round, when an insurer provides banking services to its clients. This is called *assurfinance*. Sharing of customer databases facilitates cross-selling. Cross-selling generates economies of scope through reduced client information and transaction costs and consequently higher prices and/or transaction volumes for the financial group (Schmid and Walter, 2006).

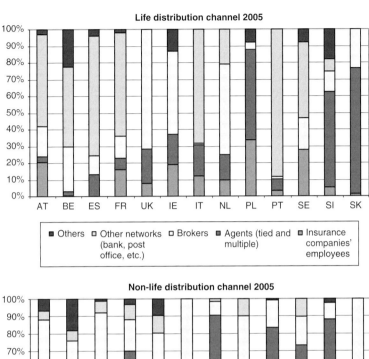

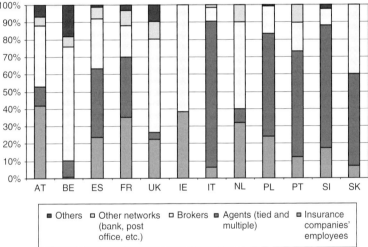

Figure 9.10   Distribution channels in Europe
Source: CEA (2007)

Second, financial integration is an important driver of financial conglomerates. There is scope for financial diversification as the risk profile of the insurance activities is different from the risk profile of banking activities. These differences in risk profile are analysed in sections 7.2 and 9.2. The question is how stable these diversification benefits are. Diversification is particularly useful in bad times. The normal distribution underestimates the downside risk, since the return series of financial assets have a fat-tailed distribution. Slijkerman *et al.* (2005) apply extreme value theory, which gives a much better description of the downside risk than the normal approximation. For a sample of European financial conglomerates, they find evidence for diversification benefits.

Third, operational integration can produce efficiencies in the back office. Operational integration generates economies of scope. Sharing of joint costs, such as IT platforms, across a diversified range of activities leads to higher levels of operating efficiency (Schmid and Walter, 2006). Another example is joint management of assets across the financial conglomerate.

There are also arguments against financial conglomerates. First, cross-subsidisation across business lines may lead to an inefficient allocation of capital and reduced performance. The profit in banking can be used for less-performing insurance activities, and vice versa. Second, opaque accounts may make it difficult to get a clear picture of the risk profile of financial conglomerates. As financial institutions report on a consolidated basis, it is difficult to detangle balance-sheet items as well as profit-and-loss items between banking and insurance business. This also gives scope for transfer of (risky) assets within a conglomerate (Schmid and Walter, 2006).

These arguments can be summarised under the heading of managerial complexity (Plantin and Rochet, 2007). A financial conglomerate is a portfolio of various business lines, which require different expertise and give rise to different risks. It is very demanding to manage such a diversified firm in a coherent way. The empirical literature finds a significant (both in statistical and economic terms) discount for non-financial conglomerates, i.e., the shares of conglomerates seem to be structurally undervalued. Although one would expect mixed financial conglomerates to be formed mainly to create added value generated by the combination of banking and insurance, this added value has thus far not been transferred to the shareholders. The main arguments for this conglomerate discount are managerial complexity and the lack of focus.

Most studies on financial conglomerates focus on the US. The US definition of a financial conglomerate is a financial institution that is active in at least two of the following areas: commercial banking (lending), investment banking (capital market transactions), insurance, and asset management. In practice, most financial conglomerates combine commercial and investment banking. Schmid and Walter (2006) and Laeven and Levine (2007) report a substantial and persistent conglomerate discount for US conglomerates. The market values of financial conglomerates that engage in multiple financial activities is about 10 per cent lower than those of comparable financial institutions that specialise in the individual activities.

Van Lelyveld and Knot (2008) focus specifically on the valuation of bank-insurance conglomerates. Using a dataset for 45 financial conglomerates, 45 banks, and 45 insurers, they compare the valuation of the three groups. Van Lelyveld and Knot (2008) do not find a structural diversification discount, but they observe considerable variability of the valuation. Large financial conglomerates face a larger discount, which is consistent with the hypothesis that larger conglomerates have more opportunities for inefficient cross-subsidisation.

On balance, the negative arguments present in financial conglomerates outweigh the positive elements. This is in line with recent market developments of large financial conglomerates. The Swiss bank, Credit Suisse, formed a financial conglomerate in 1997 with its acquisition of the insurer, Winterthur. However, in 2006, Credit Suisse sold Winterthur to the French insurer AXA. An example from the US is Citigroup, which grew out of a merger between Citicorp (banking) and Travelers (insurance) in 1998.

Box 9.5 Functional or geographical diversification?

Financial firms can pursue different diversification strategies. Functional diversification is the combination of different activities, such as banking and insurance. Swiss Re (2007b) indicates that Europe has the highest share of financial conglomerates. In particular, the combination of banking and life insurance accounts for more than half of the life-insurance market in Europe. In North America and Asia, the penetration of financial conglomerates is much lower than in Europe. This partly reflects the previously restrictive regulations on combining banking and insurance. In the US, the Gramm-Leach-Bliley Act of 1999 removed barriers between banks and insurance companies. The Japanese bancassurance market was fully liberalised only by the end of 2007.

Geographical diversification aims to spread the activities over different regions. Schoenmaker and Van Laecke (2006) show that geographical diversification of European banks exceeds that of American and Asian banks.

The two effects can be decomposed. Van Lelyveld and Knot (2008) do not find a structural discount for functional diversification, but they report that large financial conglomerates appear to trade at a discount. Functional diversification is thus predominantly value destroying for larger conglomerates. In contrast, Schmid and Walter (2006) report that geographically diversified financial firms trade at a small premium. Geographical diversification is thus value enhancing.

Table 9.9 Market share of financial conglomerates (%), 2001

	Market share of financial conglomerates (in %)		
	Share of bank deposits	Share of life premium income	Share of non-life premium income
Austria	0	0	0
Belgium	87	71	46
Denmark	24	15	37
Finland	57	61	37
France	42	20	4
Germany	14	30	29
Greece	0	11	0
Ireland	29	46	0
Italy	17	7	7
Luxembourg	17	5	0
Netherlands	31	37	22
Portugal	0	0	0
Spain	0	0	11
Sweden	18	0	0
United Kingdom	14	19	24
EU-15	27	27	19

Notes: Financial conglomerates are defined as financial services groups that have at least 10 per cent of their financial activities in each of the sectors of banking and insurance.
Source: European Commission

Citigroup has, however, divested most of its insurance underwriting business over the last few years.

Financial conglomeration is facilitated by the strong demand for long-term savings products. Growth opportunities in life-insurance and pension products lead to increasing orientation of banks towards these areas. Table 9.9 indicates that the market share of financial conglomerates in banking and life insurance amounts to 27 per cent in the EU-15. While banks have acquired a large share of the life-insurance market, where bank-distribution channels are effective, penetration in non-life is less pronounced. The market share of financial conglomerates in non-life insurance is only 19 per cent.

Turning to the country level, it appears that financial conglomerates are prominent players in Belgium, Finland, and the Netherlands, with market shares well over 30 per cent. In the southern countries of Europe, such as Italy, Greece, Portugal, and Spain, conglomerates are almost non-existent.

9.5 Conclusions

Insurance seeks to protect individuals and firms from adverse events through the pooling of risks. The business lines are very diverse. Non-life insurance includes car, property, and liability insurance, while life insurance provides cover for premature death or retirement. Insurance companies collect premiums today and make payments when adverse events happen in the future. Insurance is thus a risky business. Indeed, risk is the essence of an insurance company. This chapter has shown that the pattern of small claims, such as fire or car accidents, is fairly predictable. But larger accidents or catastrophes (like hurricanes) involve high claims with low probability. The risk of catastrophes is too big for one insurance company and is therefore divided among different insurance and re-insurance companies. Insurance companies tend to centralise risk management using internal risk-management models. Insurers and banks are converging with regard to risk-management systems and practices.

The insurance markets vary considerably across Europe. Life insurance is quite prominent in the EU-15 and can be considered a 'luxury' good. Non-life is more evenly spread across the EU and is regarded as a 'necessary' good. The figures indicate that the level of cross-border insurance has gradually increased. Insurance is sold through a variety of distribution channels. Only a minor share of insurance products is sold directly through the Internet or by employees of an insurance company. Insurance intermediaries such as brokers and agents play a dominant role, which however is expected to decrease for simple non-life insurances. A final distribution channel for insurance products is a network of banks or post offices.

Financial conglomerates combining banking and insurance have emerged in Europe. They cover about 25 per cent of the banking and insurance markets. An important driver of financial conglomerates is the cross-selling of insurance products to banking customers. Another driver is financial-diversification benefits as the risk profile of banking and insurance activities is quite different. However, this chapter also indicates that it may be difficult for managers to run a diversified firm with different business lines.

NOTES

1. Re-insurance is also used for other reasons. First, it can be used to increase an insurer's underwriting capacity. It enables the insurer to pass on part of the risk. Second, it can

be used to stabilise profits. It enables the insurer to level out the effects of poor loss performance.

2. To assess the overall risk profile of the insurance company, correlations across risk types should be taken into account, but incorporating diversification effects between risk types is still in the embryonic stage of development (Van Lelyveld, 2006).

3. In addition to interest-rate risk, bonds are subject to credit risk. The credit risk of government bonds issued by developed countries is typically very low, while the credit risk of corporate bonds is usually higher.

4. Luxembourg, with a penetration ratio of 33.4 per cent, is an outlier as it attracts life-insurance investments from other countries for tax reasons.

SUGGESTED READING

Dionne, G. (ed.) (2000), *Handbook of Insurance*, Kluwer, Dordrecht.

Drzik, J. (2005), At the Crossroads of Change: Risk and Capital Management in the Insurance Industry, *The Geneva Papers on Risk and Insurance – Issues and Practice*, 30, 72–87.

Mikosch, T. (2004), *Non-Life Insurance Mathematics: An Introduction with Stochastic Processes*, Springer-Verlag, Berlin.

Rees, R. (2008), Insurance and Re-insurance Companies, in: X. Freixas, P. Hartmann, and C. Mayer (eds.), *Handbook of European Financial Markets and Institutions*, Oxford University Press, Oxford, 414–435.

REFERENCES

Association des Assureurs Coopératifs et Mutualistes Européens (2003), *Valuing Mutuality II*, ACME, Brussels.

Comité Européen des Assurances (2007), European Insurance in Figures, CEA Statistics, No 31, CEA, Brussels.

Committee of European Insurance and Occupational Pensions Supervisors (2006), *Financial Conditions and Financial Stability in the European Insurance and Occupational Pension Fund Sector 2005–2006 (Risk Outlook)*, CEIOPS, Frankfurt am Main.

Dimson, E., P. Marsh, and M. Staunton (2002), *Triumph of the Optimists: 101 Years of Global Investment Returns*, Princeton University Press, Princeton.

Drzik, J. (2005), At the Crossroads of Change: Risk and Capital Management in the Insurance Industry, *The Geneva Papers on Risk and Insurance – Issues and Practice*, 30, 72–87.

Embrechts, P., C. Klüppelberg, and T. Mikosch (1997), *Modelling Extremal Events for Insurance and Finance*, Springer, Heidelberg.

European Commission (2007), *Business Insurance Sector Inquiry: Interim Report*, EC, Brussels.

Focarelli, D. and A. F. Pozzolo (2008), Cross-Border M&As in the Financial Sector: Is Banking Different from Insurance?, *Journal of Banking and Finance*, 32, 15–29.

Kessler, D. (2008), Insurance Market Mechanisms and Government Interventions, *Journal of Banking and Finance*, 32, 4–14.

Kohn, M. (2004), *Financial Institutions and Markets*, 2nd edition, Oxford University Press, Oxford.

Kuritzkes, A., T. Schuermann, and S. Weiner (2003), Risk Measurement, Risk Management, and Capital Adequacy in Financial Conglomerates, in: R. Herring and R. Litan (eds.), *Brookings-Wharton Papers on Financial Services: 2003*, Brookings Institution, Washington DC, 141–193.

Laeven, L. and R. Levine (2007), Is There a Diversification Discount in Financial Conglomerates?, *Journal of Financial Economics*, 85, 331–367.

Loubergé, H. (2000), Developments in Risk and Insurance Economics: The Past 25 Years, in G. Dionne (ed.), *Handbook of Insurance*, Kluwer, Dordrecht, 3–33.

Mikosch, T. (2004), *Non-Life Insurance Mathematics: An Introduction with Stochastic Processes*, Springer-Verlag, Berlin.

Niehaus, G. and A. Terry (1993), Evidence on the Time Series Properties of Insurance Premiums and Causes of the Underwriting Cycle, *Journal of Risk and Insurance*, 60, 466–479.

Oliver, Wyman and Company (2001), *Study on the Risk Profile and Capital Adequacy of Financial Conglomerates*, Oliver, Wyman and Company, London.

Plantin, G. and J.-C. Rochet (2007), *When Insurers Go Bust: An Economic Analysis of the Role and Design of Prudential Regulation*, Princeton University Press, Princeton.

Rejda, G. E. (2005), *Principles of Risk Management and Insurance*, 9th edition, Addison Wesley, Boston.

Rothschild, M. and J. Stiglitz (1976), Equilibrium in Competitive Insurance Markets: An Essay on the Economics of Imperfect Information, *Quarterly Journal of Economics*, 90, 629–649.

Schmid, M. M. and I. Walter (2006), Do Financial Conglomerates Create or Destroy Economic Value?, Working Paper 06–28, Stern School of Business, New York.

Schoenmaker, D. and C. van Laecke (2006), Current State of Cross-Border Banking, FMG Special Papers 168, London School of Economics, London.

Schoenmaker, D., S. Oosterloo, and O. Winkels (2008), The Emergence of Cross-Border Insurance Groups within Europe with Centralised Risk Management, *Geneva Papers on Risk and Insurance – Issues and Practice*, 33, 530–546.

Slijkerman, J. F., D. Schoenmaker, and C. G. de Vries (2005), Risk Diversification by European Financial Conglomerates, Discussion Paper TI2005-110/2, Tinbergen Institute, Amsterdam.

Spencer, P. D. (2000), *The Structure and Regulation of Financial Markets*, Oxford University Press, Oxford.

Swiss Re (1998), *Floods – An Insurable Risk? A Market Survey*, Swiss Re, Zurich.

Swiss Re (2007a), Natural Catastrophes and Man-Made Disasters in 2006: Low Insured Losses, *Sigma*, 2.

Swiss Re (2007b), Bancassurance: Emerging Trends, Opportunities and Challenges, *Sigma*, 5.

Van Lelyveld, I. (ed.) (2006), *Economic Capital Modelling: Concepts, Measurement and Implementation*, Risk Books, London.

Van Lelyveld, I. and K. Knot (2008), Do Financial Conglomerates Create or Destroy Value? Evidence from the EU, DNB Working Papers 174, De Nederlandsche Bank, Amsterdam.

Von Bomhard, N. (2005), Risk and Capital Management in Insurance Companies, *The Geneva Papers on Risk and Insurance – Issues and Practice*, 30, 52–59.

Part IV

Policies for the Financial Sector

10

Financial Regulation and Supervision

OVERVIEW

This chapter reviews the reasons for regulation and supervision of financial services. Regulation refers to the process of rule making and the legislation underlying the supervisory framework, while supervision refers to monitoring the behaviour of individual firms and enforcing legislation. The case for government intervention is based on market failures. A first market failure is rooted in asymmetric information: financial institutions are generally better informed than their customers. A second market failure is externalities: the failure of a financial institution may affect the stability of the financial system as a whole. A third market failure occurs when certain players in the market exert undue market power.

The chapter discusses financial supervision in more detail, distinguishing between prudential supervision and conduct-of-business supervision. Prudential supervision aims to protect consumers by ensuring the safety and soundness of financial institutions. As financial institutions are becoming more complex, supervisors are moving away from direct control to methods that provide incentives for financial institutions to behave prudently. Conduct-of-business supervision focuses on how financial institutions deal with their customers and how financial institutions behave in markets. For instance, information provisions aim to ensure that consumers get the right information about financial products. In addition, there are guidelines for objective and high-quality advice to protect the interests of customers. Conduct-of-business rules also promote fair and orderly markets.

This chapter also discusses the organisational structure of financial supervision, which is changing as most EU countries are moving from the traditional sector model (with separate banking, securities, and insurance supervisors) towards cross-sector models.

Finally, this chapter reviews the challenges for financial supervision in the EU. The newly emerging European financial landscape confronts the home and host authorities with complex coordination issues. It is therefore questionable whether national-based supervision is an adequate arrangement in an integrating market. The main proposals to establish a European supervisory structure are analysed.

 LEARNING OBJECTIVES

After you have studied this chapter, you should be able to:

- explain the main market failures in the financial system and the role of government intervention to remedy these failures
- understand the aims and instruments of prudential supervision
- understand the aims and instruments of conduct-of-business supervision
- describe the various supervisory structures
- assess the need for European financial supervision in an integrated financial market.

10.1 Rationale for government intervention

Market failure

This section reviews the reasons for regulation and supervision of financial services. Regulation refers to the process of rule making and the legislation underlying the supervisory framework, while supervision refers to monitoring the behaviour of individual firms and enforcing legislation. The case for government intervention is based on *market failures*. A market failure occurs when the private sector left to itself (i.e., without government intervention) would produce a sub-optimal outcome. Goodhart *et al.* (1998) identify three main reasons for government intervention in the financial sector:

1. *Asymmetric information*: customers are less informed than financial institutions. Financial supervision aims to protect customers against this information asymmetry. This chapter analyses how this can be done.
2. *Externalities*: the failure of a financial institution may affect the stability of the financial system. Systemic supervision aims to foster financial stability and to contain the effects of systemic failure. Chapter 11 discusses policies aimed at maintaining financial stability.
3. *Market power*: financial institutions or financial infrastructures, such as payment systems, may exert undue market power. Competition policy

aims to protect consumers against monopolistic exploitation. Chapter 12 examines this topic.

Asymmetric information arises in two cases. First, customers are generally unable to properly assess the safety and soundness of a financial institution as that requires extensive effort and technical knowledge. Establishing some sort of oversight may be needed, as financial institutions have an incentive to take too much risk. This is because high-risk investments generally bring in more revenues that accrue to the institution, while in case of failure a substantial part of the losses will be borne by the depositors. The information asymmetry creates problems of adverse selection (a riskier financial institution may make a more attractive offer to potential customers) as well as moral hazard (a financial institution may increase its risk after it has collected funds from customers). Prudential supervision aims to protect customers by ensuring the soundness of financial institutions. Moreover, governments provide direct protection to depositors through deposit insurance with a minimum cover of €20,000 (see chapter 2). However, a government safety net may provide banks with an even stronger incentive for risky behaviour. Prudential supervision is thus also needed to counter this incentive by ensuring the banks' soundness (Mishkin, 2000). Section 10.2 discusses prudential supervision in more detail.

Second, customers may not be in a position to assess properly the behaviour of a financial institution. This problem is common in professional services (Goodhart *et al.*, 1998). In most cases, private-sector mechanisms are used to mitigate this principal-agent problem. A disciplinary body of a privately run medical association can, for example, expel a member when it finds that this member has (repeatedly) failed to meet the minimum standards of the medical profession. Why, then, is government supervision of financial services needed? An important explanation draws on the fiduciary nature of financial services. A customer hands over his money today, while the service is rendered in the (sometimes far) future. For example, only after retirement does it become clear whether the advised pension savings scheme is appropriate to meet the financial needs of the retirees. Moreover, the amount of money at risk is typically larger in financial services than in other professional services. Conduct-of-business supervision focuses on how financial institutions conduct business with their customers and how they behave in markets. The focus is on the functions, regardless of the financial institution performing this function. Section 10.3 discusses conduct-of-business rules to mitigate the behaviour of financial institutions.

The second market failure that may give rise to government regulation is externalities. There is a risk that a sound financial institution may fail when another financial institution goes bankrupt (contagion). This externality is not incorporated in the decision making of the financial institution. The social costs of the failure of a financial institution thus exceed the private costs. In particular, banks are subject to contagion as their balance sheet contains illiquid assets financed by redeemable deposits. When rumours about the quality of a bank's assets spread, depositors may withdraw their deposits. The liquidity and subsequently the solvency of a bank will be threatened when it has to liquidate its assets at fire-sale prices (i.e., prices well below prices under normal market conditions). The failure of multiple banks may lead to a banking crisis. Systemic supervision aims to foster financial stability and to contain the effects of systemic failure. The task of maintaining financial stability is usually assigned to a country's central bank. Chapter 11 explains in more detail why the financial system (and especially the banking sector) is more susceptible to systemic risk than other economic sectors and discusses the role of the central bank to contain systemic risk.

The third market failure is related to market power. In a monopoly (only one firm) or an oligopoly (a few firms which may collude), firms can raise and maintain the price above the level that would prevail under (perfect) competition. The exercise of market power by firms is to the detriment of consumers who face higher prices and less choice of products or services. Lack of competition occurs in many economic sectors. In the financial sector, economies of scale (incentive for mergers) and network economies (e.g., in payment systems (see chapter 5) or stock exchanges (see chapter 3)) may reduce competition. Competition policy aims to ensure effective competition by taking a strong line against price fixing, market-sharing cartels, abuse of dominant market positions, and anti-competitive mergers. Chapter 12 explains the EU competition policy for the financial sector.

Government failure

Government failure is the public-sector analogy to market failure and occurs when government intervention causes a less efficient allocation of goods and resources than would occur without that intervention. There is thus a need to weigh problems of government failure against those due to market failure (Besley, 2007). There are various consequences of government intervention. First, government-induced protection may have a detrimental impact on incentives for consumers. Why should consumers be careful if they are protected against possible negative outcomes of their actions? Second, government regulation may lead to bureaucracy ('red tape') restricting the activities of financial institutions. Moreover, as supervisory agencies need information they generally have a more or less elaborate system of supervisory reporting in place which puts an administrative burden on the sector.

Some academics consider government failure to be a bigger problem than market failure. For instance, adherents of free banking challenge the justification for any form of government regulation of the financial system, arguing that there is nothing special about financial services that should make this sector an exception to the general rule of free trade (see, for instance, Dowd, 1996). A policy of *laissez-faire* for the financial sector is optimal as government intervention undermines the market forces that make the financial system safe. Other academics favour limited government intervention. For instance, Benston and Kaufman (1996) argue for some minimum prudential standards (in particular capital requirements) to counter externalities, but beyond these standards there is no special need for protection of customers.

In a drive for better regulation, the European Commission has embarked on a three-way programme to i) simplify existing legislation, ii) reduce the administrative burden of legislation, iii) conduct a cost–benefit analysis before proposing new rules. Similarly, national supervisors often apply principles of good regulation, reflecting their awareness of the possible negative consequences of overly regulating the financial sector. Box 10.1 illustrates how these principles are applied in the United Kingdom.

Box 10.1 Principles of good regulation

In pursuing its functions under the Financial Services and Markets Act, the Financial Services Authority (FSA) in the United Kingdom is required to have regard to the following 'principles of good regulation':

Efficiency and economy: the need to use the FSA's resources in the most efficient way. The non-executive committee of the FSA's board is required to oversee the allocation of resources and to report to the Treasury every year.

Role of management: a firm's senior management is responsible for its activities and for ensuring that its business complies with regulatory requirements. This principle is designed to guard against unnecessary intrusion by the FSA into firms' business and requires the FSA to hold senior management responsible for risk management and controls within firms.

Proportionality: the restrictions the FSA imposes on the industry must be proportionate to the benefits that are expected to result from those restrictions. In making judgements in this area, the FSA takes into account the costs to firms and consumers. One of the main techniques is cost–benefit analysis of proposed regulatory requirements.

Innovation: the desirability of facilitating innovation in connection with regulated activities. This involves, for example, allowing scope for different means of compliance so as not to unduly restrict market participants from launching new financial products and services.

International character: the FSA takes into account the international aspects of financial business and the competitive position of the UK. This involves co-operating with overseas regulators, both to agree upon international standards and to monitor global firms and markets effectively.

Competition: the need to minimise the adverse effects of regulation on competition. This covers avoiding unnecessary regulatory barriers to entry or business expansion. Competition and innovation considerations play a key role in the cost–benefit analysis work.

Source: Financial Services Authority

10.2 Prudential supervision

The current regulatory system in the EU is based on the principle of home-country control combined with minimum standards and mutual recognition. A financial institution is thus authorised and supervised in its home country and can expand throughout the EU by offering cross-border services in other EU Member States or establishing branches in these countries without additional supervision by host-country authorities (*home-country control*). The host country has to recognise supervision from the home-country authorities (*mutual recognition*), as minimum requirements for prudential supervision have been laid down in the respective EU Directives (*minimum standards*). However, financial institutions also operate through subsidiaries (separate legal entities) in other countries for reasons of taxation and limited liability (Dermine, 2006). These subsidiaries are separately licensed and supervised by the host-country authorities.

According to Lastra (2006), *prudential supervision* can be understood as a process with four stages:

1. Licensing, authorisation, or chartering of financial institutions (i.e., the entry into the business). The objective of this stage is to establish whether a person is fit and proper, i.e., before a person may obtain a licence, supervisors determine a person's integrity, honesty, reputation, and capability

to manage a financial services provider. In this respect, the Basel core principles for effective banking supervision state that 'the licensing process at a minimum should consist of an assessment of the ownership structure and governance of the bank and its wider group, including the fitness and propriety of Board Members and senior management, its strategic and operating plan, internal controls and risk management, and its projected financial condition, including its capital base' (BIS, 2006).

2. The on-going monitoring of the health of financial institutions and the financial system, in particular the asset quality, capital adequacy, liquidity, management, internal controls, and earnings. Supervision is exercised through a broad range of instruments, including off-site and on-site examinations (or inspections), auditing (internal unpublished audit and external published audits), analysis of statistical requirements, and internal controls. In case of distress in financial institutions, the supervisory authorities have to act. Box 10.2 discusses two different reactions to distress.

3. Sanctioning or imposition of penalties in case of non-compliance with the law, fraud, bad management, or other types of wrongdoing.

4. Crisis management, which comprises lender of last resort, deposit insurance, and insolvency proceedings (see chapter 11 for an in-depth discussion of crisis management).

According to the BIS (1997), banks face the following key risks (see chapter 7 for an in-depth discussion):

- *credit risk*: the risk of a loss because of the failure of a counter-party to perform according to a contractual arrangement, for instance due to a default by a borrower;
- *country risk*: the risks associated with the economic, social, and political environments of the borrower's home country;
- *market risk*: the risk due to unfavourable movements in market prices;
- *interest rate risk*: the risk related to unfavourable movements in interest rates. This risk impacts both the earnings of a bank and the economic value of its assets, liabilities, and off-balance sheet instruments;
- *liquidity risk*: this risk arises when a bank has insufficient liquid resources to meet a surge in liquidity demand. In extreme cases, insufficient liquidity can lead to the insolvency of a bank;
- *operational risk*: the risk of loss from inadequate or failed internal processes, people or systems, or from external events;[1]
- *legal risk*: risks stemming from inadequate or incorrect legal advice, changes in laws affecting the bank, new types of transactions, etc.;

Box 10.2 Forbearance versus prompt corrective action

Once a supervisory authority finds out that a financial institution is in distress there are two possible ways to react. The supervisor can intervene and resolve the distressed institution by requiring capital injections, the sale of assets, a merger with a sound institution, or liquidation once the regulatory capital ratio falls below a predetermined threshold. Alternatively, the supervisor can choose to allow the distressed financial institution to continue operation even though it is unable to meet the minimum regulatory requirements. The first response is generally called *prompt corrective action* (PCA), while the second type or response is referred to as *forbearance*. While PCA has been prescribed in the US in the 1991 Federal Deposit Insurance Corporation Improvement Act (FDICIA), in the EU Member States supervisory authorities may choose forbearance. Forbearance may dilute banks' incentives to behave prudently and induce undue liquidity support.

In view of the emergence of large cross-border banking groups, the European Shadow Financial Regulatory Committee (2005) advocates the implementation of a system of PCA as part of the supervisory process in each Member State. These procedures would reduce the likelihood of a sudden banking crisis and contribute to host-country supervisors' trust in home-country supervisors. While similar procedures are recommended, the thresholds and measures foreseen do not have to be identical in each Member State and for all banks.

Nieto and Wall (2007) identify three important aspects of the philosophy underlying PCA: (i) the primary focus of banking supervisory authorities should be on protecting the deposit-insurance fund and minimising government losses; (ii) banking supervisors should have a clear set of required actions to be taken as a bank becomes progressively more undercapitalised; and (iii) any undercapitalised bank should be closed before the economic value of its capital becomes negative. Moreover, the authors identify various institutional prerequisites for PCA: supervisory independence and accountability, adequate authority, accurate and timely information, and adequate resolution procedures. Nieto and Wall conclude that substantial changes are needed in the Member States' institutional frameworks before PCA could be adopted in the EU.

- *reputational risk*: this may arise from operational failures, failure to comply with relevant laws and regulations, or other sources. Reputational risk is particularly damaging as confidence is elementary in banking.

In order to cover the risks mentioned above, banks are required to hold a minimum level of own financial resources, i.e., *capital*. These capital requirements serve as a buffer against unexpected losses, thereby protecting depositors and the overall stability of the financial system. The challenge is to determine how much capital banks need to hold in order to ensure that they

Table 10.1 Structure of Basel II

Pillar I Minimum capital requirements	Pillar 2 Supervisory review	Pillar 3 Market discipline
Credit risk • Standardised approach; • Internal rating-based approach (foundation), and • Internal rating-based approach (advanced) *Operational risk* • Basic indicator approach; • Standardised approach, and • Advance measurement approach. *Market risk* • Value-at-Risk approach	*Economic capital* • Assessment of risk system by the supervisory authority	*Transparency* • Disclosure requirements as to amount and composition of capital relative to risk profile

Source: De Nederlandsche Bank (2003)

are sufficiently capitalised.[2] If capital levels are too low, banks may be unable to absorb potential losses but high capital levels are costly for banks.

Although it is up to banks to decide how much capital to hold, minimum requirements have been laid down by the regulatory authorities. The EU rules for supervising the capital levels are based on the Basel II framework established by the Basel Committee of Banking Supervisors. The objectives of Basel II include creating a better link between minimum regulatory capital and risk, enhancing market discipline, and supporting a level playing field in an increasingly integrated global financial system. The Basel II framework has a three-pillar structure, namely minimum capital requirements (Pillar 1), the process of supervisory review (Pillar 2), and market discipline (Pillar 3). While capital requirements used to be specified in detail by the regulatory authorities in the previous Basel Accord of 1988 (generally referred to as Basel I), the new Basel II framework allows banks to use their internal risk management models for the calculation of the required amount of capital. Basel II acknowledges that it is difficult for regulatory and supervisory authorities to identify and monitor all risks to which banks are exposed. It therefore intends to provide banks with an incentive to develop and maintain state-of-the-art models for their risk and capital management. Table 10.1 provides a stylised overview of the Basel II framework.

The first pillar covers the minimum capital requirements for credit risk, operational risk, and market risk. There are three methods for calculating the solvency requirements for credit risks depending on the sophistication of the internal risk-management systems of the respective bank:

- The standardised approach is the least complex method, which makes use of fixed risk weights, i.e., different categories of assets are assigned fixed risk weights. This approach is somewhat similar to the minimum capital requirements set out in Basel I. However, external credit ratings may be used so that capital requirements should more closely match the actual risk profile.
- Under the internal rating-based approach, banks may use their own internal rating methods to calculate credit risk. In the foundation version, a bank independently calculates the probability of default, while other factors are prescribed by the supervisor. In the advanced version, all factors which are used to determine credit risk are calculated by the bank itself.

One of the new features introduced by the Basel II framework is capital requirements for operational risk. Here, too, different approaches are allowed for calculating the risk. The basic indicator approach makes use of a single indicator for quantifying operational risk for the overall operations of the bank. The standardised approach, meanwhile, makes a distinction between the different business lines of the bank. Finally, the advance-measurement approach enables a bank to use internal and external data on operational losses to calculate the required level of capital. The preferred approach to measure market risk is the Value-at-Risk (VaR) method (see chapter 7).

Pillar 2 of the Basel II framework is the supervisory review. Pillar 2 requires each bank to develop its own internal process for assessing capital adequacy. To check the accuracy of the capital assessment, banks have to perform regular back-tests of realised outcomes against model estimates and stress tests of certain scenarios (e.g., a 10 per cent downturn of the stock market and/or a 2 per cent increase in interest rates). The supervisory review entails supervisory authorities examining the activities and risk profile of the bank in order to see whether there is a need for banks to hold additional capital (on top of the level of capital calculated under Pillar 1). Moreover, the supervisory review enables the supervisor to take account of risks which are not covered in Pillar 1, e.g., concentration risk, interest rate risk, legal risk, and liquidity risk. With respect to the latter, the Basel Committee will come forward with new initiatives to strengthen liquidity-risk management in banking groups (see Box 10.3).

The objective of Pillar 3 is to enhance market discipline by increasing the transparency of the amount and composition of a bank's capital relative to that bank's risk profile. According to the BIS (2001), Pillar 3 recognises that market discipline has the potential to reinforce minimum capital requirements (Pillar 1) and the supervisory review process (Pillar 2), thereby promoting the

---

> ## Box 10.3 Liquidity-risk management
>
> *Liquidity* is the ability to fund increases in assets and meet obligations as they come due (at reasonable cost). Liquidity risk management seeks to ensure a bank's ability to continue to do so. In 2000, the BIS laid down the following principles for the assessment of liquidity management in banks:
>
> - a bank should have a strategy for day-to-day management of liquidity;
> - a bank must have adequate systems for measuring, monitoring, controlling, and reporting liquidity risk;
> - a bank should perform stress tests for liquidity using a variety of "what if" scenarios;
> - a bank must periodically review the diversification of liabilities (i.e., different sources of funding) and its capacity to sell assets;
> - a bank should have contingency plans to handle a liquidity crisis, including procedures for making up cash-flow shortfalls in emergency situations;
> - supervisors should conduct an independent evaluation of a bank's management of liquidity.
>
> The sub-prime mortgage market crisis that started in mid-2007 has highlighted the importance of market liquidity to the banking sector. The contraction of liquidity in certain structured product markets (e.g., the market for collateralised debt obligations) and the inter-bank markets put a severe strain on the banks' ability to attract liquidity. Central banks intervened to provide large amounts of liquidity to the banking system. At the height of the crisis, the ECB injected €95 billion into the overnight money market.
>
> The BIS (2008) has drawn several lessons from this episode. First, banks should conduct stress tests not only for bank-specific shocks but also for system-wide shocks such as disruptions in the inter-bank market. Second, banks should strengthen their contingency funding plans and review the underlying assumptions. In particular, the assumptions about asset-market liquidity should be modified. Third, banks should incorporate the liquidity risk of off-balance-sheet activities and contingent commitments in their stress tests. The Basel Committee was planning to update and strengthen its principles for liquidity-risk management later in 2008.

safety and soundness of banks. It is argued that market discipline imposes strong incentives on banks to conduct their business in a safe, sound, and efficient manner, including an incentive to maintain a strong capital base.

In the EU, the Basel II framework was implemented as of 2008 by means of the Capital Requirements Directive (CRD, 2006/48/EC and 2006/49/EC). However, while the Basel II framework has been developed for large internationally active banks, the CRD is being applied to all banks as well as investment firms. Among other things, the CRD enhances the role of the 'consolidating supervisor', i.e., the supervisor in the Member State where the group's parent institution is authorised. This supervisor is responsible for group-level supervision of capital adequacy, concentration risk, and systems and controls. Moreover, the consolidating supervisor has specific responsibilities and powers in coordinating supervision of a cross-border banking group. In 2008, the European Commission (2008) came forward with proposals for further refinement of the CRD.

The European Commission has also proposed a somewhat similar system for the regulatory capital of insurance companies, the draft Solvency Directive (SEC/2007/840 and SEC/2007/841). This draft directive, nicknamed Solvency II, introduces more sophisticated solvency requirements for insurers, in order to guarantee that they have sufficient capital to withstand adverse events, such as floods, storms, or big car accidents. This will help to increase their financial soundness. Currently, EU solvency requirements cover insurance risks only, whereas in the future insurers would be required to hold capital also against market risk, credit risk, and operational risk. The Solvency II Directive draws on the experiences from banking and follows the three-pillar approach of the Capital Requirements Directive.

Critics of the Basel II framework argue that the Basel II framework has failed to address many of the shortcomings in the regulatory system and even creates potential new sources of risk. First, critics question whether the heavy reliance on credit rating agencies is sensible, as these are unregulated entities and it is difficult to assess the quality of their assessments. Conflict of interest may arise as there is a close (financial) relationship between crediting rating agencies and the entities under examination (see chapter 3).

Second, the pro-cyclical effects of Basel II have been criticised. Financial regulation is inherently pro-cyclical, because capital requirements imply that financial institutions have to hold more capital when credit risk increases, which is generally the case in an economic downturn. If financial institutions have to increase capital, they can lend less to firms and households, thereby stimulating the downswing. The reverse reasoning applies in case of economic upswing (see Box 10.4 for a further discussion on pro-cyclicality in bank lending). Danielsson *et al.* (2001) argue that the Basel II framework will exacerbate this tendency significantly. They argue that risk assessments, whether based on credit rating agencies' assessment or internal ratings, do not assess risk 'through the cycle'.

However, Taylor and Goodhart (2006) argue that the impact of regulation on pro-cyclicality depends on the time horizon over which banks assess risk.

Box 10.4 Pro-cyclicality in bank lending?

The business cycle determines the prospects for business. The default rate of companies is low during an economic boom, while the default rate is high during a recession. The business cycle is thus an important driver of credit risk.

The probability of default and the related recovery rate (i.e., the part of the loan that is recovered in case of default) are not constant in time. In expanding economies, default probabilities decline and recovery rates improve. This results in declining rates on loans due to declining risk premiums. As loan rates go down, further loans are granted, fuelling the economic expansion. This is an example of pro-cyclicality. The reverse process can also happen. Increasing loan rates (due to rising default probabilities) in a recession cause a decline in new loans.

There is also a second effect. Losses in the loan book lower a bank's profitability. A bank's capital is then reduced as profits are added to capital and, worse, losses are deducted from capital. At the same time, capital requirements for loans increase as the credit risk on loans goes up. If banks are capital-constrained, they cannot grant new loans. This process could end in a full-blown 'credit crunch', where banks are no longer able to provide business with new credit.

The Basel Committee has recognised the problem of pro-cyclicality. The solution is to take the default probability (and related recovery rate) as an average of the default probability through the economic cycle, rather than an estimate at one point in time. However, when default probabilities are estimated in this manner the systemic component of default risk might be ignored. So except for an 'average year', regulatory capital will not reflect the actual risk and may overstate the true risk in economic booms and understate risk in an economic downturn.

The cyclical bias also has a psychological component. Guttentag and Herring (1984) have introduced the concept of 'disaster myopia', which means that the subjective probability of a major shock is a negative function of the time since the last shock happened. A good example is air travel. Passengers' feeling of safety decreases after one or more reported airplane crashes, while the safety feeling increases after a prolonged period with no major crashes. Similarly, it is possible that subjective probabilities of default decline during an economic boom (no major defaults), while actual probabilities remain constant.

Point-in-time estimates of the probability of default are likely to be more pro-cyclical, as banks hold less capital or lend too much in economic booms and hold on to too much capital or do not lend enough in economic downturns. Through-the-cycle estimates of default risk (i.e., the average default risk over the cycle) may slow credit growth by building up capital in booms, which will be available to cushion losses and limit the contraction of credit in downturns.

According to Taylor and Goodhart (2006), supervisors should consider using the discretion provided by Pillar II to encourage banks to take a longer perspective in order to lessen the possible pro-cyclical effects of Basel II.

Finally, Slijkerman *et al.* (2005) point out that the Basel II framework does not take into account any diversification benefits, i.e., a reduction of risk as a result of the allocation of funds in multiple investments. They recommend exploring the properties for risk diversification by financial conglomerates in future work on capital requirements.

10.3 Conduct-of-business supervision

Conduct-of-business supervision focuses on how financial institutions conduct business with their customers and how they behave in markets, by prescribing rules about appropriate behaviour and monitoring behaviour that can be harmful to customers and to the functioning of markets. It is a relatively new activity, which became prominent after the liberalisation of financial markets. In the Big Bang in 1986, fixed commissions for trading at the London Stock Exchange were abolished. The Big Bang was the start of a process of liberalising financial markets across Europe. Liberalisation promotes entry of new players and may thereby lead to a wider choice of products and services (at lower prices). Conduct-of-business rules ensure a fair treatment of, in particular, retail customers in these liberalised markets.

The focus of conduct-of-business regulation is on the activities of financial institutions. The dividing lines between the sub-sectors of banking, insurance, and securities are blurring; the same type of product is increasingly offered by different financial institutions. Merton (1995) proposes a functional approach towards regulation to prevent regulatory arbitrage between different types of financial institutions. So, in his view the same conduct-of-business rules should apply to whoever (a bank, an insurer, or an investment firm) is offering, for example, long-term savings products to retail customers.

Protecting retail customers

Conduct-of-business rules protecting retail customers comprise the following elements (Llewellyn, 1999):[3]
- mandatory information provision;
- objective and high-quality advice;
- duty of care.

Mandatory information provisions ensure that customers get the right information at the right time. Selecting an inappropriate product can have adverse consequences for retail customers and an important safeguard against this is proper disclosure and sufficient information (*transparency*). Good information helps customers to understand the key features of a financial product, including the risks, potential returns, and costs. Mandatory information provisions specify the (minimum) information needed to understand products. These provisions also require financial institutions to present this information in a consistent format to compare products.

Developing customers' literacy in financial matters is becoming increasingly important, as individuals take many decisions affecting their financial security and capital markets have become more accessible to consumers. The European Commission (2007) reports that international surveys demonstrate a low level of understanding of financial matters on the part of customers. There is a strong correlation between low levels of financial literacy and the ability to make appropriate financial decisions. Customers with poor financial literacy find it hard to understand and make use of the information they receive when purchasing financial services.

Conduct-of-business rules can also give guidelines for the quality and objectivity of advice. Providing advice is distinct from providing information. Whilst information merely describes the (essential) characteristics of a product or service, *advice* implies a recommendation to a given customer to opt for a specific product. A financial institution must take steps to ensure that a recommendation is suitable for its customer. This can, for example, be done by making a customer's profile containing information about the customer's knowledge and experience relevant to the specific type of financial product, financial situation, and investment objectives. When advice is given, it should be objective, based on the profile of the customer, and commensurate with the complexity of the products and the risks involved. The requirement of objectivity aims to minimise potential conflicts of interests when financial institutions are better informed than customers. Customers in some countries rely on independent advice to make appropriate decisions.

More generally, financial institutions have a duty of care towards their customers. A *duty of care* is an obligation imposed on financial institutions requiring that they adhere to a reasonable standard of care while dealing with customers. It aims to enhance responsible behaviour of financial institutions. A financial institution breaches its duty of care when it sells, for example, a high-risk investment product to a customer who cannot afford to bear the financial risk (e.g., a low-income household with limited savings).

To sum up, on the one hand conduct-of-business rules require proper information provision (transparency) to (potential) customers. This should enable customers to take better decisions. On the other hand conduct-of-business rules set minimum standards for advice and introduce a duty of care for financial institutions. The challenge for policy makers is to find the right balance between empowering customers by providing information and education (fostering financial literacy) and protecting customers by setting minimum standards for financial institutions' behaviour.

Since conduct-of-business rules are relatively new, they are not (yet) applied to all financial activities at the level of the EU. So far, rules for consumer credit and mortgage credit have been largely left to the national authorities. There is an early Directive on Consumer Credit (87/102/EEC), which contains minimal common rules on consumer protection and permits Member States to add national rules. Proposals for further-going EU rules were being prepared at the time of writing.[4]

In the insurance markets, intermediaries play a vital role in selling insurance products. They also play a role in protecting the interests of insurance customers, primarily by offering them advice and assistance and by analysing their specific needs. At the same time, insurance intermediaries face incentives to sell products on which they earn a high commission, while these products are not always suitable for the customer. The Insurance Mediation Directive (2002/92/EC) contains rules to ensure a high level of professionalism and competence among insurance intermediaries whilst guaranteeing a high level of protection of customers' interests.

EU rules are most advanced in the field of securities. The Markets in Financial Instruments Directive (MiFID; 2004/39/EC), which replaced the Investment Services Directive (93/22/EEC), comprises a comprehensive set of operating conditions applicable to both banks and investment firms that regulates the relationship between these firms and their clients. This framework consists of a set of conduct-of-business, best-execution, and client-order-handling rules, as well as inducements and conflicts-of-interest provisions. Specific attention is paid to retail clients for whom a specific regime has been established, which entails reinforced fiduciary duties upon the firm.

Another set of EU rules in the investment-services field are contained in the Undertakings for Collective Investments in Transferable Securities Directive (UCITS; 2001/107/EC and 2001/108/EC). UCITS are a set of EU directives that allow collective-investment schemes to operate freely throughout the EU on the basis of a single authorisation. A collective-investment fund may apply

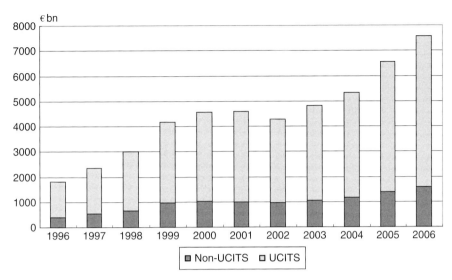

Figure 10.1   Assets of European investment funds (€ billion), 1996–2006
Source: EFAMA (2007)

for UCITS status in order to allow EU-wide marketing. Figure 10.1 illustrates that the vast majority of European investment funds is operating under a UCITS licence.

Market functioning

Conduct-of-business regulation promoting fair and orderly markets contain the following elements:

- transparency of trading;
- prohibition of insider trading and market manipulation;
- information requirements for issuers, including prospectus and financial reporting, and for shareholders.

Rules on the *transparency of trading* require disclosure of quotes, i.e., prices at which traders are prepared to sell or buy securities, and of prices at which trades have taken place. Potential investors can only analyse and compare trading conditions for securities when quotes (pre-trade transparency) are published. Post-trade transparency is also important to get timely insight into the movement of prices. The transparency requirements seek to achieve an adequate price-formation process, to ensure best execution and to provide for a level playing field between the different types of trade venue (see also Box 3.3).

Insider trading and market manipulation undermine the proper functioning and integrity of markets. *Insider-trading rules* put a ban on trading with inside information, i.e., material information on the firm that has not yet been made public. The use of this information by insiders, such as management or employees, may influence the price of the firm's securities. To speed up the release of new information (and thus reduce the potential for insider trading), insider-trading rules require listed firms to disclose inside information as soon as possible. It thus promotes transparency and equal treatment of investors. *Market-manipulation rules* prohibit the spread of rumours to influence (i.e., 'manipulate') the price of a security.

Firms that issue securities are required to publish information on a regular basis. First, firms have to publish a prospectus when they are issuing securities. A *prospectus* commonly provides investors with material information about the firm's business, financial statements, biographies of officers and directors, detailed information about their compensation, any litigation that is taking place, a list of material properties, and any other material information. Next, listed firms have to provide annual financial reports. In addition, half-yearly or quarterly financial reports may be required. The purpose of financial reporting is to ensure comparable, transparent, and reliable information about firms. Finally, shareholders have to disclose acquisitions (and disposals) of shareholdings beyond the 5 per cent threshold. In that way, firms can identify their major shareholders.

The conduct-of-business rules for markets are laid down in a raft of EU directives. The Markets in Financial Instruments Directive (MiFID; 2004/39/EC) contains inter alia rules on transparency of trading. MiFID expands trading from regulated markets (i.e., stock exchanges) to multi-trading facilities (MTFs), i.e., systems that bring together multiple parties (e.g., retail investors or other investment firms) that are interested in buying and selling financial instruments and enable them to do so. MiFID also facilitates in-house matching. Under certain conditions regarding pre-trade transparency and best execution, banks and investment firms are allowed to 'match' trades of customers internally. MiFID came into force on 1 November 2007 and is widely expected to have an impact on the structure of equity markets (see section 2.4).

The Market Abuse Directive (2003/6/EC) harmonises the rules for insider trading and for market abuse. It requires closer co-operation and a higher degree of exchange of information between national authorities, thus ensuring the same framework for enforcement throughout the EU and reducing potential inconsistencies, confusion, and loopholes. The Prospectus Directive

(2003/71/EC) requires that prospectuses provide investors with clear and comprehensive information. This directive makes it easier and cheaper for companies to raise capital throughout the EU on the basis of a single prospectus approved by a regulatory authority ('home supervisor') in one Member State.

Finally, the Transparency Directive (2004/109/EC) requires that all securities issuers must provide annual financial reports within four months of the end of the financial year. As for the contents of the financial reports, the EU has adopted the International Accounting Standards (IAS) – now referred to as International Financial Reporting Standards (IFRS) – through the IAS Regulation (1606/2002/EC). As explained in chapter 2, the IAS provides a single set of comparable global accounting standards issued by the International Accounting Standards Board (IASB).

10.4 Supervisory structures

The organisational structure of financial supervision is in the process of change in most EU Member States. All countries used to have a sectoral model of financial supervision with separate supervisors for banking, insurance, and securities reflecting the traditional dividing lines between financial sectors. However, as documented in chapter 9, financial conglomerates represent about 25 per cent of the banking market and the insurance market. Furthermore, financial products are converging. Banking as well as life-insurance products, for example, serve the market for long-term savings. Because of the blurring of the dividing lines between financial sectors, cross-sector models of supervision have emerged. There are two main cross-sector models of supervision: a functional (or 'twin peaks') model and an integrated model.

In the *functional model*, there are separate supervisors for each of the supervisory objectives: prudential supervision and conduct of business (see column (2) in Table 10.2). Referring to these two objectives, the functional model is also known as the 'twin-peaks' model (Taylor, 1995). In some countries, especially in the euro area where central banks have transferred their responsibility for monetary policy to the ECB, the central bank is responsible for prudential supervision. In other countries (e.g., Australia), a separate agency is responsible for prudential supervision.

In the *integrated model*, there is a single supervisor for banking, insurance, and securities combined (or, put differently, one supervisor for prudential supervision and conduct of business combined). There are two modes of the

Table 10.2 Organisational structure of financial supervision

Countries	(1) Sectoral	(2) Cross-sector: Functional	Basic models (3a) Cross-sector: Integrated without central bank role in banking supervision	(3b) Cross-sector: Integrated with central bank role in banking supervision
European Union	Bulgaria	France (2003)	Belgium (2004)	Austria (2002)
	Cyprus	Italy (1999)	Denmark (1988)	Czech Republic (2006)
	Finland	Netherlands (2002)	Estonia (2002)	Germany (2002)
	Greece	Portugal (2000)	Hungary (2000)	Ireland (2003)
	Lithuania		Latvia (2001)	Slovakia (2006)
	Luxembourg		Malta (2002)	
	Romania		Poland (2008)	
	Slovenia		Sweden (1991)	
	Spain		United Kingdom (1997)	
Outside EU		Australia (1998)	Japan (2000)	
		Canada (1987)		
		United States (1999)		

Note: In parentheses the year of establishment of the new cross-sector supervisor(s) is shown.
Source: Schoenmaker (2005) and ECB (2006)

integrated model. Scandinavia and the UK have adopted a fully integrated model without central bank involvement in financial supervision (see column (3a) in Table 10.2). In Germany and Austria, the central bank still has a role in banking supervision. The findings of the central bank are provided to the integrated supervisor, who has final authority (see column (3b) in Table 10.2). Box 10.5 provides an overview of country experiences with the various models.

The functional model combines the objectives of systemic supervision and prudential supervision, leaving conduct-of-business supervision as a separate function. The integrated model combines the objectives of prudential supervision and conduct-of-business supervision, leaving systemic supervision (financial stability) as a separate function that is usually performed by the central bank.

Kremers *et al.* (2003) have developed a framework to analyse the trade-offs by listing the synergies and conflicts of supervisory interests of both models. Figure 10.2 summarises these potential synergies and conflicts. The first synergy in the left panel of Figure 10.2 results from combining systemic supervision and prudential supervision of financial institutions. The synergy

---

Box 10.5 Country experiences

In 2002, the Netherlands adopted the functional model. In the Netherlands, the prudential and financial stability functions are delegated to the central bank, De Nederlandsche Bank (DNB). The Dutch model acknowledges the close linkage between systemic stability and prudential supervision of the larger financial institutions. A separate supervisor, Autoriteit Financiële Markten (AFM), is responsible for the conduct-of-business standards. In a similar way, France has merged its securities-market supervisors, Commission des Opérations de Bourse (COB) and Conseil des Marchés Financiers (CMF), into one agency, the Autorité des Marchés Financiers (AMF), while the prudential supervisors, the Commission Bancaire (CB) based at the Banque de France and the Autorité de Contrôle des Assurances et des Mutuelles (ACAM), are approaching each other. Italy has an objectives-based model of supervision, since the government changed the division of labour between CONSOB, the securities supervisor, and the Banca d'Italia (the Italian central bank) in 1999. In this new setting, CONSOB is responsible for transparency and proper conduct and the Banca d'Italia is responsible for prudential supervision of banks and securities firms as well as financial stability. The Banca d'Italia co-operates with the insurance supervisor, ISVAP.

The supervisory model in the US also has some features of the functional model (Padoa-Schioppa, 2003), although a sectoral orientation has been kept in place. The central bank is responsible for systemic stability and has extensive prudential supervisory responsibilities, while other agencies (notably the Securities and Exchange Commission (SEC)) are entrusted with the task of protecting the investor's interests. The overall supervisory landscape in the US is fragmented, with, for example, multiple supervisors for banks (the Federal Reserve, the Office of the Comptroller of the Currency, the Federal Deposit Insurance Corporation, as well as state banking supervisors). The US Treasury (2008) has issued a blueprint for a modernised financial regulatory structure, which proposes to consolidate the various supervisory agencies into a prudential financial regulator and a conduct-of-business regulator. Canada also applies the functional model, with a prudential supervisor (OSFI) at the federal level and securities supervisors at the state level.

The integrated model started in Scandinavia in the late 1980s and early 1990s, while in the United Kingdom the Financial Services Authority was established in 1997. The consolidation of financial supervision in the UK was a response to the scattered framework of nine different supervisors with overlapping responsibilities (including the Bank of England and the Building Societies Commission for banking supervision, the Securities and Investments Board (SIB) with its multiple self-regulatory organisations for securities and conduct-of-business supervision, and the Department of Trade and Industry for insurance supervision). The integrated model shares its cross-sector approach towards financial conglomerates with the functional model.

Germany also used to have a sectoral framework: the Bundesaufsichtsamt für das Kreditwesen (in conjunction with the Bundesbank) was responsible for banking supervision, the Bundesaufsichtsamt für das Versicherungswesen for insurance supervision, and the Bundesaufsichtsamt für den Wertpapierhandel for securities supervision. These three supervisory agencies were merged into one agency, the new Bundesanstalt für Finanzdienstleistungaufsicht (BaFin), in 2002. Similarly, a single supervisor, the Finanzmarktaufsichtbehörde, was established in Austria. In the German and Austrian versions of the integrated model, the central bank still has some involvement in banking supervision.

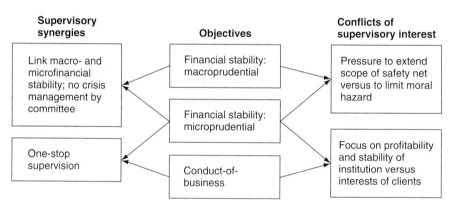

Figure 10.2   Supervisory synergies and conflicts
Source: Kremers *et al.* (2003)

between stability issues on a micro level (at the level of the financial institution) and a macro level (economy-wide) refers to the possibility to act decisively and swiftly in the event of a crisis situation. Crisis management usually requires key decisions to be taken within hours rather than days. Combining both micro- and macro-prudential supervision within a single institution ensures that relevant information is available at short notice and that a speedy decision to act can be taken if necessary.[5]

The second synergy in Figure 10.2 is 'one-stop supervision', i.e., the synergy between prudential supervision and conduct of business. This relates to the fact that it confronts all types of financial institutions with one supervisor only for prudential and conduct-of-business supervision. Furthermore, synergies in the execution of supervision are exploited by combining different supervisory activities within one institution.

The first potential conflict of interest between systemic supervision and prudential supervision relates to the possibility of lender-of-last-resort operations (LOLR) by the central bank. How to balance the pressure to extend the benefits of LOLR operations (avoiding systemic risk, like a financial panic or bank runs) to all financial institutions against its costs (moral hazard)? The answer adopted by many central banks is to limit the possibility of LOLR operations to banks, which are subject to systemic risk (see chapter 7). Then LOLR operations are not available to insurance companies. However, when financial groups integrate, it may become more difficult to separate the banking part of financial institutions that justify the possibility of LOLR operations.

The second potential conflict of interest between prudential supervision and conduct-of-business supervision relates to the different nature of their objectives. The prudential supervisor will be interested in the soundness of financial institutions including profitability, while the conduct-of-business supervisor will focus on the interests of clients. Mixing up both responsibilities of financial stability and conduct of business could lead to incentives for the supervisor to give prevalence to one objective over the other. By separating the supervisory functions, the conduct-of-business supervisor is ideally situated to supervise possible conflicts of interest between a financial institution and its clients, since it will focus only on the interests of the clients. Furthermore, the stability objective is consistent with preserving public confidence and may require discretion and confidentiality, which could be counter-productive to the transparency objective.

10.5 Challenges for financial supervision

The problem

A key element in the design of the institutional framework for financial supervision is the appropriate level of (de)centralisation. To date, national supervisory agencies in the EU Member States are in charge of the supervision of financial institutions. As explained in chapter 2, they co-ordinate their activities through European supervisory committees. The aim of these supervisory committees is to promote the convergence of supervisory standards and practices across the EU. While supervisors co-ordinate at the European level, they operate on the basis of a national mandate embedded in national legislation. This raises questions of efficiency and effectiveness.

The European Commission and the European Council have therefore presented a number of suggestions on how to strengthen the functioning of the European supervisory committees. The key objectives are to reinforce the political accountability of these committees, improve their internal decision-making procedures (by introducing qualified majority voting), and revise the national mandates of the supervisory authorities, to ensure that they are required to contribute to the regulatory convergence process at the EU level (FSC, 2008).

Schüler and Heinemann (2005) have calculated the cost of fragmentation of financial supervision in the EU-15. Their results indicate increasing economies of scale in supervision. Comparing a structure with 15 national supervisors with a cost-efficient European supervisory framework, they predict cost savings of some 15 per cent.

Another drawback of national-based supervision is the potential for conflicts of interest among national supervisors. While large cross-border financial institutions increasingly operate on an integrated basis, with key decisions taken at headquarters, supervisors are still examining the national parts of these institutions. The home supervisor as consolidated supervisor is coordinating the national supervisory efforts to minimise the potential for regulatory and supervisory arbitrage. The national supervisors also perform joint risk assessments of the large cross-border financial institutions, resulting in a joint supervision plan. But there are no legally binding mechanisms to deal with potential conflicts of national interest.[6]

An example of a potential conflict is the distribution of capital (or liquidity) in a financial services group. The host supervisor may request full capitalisation of the host subsidiary, while the home supervisor may request to maintain capital at the group level and to keep the capitalisation of subsidiaries at the minimum level. Supervisors may also have diverging views on how to remedy shortcomings of a financial institution. Supervisors can easily settle on a joint action when they agree. But when there are (lasting) differences, the various supervisors all have the legal power to take enforcement action under their national mandate and this may result in sub-optimal outcomes.

These co-ordination problems pose the question whether supervision should be done at the national level or the European level. The basic argument in favour of moving to a European structure is that it might be difficult to achieve simultaneously an integrated and a stable financial system, while preserving a high degree of national-based supervision and crisis management with only decentralised efforts at harmonisation (Thygesen, 2003). This is an application of the classical trilemma in monetary policy in which policy

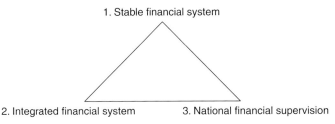

1. Stable financial system

2. Integrated financial system   3. National financial supervision

Figure 10.3   The trilemma in financial supervision

makers are confronted with three desirable, yet contradictory, objectives: fixed exchange rates, capital mobility, and independent monetary policy. Only two out of the three objectives are mutually consistent, leaving policy makers with the decision about which one they wish to give up: the 'trilemma'.

A similar trilemma occurs in financial supervision (Schoenmaker, 2005). Figure 10.3 illustrates the three incompatible objectives: (1) a stable financial system; (2) an integrated financial system; and (3) independent national financial supervision. An argument against moving to a European solution for financial supervision at the present time could be that the degree of financial integration does not yet justify such a move. However, as shown in previous chapters, many financial markets (in particular wholesale markets) are almost fully integrated. The infrastructures to support financial markets are also integrating, albeit at a slower pace. There is also evidence for increasing cross-border penetration of banks and insurers. Emerging pan-European financial institutions give rise to cross-border externalities arising from the (potential) failure of these institutions. The increasing presence of financial institutions from other EU countries undermines the capacity of host authorities to manage effectively the stability of their financial system (see chapter 11 for more details).

Policy options

Different proposals to establish a European structure of financial supervision have been put forward, as documented by Fonteyne and Van der Vossen (2007) and Schoenmaker and Oosterloo (2008). The three main policy options are:

1. Appoint a lead supervisor for the supervision of cross-border financial groups. In practice, this will mean that the home-country authority of a pan-European financial group is given full responsibility for the EU-wide operations, both branches and subsidiaries.

2. Establish a single EU supervisor either for all EU banks or merely for the large cross-border banking groups (i.e., a two-tier system).
3. Establish a European System of Financial Supervisors, in which a central agency works in tandem with national supervisors. The role of the central agency is to foster cooperation and consistency among members of the System, but could leave the day-to-day supervision of cross-border financial groups with the consolidating supervisor.

Lead supervisor

According to the European Financial Services Round Table (EFR, 2005, 2007), a clearly defined lead supervisor (usually the home supervisor) for prudential supervision of large cross-border financial institutions would be an important step towards a more coherent and efficient supervisory framework in the EU. The lead supervisor should in particular be the single point of contact for all reporting schemes, validate and authorise internal models, approve capital and liquidity allocation, approve cross-border set-up of specific functions, and decide about on-site inspections. Furthermore, the lead supervisor should be responsible for supervision not only on a consolidated level but also on the level of individual subsidiaries.

The EFR agrees that host countries should be involved in the supervisory process, as local supervisors generally have a better understanding of the local market conditions. The EFR suggests forming colleges of supervisors (one for each specific group) in which all supervisors involved share relevant group-wide and local information regarding the financial group in question. The lead supervisor, who is the home supervisor of the parent company, would chair the college of supervisors that would comprise, at a minimum, all supervisory agencies in whose jurisdictions the financial institution has sizeable operations. The lead supervisor would make intelligent use of the expertise and knowledge of the local supervisors in the college and entrust tasks to them by means of the delegation of tasks and, where appropriate, responsibilities. A mediation mechanism would be available if disagreements were to arise between the lead supervisor and other members of the college.

In comparison with the current situation, the efficiency of supervision is enhanced under this option as duplication is eliminated. Nevertheless, the lead supervisor does poorly with respect to financial stability, as its national mandate does not induce the lead supervisor to incorporate the cross-border externalities of a failure of a financial institution in its decision making.

Single supervisor

Some have argued that developments in the EU banking sector call for establishing a single pan-European supervisor (e.g. Schüler, 2002), which should assume full responsibility for the supervision of both branches and subsidiaries of all EU banks. There may indeed be merit in centralising day-to-day supervision and pooling of information, allowing for effective market surveillance of European-wide systemic risks. A major drawback of a central European supervisory authority could, however, be that the distance between the central authority and the supervised institutions may be too large – both physically and in terms of familiarity with local circumstances. Bank supervision may therefore be better executed at the local level, because of the availability of specific expertise of the local market. The EU Treaty nevertheless offers the possibility to centralise prudential tasks within the ECB, i.e., article 105.6 states that 'the Council may, acting unanimously on a proposal from the Commission and after consulting the ECB and after receiving the assent of the European Parliament, confer upon the ECB specific tasks concerning policies relating to the prudential supervision of credit institutions and other financial institutions with the exception of insurance undertakings.

Another option would be to set up a two-tier system, i.e., a system in which large cross-border banking groups are supervised by a central pan-European supervisory authority, while local banks are supervised by the existing national supervisory authorities. This option may, however, risk creating an un-level playing field in supervision between pan-European banks and banks operating at the national level, while both are competing on the same market. The potential problems with respect to the distance to the activities of the large cross-border banking groups may also be applicable to this option.

European System of Financial Supervisors

Vives (2001) and Schoenmaker and Oosterloo (2008) propose to establish a European System of Financial Supervisors (ESFS) with a European Financial Agency (EFA) at the centre of the system and national supervisors in the different countries. Such a system could be set up along the lines of the European System of Central Banks. A key issue is the appropriate level of (de)centralisation of the central agency. Supervision is primarily a micro policy as day-to-day supervision should be conducted close to supervised institutions. Nevertheless, there may be some merit in centralising policy making and pooling information, allowing effective market surveillance of European-wide systemic risks. The drawback of a central European supervisor could be that the distance between the central agency and the supervised

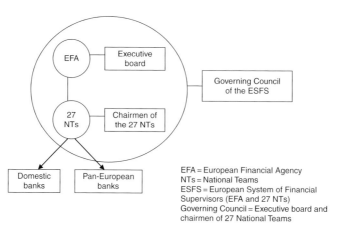

EFA = European Financial Agency
NTs = National Teams
ESFS = European System of Financial
Supervisors (EFA and 27 NTs)
Governing Council = Executive board and
chairmen of 27 National Teams

Figure 10.4   A decentralised European System of Financial Supervisors (ESFS)
Source: Schoenmaker and Oosterloo (2008)

institutions may be too large – physically and in terms of familiarity with local circumstances.

A decentralised ESFS could combine the advantages of a European framework with the expertise of local supervisory bodies. Figure 10.4 illustrates such a framework with an EFA at the centre working in tandem with the 27 decentralised national auxiliary branches. A crucial element of the proposal is that the ESFS operates under a European mandate. In this proposed system, small and medium-sized banks (as well as insurers) which are primarily nationally oriented are supervised by one of the 27 (teams of) national supervisors. Pan-European banks are supervised by the consolidating or lead supervisor (usually the supervisory team of the home country). This national supervisor will be the single point of contact for all reporting schemes (no reporting to the host authorities), validate and authorise internal models, approve capital and liquidity allocation, approve cross-border set-up of specific functions, and decide about on-site inspections. With respect to the latter, the lead supervisor can ask host authorities to perform on-site inspections on its behalf. The lead supervisor is compelled to inform host authorities about its activities and host authorities should have access to all reporting schemes (i.e., a common database of the ESFS). If a host authority feels the lead supervisor does not take account of its interests and no agreement can be reached, it can present its concerns to the EFA. If necessary, the EFA can overrule the lead supervisor and enforce the European mandate.

Crisis management is also done on a European basis. While the national team in the home country takes the lead during a crisis at an individual institution (gathering information, making an assessment of the situation), the ESFS is involved to ensure an adequate EU-wide solution. When a crisis hits more (large) financial institutions at the same time, the involvement of the EFA (in close co-operation with the European Central Bank) will be intensified.

Key supervisory decisions (for example, the assessment of potential cross-border mergers and acquisitions or crisis-management decisions) as well as the design of policy are done at the centre by the Governing Council consisting of the executive board of the EFA and the chairmen of the 27 National Teams (in the same way as the ESCB takes decisions on monetary policy). In this way, host-country authorities are fully involved and the interests of their depositors are fully taken into account (i.e., potential cross-border externalities are incorporated). Day-to-day supervision is conducted by one of the 27 national teams close to the financial firms. The EFA will be responsible for information pooling and is therefore best equipped to perform EU-wide peer-group analysis of large European financial groups.

The EFA is responsible for the correct and uniform application of supervisory rules (level playing field) and it can also act as a mediator in case of problems between home- and host-country authorities. In doing so, it may give instructions to the 27 national teams. This mediation role for the EFA could evolve from the mediation mechanisms which are currently set up for the European supervisory committees at level 3 (FSC, 2005). A drawback of a system with a central agency and 27 national teams is that decision-making structures can be complicated.

How to get there?

There are two comparable, but differing, possibilities to create a European system. The first is the revolutionary option. The role of DG Competition in competition-law enforcement started from scratch at the time of the creation of the European Coal and Steel Community (ECSC), because many Member States did not then have a competition authority. It is interesting to see that Member States have now established their own competition authority. This has led to the ex-post creation of the European Competition Network in 2004 to introduce decentralised elements of competition-law enforcement (see chapter 12).

The second is the evolutionary option. As all Member States had a fully functioning central bank at the time, the European System of Central Banks was created on top of the national central banks, even though Member States had to adjust their central bank laws to ensure full independence of their central bank as enshrined in the Maastricht Treaty. The ESCB was created in different stages. The Committee of EU Central Bank Governors (stage 1) was turned into the European Monetary Institute (EMI) to prepare the ground for a single monetary policy (stage 2). The EMI was subsequently turned into the ESCB, comprising the ECB and the national central banks of the Member States participating in the euro area (stage 3). In a similar vein, a European System of Financial Supervisors could evolve from the current European supervisory committees at level 3. The European Commission has clearly indicated favouring an evolutionary approach to supervision. The proposals to refine EU banking supervision are in line with this idea (see Box 10.6).

A final question is to choose the appropriate organisational structure of supervision at the European level. The current level 3 supervisory committees are set up along sectoral lines. The disappearance of sectoral boundaries would suggest that a cross-sector model (functional or integrated) is more suitable. Given the lack of a dominant model with a convincing track record, policy competition between the different models could facilitate the discovery of a 'superior' model (Fender and Von Hagen, 1998). Superior refers in this case to achieving the objectives of supervision: financial stability, prudential supervision, and conduct of business. In addition, market developments are key

---

Box 10.6 Evolutionary approach to refine EU banking supervision

In 2008, the European Commission proposed to amend the Capital Requirements Directive (CRD). Among other things, these proposed amendments aimed to:
- improve information rights of host supervisors of systemically relevant branches;
- reinforce supervisory cooperation and clarify supervisors' tasks and responsibilities;
- require supervisors to have regard to financial stability concerns in all Member States involved;
- clarify the legal framework for transmitting information to ministries of finance and central banks.

While not modifying the allocation of responsibilities between the home and the host supervisors, the suggested amendments aimed to reinforce the efficiency and effectiveness of supervision of cross-border banking groups by requiring (1) the establishment of colleges of supervisors, (2) agreement within colleges on key home/host issues, e.g., capital add-on on subsidiaries and reporting requirements, and (3) referrals to CEBS in case of disagreement within colleges. Colleges would also be required for supervisors overseeing cross-border structures that do not have subsidiaries in other Member States but that do have systemically important branches.

Source: European Commission (2008)

Box 10.7 A European SEC?

Lee (2005) analyses the factors influencing whether a European Securities and Exchange Commission will be created. While public policy is determined by the trinity of economics, law, and politics, Lee argues that political factors matter most.

First, there is a need for identical supervisory practices. A clear example is the oversight of international accounting standards. Under the IAS Regulation, European firms listed at a regulated market have to follow the same international accounting standards for financial reporting, as of January 2005. The oversight of these uniform standards is currently carried out by national supervisors, leaving scope for diverging supervisory practices. The political call for identical supervisory practices implies the need for a single supervisor.

Second, the possible future models for regulating EU securities markets require that some power is centralised at the EU level. An example is the creation of Euronext, combining the stock exchanges (cash and derivatives) of Paris, Amsterdam, Brussels, Lisbon, and the derivatives market of London (see chapter 3). The recent merger with the New York Stock Exchange reinforces the need for European supervisors to speak with one voice with their American counterpart, the SEC.

Third, a majority of policy makers in the EU view the notion of regulatory competition as intrinsically harmful to the authority of supervisors. In particular supervisors in continental Europe are concerned that competition between regulatory regimes may encourage the adoption of Anglo-American practices and cultures in securities markets.

Finally, Lee (2005) concludes that these factors will inevitably lead to the creation of a European SEC. He notes that the political support (e.g., in the European Parliament and France) for a European SEC is growing.

---

drivers for change in the organisational structure of supervision. Lee (2005) argues that developments in securities markets will inevitably lead to the creation of a European Securities and Exchange Commission, i.e., a pan-European supervisor similar to the US SEC (see Box 10.7).

10.6 Conclusions

This chapter has identified three market failures in financial services that justify government intervention. First, consumers may be less informed than financial institutions. Financial supervision (both prudential supervision and conduct-of-business supervision) addresses this problem of asymmetric information.

Second, the malfunctioning of a part of the financial system may have an adverse impact on the financial system as a whole. Systemic supervision aims to foster financial stability and to contain the effects of systemic failure. Third, certain players in the market may exert undue market power. Competition policy seeks to protect consumers against exploitation of market power.

Prudential supervision aims to protect consumers by ensuring the safety and soundness of financial institutions. As financial institutions are becoming more complex, supervisors are moving away from direct control to methods that provide incentives to financial institutions to behave prudently. The new Basel II capital-adequacy framework allows banks to use their internal models to manage the risks and to assess the minimum capital required as a buffer against these risks. Conduct-of-business supervision focuses on how financial institutions deal with their customers. Information provisions ensure that consumers get the right information about financial products. In addition, there are guidelines for objective and high-quality advice to protect the interests of customers. Conduct-of-business rules also promote fair and orderly markets.

The organisational structure of supervision is changing across the EU. Countries are increasingly moving from the traditional sectoral structure (with separate banking, insurance, and securities supervisors) to a functional model (with a prudential and a conduct-of-business supervisor) or an integrated model (with only one supervisor). The functional and integrated models can better cope with market developments, such as the development of complex financial products and the emergence of financial conglomerates.

Finally, the European financial landscape is integrating. So far, the response of national supervisory authorities has been to cooperate their efforts in EU-wide supervisory committees. But further consolidation of national supervisors at the European level may be needed in view of emerging cross-border financial institutions and markets. Three proposals have been discussed. The first is to appoint a lead supervisor for the supervision of cross-border financial groups. In practice, this means that the home country authority of a pan-European financial group is given full responsibility for the EU-wide operations, both branches and subsidiaries. The second option is to establish a central pan-European supervisory authority for all European banks or exclusively for large cross-border groups. The third is to establish a European System of Financial Supervisors, in which a central agency works in tandem with national supervisors. The role of the central agency is to foster cooperation and consistency among members of the system, but could leave the day-to-day supervision of cross-border financial groups with the consolidating supervisor.

NOTES

1. The €5 billion loss at Société Générale in 2007 due to the alleged fraud of a rogue trader is an exceptional example of the failure of internal controls in a bank.
2. While prudential supervision aims to minimise the risk of failure, it cannot eliminate the risk of a failing bank in a market economy.
3. The integrity and competence of financial institutions is not listed here as a specific conduct-of-business element. Fit and proper rules are general requirements that are applied in both prudential and conduct-of-business regulation. Section 10.2 explains these rules.
4. The European Parliament and the Ecofin adopted the Consumer Credit Directive in early 2008. The European Commission published a White Paper on the Integration of EU Mortgage Credit Markets (COM/2007/807).
5. The Northern Rock crisis in 2007 indicates that crisis management by two institutions may not be very effective. According to Buiter (2007), the coordination between the Bank of England and the FSA has been wanting.
6. The level 3 European supervisory committees are introducing a mediation mechanism (FSC, 2005).

SUGGESTED READING

Goodhart, C. A. E., P. Hartmann, D. T. Llewellyn, L. Rojas-Suarez, and S. Weisbrod (1998), *Financial Regulation: Why, How and Where Now?*, Routledge, London.

Mishkin, F. S. (2000), Prudential Supervision: Why is It Important and What are the Issues?, NBER Working Paper 7926.

Schoenmaker, D. and S. Oosterloo (2008), Financial Supervision in Europe: A Proposal for a New Architecture, in: L. Jonung, C. Walkner, and M. Watson (eds.), *Building the Financial Foundations of the Euro – Experiences and Challenges*, Routledge, London, 337–354.

REFERENCES

Bank for International Settlements (1997), *Core Principles for Effective Banking Supervision*, BIS, Basel.

Bank for International Settlements (2001), *Working Paper on Pillar 3 – Market Discipline*, BIS, Basel.

Bank for International Settlements (2006), *Core Principles for Effective Banking Supervision*, BIS, Basel.

Bank for International Settlements (2008), *Liquidity Risk: Management and Supervisory Challenges*, BIS, Basel.

Benston, G. J. and G. G. Kaufman (1996), The Appropriate Role of Bank Regulation, *The Economic Journal*, 106, 688–697.

Besley, T. (2007), The New Political Economy, *The Economic Journal*, 117, 570–587.

Buiter, W. (2007), Lessons from the 2007 Financial Crisis, CEPR Discussion Paper 6596.

Danielsson, J., P. Embrechts, C. Goodhart, C. Keating, F. Muennich, O. Renault, and H. Song Shin (2001), An Academic Response to Basel II, FMG Special Papers 130, London School of Economics, London.

De Nederlandsche Bank (2003), *Quarterly Bulletin*, September, DNB, Amsterdam.

Dermine, J. (2006), European Banking Integration: Don't Put the Cart before the Horse, *Financial Markets, Institutions & Instruments*, 15(2), 57–106.

Dowd, K. (1996), The Case for Financial Laissez-Faire, *The Economic Journal*, 106, 679–687.

European Central Bank (2006), *Recent Developments in Supervisory Structures in EU and Acceding Countries*, ECB, Frankfurt am Main.

European Commission (2007), *Green Paper on Retail Financial Services in the Single Market*, EC, Brussels.

European Commission (2008), *Public Consultation for Potential Refinements to the Capital Requirements Directive*, EC, Brussels.

European Financial Services Round Table (2005), *On the Lead Supervisor Model and the Future of Financial Supervision in the EU*, EFR, Brussels.

European Financial Services Round Table (2007), *Monitoring Progress in EU Prudential Supervision*, EFR, Brussels.

European Fund and Asset Management Association (2007), *Fact Book 2006*, EFAMA, Brussels.

ESFRC (2005), Reforming Banking Supervision in Europe, Statement No. 23, Frankfurt am Main.

Fender, I. and J. von Hagen (1998), Central Bank Policy in a More Perfect Financial System, *Open Economies Review*, 9, 493–531.

Financial Services Committee (2005), *Report on Financial Supervision* (Francq Report), FSC, Brussels.

Financial Services Committee (2008), *Report of the FSC on Long-Term Supervisory Issues* (Ter Haar Report), FSC, Brussels.

Fonteyne, W. and J.-W. Van der Vossen (2007), Financial Integration and Stability, in: J. Decressin, H. Faruqee, and W. Fonteyne (eds.), *Integrating Europe's Financial Markets*, IMF, Washington DC, 199–237.

Goodhart, C. A. E., P. Hartmann, D. T. Llewellyn, L. Rojas-Suarez, and S. Weisbrod (1998), *Financial Regulation: Why, How and Where Now?*, Routledge, London.

Guttentag, J. and R. Herring (1984), Credit Rationing and Financial Disorder, *Journal of Finance*, 39, 1359–1382.

Kremers, J. J. M., D. Schoenmaker, and P. J. Wierts (2003), Cross-Sector Supervision: Which Model?, in: R. Herring and R. Litan (eds.), *Brookings-Wharton Papers on Financial Services: 2003*, Brookings Institution, Washington DC, 225–243.

Lastra, R. M. (2006), *Legal Foundations of International Monetary Stability*, Oxford University Press, Oxford.

Lee, R. (2005), Politics and the Creation of a European SEC, FMG Special Paper 161, London School of Economics, London.

Llewellyn, D. (1999), The Economic Rationale for Financial Regulation, FSA Occasional Paper 1, Financial Services Authority, London.

Merton, R. C. (1995), Financial Innovation and the Management and Regulation of Financial Institutions, *Journal of Banking and Finance*, 19, 461–481.

Mishkin, F. S. (2000), Prudential Supervision: Why is It Important and What are the Issues?, NBER Working Paper 7926.

Nieto, M. J. and L. D. Wall (2007), Preconditions for a Successful Implementation of Supervisors' Prompt Corrective Action: Is There a Case for a Banking Standard in the EU?, Banco de España Working Paper 0702.

Padoa-Schioppa, T. (2003), Financial Supervision: Inside or Outside Central Banks?, in: J. J. M. Kremers, D. Schoenmaker, and P. J. Wierts (eds.), *Financial Supervision in Europe*, Edward Elgar, Cheltenham, 160–175.

Schoenmaker, D. (2005), Central Banks and Financial Authorities in Europe: What Prospects?, in: D. Masciandaro (ed.), *The Handbook of Central Banking and Financial Authorities in Europe*, Edward Elgar, Cheltenham, 398–456.

Schoenmaker, D. and S. Oosterloo (2008), Financial Supervision in Europe: A Proposal for a New Architecture, in: L. Jonung, C. Walkner, and M. Watson (eds.), *Building the Financial Foundations of the Euro – Experiences and Challenges*, Routledge, London, 337–354.

Schüler, M. (2002), The Threat of Systemic Risk in European Banking, *Quarterly Journal of Business and Economics*, 41, 145–165.

Schüler, M. and F. Heinemann (2005), The Costs of Supervisory Fragmentation in Europe, ZEW Discussion Paper, No. 05-01, Mannheim University, Mannheim.

Slijkerman, J. F., D. Schoenmaker, and C. G. De Vries (2005), Risk Diversification by European Financial Conglomerates, Tinbergen Institute Discussion Paper 2005-110/2.

Taylor, M. (1995), *Twin Peaks: A Regulatory Structure for the New Century*, Centre for the Study of Financial Innovation, London.

Taylor, A. D. and C. A. E. Goodhart (2006), Procyclicality and Volatility in the Financial System: The Implementation of Basel II and IAS39, in: S. Gerlach and P. Gruenwald (eds.), *Procyclicality of Financial Systems in Asia*, Palgrave Macmillan, Basingstoke, 9–37.

Thygesen, N. (2003), Comments on The Political Economy of Financial Harmonisation in Europe, in: J. J. M. Kremers, D. Schoenmaker, and P. J. Wierts (eds.), *Financial Supervision in Europe*, Edward Elgar, Cheltenham, 142–150.

US Treasury (2008), Blueprint for a Modernized Financial Regulatory Structure, Washington DC.

Vives, X. (2001), Restructuring Financial Regulation in the European Monetary Union, *Journal of Financial Services Research*, 19, 57–82.

11

Financial Stability

OVERVIEW

While prudential supervision aims at the proper management of individual financial institutions, maintaining financial stability is primarily concerned with systemic risks, i.e., events that will trigger a loss of economic value or confidence in, and attendant increases in uncertainty about, a substantial portion of the financial system that is serious enough to have significant adverse effects on the real economy. In addition to prevention, maintaining financial stability implies taking the necessary steps to restore financial stability after a crisis has occurred. Prudential and systemic concerns may overlap when large financial intermediaries face bankruptcy.

The policy objective of maintaining financial stability has gained importance in recent decades. The greater emphasis on financial stability is mainly related to the expansion and liberalisation of financial systems. First, financial systems have grown faster than the real economy. Given the size of the financial system and its importance to the real economy, a financial crisis can have substantial fiscal costs and output losses. Second, financial systems have become more complex in recent decades, and as a result it is much more difficult to assess financial risks and vulnerabilities. For example, as a result of financial innovation, banks (and other providers of credit) increasingly transfer the credit risk to other market parties. This has increased the opaqueness of the financial system, as was painfully exposed by the sub-prime mortgage crisis of 2007/2008. Third, as a result of the blurring of distinctions between different types of financial intermediaries (e.g., the emergence of financial conglomerates) as well as increasing cross-border integration, financial systems have become more interlinked. Especially in the EU, the emergence of large cross-border financial groups poses new challenges for policy makers.

This chapter explains why maintaining financial stability is a policy objective and who is in charge of this policy objective in the EU.

LEARNING OBJECTIVES

After you have studied this chapter, you should be able to:
- explain the concepts of financial stability and systemic risk
- explain why financial stability is a policy concern
- explain how financial stability can be maintained
- explain the challenges for policy makers in the EU as a consequence of financial integration.

11.1 Financial stability and systemic risk

There is no unambiguous definition of financial stability. To quote the former president of the ECB, Wim Duisenberg (2001): 'Monetary stability is defined as stability in the general level of prices, or as an absence of inflation or deflation. Financial stability does not have as easy or universally accepted a definition. Nevertheless, there seems to be a broad consensus that financial stability refers to the smooth functioning of the key elements that make up the financial system.'

There exist various theories on the causes of financial crises (see Table 11.1). Because of the lack of an unambiguous definition of financial stability, many analyses of financial crises follow an approach which is essentially empirical. Kindleberger (2000) presents a historical overview of financial crises and provides an autonomy of a typical financial crisis building on a model by Minsky. In the Kindleberger–Minsky model the events leading up to the crisis start with a 'displacement', some exogenous, outside shock to the macroeconomic system. Subsequently there are five stages to the boom and eventual bust:
- credit expansion, characterised by rising assets prices;
- euphoria, characterised by overtrading;
- distress, characterised by unexpected failures;
- discredit, characterised by liquidation; and
- panic, characterised by the desire for cash.

According to the Keynesian approach the determining factor for financial crises is insufficient aggregate demand. This school of thought stresses the importance of cyclical factors to financial (in)stability. Monetarists like Friedman and Schwartz (1963) explicitly link financial crises to *banking panics*, i.e. situations where the public loses confidence in the ability of

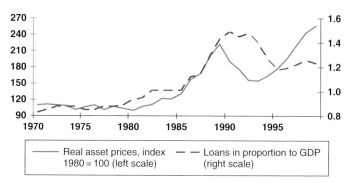

Figure 11.1   Real asset prices and total loans in proportion to GDP, Sweden, 1970–1999
Source: Bäckström (1999)

In all but the most highly concentrated financial systems, systemic risk is usually associated with a contagious loss of value or confidence that spreads throughout the financial system and leads to additional failures (*domino effects*). However, in highly concentrated financial systems the collapse of a single firm or market can be sufficient to create a systemic crisis;

- in the absence of an adequate policy response, a systemic shock induces undesirable effects to the real economy (e.g., substantial reductions in output and employment). A financial shock, no matter how large, that has no effect on the real economy is not a systemic event.

A good example of a systemic shock was the financial crisis in Sweden at the beginning of the 1990s. The deregulation of the Swedish credit and currency markets in the 1980s was followed by a rapid expansion of credit, strong price increases of assets, and eventually a bursting of the bubble (see Figure 11.1). As a result of the subsequent banking and exchange rate crisis, GDP fell for three consecutive years (from 1991 to 1993), by a total of 6 per cent, and unemployment shot up. This financial crisis was not confined to Sweden but hit other Nordic countries (see Box 11.1 for an overview of the Nordic banking crisis).

Shocks may propagate from one financial institution or market to another (*contagion*). There are two main channels of contagion (De Bandt and Hartmann, 2002). The first is the *real* or *exposure channel*, which refers to the 'domino effects' resulting from real exposures in the interbank markets and/or in payment systems. The second is the *information channel*, which relates to the contagious withdrawals when depositors are imperfectly informed about the type of shocks hitting banks and about their physical exposure to each other (*bank run*).

Box 11.1 The Nordic banking crisis

In the late 1970s, most developed countries initiated a period of deregulation of financial markets. In Finland, Norway, and Sweden the hasty deregulation process created incentives for financial institutions to take on too much risk (e.g., lending growth got out of hand and speculative assets were financed in a dangerous way), which made the financial system more vulnerable to shocks. An exception was Denmark, where financial stability was maintained because of a much smoother deregulation process and early interventions.

In Norway, the first half of the 1980s was characterised by a strong boom and large increases in the volume of credit. In 1985–1986, a drop in oil prices brought on a severe downturn spurred by tight economic policies. Problems soon spread to the banking system and a banking crisis occurred. During 1987 and 1992, losses in the banking sector amounted to NOK 76 billion. The three largest Norwegian commercial banks lost all their equity and were rescued by the government.

In the first half of the 1990s, Finland had the deepest crisis of the century. Increasing interest rates and the collapse of trade to the imploding Soviet Union turned a boom, fuelled by large increases in the volume of credit, into a recession. A banking crisis erupted and later also a currency crisis as the marka was allowed to float in 1992. Declining GDP and massive unemployment were the result of a debt-deflation spiral.

Sweden suffered from a crisis almost as severe as the Finnish one. The period between 1990 and 1994 was characterised by banking crisis, currency crisis, decreasing GDP, lower inflation rates, higher unemployment, and large budget deficits. Once again the government stepped in to reinstate the stability of the financial system.

Source: Jonung and Hagberg (2005).

Why is the financial system (and especially the banking sector) more susceptible to systemic risk than other economic sectors? There are three characteristics of financial systems that make them prone to systemic risk:

- The activities of banks, i.e., banks take deposits that can be withdrawn at a very short notice, while this money is lent long-term to other individuals and firms (see chapter 7). In normal situations, only a small portion of a bank's assets need to be held in liquid reserves in order to meet deposit withdrawals. However, in exceptional situations, when there are extremely high withdrawals and long-term loans cannot be liquidated, liquidity problems and even default may occur (even when the bank is solvent in the long run).
- Due to the interconnection of financial institutions and markets – through the interbank money market, the large-value (wholesale) payment and

security-settlement systems – problems can spread from one institution or market to others.

● The information intensity of financial contracts and related credibility problems may lead to sudden price swings. Financial prices are based on expectations of future cash flows. When uncertainty increases or the credibility of financial commitments is being questioned, market expectations can suddenly shift and, due to herding behaviour, lead to large asset-price fluctuations.

Relevance of financial crises

Banking crises are not a new phenomenon, but their frequency has increased during recent decades. According to Caprio and Klingebiel (2003), 117 systemic banking crises have occurred since the late 1970s. Moreover, 51 borderline and smaller (non-systemic) banking crises occurred during the same period. Well-known examples of systemic banking crises include the Nordic banking crisis of the early 1990s (see Box 11.1), the Japanese banking crisis of the 1990s, the Mexican Tequila crisis in 1995, the Asian crisis of 1997–1998, the Argentinian banking crisis of 2001–2002, and the sub-prime crisis of 2007/2008. Figure 11.2 gives an overview of the number of systemic crises in the period 1980–2002.

Since total financial assets often represent a multiple of GDP – especially in industrial countries – the cost of systemic banking crises can be substantial. Crockett (2005) argues that '[t]he direct losses to shareholders, creditors, uninsured depositors, insurance funds and employees would be enormous.

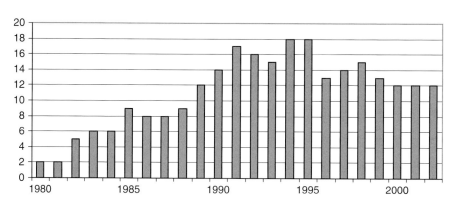

Figure 11.2   Number of systemic banking crises, 1980–2002
Note: The figure shows the number of crises that are in progress in the respective years.
Source: Caprio and Klingebiel (2003)

Table 11.2 Costs of banking crises, 1994–2003

	Number of banking crises (1994–2003)	Average crisis length (years)	Fiscal costs of banking resolution (% of GDP)	Average cumulative output losses (% of GDP)
All countries	30	3.7	18	17
Emerging market countries	23	3.3	20	14
Developed countries	7	4.6	12	24
Banking crises alone	11	3.3	5	6
Banking and currency crises	19	4.1	25	30

Source: Carstens *et al.* (2004)

But they would be only the tip of a very large iceberg'. This is because next to these direct losses, banking crises can lead to substantial fiscal costs, as the government can be forced to undertake a major and expensive restructuring of the banking system. Furthermore, banking crises can lead to a *credit crunch*, i.e., a situation in which it is nearly impossible for firms to borrow, as there are few lenders and/or the borrowing rates are (too) high. This can subsequently depress economic activity and even impair the ability of financial markets to channel savings to the most productive investments.

Table 11.2 shows estimates of the fiscal costs and output losses of 30 banking crises in the period 1994–2003. The average fiscal costs of banking resolution is 18 per cent of GDP, while the average cumulative output losses on average are nearly 17 per cent of GDP. Honohan and Klingebiel (2000) argue that some crises have led to much larger costs: governments in Argentina and Chile have spent as much as 40–55 per cent of GDP in the early 1980s crises. Most of the costs of the Asian banking crises (estimated at 20–55 per cent of GDP for the three worst-affected countries) will fall on the budget of the respective countries. The authorities in Japan spent more than 20 per cent of GDP on the restructuring of the Japanese banking system. As follows from Table 11.2, a combination of a banking and currency crisis has the most detrimental effect, i.e., the average fiscal costs are 25 per cent of GDP and average cumulative output losses are almost 30 per cent.

Financial crises have occurred throughout history (see Kindleberger (2000) for an in-depth discussion of the history of financial crises). The high number of financial crises that have occurred in recent decades have coincided with a period of structural changes in the global financial system. From the 1980s, financial liberalisation led to an accelerated expansion of cross-border financial activity, new interdependencies among market participants, markets, and financial systems, greater international mobility of capital, enhancement in efficiency in international markets, greater complexity of financial instruments and trading strategies, and faster adjustments of financial flows and asset prices (Schinasi, 2006). Although financial liberalisation has brought undisputable gains (such as cheaper sources of finance, new opportunities for risk sharing, and more efficient allocation of capital), it also makes it more challenging to maintain financial stability. Due to the growing complexity of the international financial system it is much more difficult to assess financial risks and vulnerabilities. As complex interdependencies arise, it becomes harder to assess the distribution of financial risks and financial disturbances can swiftly be transmitted from one party to another. The increased opaqueness of the financial system was painfully exposed by the sub-prime mortgage crisis of 2007/2008 (see Box 11.2). Rising defaults on sub-prime mortgages in the US triggered a global financial crisis as losses were transmitted partly via complex securitisation products to financial institutions around the world.

Box 11.2 Sub-prime mortgage crisis of 2007/2008

Sub-prime mortgages are housing loans to high-risk borrowers with a weak or a bad credit history who do not qualify for a conventional mortgage. Although these loans are relatively risky, sub-prime mortgages represented about 20 per cent of all newly issued mortgages in the US in 2005/2006. The mortgages were initially sold at bargain rates, but would be reset after some time (i.e., these contracts had a low or zero starting interest rate, which would rise significantly after a year or two). Due to the housing boom in the US – which began around 2001 – these mortgages could be refinanced before the interest rates were reset at market rates (thereby averting the high interest costs). However, when housing prices started to fall in 2006, many sub-prime owners could not refinance their mortgage and a significant number of them were unable to continue payments. This resulted in many defaults among sub-prime borrowers.

But why did financial institutions provide these mortgages? And how did problems in the US housing market lead to a global financial crisis? After the dot-com bubble of the 1990s, central banks – and especially the US Federal Reserve – aggressively cut interest rates to prevent a potential recession. This resulted in a situation in which inflation exceeded nominal interest (i.e., the real interest rate was negative), which caused the economy to expand and markets – especially the housing market – to boom. Because of the historically low interest rate and the benign global macroeconomic conditions, sub-prime loans became interesting as a relatively high interest rate could be charged while (at that time) the default rate was very low because of the housing boom.

There is one particular aspect of the sub-prime crisis that makes this crisis different from previous financial crises. As discussed in chapter 7, banks traditionally finance their mortgage loans through the deposits received from depositors and keep the mortgage loans (as well as the associated risks) on their balance sheet. In return, banks receive an upfront fee as well as interest income. However, in this case the providers of sub-prime loans (which were often unregulated US mortgage companies) bundled the mortgage loans and sold them to investors as mortgage-backed securities. As these mortgage providers were merely interested in receiving the upfront fee, they tried to sell as many mortgages as possible and there was no incentive to perform a proper credit check as the risks were transferred to third parties.

The process of packaging, pooling, and reselling the loans as securities is referred to as securitisation (see Box 7.1). New structured finance products (such as 'collateralised-debt obligations' (CDOs) and 'asset-backed securities' (ABS)) were created by combining different types or tranches of debt (each of them having a different maturity and risk). The securitisation process made it much easier to transfer (credit) risks and fund additional borrowing.

Before the CDOs were sold, they were rated by credit-rating agencies. However, the CRAs did not adequately assess the risks related to the sub-prime mortgages (see chapter 3). Moreover, there was poor investor due diligence as investors excessively relied on credit ratings without taking account of any other risks (apart from credit risk). The poor credit assessment by CRAs and over-reliance on credit ratings by investors clearly contributed to the build-up of the crisis.

But how were banking groups in the EU hit? Many EU banks established structured investment vehicles (SIVs), i.e., (unregulated) off-balance sheet entities, which borrow money by issuing short-term debt at low interest rates and lend money by buying long-term securities at a higher interest rate. These SIVs (as well as banking groups themselves) invested heavily in CDOs and as a result the risks related to the sub-prime loans spread around the globe. It should be stressed, however, that not only banks but also hedge funds, pension funds, and insurance companies invested in these financial instruments.

What was the actual trigger of the sub-prime crisis (i.e., why did housing prices decline)? As of 2004, the US Federal Reserve began to raise interest rates gradually from 1 per cent to 5.25 per cent in order to cool down the economy and keep inflation under control. As a result, it became more expensive to buy a house as mortgage rates started to rise substantially. This led to a slowdown in the housing market and eventually a housing-price crash. As the sub-prime mortgages were sold under the (false) assumption that housing prices would continue to increase, many sub-prime mortgages holders defaulted as they were unable to refinance their loans. This created a domino effect, as a result of which problems spread through the financial system.

Although the securitisation of the loans had allowed risks to be spread (evenly) across the financial system, it had also increased the opaqueness of financial markets. Due to the complexity of the financial instruments that were sold, it was unclear who was actually affected by these losses. Buiter (2007) illustrates this by arguing that by the time a hedge fund, owned by a French commercial bank, sells ABSs backed by US sub-prime residential mortgages to a conduit owned by a small German bank specialising in lending to small and medium-sized German firms, neither the buyer nor the seller of the ABS has any idea as to what is really backing the securities that are being traded. The uncertainty as to whom was exposed to these risks disturbed the functioning of many financial markets, including the interbank money market. Problems started to occur in the money market due to the damage done to two hedge funds affiliated with the US investment bank Bear Strearns. Increasingly, banks started to be reluctant to lend to each other (which resulted in a liquidity crisis). Increased risk aversion and de-leveraging amplified the initial shock. Central banks were forced to inject liquidity into the financial system to ensure that banks were not exposed to long periods of tight liquidity. Banks reported substantial losses as they had invested directly in CDOs or mortgage-backed securities or had contracts requiring them to support SIVs. Many firms were, however, unable to rapidly assess their exposures as their assets had become illiquid (since the underlying market had imploded).

In the summer of 2008 problems worsened and the US authorities were forced to bail out Bear Stearns and nationalise the US mortgage agencies Fannie Mae and Freddy Mac – the latter two accounted for nearly half of the outstanding mortgages in the US. Subsequent problems in the US investment bank Lehman Brothers forced the authorities to persuade rival institutions to take over the troubled firm. In the absence of a buyer, the government felt that an example had to be set to combat 'moral hazard', and decided to allow Lehman Brothers to fail. The subsequent fears over counterparty risk turned into panic and brought the global money markets close to breakdown. Central banks had to step in and eventually became vital suppliers in the money market. However, as they can only lend for short periods and against adequate collateral, not all financing problems could be addressed.

Both in the EU and the US, authorities were eventually forced to rescue financial institutions to prevent a systemic meltdown. The world's largest insurance company, American International Group (AIG), received an emergency loan in return for an 80 per cent public stake in the firm. The landscape of American finance was changed radically. The investment bank Merrill Lynch was bought by Bank of America. The two remaining free-standing investment banks, Goldman Sachs and Morgan Stanley, converted themselves into commercial banks. In a rescue deal backed by US authorities, Washington-Mutual and Wachovia were sold to JPMorgan Chase and Citigroup respectively. In Europe, Benelux authorities had to bail out Fortis. Eventually the Dutch activities of Fortis were nationalised by the Dutch government, while the other activities were sold to the French banking group PNB Paribas. The French, Belgian, and Luxembourg authorities also had to recapitalise the financial conglomerate Dexia. In the UK, the authorities were forced to take over the mortgages and loans of Bradford & Bingley, while its savings operations and branches were sold to the Spanish banking group Santander. Germany's Hypo Real Estate, a large commercial property lender, received a €50 billion secured-credit facility by a consortium of German banks and the government. The Icelandic authorities had to nationalise their entire banking system, leading to a near bankruptcy of the country itself.

In the absence of more widespread and permanent government support fears grew about the implications of the financial crisis on the real economy. After the US House of Representatives rejected a $700 billion rescue package, global stock markets crashed on Monday 29 September 2008. A few days later the US President was finally able to sign into law the rescue package which, among other things, authorised the Secretary of Treasury to establish a Troubled Asset Relief Programme (TARP) to purchase toxic assets from financial institutions. The passage of the rescue package did little to halt the widespread panic and on Monday 6 October stock markets witnessed their steepest fall in two decades. In Europe the response started off in a rather unco-ordinated fashion, with Member States putting forward different rescue plans and guarantees. However, on 12 October euro area leaders put forward a concerted and unprecedented action plan (based on the a rescue plan initiated by the UK authorities). This plan, endorsed by the European Council, aimed at: (i) ensuring appropriate liquidity conditions by central banks for financial institutions; (ii) facilitating the funding of banks by full government guarantees for new short- and medium-term debt; (iii) allowing for an efficient recapitalisation of distressed banks by governments; and (iv) ensuring sufficient flexibility in the implementation of accounting rules. In total, EU governments made €1,400 billion available for guaranteeing ST and MT funding and €200 billion for recapitalising banks (by taking equity stakes). While the initial US rescue package had a strong focus on buying up troubled assets, US authorities soon followed the EU approach and started to take equity stakes in financial institutions.

At the time of writing, the financial crisis was still ongoing. This financial crisis was the largest since the Great Depression of the 1930s and had its roots in a housing and credit bubble fuelled by lax monetary policy. The IMF reckoned that worldwide credit-related losses of banks would eventually reach $1.4 trillion. To give a complete overview of the crisis, the website accompanying this textbook provides an update of the events after mid-October 2008.

Since financial distress can seriously harm the economy, public authorities take great interest in maintaining financial stability. But can financial stability be regarded as a public good? A *public good* has the following two characteristics:

- the producer of the good is unable to control who benefits from consumption of the good (*non-excludability*); and
- consumption of the good by one consumer does not affect the potential benefits available for other consumers (*non-rivalrous consumption*).

Because of the private and social costs involved, it is in the interests of everyone to maintain financial stability. Financial stability is to the benefit of all individuals, i.e., financial stability is non-excludable. Moreover, the benefit to one person does not prevent others from benefiting as well, i.e., financial stability is non-rivalrous. This means that financial stability can be regarded as a public good and there is a role for public authorities to safeguard financial stability.

11.2 How can financial stability be maintained?

In order to maintain financial stability, public authorities should have a structure in place enabling them to (i) identify potential vulnerabilities at an early stage, (ii) take precautionary measures, which make it less likely that costly financial disturbances occur, and (iii) undertake actions to reduce the costs of disturbances and restore financial stability after a period of distress. Figure 11.3 shows such a framework.

The public authorities need to monitor and analyse all potential sources of risks and vulnerabilities, which requires systematic monitoring of individual

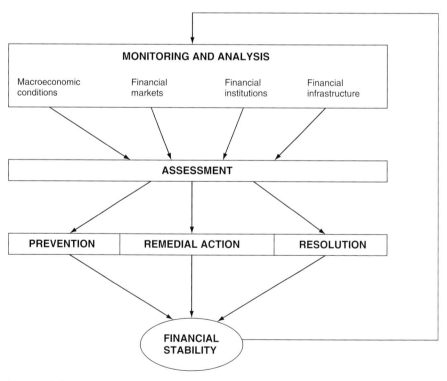

Figure 11.3 Framework for maintaining financial stability
Source: Houben *et al.* (2004)

parts of the financial system (financial markets, intermediaries, and infrastructure), the interplay between these individual elements, as well as the macro-economic conditions. To come up with a comprehensive view of the stability of the financial system, different steps have to be taken. First, the authorities assess the individual and collective robustness of the intermediaries, markets, and infrastructure that make up the financial system. For a long time, central banks had no standard framework to analyse financial stability. In an effort to improve the quality and comparability of data, the International Monetary Fund (IMF) has developed a set of Financial Soundness Indicators (FSIs) as a key tool for macro-prudential surveillance (see IMF, 2004).

The authorities need to identify the main sources of risk and vulnerability that could pose challenges for financial system stability in the future (see Table 11.3 for an overview of the potential sources of risk) and assess the ability of the financial system to cope with a crisis should these risks materialise. The overall assessment will make clear whether any (remedial) action is needed.

If the assessment does not suggest any immediate dangers, continued supervision, surveillance, and macroeconomic policies are key to preserving the stability of the financial system. In addition, communicating on these

Table 11.3 Potential sources of risk to financial stability

Endogenous	Exogenous
Institutions-based:	*Macroeconomic disturbances*:
Financial risks	Economic-environment risk
Operational risk	Policy imbalances
Legal/integrity risk	
Reputation risk	*Event risk*
Business strategy risk	Natural disaster
	Political events
Market-based:	Large business failure
Counterparty risk	
Asset-price misalignment	
Run on markets	
Contagion	
Infrastructure-based:	
Clearance, payment, and settlement-system risk	
Infrastructure fragilities	
Collapse of confidence leading to runs	
Domino effects	

Source: Houben *et al.* (2004)

issues is important. There are various ways of communicating to the public on financial stability policies. One such method is the publication of a Financial Stability Review (FSR). The purpose of publishing a FSR is to promote awareness in the financial industry and among the public of issues that are relevant for safeguarding the stability of the financial system. By providing an overview of the possible risks to and vulnerabilities of the financial system, the FSR can also play a role in preventing financial crises. In this respect, Svensson (2003, pp. 26–27) argues that publication of a FSR serves 'to assure the general public and economic agents that everything is well in the financial sector when this is the case. They also serve as early warnings for the agents concerned and for the financial-regulation authorities when problems show up at the horizon. Early action can then prevent any financial instability to materialize, keeping the probability of future financial stability very low'. The growing interest of central banks in monitoring and analysing risks and threats to the stability of the financial system has spurred the publication of FSRs. During the last decade, the number of central banks that publish a FSR increased rapidly from 1 in 1996 to over 40 in 2005 (see Figure 11.4).

If there are any indications of possible financial distress, it is up to the competent authorities to react properly. The public authorities can take informal action through correspondence and discussion with the affected institutions(s) to solve these problems. They can also use informal pressure to influence the behaviour of financial players. Generally, the public authorities might exert moral suasion in two different situations – first, when they want to influence expectations of the general public through external statements or

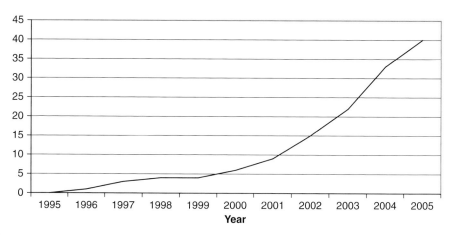

Figure 11.4   Number of central banks that publish a FSR, 1995–2005
Source: Oosterloo *et al.* (2007)

speeches, and second, when they attempt to persuade financial intermediaries to modify their behaviour in the interest of the sound development of markets. If moral suasion fails, other policy instruments, such as surveillance and supervision, need to be intensified in order to correct the situation at hand. The authorities might also strengthen the existing safety nets, in order to avert any risks related to bank and liquidity runs.

If a financial crisis occurs, one cannot pinpoint a single set of instruments that should be used. Generally, crises are never exactly alike and options differ as to which particular approach is 'best' for resolving them. Although there is no blueprint for crisis resolution, generally four reactive instruments can be considered:

  (i) private-sector solutions;
 (ii) liquidity-support measures;
(iii) public-intervention tools; and
 (iv) winding down.

Private-sector solutions

If a financial crisis occurs, authorities often try to involve the private sector as much as possible in its resolution. Two types of private-sector solutions can be distinguished:

- ad-hoc mechanisms, such as liquidity provision, a merger or acquisition (capital infusion), or other rescue operations, which may be considered in case of an emergency. These solutions can be promoted by the authorities acting as honest broker, especially given the time constraints under which most crises have to be solved and the potential information asymmetries that then exist;

- predetermined mechanisms aimed at preventing spill-over effects of financial crises. An example is the German Liquidity Consortium Bank (LIKO-bank), a semi-private institution that was founded in 1974 after the failure of the Herstatt Bank in order to bridge possible liquidity shortages of individual banks that are financially sound. However, as a 'lender of penultimate resort' the LIKO-bank may not lend to insolvent institutions.

If a private-sector solution is not immediately at hand, the public authorities can bridge the gap between failure and resolution by a third party (*bridge banking*).

Liquidity-support measures

According to Frydl and Quintyn (2000), liquidity support from the public authorities to troubled financial institutions starts long before the systemic nature of a banking crisis has been recognised. When a bank, or several banks, start experiencing substantial withdrawals from depositors and creditors, and they cannot borrow directly (or only at high rates) in the interbank market, the public authorities (usually the central bank) can become their Lender of Last Resort (LoLR). In principle, central banks should support only illiquid but still solvent banks. Yet during the early stages of an unfolding crisis, it is very difficult to distinguish illiquidity from insolvency. It often turns out that banks resorting to the central bank for liquidity support have been insolvent for a while, without this being known. In a crisis situation it is hardly possible to distinguish between illiquidity and insolvency. So, the LoLR interventions by the public authorities mostly involve high-risk loans, which eventually may lead to huge costs to the taxpayer. Apart from liquidity support to individual financial institutions, liquidity support can also be given to the market as a whole. Emergency assistance to the market is provided temporarily to relieve market pressure following an adverse exogenous shock (for example, the 9/11 terrorist attacks and the sub-prime mortgage crisis of 2007/2008). In Europe, this is typically a task of the ECB. But what would happen if a pan-European banking group should suddenly experience a liquidity shock? Decisions to provide emergency liquidity assistance are up to the national central banks in the respective countries where banking groups are licensed and operate. However, this national responsibility can lead to multiple co-ordination problems. Section 11.4 offers a discussion on the present ambiguity regarding the allocation of LoLR responsibilities in the EU.

Public-intervention tools

Once the true nature of a crisis has been identified and bank insolvency has been revealed as widespread, facilities such as deposit-insurance schemes may act as stabilisers to the financial system. There are two rationales for deposit insurance (MacDonald, 1996):

- consumer protection: deposit insurance protects depositors against the consequences of the failure of a bank. It is difficult for (potential) depositors to assess the financial health of banks. Only a small part of the information necessary to make an effective assessment of a bank is publicly available and even then the general public may have difficulties in interpreting such information;
- reducing the risk of a systemic crisis: without deposit insurance, uninformed depositors might remove their deposits from sound banks in reaction to problems at a single bank (bank run). In order to meet these withdrawals, banks have to liquidate their asset portfolio at a loss, and eventually might fail. If depositors know that their money is safe because of the insurance, they

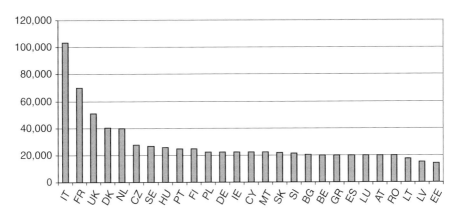

Figure 11.5   The level of coverage of deposit insurance in the EU (in €)
Source: European Commission (2007)

will have no reason to withdraw it. Deposit insurance can thus be seen as a preventative instrument as well. However, this requires a high coverage level (e.g., 100 per cent deposit guarantee) and rapid payout.

Although deposit insurance funds were originally aimed at preventing bank runs, in some countries these funds may also be used for restructuring of failing banks. It is, however, questionable whether this should be the objective of deposit insurance. Quite often countries have established limited deposit insurance funds (see Figure 11.5 for an overview of the level of coverage in the EU). For example, the EU Deposit Guarantee Directive required a minimum coverage rate of €20,000. Moreover, the home country scheme has to cover depositors of EU branches of banking groups. Experience has shown that limited deposit insurance schemes are inadequate to maintain or restore confidence during a (systemic) banking crisis. In order to prevent or stop bank runs, countries can resort to the announcement of full protection for depositors and creditors. However, such a blanket guarantee can come at great costs (as the liability is against assets of uncertain value). During the sub-prime mortgage crisis several Member States decided to provide full protection to their depositors. In order to harmonise EU practices, the European Commission subsequently tabled a proposal to revise the existing Directive, with the aim of (i) increasing the minimum coverage level first to €50,000 and within a further year to €100,000, (ii) substantially shortening the pay-out period (i.e., a maximum of three days), and (iii) abolishing co-insurance (i.e., the practice whereby the depositor bears part of the losses).

When the failure of a financial institution could create systemic problems, the government may decide to recapitalise (or even nationalise) the institution. This option is optimal if the costs of recapitalisation are lower than the social benefits of preserving financial stability. Recapitalisation may consist of a direct capital injection or the purchase of troubled assets. As the provision of solvency support puts taxpayers' money at risk, the decision to recapitalise is normally taken by the government and not by the central bank. Initially, the fiscal costs of nationalisation will be relatively high, but the government can try to sell the nationalised institution at a later date. Often a Banking Restructuring Agency (BRA) is established to restore the health of the banking system (see Box 11.3). In order to protect the BRA from political interference, Enoch *et al.* (2001) argue

---

Box 11.3 Resolving banking crises: experiences of the Nordic countries and Japan

The Nordic countries and Japan experienced severe banking crises in the 1990s. While there are many comparisons that can be made between the Nordic and Japanese banking crises, the approach that was taken to resolve these crises and the actual outcomes differed considerably. While the Nordic authorities reacted promptly, the response of the Japanese authorities was slow. As a result, the Nordic banking crisis was resolved relatively quickly, while the Japanese banking crisis continued for more than a decade. While the costs of the Nordic banking crisis amounted to a fiscal cost of 8 per cent of GDP, the Japanese authorities spent more than 20 per cent of GDP on the restructuring of their banking system.

There are a number of substantial differences between the approaches pursued in the Nordic countries and those pursued in Japan. First, the Banking Restructuring Agencies formed in the Nordic countries were much more aggressive in disposing of, and restructuring, troubled loans. Klingebiel (2000) reports that the percentages of assets transferred by the asset-management companies (or bank-restructuring agency) in Finland and Sweden were 64 and 86 per cent, respectively. In each case, the initial amount of assets transferred was about 8 per cent of GDP. Both restructuring agencies accomplished their loan disposals within five years of establishment.

Second, there was a significant contrast in the willingness to shrink the banking sector. Hoshi and Kashyap (2004) show that in Finland total domestic bank assets fell by 33 per cent between 1991 and 1995, while in Sweden domestic commercial bank assets dropped 11 per cent between 1991 and 1993. In contrast, total domestic bank assets in Japan fell less than 1 per cent between 1993 and 2003.

Third, when the downsizing and loan disposal occurred in the Nordic countries, the financial institutions were decisively recapitalised and management typically was changed. Such a firm line was absent in Japan. There was little public support for banks in Japan. This restricted the ability of the Japanese Ministry of Finance to recapitalise banks (Hoshi and Kashyap, 2004).

that the BRA should be functionally independent from the government and publicly accountable.

Winding down

When systemic risks are negligible, or when the costs of intervention are higher than the potential social benefits, the authorities will opt for the winding down of the troubled institution. However, the closure of a financial institution creates potential for disruption, especially to market functioning and liquidity. Therefore, the authorities should ensure that the winding down is managed in an orderly manner. One way to contain the negative effects is by liquidity support to other intermediaries. However, 'when financial distress has been broad-based or has involved systemically important institutions, liquidation has rarely been the preferred option' (OECD, 2002, p. 131). The expectation that large financial institutions are 'too big to fail' may give rise to moral hazard, i.e., the risk that once people know there is some sort of safety net or insurance they take greater risk than they would do without this protection.

11.3 The current organisational structure

Maintaining financial stability involves a number of different public authorities that share responsibilities, i.e., the central bank, the supervisory authority, and the Ministry of Finance.

According to Healey (2001), central banks are interested in the stability and health of the financial system because of their responsibility for monetary policy making. Often, but not always, this has resulted in the central bank supervising and, if necessary, regulating the banking system. For example, supervision issues in the Netherlands can rapidly take on systemic dimensions because of the presence of a few large and complex financial intermediaries. In such a situation, there are various advantages in making the central bank responsible for both banking supervision and financial stability, such as an easier and timelier exchange of information, especially necessary in crisis situations, and a closer co-ordination of the use of monetary and prudential instruments.

In other countries, such as the UK, a noticeable change in the institutional structure of maintaining financial stability in the last decade has been the move to consolidate financial supervision in a separate agency (see Table 11.4). As a consequence, different policy makers are responsible for prudential supervision and maintaining financial stability. While the central bank in

Table 11.4 Tasks of central banks in the EU

Country	Central bank responsible for financial stability?	Banking supervisor	Central banking model[1]	Central bank involved in management of banking supervisor?[2]	Shared staff and/or financial budget resources
Austria	Yes	Financial Market Authority	Intermediate	No	No
Belgium	Yes	Banking and Finance Commission	Narrow	Yes	Staff and budget
Bulgaria	Yes	Bulgarian Central Bank	Broad	–	–
Cyprus	Yes	Central Bank of Cyprus	Broad	–	–
Czech Republic	Yes	Czech National Bank	Broad	–	–
Denmark	Yes	Danish Financial Supervisory Authority	Narrow	No	No
Estonia	Yes	Estonian Financial Supervisory Authority	Narrow	Yes	No
Finland	Yes	Finnish Financial Supervisory Authority	Narrow	Yes	No
France	Yes	Banque de France / Commission Bancaire	Narrow	Yes	Staff and budget
Germany	Yes	Bundesanstalt für Finanzdienstleistungsaufsicht	Intermediate	No	No
Greece	Yes	Bank of Greece	Broad	–	–
Hungary	Yes	Hungarian Financial Supervisory Authority	Intermediate	No	No
Ireland	Yes	Central Bank of Ireland	Intermediate	No	Only staff
Italy	Yes	Banca d'Italia	Broad	–	–
Latvia	Yes	Financial and Capital Market Commission	Intermediate	Yes	Staff and budget
Lithuania	Yes	Bank of Lithuania	Broad	–	–
Luxembourg	Yes	Commission de Surveillance du Secteur Finance	Narrow	No	No
Malta	Yes	Malta Financial Services Authority	Narrow	No	No
Netherlands	Yes	De Nederlandsche Bank	Broad	–	–
Poland	Yes	Commission for Banking Supervision	Narrow	Yes	Staff and budget
Portugal	Yes	Banco de Portugal	Broad	–	–
Romania	Yes	National Bank of Romania	Broad	–	–
Slovakia	Yes	Slovak National Bank	Broad	–	–
Slovenia	Yes	Bank of Slovenia	Broad	–	–
Spain	Yes	Banco de España	Broad	–	–
Sweden	Yes	Swedish Financial Supervisory Authority	Narrow	Yes	No
United Kingdom	Yes	UK Financial Services Authority	Narrow	Yes	No

Source: Update and extension of Oosterloo and De Haan (2004) and ECB (2006b).

these countries focuses primarily on the systemic-risk aspects of the financial system, the authorities responsible for prudential supervision focus on supervising individual institutions' risks. In crisis situations, the different authorities need to congregate and coordinate their actions.

A distinction can be made between three basic models of central banking (Healey, 2001):

- the *narrow model* in which the central bank focuses on the stability of the financial system, including payment system oversight, payments processing, and emergency liquidity assistance. Under this model, the remaining financial stability functions are carried out by other government or private entities;
- an *intermediate model* in which the central bank has the core functions plus some role in crisis resolution and supervision of individual banks;
- a *broad model* in which the tasks of the central bank include the core functions plus various safety-net/crisis-resolution functions as well as the sole responsibility for the supervision of banks (and in particular cases also non-bank financial institutions).

As Table 11.4 shows, all three models are present in the EU. Note that even in the narrow model there can be a close relationship between the central bank and the supervisory authority as the central bank may be involved in the management of the supervisory authority or both institutions share staff and/or budgetary resources.

In addition to the central bank and the supervisory authority, the third party involved in the process of maintaining financial stability is the government, which is in most cases represented by the Ministry of Finance. Generally, the Minister of Finance has two responsibilities. He/she is (politically) responsible for the functioning of the financial system, which comes down to the responsibility for the overall structure of supervision and regulation and the allied legislation. Furthermore, the Minister of Finance is the guardian of the public purse and he/she will therefore take decisions on the use of public money in crisis resolution (Goodhart and Schoenmaker, 1995).

The ECB also has a responsibility for maintaining financial stability. In Article 105 of the Maastricht Treaty, the European Union assigned the ECB the task of contributing 'to the smooth conduct of policies pursued by the competent authorities relating to the prudential supervision of credit institutions and the stability of the financial system'. This task does not merely apply to the euro area but to the entire European Union, as most systemic banking groups operate on a pan-European scale. The ECB has three specific tasks in this field:

- it systematically monitors cyclical and structural developments in the EU banking sector and in other financial sectors. The purpose is to assess possible vulnerabilities in the financial sector, and its resilience to potential shocks. A tangible outcome is the publishing of the bi-annual FSR which discusses developments in the euro-area financial system;

- it contributes its technical expertise to financial supervision; and
- it promotes co-operation between central banks and supervisors authorities in the EU.

Although the EC Treaty leaves open the possibility of granting the ECB prudential supervisory tasks (see Article 105, subsection 6), the relevant national authorities are in charge in case of any disruptions in the financial system. The operational tasks of the ECB are currently confined to the provision of liquidity support to the market as a whole, e.g., in case of problems in the euro-area interbank market.

11.4 Challenges for maintaining financial stability

Cross-border externalities

Especially in Europe, an important challenge for maintaining financial stability arises from cross-border banking. Pan-European banks may create cross-border externalities in case of (potential) failure. There are at least 46 EU banking groups with significant cross-border activities, accounting for 68 per cent of overall consolidated EU banking assets (see also chapter 7). Until recently there were just a few regional cross-border retail banks, such as Nordea (see Table 11.5) and Fortis. Other cross-border operations focused on wholesale activities, often involving securities and derivatives operations in London.

Table 11.5 Nordea's market shares in the Nordic countries (%)

	Denmark	Finland	Norway	Sweden
Mortgage lending	17	32	12	16
Consumer lending	15	31	11	9
Personal deposits	22	33	8	18
Corporate lending	19	35	16	14
Corporate deposits	22	37	16	21
Investment funds	20	26	8	14
Life and pension	15	28	7	3
Brokerage	17	5	3	3

Source: Vesala (2006)

However, recently some retail mergers have taken place. Striking examples include Santander–Abbey National in 2004, UniCredit–HypoVereinsbank in 2005, and the takeover of ABN Amro in 2007 by a consortium of banks consisting of Fortis, Royal Bank of Scotland, and Banco Santander. Cross-border banking occurs across the EU and is not confined to the euro area (see Box 11.4). Financial intermediaries from the UK particularly are central players. Moreover, banks from other EU countries own most banking assets in the new EU Member States (see chapter 8).

The interaction of highly penetrated banking systems with national regulations and burden allocation might be a dangerously weak institutional feature (Goodhart, 2005). The reason is that national authorities have a mandate for maintaining financial stability in their own system and they may therefore be reluctant to help solve problems in other EU Member States, thus neglecting cross-border externalities caused by financial institutions under their jurisdiction. Current national-based arrangements may therefore undervalue externalities related to the cross-border business of financial institutions. To formalise this issue, two different models of recapitalising banks are examined: a single-country and a multi-country model.

Single-country model of bailout

Freixas (2003) presents a model of the costs and benefits of a bailout. The model considers the ex-post decision whether to recapitalise or to liquidate a bank in financial distress. The choice to continue or to close the bank is a variable x with values in the space $\{0, 1\}$. Moreover, θ denotes the social benefits of a recapitalisation and C its costs. The benefits of a recapitalisation include those derived from avoiding contagion and maintaining financial stability. The direct cost of continuing the bank activity is denoted by C_c and the cost of stopping its activities by C_s and the difference is $C = C_c - C_s$. The case $C < 0$ is obviously possible, but is a case where continuing the bank's operations are cheaper than closing it, so that continuation is preferred and the recapitalisation decision is simplified. In this situation, private-sector solutions are possible and the central bank can play the role of 'honest broker'.

The optimal decision for the authorities will be to maximise:

$$x^*(\theta - C)$$

so that x^*

$$\begin{cases} x^* = 1 \ if \ \theta - C > 0 \\ x^* = 0 \ if \ \theta - C < 0 \end{cases} \tag{11.1}$$

Box 11.4 Financial stability: a euro-area or a European Union concern?

Most authors agree that financial stability should be managed at the European level, but there is no agreement on the precise scope. Some argue that financial stability is primarily a concern for the euro area (Pisani-Ferry *et al.*, 2008), while others consider financial stability as an issue for the EU as a whole (Goodhart and Schoenmaker, 2009; Nieto and Schinasi, 2007).

There are three arguments for focusing on the euro area (Pisani-Ferry *et al.*, 2008). First, financial integration is deeper in the euro area. Banks in the euro area are more closely linked. Second, central banks' emergency provision of liquidity to banks affects the Eurosystem as a whole. Ring-fencing turmoil in national money markets is not possible in an integrated euro area. Third, the political support for European co-ordination of financial stability arrangements is larger in the euro-area than in the non-euro-area countries.

The choice for the EU is based on different arguments. First, it is difficult to manage financial stability in Europe without incorporating its financial centre, London (Goodhart and Schoenmaker, 2009). Large banks conduct a significant part of their business in the London wholesale market (e.g., Deutsche Bank has 30 per cent of its assets in London). Second, financial stability is a particular concern for the new Member States as a large part of their banking system is owned by banks from other EU countries (see chapter 8). Third, financial stability is related to the wider regulatory and supervisory framework of the EU Single Market, which allows banks to expand throughout the EU without additional supervision by the host countries (see chapter 10).

Reviewing the arguments, it is not clear from the data that banks are more linked in the euro area. There are a few Scandinavian banks (e.g., Nordea (see Table 11.5) and Danske Bank) that operate throughout the region, both in the ins (Finland) and in the outs (Denmark and Sweden). The merger of Banco Santander (Spain) and Abbey National (UK) and the takeover of ABN Amro (Netherlands) by a consortium of banks consisting of Fortis (Belgium), Santander (Spain), and Royal Bank of Scotland (UK) indicate that cross-border consolidation is not confined to the euro area. Finally, the financial stability function is more closely related to the regulatory and supervisory function than to the monetary function. On the supervisory side, the soundness of financial institutions is monitored by financial supervisors. The focus of financial stability is on the wider financial system, of which financial institutions, financial markets, and financial infrastructures are key components. There is thus a continuous flow of information between financial supervisors and central banks responsible for financial stability that is intensified in times of crisis. On the monetary side, it is sufficient when the ECB and the non-euro-area central banks co-operate to provide emergency liquidity assistance to the European banking system in times of crisis.

This simple model shows that a bank will be recapitalised whenever the total benefits of an intervention are larger than the net costs. In the case of a bailout, the authorities will contribute C.

Multi-country model of bailout

In the multi-country model, Freixas (2003) considers the case where the mechanism is set in such a way that the bank is recapitalised only if a sufficient contribution from the different countries can be collected. This is an interpretation of improvised co-operation: the different countries meet to find out how much they are ready to contribute to the recapitalisation, denoted by t.[3] If the total amount they are willing to contribute is larger than the cost, the bank is recapitalised. The decision is:

$$\begin{cases} x^* = 1 \ if \ \sum_j(t_j - C_j) > 0 \\ x^* = 0 \ if \ \sum_j(t_j - C_j) < 0 \end{cases} \tag{11.2}$$

and the j-country objective will be to maximise:

$$x^*(\theta_j - t_j) \tag{11.3}$$

This game may have a multiplicity of equilibria and, in particular, the closure equilibrium $t_j = 0, x^* = 0$ will occur provided that for no j we have:

$$\theta_j - \sum_j {}_jC_j > 0 \tag{11.4}$$

that is, no individual country is ready to finance the recapitalisation itself. Obviously, if this equilibrium is selected, the recapitalisation policy is inefficient as banks will almost never be recapitalised.

That in most cases the closure equilibrium will occur can be explained by the fact that part of the externalities fall outside the home country (although it is safe to assume that in the current setting the country with the highest social benefits of a recapitalisation is the home country). The countries are grouped as follows: the home country denoted by H, all other European countries denoted by E, and all other countries in the world denoted by W. The social benefits can then be decomposed into the social benefits in the home country ($h \cdot \theta = \theta_h$), the rest of Europe ($e \cdot \theta = \theta_e$), and the rest of the world ($w \cdot \theta = \theta_w$):

$$\sum_{j=1}^{W} \theta_j = \theta_h + \sum_{j \notin H}^{E} \theta_{e,j} + \sum_{j \notin E}^{W} \theta_{w,j} \tag{11.5}$$

In this equation h, e, and w are indexes for the social benefits (i.e., externalities caused by the possible failure of a financial institution) in the home country, the rest of Europe, and the rest of the world. The sum of h, e, and w is 1. When the total social benefits are close (or equal) to the social benefits of the home country (θ is close to θ_h, so h is close to 1), the home country will be willing to bail out the financial institution. In all other cases ($h < 1$), the home country will deal with the social benefits only within its territory, while host countries expect the home country to pay for (a part of) the costs in the host country.[4] Current national-based arrangements undervalue externalities related to the cross-border business of financial institutions. As a result, insufficient capital will be contributed and the financial institution will not be bailed out. This model pinpoints the public-good dimension of collective bailouts and shows why improvised co-operation will lead to an under-provision of public goods, that is, to an insufficient level of recapitalisations. Countries have an incentive to understate their share of the problem so as to incur a smaller share of the costs. This leaves the largest country, almost always the home country, with the decision whether to shoulder the costs on its own or let the bank close and possibly be liquidated. Schinasi (2007) provides another interesting model on decision-making problems related to EU financial-crisis management.

Cross-border co-operation

The model of Freixas (2003) shows that ex-post negotiations on burden sharing lead to an underprovision of recapitalisation, and therefore more efficient mechanisms for the management and resolution of cross-border financial crises need to be developed. This is because national authorities (central banks and Ministries of Finance) merely have a mandate for maintaining national financial stability and may therefore be reluctant to provide liquidity or solvency support to banks in other EU countries. They do not take into account cross-border externalities caused by financial institutions under their jurisdiction. Current national-based arrangements may undervalue externalities related to the cross-border business of financial institutions. Table 11.6 shows in which situations there is a potential conflict of interest and possible co-ordination problems. If the position of the financial group is significant in the host country, potential conflicts of interest and co-ordination problems can occur. In this respect, the Swedish Riksbank argues that '[t]o mitigate the impact of a future financial crisis it is important to maintain a good state of preparedness. Crises can arise unexpectedly

Table 11.6 The home-host relationship

Systemic relevance in HOME country	Systemic relevance in HOST country	
	Significant	Non-significant
Significant	Potential conflicts of interest and co-ordination problems	Not a big problem
Non-significant	Potential conflicts of interest and co-ordination problems	Not a big problem

Source: Srejber (2005)

and spread rapidly to other parts of the financial system. If a crisis breaks out it is crucial to quickly establish effective communication channels and to have an explicit delineation of responsibilities between public authorities'.[5] How can these conflicts of interest and co-ordination problems be removed?

The current mechanisms for the management and resolution of financial crises in the EU are based on voluntary agreements. Such voluntary co-operation often takes the form of a Memorandum of Understanding (MoU). These MoUs, which set out procedures for cooperation and information sharing, have been adopted at the EU, regional, and national levels. According to the ECB (2007), '[t]he MoUs on crisis management are a key component of the EU institutional framework for safeguarding financial stability. They are generally designed to provide basic principles and practical arrangements for cross-border co-operation between authorities in the event of disturbances with cross-border systemic implications'. At the EU level, there are at the time of writing two multilateral MoUs specifically focusing on financial-crisis management (see Box 11.5 for an overview).

Next to these pan-European MoUs, regional agreements have emerged (see Box 11.6). Both in the Nordic and the Benelux countries, the authorities have come to the conclusion that the financial systems in these respective regions have become integrated in such a way that more specific agreements are needed. As for the Nordic countries, their recent experience with systemic banking crises also played a role. According to the Riksbank (2003), '[t]he experience gained from banking problems in some Nordic countries in the early 1990s clearly showed the need for central banks to act quickly in a bank crisis situation. In recent years, a number of banks have established themselves outside their countries of domicile – including several banks in the Nordic

Box 11.5 Multilateral Memoranda of Understanding at the EU level

The first EU-wide MoU on cooperation in crisis-management situations was adopted in March 2003 under the auspices of the ESCB's Banking Supervision Committee (BSC). This MoU was designed to contribute to effective crisis management by ensuring a smooth interaction between the authorities concerned, thus facilitating an early assessment of the systemic scope of a crisis at both the national and EU levels. It sets out specific principles and procedures for the identification of the authorities responsible for the management of a crisis in the EU. It also indicates the required flows of information between banking supervisors and central banks, and the practical arrangements for sharing information across borders. It establishes a framework for cross-border communication between banking supervisors and central banks, including a list of emergency contacts.

The second MoU was adopted by the EU banking supervisors, central banks, and Ministries of Finance in May 2005. This MoU provides a set of principles and procedures for sharing information, views, and assessments in order to assist the signatory authorities in pursuing their respective policy functions and to preserve the overall stability of the financial systems of individual Member States and of the EU as a whole. In particular, the authorities concerned should be in a position, if need be, to engage in informed discussions among themselves at the cross-border level through existing networks and committees. To further support cooperation between authorities, the 2005 MoU includes arrangements for the development of contingency plans for the management of crisis situations, along with stress-testing and simulation exercises. Finally, the MoU includes an explicit statement that it should not be construed as representing an exception to (i) the principle of the firm's owners'/shareholders' primary financial responsibility, (ii) the need for creditor vigilance, and (iii) the primacy of market-led solutions when it comes to solving crisis situations in individual institutions. In view of the challenges posed by the EU integration process as well as the globalisation of financial markets, the latter MoU was revised in June 2008.

Source: European Central Bank (2007)

area – and this makes it necessary for central banks to undertake joint analysis, discussion and action in the event of a financial crisis'.

While these MoUs address co-operation and information-sharing arrangements between supervisors, central banks, and Ministries of Finance, they are legally non-binding and do not address the present ambiguity with respect to the allocation of LoLR responsibilities between the national central banks and the ECB. Both supervisory and LoLR arrangements remain fragmented, with primary responsibilities at the national level. It is, however, questionable

---

Box 11.6 Regional Memoranda of Understanding

The Nordic MoU – which was signed in 2003 by the governors of the central banks of Denmark, Finland, Iceland, Norway, and Sweden – is applicable to financial crises in Nordic banking groups with cross-border establishments in other Nordic countries. The focus of the Nordic MoU is on practical arrangements. It states that any central bank may call for a meeting of a 'crisis-management group' comprising high-level central bank officials. Furthermore, it indicates which central bank should take the leading role and outlines the contacts that need to be made with bank supervisors, Ministries of Finance, bank managers, and other parties. The MoU also specifies which information should be obtained and analysed from the bank concerned. Finally, the MoU calls for co-ordination of the information that the central banks provide to outside parties.

In a similar vein, the National Bank of Belgium, the Belgian Banking, Finance and Insurance Commission, and De Nederlandsche Bank signed an MoU in 2006, reinforcing their cooperation in the area of supervision. To that end, the MoU stipulates that a crisis-management committee consisting of the three authorities will be convened if an emergency situation arises. This committee deals with the consultation and co-ordination between the authorities, collects information, prepares decisions, and maintains contacts with the institution and market participants.

Source: European Central Bank (2007).

---

whether national central banks are able to take into account the pan-European systemic problems that may arise in a crisis situation. Boot (2006) argues that this national authority diffuses the command structure, while the LoLR should be at the heart of crisis management.

When discussing the regulatory response to the 2007/2008 financial crisis, Goodhart (2008) argues that financial regulators and supervisors have been fortunate that there has been no failure thus far of a bank, or other financial institution, involving significant cross-border consequences. Northern Rock, IKB, and SachsenLB were all primarily domestic. He stresses that 'war games' (i.e., crisis-management exercises) have led us to believe that the exercise could be difficult, messy, and protracted, while in a crisis speed is usually essential.

Considering the pan-European nature of systemic concerns, the ECB has already started a European-wide financial stability assessment and as of 2004 it started to publish the outcome of this assessment in its FSR. Next to this European-wide structure for monitoring systemic risk, there could also be a need for a more centralised approach to LoLR activities. With respect to the latter, it seems natural to grant the ECB explicit responsibility over the LoLR function.

Burden sharing

Some authors also argue in favour of explicit burden-sharing arrangements to cover potential losses in those operations. Goodhart and Schoenmaker (2009) argue that MoUs will not be sufficient to solve potential conflicts of interest and co-ordination problems, as MoUs are not enforceable. Moreover, these MoUs do not solve the issue of negotiations on burden sharing.

As the funding for recapitalisation is exclusively available at the domestic level, no one knows how the loss burden arising from the failure of a cross-border financial group might be handled. Countries have an incentive to understate their share of the problem so as to incur a smaller share in the costs. This leaves the largest country, generally the home country, with the decision whether to bear the burden or to let the bank close and possibly be liquidated.

To counter moral hazard, crisis-management arrangements for LoLR and solvency support could not be specified in advance. Constructive ambiguity regarding the decision whether or not to recapitalise can be useful to contain moral hazard. However, it is clear that ambiguity over burden sharing will lead to fewer recapitalisations than is socially optimal. It is therefore desirable to attain the same clarity at the European level as currently exists at the national level where the financial risk of support operations is carried by the Ministry of Finance and the central bank. Clarity at the European level about how to share the costs among treasuries (and central banks) does not increase moral hazard.

In designing ex-ante mechanisms for burden sharing, the following issues arise. First, should all countries join in the burden sharing (in a banking crisis, every country pays relative to its size) or only the countries involved (countries pay relative to the national presence of the problem bank)? Second, should the burden be shared according to a fixed or a flexible key (accommodating the specific circumstances)?

The general-fund mechanism is an example of generic burden sharing by countries. Under this mechanism, the costs of recapitalisation are distributed among the participating countries, irrespective of the location of the failing bank. However, there are two substantial problems with such a mechanism. First, this construction will lead to international transfers between countries (a country may have to contribute its share to the recapitalisation of a problem bank that does not operate in its jurisdiction). Second, general burden sharing generates adverse selection and moral-hazard problems. Countries with weak banking systems will profit from such a scheme and countries with strong banks are therefore less inclined to sign up (adverse selection). As the link between payment for a recapitalisation and responsibility for supervision is weakened, supervisory authorities may have fewer incentives to provide an adequate level of supervisory effort (moral hazard).

Alternatively, the burden may be shared only by countries in which a failing bank is present. Each country involved pays part of the burden that reflects the relative presence of the bank in the country concerned. An important advantage of specific sharing arrangements is that there are almost no international transfers. The specific sharing scheme is also incentive compatible: the fiscal authorities (the principal) will require from the supervisor (the agent) adequate supervision.

Finally, there are some concerns surrounding both burden-sharing mechanisms. First, burden-sharing arrangements face a free-rider problem. Countries that do not sign up to burden sharing still benefit from it, as the stability of the European financial system is a public good. Second, there is a concern with foreign banks in small countries. If such a bank is systemic in the host country but not in the home country, the bank might not be rescued. This could be a problem for the new EU Member States in particular. Third, it could be difficult to organise burden sharing for truly international banks, which have a large part of their business outside Europe. Moreover, such mechanisms fail to address crisis problems caused by the failures of banks headquartered outside Europe. Fourth, a common agreement on burden sharing will need political commitment. The appetite of European politicians for adopting explicit burden-sharing arrangements is currently, however, limited (Pauly, 2008).

11.5 Conclusions

Financial stability refers to a situation in which the financial system is capable of successfully performing its key functions and is robust to financial and real economic disturbances. A fundamental underlying concept for the study of financial (in)stability is the concept of 'systemic risk'. Although virtually any systemic event can be labelled as an episode of financial instability, the converse will not necessarily hold. A financial shock, no matter how large, without measurable effects on the real economy is not a systemic event.

Since financial distress can seriously harm the economy, it is natural that public authorities take great interest in maintaining financial stability. Despite substantial differences across the EU Member States in terms of the supervision of financial intermediaries, in all countries the central bank considers maintaining financial stability as an important task. In addition, the ECB has to contribute to the smooth conduct of policies relating to the prudential supervision of credit institutions and the stability of the financial system.

In order to maintain financial stability, public authorities should (i) identify potential vulnerabilities at an early stage, (ii) take precautionary measures, which make it less likely that costly financial disturbances occur, and (iii) undertake actions to reduce the costs of disturbances and restore financial stability after a period of distress. With respect to the latter, four important reactive instruments can be distinguished: private-sector solutions, liquidity-support measures, public-intervention tools, and winding down of a financial institution.

The potential for a pan-European crisis raises the thorny issue of dividing the fiscal costs of possible bailouts between the Member States involved. As countries have an incentive to understate their share of the problem in order to have a smaller share in the costs, negotiations on burden sharing will likely lead to an underprovision of recapitalisations. This leaves the largest country, generally the home country, with the decision whether to bear the costs on its own or to let the bank close. An alternative to negotiations after a crisis has occurred is to agree ex ante on some burden-sharing mechanisms, be it generic or specific burden sharing.

Current arrangements (such as Memoranda of Understanding) address co-operation and information-sharing arrangements between supervisors, central banks, and Finance Ministries, but do not address the present ambiguity with respect to the allocation of LoLR responsibilities between the national central banks and the ECB. Many authors therefore argue in favour of a more prominent role for the ECB in LoLR operations and crisis management.

NOTES

1. In Austria, the central bank carries out on-site inspections when commissioned to do so by the FMA. In Germany, the Bundesbank and the BaFin are entrusted by law to co-operate closely in the area of banking supervision, while in Ireland, Latvia, and Hungary the central bank has the power to carry out on-site inspections and/or review the capital and risk management systems of supervised entities.

2. The central bank proposes the appointment of some of the members of the banking supervisor's management board in Belgium, Finland, and Latvia. The central bank is involved ex officio in the management of the banking supervisor in Belgium, Estonia, France, Poland, Sweden, and the UK.

3. The term 'improvised co-operation' has been coined to convey the view of an efficient although adaptive exchange of information and decision taking. It relies on the idea that maintaining financial stability is a goal that every individual country is interested in achieving, so there are good grounds for co-operation (Freixas, 2003). It can be argued that improvised co-operation corresponds to the current situation in the EU.

4. We assume that the country with the highest social benefits of a bailout is the home country. This assumption is consistent with the post-BCCI Directive that stipulates that banks have to be headquartered in the country where most of their business is conducted.

5. Quote obtained from the website of the Swedish Riksbank (www.riksbank.se).

SUGGESTED READING

De Bandt, O. and P. Hartmann (2002), Systemic Risk: A Survey, in: C. Goodhart and G. Illing (eds.), *Financial Crises, Contagion, and the Lender of Last Resort – A Reader*, Oxford University Press, Oxford, 249–297.

Kindleberger, C. P. (2000), *Manias, Panics, and Crashes: A History of Financial Crises*, 4th edition, John Wiley & Sons, Inc., New York.

Mishkin, F. S. (1992), Anatomy of a Financial Crisis, *Journal of Evolutionary Economics*, 2(2), 115–130.

Oosterloo, S. and J. de Haan (2004), Central Banks and Financial Stability: A Survey, *Journal of Financial Stability*, 1(2), 257–273.

Schinasi, G. J. (2006), *Safeguarding Financial Stability: Theory and Practice*, International Monetary Fund, Washington DC.

REFERENCES

Bäckström, U. (1999), *International Financial Turbulence in the 1990s*, Sveriges Riksbank, Stockholm.

Boot, A. W. A. (2006), Supervisory Arrangements, LoLR and Crisis Management in a Single European Banking Market, *Economic Review*, Sveriges Riksbank, Stockholm, 2, 15–33.

Buiter, W. H. (2007), Lessons from the 2007 Financial Crisis, CEPR Policy Insight, No. 18, London.

Caprio, G. and D. Klingebiel (2003), *Episodes of Systemic and Borderline Financial Crises*, World Bank data set available at http://econ.worldbank.org/view.php?id=23456

Carstens A. G., D. C. Hardy, and C. Pazarbasioglu (2004), Avoiding Banking Crises in Latin America, *Finance and Development*, September, 30–33.

Crockett, A. (2005), Dealing with Stress in Large and Complex Financial Institutions, in: D. Evanoff and G. G. Kaufman (eds.), *Systemic Financial Crises; Resolving Large Bank Insolvencies*, World Scientific Publishing Company, Singapore, 17–27.

De Bandt, O. and P. Hartmann (2002), Systemic Risk: A Survey, in: C. E. A. Goodhart and G. Illing (eds.), *Financial Crisis, Contagion and the Lender of Last Resort*, Oxford University Press, Oxford, 249–297.

Duisenberg, W. F. (2001), The Contribution of the Euro to Financial Stability, in: *Globalisation of Financial Markets and Financial Stability – Challenges for Europe*, Nomos Verlagsgesellschaft, Baden-Baden, 37–51.

Enoch, C., G. Garcia, and V. Sundararajan (2001), Recapitalising Banks with Public Funds, *IMF Staff Papers*, 48(1), 58–110.

European Central Bank (2006a), *Financial Stability Review*, December, ECB, Frankfurt am Main.

European Central Bank (2006b), *Recent Developments in Supervisory Structures in EU and Acceding Countries*, ECB, Frankfurt am Main.

European Central Bank (2007), The EU arrangements for financial crisis management, *ECB Monthly Bulletin*, February, 73–84.

European Commission (2007), *Scenario Analysis: Estimating the Effects of Changing the Funding Mechanisms of EU Deposit Guarantee Schemes*, EC, Brussels.

Freixas, X. (2003), Crisis Management in Europe, in: J. J. M. Kremers, D. Schoenmaker, and P. Wierts (eds.), *Financial Supervision in Europe*, Edward Elgar, Cheltenham, 102–119.

Friedman, M. and A. J. Schwartz (1963), *A Monetary History of the United States, 1867–1960*, Princeton University Press, Princeton.

Frydl, E. and M. Quintyn (2000), The Benefits and Costs of Intervening in Banking Crises, IMF Working Paper 00/147.

Goodhart, C. A. E. (2005), How Far Can a Central Bank Act as a Lender of Last Resort Independently of Treasury (Ministry of Finance) Support?, paper presented at the Norges Bank conference on Banking Crisis Resolution – Theory and Policy, 16–17 June, Oslo.

Goodhart, C. A. E. and D. Schoenmaker (1995), Should the Functions of Monetary Policy and Banking Supervision Be Separated?, *Oxford Economic Papers*, 47, 539–560.

Goodhart, C. A. E. and D. Schoenmaker (2009), Fiscal Burden Sharing in Cross-Border Banking Crises, *International Journal of Central Banking*, 5, forthcoming.

Goodhart, C. A. E. (2008), The Regulatory Response to the Financial Crisis, CESifo Working Paper Series No. 2257, Munich.

Group of Ten (2001), *Consolidation in the Financial Sector*, Basel, BIS.

Healey, J. (2001), Financial Instability and the Central Bank – International Evidence, in: *Financial Stability and Central Banks – A Global Perspective*, Centre for Central Bank Studies, Bank of England, London, 19–78.

Hoshi, T. and A. K. Kashyap (2004), Solutions to the Japanese Banking Crisis: What Might Work and What Definitely Will Fail, Hi-Stat Discussion Paper Series D04-35, Institute of Economic Research, Hitotsubashi University.

Houben, A., J. Kakes, and G. J. Schinasi (2004), Towards a Framework for Financial Stability, De Nederlandsche Bank, Occasional Study, No. 2(1).

Honohan, P. and D. Klingebiel (2000), Controlling the Fiscal Costs of Banking Crises, World Bank Policy Research Working Paper 2441.

Ingves, S. (2007), Cross-border Banking Regulation – A Way Forward for Europe, in: D. Evanoff and G. Kaufman (eds.), *International Financial Instability: Cross-Border Banking and National Regulation*, World Scientific Publishing Company, Singapore, 3–11.

International Monetary Fund (2004), *Compilation Guide on Financial Soundness Indicators*, IMF, Washington DC.

International Monetary Fund (2008), *Global Financial Stability Report – Containing Systemic Risks and Restoring Financial Soundness*, IMF, Washington DC.

Jonung, L. and Hagberg, T. (2005), How Costly Was the Crisis of the 1990s?, unpublished manuscript.

Kindleberger, C. P. (2000), *Manias, Panics, and Crashes: A History of Financial Crises*, 4th edition, John Wiley & Sons, Inc., New York.

Klingebiel, D. (2000), The Use of Asset Management Companies in the Resolution of Banking Crises, World Bank Policy Research Paper No. 2284.

MacDonald, R. (1996), *Deposit Insurance*, Centre for Central Bank Studies, Bank of England, London.

Mishkin, F. S. (1992), Anatomy of a Financial Crisis, *Journal of Evolutionary Economics*, 2(2), 115–130.

National Bank of Belgium (2000), *Economic Review II*, Brussels.

Nieto, M. J. and G. J. Schinasi (2007), EU Framework for Safeguarding Financial Stability: Towards an Analytical Benchmark for Assessing its Effectiveness, IMF Working Paper 07/260.

Oosterloo, S. and J. de Haan (2004), Central Banks and Financial Stability: A Survey, *Journal of Financial Stability*, 1(2), 257–273.

Oosterloo, S., J. de Haan, and R. M. Jong-A-Pin (2007), Financial Stability Reviews: A First Empirical Analysis, *Journal of Financial Stability*, 2(4), 337–355.

Organisation for Economic Co-operation and Development (2002), Experiences with the Resolution of Weak Financial Institutions in the OECD Area, OECD, *Financial Market Trends*, No. 82.

Pauly, L. W. (2008), Financial Crisis Management in Europe and Beyond, *Contributions to Political Economy*, 27, 73–89.

Pisani-Ferry, J., P. Aghion, M. Belka, J. von Hagen, L. Heikensten, and A. Sapir (2008), Coming of Age: Report on the Euro Area, Bruegel Blueprint No. 4, Brussels.

Riksbank (2003), Nordic Central Banks Conclude MoU on Financial Crisis Management, Press Release, Sveriges Riksbank, Stockholm.

Srejber, E. (2005), The Divorce between Macro Financial Stability and Micro Supervisory Responsibility: Are We Now in For a More Stable Life?, speech at the 33rd Economics Conference of the Oesterreichische Nationalbank, 12–13 May, Vienna.

Schinasi, G. J. (2006), *Safeguarding Financial Stability: Theory and Practice*, International Monetary Fund, Washington DC.

Schinasi, G. J. (2007), Resolving EU Financial-Stability Challenges: Is a Decentralised Decision-Making Approach Efficient?, paper presented at the 2nd Conference of Banking Regulation – International and Financial Stability hosted by the Centre for European Economic Research (ZEW), Mannheim.

Svensson, L. E. O. (2003), Monetary Policy and Real Stabilization, NBER Working Paper 9486.

Vesala, J. (2006), Remarks at a workshop organised by National Bank of Belgium on Financial Stability Monitoring and Assessment in a Multilateral Environment, available at www. rahoitustarkastus.fi/NR/rdonlyres/9F7E459B-F462-4EE6-A029-CFD2586650FC/0/ Vesala_Brussels_notes_140606.pdf

12

European Competition Policy

OVERVIEW

This chapter provides a concise overview of European competition policy, with a focus on financial services. The chapter first defines competition and describes the objectives of EU competition policy, i.e., the maintenance of competitive markets in the EU, as well as the single-market objective. The ultimate goal of competition is to offer consumers greater choice of products and services at lower prices (i.e., to enhance consumer welfare).

The second part of the chapter analyses the economic rationale for competition policy by examining the difference between a perfectly competitive market and a monopoly. In a competitive market, prices are 'competed' down and goods or services are produced in the least costly way. Firms are price takers. In a monopoly, there is a single seller in the market who can exert undue market power. The monopolist thus has significant power over the price and is a price setter.

The third part of the chapter elaborates on the four tools of EU competition policy, i.e., the elimination of agreements that restrict competition and abuse of a dominant position, the control of mergers and acquisitions, the liberalisation of monopolistic sectors, and monitoring of state aid. The relevance of these tools is illustrated by a number of practical cases in financial services related to the alleged dominance of MasterCard and the illegal state aid to German, Austrian, and French public banks.

The fourth part of the chapter discusses a framework for investigating abuse of dominance. One of the elements of this framework is the so-called 'small, but significant non-transitory increase in prices' (SSNIP) methodology, which is used to define the smallest market in which a hypothetical monopolist would be able to impose a small but significant non-transitory price increase (the relevant market). The relevant market for various financial services is discussed.

The final part of the chapter provides a brief description of the dual legislative and enforcement system for competition policy in the EU.

LEARNING OBJECTIVES

After you have studied this chapter, you should be able to:

● describe competition and competition policy
● explain the economic arguments for having competition policy
● reproduce the different tools of EU competition policy and explain how these relate to financial markets
● describe the process of assessing a dominant position
● understand the institutional structure of competition policy in the EU.

12.1 What is competition policy?

Competition can be defined as a market situation in which firms or sellers independently strive for the patronage of buyers in order to achieve a particular business objective, e.g., profits, sales, and/or market share (OECD, 1993). Competition forces firms:

● to become (more) efficient;
● to offer greater choice of products and services; and
● to offer these products and services at lower prices.

Ultimately, competition gives rise to increased consumer welfare and allocative efficiency (the latter will be discussed in more detail in section 12.3). Moreover, the level of competition is an important aspect of financial-sector development and, in turn, economic growth (Claessens and Laeven, 2005).

Generally, *competition policy* aims to ensure that competition in the marketplace is not restricted in a way that is detrimental to society (Motta, 2004). In practice, authorities establish a set of rules and policies aimed at safeguarding competition, as a means of enhancing economic welfare and ensuring efficient allocation of resources. However, the aim of competition policy should not be to eliminate market power, as the prospect of enjoying market power is an important driver for innovation and efficiency. Still, as will be discussed in section 12.4, firms are prohibited from abusing market power.

Competition policy is one of the pillars of the EU's internal market policy. By combating distortions of competition between firms, competition policy creates the preconditions for the proper market functioning with the aim to enhance overall consumer welfare. Moreover, safeguarding competition in the EU is an important instrument to promote further market integration, e.g., by taking away barriers for entry or exit, and the application of non-discrimination principles for new entrants. The objective of EU competition policy is therefore twofold (European Commission, 2000): 'The first objective of competition policy is the maintenance of competitive markets. Competition policy serves as an instrument to encourage industrial efficiency, the optimal allocation of resources, technical progress and the flexibility to adjust to a changing environment. In order for the Community to be competitive on worldwide markets, it needs a competitive home market. Thus, the Community's competition policy has always taken a very strong line against price-fixing, market-sharing cartels, abuses of dominant positions, and anti-competitive mergers. It has also prohibited unjustified State-granted monopoly rights and State aid measures which do not ensure the long-term viability of firms but distort competition by keeping them artificially in business. The second is the single market objective. An internal market is an essential condition for the development of an efficient and competitive industry . . . The Commission has used its competition policy as an active tool to prevent this (i.e., the erection of barriers to trade), prohibiting, and fining heavily the parties to two main types of agreement: distribution and licensing agreements that prevent parallel trade between Member States, and agreements between competitors to keep out of one another's "territories".' The provisions of the Maastricht Treaty specifically require EU policy makers to 'act in accordance with the principle of an open market economy with free competition, favouring an efficient allocation of resources'. Roeller and Stehmann (2006) argue that with the progress made towards realisation of the internal market, the relative importance of the market integration goal has declined. As a result, policy statements increasingly focus on efficiency, consumer welfare, and competitiveness. Nevertheless, competition policy may be an effective instrument to strengthen integration in certain segments of the financial market.

At the EU level, competition law is enforced by the European Commission (more specifically, the Directorate General for Competition), while at the national level the National Competition Authorities are responsible. Section 12.5 will discuss the organisation of EU competition policy in more detail.

12.2 The economic rationale for competition policy

According to Motta (2004), the basis of competition policy is the idea that monopolies are 'bad'. Although this might sound somewhat simplistic, examining the difference between perfect competition and a monopoly (i.e., the two

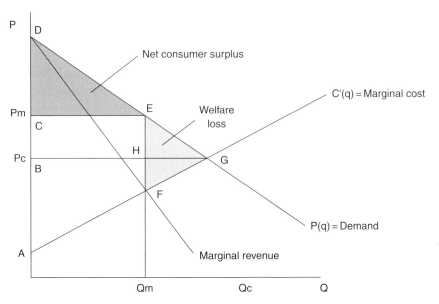

Figure 12.1 Welfare loss from monopoly
Source: Tirole (1988)

extremes in a market place) is useful to explain the economic rationale for competition policy.

A *monopoly* can be defined as a situation where (i) there is a single seller in the market, (ii) there are no (close) substitute products or services, and (iii) there are barriers to entry for potential sellers. As a result of these characteristics, a monopolist has significant power over the price, i.e., he is a *price setter* rather than a price taker. The ability of a monopolist to raise and maintain a price above the level that would prevail under (perfect) competition is referred to as *market* or *monopoly power*. Generally, the exercise of market power leads to reduced output and loss of economic welfare. However, monopolies do not necessarily have to be a bad thing. A good example is a *natural monopoly* where a single firm can produce at lower costs than a situation in which there are two or more firms. According to the OECD (1993), natural monopolies are characterised by steeply declining long-run average and marginal-cost curves such that there is room for only one firm to fully exploit available economies of scale and supply the market.

Figure 12.1 shows the welfare effects of market power, by comparing the total surplus at the monopoly price with that at the perfect competitive (marginal-cost) price.[1] Under perfect competition, the price of the goods or services produced equals marginal cost (P_c = MC) and the goods or services will be produced in the least costly way. At the opposite, the monopolist sets output at the level where marginal cost equals marginal revenue (MC = MR) in order to maximise its profits. Tirole (1988) shows that the total surplus is equal to the sum of the consumer surplus and the producer surplus (or profit), or to the difference between total consumer utility and production costs. In Figure 12.1 this surplus is represented by the area DGAD under marginal-cost pricing and by the area DEFAD under monopoly pricing. The difference between the total surplus under monopoly and the surplus under marginal-cost pricing is the *welfare or deadweight loss* (given by triangle EFG in Figure 12.1). This welfare loss represents the overall opportunity costs to society arising from monopoly pricing. In addition, part of the consumer surplus under perfect competition, BCEH, is transferred to the monopolist in the form of excess profits.

So what does this entail in practice for competition policy? Figure 12.1 shows that having one firm (or very few firms) serving the market generally leads to a welfare loss for society. Competition policy should, however, not try to maximise the number of firms that operate in a market, because firms will then not be able to optimise the scale or magnitude of their output, which results in an average cost per unit of output that is higher than would be the case in a more concentrated market. Motta (2004) stresses that:

  (i) competition policy is not concerned with maximising the number of firms; and

  (ii) competition policy is concerned with defending market competition in order to increase welfare, not defending competitors.

Should competition authorities then strive for perfect competition? Since the notion of perfect competition can in practice be highly restrictive in terms of policy making (OECD, 1993), the goal of competition policy should be a more realistic target such as *workable competition*, i.e., trying to create the preconditions for the proper operation of markets and ensure that firms do not abuse a dominant position. Although there is no generally accepted definition of workable competition, all authorities involved in competition policy seem to make use of some version of this concept. According to the OECD (1993), workable competition is a notion which arises from the observation that since perfect competition does not exist, theories based on it do not provide reliable guides for competition policy. Criteria for judging whether competition was workable are wide ranging, e.g., the number of firms should be at least as large as economies of scale permit, promotional expenses should not be excessive, and advertising should be informative.

For competition authorities it is important to have insight into the market power of firms and the level of competition in a specific market. There are various ways to quantify the level of market power. A well-known indicator is the *Lerner Index* (LI), which measures the degree to which a firm is able to price its products above marginal costs. The Lerner Index is a more accurate measure of market power than concentration measures (such as the Herfindahl Index and the CR5 ratio). Nevertheless, it poses some challenges. For instance, if the LI is relatively high it may still be hard to judge whether this indicates market power or superior efficiency. Moreover, in practice the LI is hard to calculate as information on marginal costs is often not readily available. The LI is given by the following formula:

$$LI = (Price - Marginal\ Cost)/Price = 1/\varepsilon \tag{12.1}$$

where ε is the price elasticity of demand $[\varepsilon = - (\Delta Q/\Delta P)(P/Q)]$. The key determinant of market power is the elasticity of demand. The greater is ε, the greater will be the reduction in quantity demanded when the price rises. This entails that the higher the elasticity of demand, the lower the market power of the respective firm. In the case of perfect competition, P = MC and the LI equals zero. The higher the value of LI, the greater is the firm's market power. De Guevara and Maudos (2004) estimate the LI for the European banking system and argue that, in spite of the process of deregulation, market power increased during the 1990s in ten of the EU-15 countries (see Table 12.1). The authors estimate the associated welfare loss at close to 2.5 per cent of EU GDP.

A method to assess competition in a market is the H-statistic of Panzar and Rosse (1987). This test statistic examines the relationship between a change in a firm's input prices and the revenue earned. The basic idea behind this indicator is that firms employ different pricing strategies in response to changes in input costs depending on the market structure in which they operate. Table 7.3 provides an overview of the level of competition in the EU banking sector in the period 1990–2005. (See Bikker and Bos (2008) for a further discussion on competition and concentration in the banking sector.)

Even in the absence of a monopoly, dominant positions might arise (Motta, 2004). The latter can, for example, be due to *sunk costs*, i.e., costs which, once incurred, cannot be (easily) recovered. Sunk costs lead to barriers to entry as well as to exit, as the existence of these costs increases an incumbent's commitment to the market and may signal a willingness to respond aggressively to entry (OECD, 1993). In this respect, offering financial services via the Internet or via intermediaries has the potential to improve contestability of markets by lowering sunk costs and barriers. Dermine (2005) discusses the online activities of ING Direct, offering a standard package of a savings account, a mortgage, and a selection of mutual funds to customers in

Table 12.1 Lerner Index for banks in the EU-15, 1993–2000

	1993	1994	1995	1996	1997	1998	1999	2000
Belgium	4.32	4.73	5.57	6.25	7.44	9.97	9.61	8.25
Denmark	12.07	16.66	12.72	13.17	13.89	10.45	13.89	11.28
Germany	11.32	13.33	12.79	12.67	11.08	10.63	8.97	9.19
Greece	2.48	4.29	4.73	5.59	9.72	9.50	17.10	15.60
Spain	12.24	10.15	10.14	9.64	12.50	14.66	16.20	15.74
France	7.70	5.52	4.68	5.34	6.08	5.91	8.53	7.87
Ireland	9.13	11.44	9.37	11.69	10.22	13.11	8.19	4.20
Italy	10.83	3.02	7.45	7.13	9.11	16.00	15.13	18.42
Luxembourg	8.72	7.13	6.95	8.34	8.09	9.12	7.48	6.46
Netherlands	6.56	8.81	5.85	5.13	9.99	9.42	7.14	6.86
Austria	7.81	8.23	9.10	10.48	11.24	12.09	8.24	11.02
Portugal	12.34	8.08	8.52	9.83	12.36	15.97	17.16	14.66
Finland	9.81	7.85	5.84	14.23	19.37	20.85	20.47	25.39
Sweden	14.62	12.74	15.60	16.84	13.71	12.82	5.54	8.18
United Kingdom	16.15	15.31	14.26	16.52	14.69	14.18	18.65	19.96
EU-15	10.21	9.17	8.91	9.47	9.84	10.86	11.36	11.92

Source: De Guevara and Maudos (2004)

Europe, Australia, and North America. Dermine argues that the online banking operations of this Dutch banking group stand as a prime example of how a newcomer competing against a host of well-established banks can gain the upper hand through creative application of a relatively new technology (i.e., Internet services), and a basic but widely appealing package of services. Moreover, ING's market strategy aims at worldwide name recognition to support its online operations. The ING brand is ranked 43 in the global Top 100 Brand Ranking 2008 (Millward Brown, 2008).

In other cases a dominant position may arise as a result of *lock-in effects* or *switching costs*. These are costs that customers face when changing from one supplier to the other. The higher these costs, the more difficult it becomes to switch. The existence of switching costs can give substantial market power to existing suppliers. For example, the absence of account number portability increases switching cost of customers who would like to change banks. Finally, dominant positions can be a result of *network effects*. As shown in chapter 5, the addition of a new participant to a network increases its value for all participants. This means that the value of the services and products offered to the participants depends on the number of other participants purchasing the same services and products. The existence of network externalities can lead to lock-in effects and make it hard for potential competitors to successfully enter the market.

According to Motta (2004), competition policy is also needed because firms may resort to actions that increase their profits but harm society. One example of such behaviour is *collusion*, which refers to any formal or informal agreements to raise or fix prices or to reduce output in order to increase profits. When explicitly formalised, these agreements are referred to as *cartels*. Firms may also display *predatory behaviour*, which refers to the situation in which one firm drives out its competitors by setting very low prices (sometimes even below costs). As soon as the predatory firm has driven out its competitors and has discouraged new entry into the market, it can raise prices and earn higher profits. Other types of *exclusionary behaviour* include investing in extra capacity, foreclosing access of rivals to crucial inputs, tying and bundling, and price discrimination. *Tying* refers to the practice of making the purchase of product A conditional on the purchase of product B. *Bundling* refers to the practice of selling two or more products or services in a package. *Price discrimination* occurs when customers in different segments are charged different prices for the same good or service, for reasons unrelated to costs (OECD, 1993). However, this type of exclusionary behaviour is effective only if customers cannot profitably re-sell the goods or services to other customers. Finally, as will be discussed in the next section, mergers and acquisitions may also reduce competition.

12.3 Pillars of EU competition policy

The objective of EU competition policy was first set out in the Treaty of Rome (1957), where it was indicated that one of the activities of the Community includes establishing 'a system ensuring that competition in the internal market is not distorted'. In general, EU competition policy has the following objectives:
- the elimination of agreements which restrict competition and of abuses of a dominant position (*antitrust*);
- the control of mergers and acquisitions between firms;
- the liberalisation of monopolistic economic sectors; and
- the monitoring of state aid.

Antitrust

The two main pillars of EU competition law are Articles 81 and 82 of the EC Treaty.[2] Article 81 prohibits agreements and concerted practices with an anti-competitive object or effect on the market, while Article 82 prohibits abuse of a dominant position.

The EC Treaty prohibits 'all agreements between undertakings, decisions by associations of undertakings and concerted practices which may affect trade between Member States and which have as their object or effect the prevention, restriction or distortion of competition within the common market'. Actions prohibited under article 81 can take the form of:

- direct or indirect fixing of purchase or selling prices or any other trading conditions;
- limiting or controlling production, markets, technical development, or investment;
- sharing markets or sources of supply;
- applying dissimilar conditions to equivalent transactions with other trading parties, thereby placing them at a competitive disadvantage; or
- making the conclusion of contracts subject to acceptance by the other parties of supplementary obligations which, by their nature or according to commercial usage, have no connection with the subject of such contracts.

Box 12.1 provides two recent decisions in the domain of Article 81. The first example is the decision of the European Commission to prohibit MasterCard's multilateral interchange fees[3] (see chapter 5 for a discussion on interchange fees). The second example is related to the price measures by the Groupement des Cartes Bancaires in France that – according to the Commission – hindered the issuing of cards at competitive rates. It should, however, be stressed that some of these decisions are still subject to judicial review at the time of writing.

Article 81 applies to horizontal as well as vertical agreements. *Horizontal agreements* are made between competitors in the same product market, while *vertical agreements* are made between firms operating at different stages of a certain production or distribution chain. However, exceptions can be made for those agreements that improve the production or distribution of goods or that promote technical or economic progress. Moreover, such agreements should benefit consumers and should not unnecessarily eliminate competition.

Article 82 prohibits abuse of a dominant position. This article states that '[A]ny abuse by one or more undertakings of a dominant position within the common market or in a substantial part of it shall be prohibited as incompatible with the common market in so far as it may affect trade between Member States'. A firm is in a dominant position if it has the ability to (European Communities, 2003):

- set prices above the competitive level;
- sell products of an inferior quality; or
- reduce its rate of innovation below the level that would exist in a competitive market.

Box 12.1 Article 81 cases: MasterCard and Groupement des Cartes Bancaires

MasterCard's intra-EEA Multilateral Interchange Fees

Chapter 5 indicates that the use of interchange fees is the subject of several regulatory and antitrust investigations. In December 2007, the European Commission published its findings on the multilateral interchange fees (MIF) for cross-border payment card transactions with MasterCard and Maestro branded debit and consumer credit cards in the European Economic Area. The Commission concluded that MasterCard violated EC Treaty rules on restrictive business practices, as its MIF inflated the cost of card acceptance by retailers without leading to proven efficiencies. It was, however, stressed that MIFs are not illegal as such. According to the Commission, a MIF in an open-payment card scheme such as MasterCard's is compatible with EU competition rules only if it contributes to technical and economic progress and benefits consumers. In 2008 the European Commission also opened formal antitrust proceedings against Visa in order to establish whether its MIF constituted infringements of Article 81.

Price measures by Groupement des Cartes Bancaires

In 2007 the Commission decided that the Groupement des Cartes Bancaires (France) had infringed the EC Treaty rules prohibiting practices which restrict competition. The Groupement had adopted price measures that hinder the issuing of cards in France at competitive rates by certain member banks, thereby keeping the price of payment cards artificially high to the benefit of the major French banks. According to the Commission, consumers were the victims of this illegal practice, depriving them of cheaper cards and a more diversified product offering. The decision ordered the Groupement to annul the measures concerned with immediate effect and to avoid taking any measures with a similar purpose or effect in the future.

Source: European Commission (2007a, b)

However, it is not illegal under EU competition law to hold a dominant position, since this can be obtained by legitimate means of competition. Still, competition rules forbid companies to abuse their dominant position. The next section will discuss a framework for investigating abuse of dominance. A well-known example of an article 82 case was the decision of the European Commission that Microsoft had abused its dominant market position by leveraging its near monopoly in the market for PC operating systems onto the markets for work-group-server operating systems and for media players (European Commission, 2007c). Microsoft was fined €497 million for infringing the EC Treaty rules on abuse of a dominant market position. Because of non-compliance with certain requirements set out by the European Commission, the fine was subsequently raised to €899 million in 2008.

Examining mergers

The second element of the EU's competition policy is the examination of mergers, in order to assess whether they may lead to less competition. Merger control regulation has existed since 1989. The EC Merger Regulation[4] adopted in 2004 sets out rules for mergers and acquisitions of companies, which could have the possibility to restrict competition. In this respect, article 2(3) of the Regulation states that: '[A] concentration which would significantly impede effective competition, in the common market or in a substantial part of it, in particular as a result of the creation or strengthening of a dominant position, shall be declared incompatible with the common market.' *Dominance* has been defined by the European Court of Justice (ECJ) as 'a position of economic strength enjoyed by an undertaking which enables it to prevent effective competition being maintained on the relevant market by affording it the power to behave to an appreciable extent independently of its competitors, customers and ultimately of its customers'.[5] However, the new EC Merger Regulation prohibits every merger which significantly impedes effective competition, i.e., the ban is not confined to 'dominant firms'. It therefore takes account of the argument that even in the absence of a dominant position a merger may also have serious anti-competitive effects.

As for the enforcement of merger rules, general principles have been established to ensure an efficient division of work. Mergers with a Community dimension are investigated by the European Commission. The main requirement for a merger having a Community dimension is that the combined aggregate worldwide turnover of the merging companies is over €5 billion and that the aggregate Community-wide turnover of each of at least two of the undertakings concerned is more than €250 million.

A merger may also have a Community dimension if the following turnover criteria are met: the combined aggregate worldwide turnover of all undertakings is more than €2.5 billion, and the aggregate Community-wide turnover of each of at least two of the undertakings concerned is more than €100 million, and in each of at least three Member States the combined aggregate turnover of all the undertakings concerned is more than €100 million, and in each of at least three of these Member States the aggregate turnover of each of at least two of the undertakings concerned is more than €25 million. A merger of such a dimension can subsequently be assessed in a single procedure by the European Commission (one-stop-shop principle), instead of different assessments by the Member States involved.

But if each of the undertakings involved achieves more than two-thirds of its Community-wide turnover within one and the same Member State, the

Table 12.2 Community dimension – threshold I

Undertaking	A	B	A+B
Worldwide turnover			> €5 billion
Community turnover (CT)	> €250 million Not 2/3 of CT in one and the same Member State	> €250 million Not 2/3 of CT in one and the same Member State	

Table 12.3 Community dimension – threshold II

Undertaking	A	B	A+B
Worldwide turnover			> €2.5 billion
Community turnover (CT)	> €100 million Not 2/3 of CT in one and the same Member State	> €100 million Not 2/3 of CT in one and same Member State	
Turnover Member State 1	> €25 million	> €25 million	> €100 million
Turnover Member State 2	> €25 million	> €25 million	> €100 million
Turnover Member State 3	> €25 million	> €25 million	> €100 million

merger is in principle examined by the competition authority of that country (as it is supposed to be better placed to examine the potential effects). Both merger-regulation thresholds are summarised in Tables 12.2 and 12.3. Below these thresholds, the national competition authorities in the EU Member States may review the merger. However, the European Commission can also examine mergers, which are referred to it by the national competition authorities or the undertakings involved. In the latter case, agreement of all relevant national competition authorities is needed.

Apart from competitive reasons, potential mergers and acquisitions between financial institutions may also be blocked for prudential reasons. The 'prudential carve-out' allows supervisory authorities to block proposed mergers and acquisitions if the 'sound and prudent management' of the targeted firm(s) could be put at risk. Initially, the margins of this requirement were defined rather broadly and on several occasions the carve-out was used in a protectionist manner. After the takeover battle for the Italian bank Antonveneta in 2005, in which then-governor of the Italian Central Bank Antonio Fazio tried to block the purchase of

Antonveneta by ABN Amro, the Council and the European Parliament endorsed a proposal in 2007 to tighten the procedures that supervisory authorities have to follow when assessing proposed mergers and acquisitions. The new directive (2007/44/EC) foresees a list of criteria on the basis of which prudential supervisory authorities should assess the acquiring company, e.g., reputation of the proposed acquirer, reputation and experience of the management, financial soundness, compliance with EU Directives, and risks related to money laundering and terrorism financing. Moreover, the assessment period is reduced from three months to 30 days.

Liberalisation of monopolistic economic sectors and state aid

Governments can also introduce restrictions on competition by granting national businesses exclusive rights to provide certain goods or services, or by providing public aid to businesses.

Based on article 86 of the EC Treaty, the European Commission is responsible for monitoring public undertakings and undertakings to which Member States grant special or exclusive rights (thereby establishing monopolistic sectors). The European Commission also has the power to address government actions which may distort competition in the internal market. Under this heading, the European Commission plays a pivotal role in opening up markets such as transport, energy, postal services, and telecommunications to competition.

Firms receiving support from their government are likely to obtain an unfair advantage over their competitors. State aid is therefore forbidden, unless it is justified by reasons of general economic development. The rules concerning state aid have been laid down in Articles 87, 88, and 89 of the EC Treaty. In order to ensure that these rules are respected and exemptions are applied equally across the EU, the European Commission is in charge of monitoring state aid. Box 12.2 presents two different cases in which the Commission had to examine whether or not government support to banks was in line with the EC Treaty.

12.4 Assessment of dominant positions

Under article 82 and the EC Merger Regulation, competition authorities need to examine abuse of dominance. This section discusses how competition authorities may examine (potential) abuse of dominant positions, using a

Box 12.2 State aid to banks

State aid to German, Austrian, and French public banks

The German and Austrian Landesbanken obtained guarantees from their governments protecting them from bankruptcy. These guarantees allowed the public banks to grant loans on more favourable conditions than their commercial competitors, i.e., provide cheaper funding. After an investigation, the European Commission concluded that the guarantees constituted illegal state aid and negotiated their phasing out with the German and Austrian governments. A similar decision was taken with regard to a guarantee by the French government to the public financial institution Caisse des Depots et Consignations (CDC) to support its commercial banking activities. The Commission also demanded the phasing out of the guarantee, thereby forcing CDC to operate under the same conditions as its competitors.

UK rescue-aid package for Northern Rock

In 2007 Northern Rock was the UK's fifth largest UK mortgage bank with a balance-sheet total of €150 billion (as of 31 December 2006). Its core activity was residential mortgage lending, which represented more than 90 per cent of all outstanding loans made by the bank. As a consequence of the ongoing turbulence in the world's financial markets in 2007 (see Box 11.2 for further details), a significant rationing of funds in the sterling money markets occurred in August and September 2007 and the mortgage-securitisation market virtually closed. This created severe liquidity difficulties for Northern Rock whose business model was particularly reliant on raising finance in these markets.

When Northern Rock was unable to meet its funding needs it requested the support of the Bank of England for emergency liquidity assistance pending a longer-term solution for its difficulties. On 14 September, the Bank of England granted emergency liquidity assistance to Northern Rock against sufficient collateral and a penal interest rate. The difficulties of Northern Rock were aggravated by a bank run, which started after the news of the Bank of England granting support to Northern Rock was made public. In order to stop the bank run and to avoid contagious effects leading to a wider banking crisis, the UK Treasury announced guarantee arrangements for all existing accounts in Northern Rock on 17 September 2007. Further, the UK Treasury clarified the assumed liability guarantee backed by state resources via a publication on its website on 20 September 2007.

On 9 October 2007 the Treasury extended the guarantee to new retail deposits and, together with the Bank of England, modified the terms and conditions of the emergency liquidity assistance, losses from which were from that date also covered by a Treasury indemnity. The European Commission authorised the UK authorities' package of measures to support Northern Rock under strict conditions and concluded that the measures complied with EU rules on aid for rescuing and restructuring firms in difficulty. Under these rules, rescue aid must be given in the form of loans or guarantees lasting no more than six months, although there are certain exceptions to these rules related to prudential requirements. However, in February 2008 the UK authorities announced the nationalisation of Northern Rock, as this was seen as the best way to protect the £55 billion of taxpayers' money provided in loans and guarantees. Shortly thereafter (in April 2008) the European Commission opened a formal investigation into the support provided by the UK authorities. Similar investigations were launched into the bail-out of two German banks (IKB and SachsenLB).

Source: European Commission (2004a, 2007d)

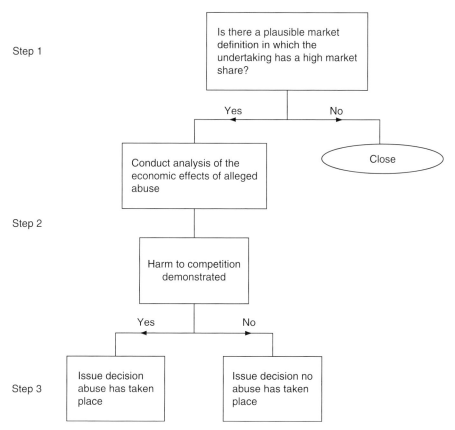

Step 1

Step 2

Step 3

Figure 12.2   Flowchart for undertaking abuse-of-dominance investigations
Source: Office of Fair Trading (2001)

framework suggested by the UK Office of Fair Trading (OFT, 2001). This approach consists of three steps (see Figure 12.2):
1. Assess whether there is a plausible market definition under which the firm under investigation has a high market share.
2. If there is a plausible market in which the firm might be dominant, conduct a full analysis of the economic effects of the practice under investigation.
3. If competition is likely to have been significantly damaged or if there is a prospect of such damage, issue a decision that describes and demonstrates the adverse economic effects of the business practice. Alternatively, if the conduct is not harmful, issue a decision giving the reasons why the business practice under investigation does not constitute an abuse of a dominant position.

The three steps will be discussed in more detail. Although Figure 12.2 depicts an ex-post investigation of possible abuse of dominance, similar investigations can be done ex ante in case of a proposed merger or acquisition.

Step 1: Identify the relevant market

The main purpose of market definition is to identify in a systematic way the competitive constraints that the firms involved face. A market is defined in both its product and geographical dimension (European Commission, 1997). The relevant *product market* is said to 'comprise all those products and/or services which are regarded as interchangeable or substitutable by the consumer, by reason of the products' characteristics, their prices and their intended use'. Moreover, the relevant *geographical market* 'comprises the area in which the undertakings concerned are involved in the supply and demand of products or services, in which the conditions of competition are sufficiently homogeneous and which can be distinguished from neighbouring areas because the conditions of competition are appreciably different in those areas'.

A very common methodology to define the relevant geographical market is the *Small, but Significant Non-transitory Increase in Prices* methodology (European Commission, 2004b). The SSNIP methodology is used to examine whether some goods produced within a specific area constitute their own relevant geographical market. The first step is to assume that the respective goods or services are produced by a hypothetical monopolist. Subsequently, the question is asked whether it is likely that this monopolist can earn a profit by increasing prices by 5–10 per cent (i.e., small but significant) for a period of not less than 12 months (i.e., non-transitory).

If the answer is yes, then the candidate goods form their own relevant geographic market. If on the other hand the answer is no, because consumers substitute away from the candidate markets as they are able to purchase the same good in neighbouring regions or because producers from other regions enter the market, then the relevant geographical market is larger than the goods for the candidate market. The thought experiment is subsequently repeated with a larger geographical area and continued until the answer to the question posed is affirmative. At that stage, the relevant geographical market is composed of all areas included in the last experiment. When it is difficult to assess whether goods which meet the same needs of the consumer belong to the same market or not, price tests (looking at price co-movements) can be used to evaluate the extent of the relevant candidate market.

Whether or not a price increase is profitable depends on the sales volume that is lost following the price increase, i.e., the extent to which a consumer can substitute away from the candidate market (see Box 12.3 which explains the algebra of the SSNIP methodology). The quantity of lost sales depends on the following two aspects:

Box 12.3 Algebra of the SSNIP methodology*

Profits (π) beforehand (denoted with subscript 0) are equal to revenue (price (P) times quantity (Q)) minus total costs (average costs (C) times Q):

$$\pi_0 = (P_0 - C_0)Q_0 \tag{12.2}$$

A change in the price ($\Delta P = P_1 - P_0$) leads to a change in quantity demanded ($\Delta Q = Q_1 - Q_0$) and may also lead to a change in the average costs of production ($\Delta C = C_1 - C_0$). This gives a new level of profits:

$$\pi_1 = (P_1 - C_1)Q_1 \tag{12.3}$$

The change in profit is given by:

$$\Delta \pi = \pi_1 - \pi_0 = (P_1 - C_1)Q_1 - (P_0 - C_0)Q_0$$
$$= \Delta PQ_1 + (P_0 - C_0)\Delta Q - Q_1 \Delta C \tag{12.4}$$

Note that when $\Delta P > 0$, it is expected that $\Delta Q < 0$. The issue is when $\Delta \pi$ will be less than zero. It is convenient to rewrite (12.4) by dividing through P_0 (note that this does not matter as $\Delta \pi < 0$ if $\Delta \pi / P_0 < 0$), yielding

$$\frac{\Delta \pi}{P_0} = \frac{\Delta P}{P_0} Q_1 + \frac{P_0 - C_0}{P_0} \Delta Q - \frac{Q_1}{P_0} \Delta C. \tag{12.5}$$

Suppose average costs is constant (i.e., it does not depend on the amount produced) so that $\Delta C = 0$. Then,

$$\frac{\Delta \pi}{P_0} = \frac{\Delta P}{P_0} Q_1 + \frac{P_0 - C_0}{P_0} \Delta Q \tag{12.6}$$

Thus, a price rise will be profitable if:

$$\frac{\Delta P}{P_0} Q_1 > \frac{P_0 - C_0}{P_0} - \Delta Q \tag{12.7}$$

that is, if the increased price charged on the new (lower) quantity is greater than the lost margin on the decrease in quantity. If there are economies of scale, it is also necessary to work out:

$$\frac{Q_1}{P_0} \Delta C. \tag{12.8}$$

if for example, $\Delta C > 0$ when $\Delta Q < 0$, the increase in price on the new quantity needs to be greater than the lost margin on the decreased quantity plus the higher costs of the new quantity.

Source: Geroski and Griffith (2004)

- the availability of substitute products (i.e., *demand-side substitutes*); and
- the ability of other firms to supply these products (i.e., *supply-side substitutes*).

Once the relevant market has been defined, market shares and concentration indices have to be calculated. There are no thresholds for defining dominance set by law, but the European Court of Justice has argued that dominance can be presumed in the absence of evidence to the contrary if a firm has a market share persistently above 50 per cent. However, a firm with lower market shares may also be dominant, particularly if it faces competitors that are much smaller. The OFT (2001) stresses that despite having a high market share, a firm may not be dominant if one or more of the following conditions hold:

- there are very low barriers to entry into the relevant market and the threat of potential entry is sufficient to discipline firms with high market shares;
- the nature of competition within the market is such that very intense competition exists even where there are very few players; and
- the nature of the buyers in a market and the volumes that they purchase are such that they can exert significant countervailing power against a firm with a high market share.

Also, a high concentration ratio does not necessarily point towards a lack of competition. Claessens and Laeven (2004) estimate competitiveness indicators for banks in a large cross-section of countries and find no evidence that banking-system concentration is negatively associated with competitiveness. In fact, they find some evidence that more concentrated banking systems are more competitive. The latter may be the result of fierce competition in the preceding period, as a result of which the overall banking system has become relatively efficient. Claessens and Laeven (2004) conclude that a contestable system may be more important to assure competitiveness than a system with low concentration (see chapter 7).

Step 2: Abuse of dominance?

Once it is clear that a market can be defined in which the respective firm has a dominant position, the economic effects of (possible) abuse should be examined. Abusive conduct generally falls into one of the following categories (OFT, 2004):

- conduct which exploits customers or suppliers (for example, through excessively high prices); or
- conduct which amounts to exclusionary behaviour, because it removes or weakens competition from existing competitors, or establishes or strengthens entry barriers, thereby removing or weakening potential competition.

In the first case, it may be possible to identify abuse by analysing the profitability of the respective firm. However, profitability figures may be hard to interpret (OFT, 2003). For example, when are profits too high or too low, and what is the relevant time period to consider? And if high profits are found, are they due to market power or to superior efficiency? Profitability figures should therefore be cautiously interpreted and other economic indicators – such as productivity, the advertise-to-sale ratio, prices, and the level of innovation – should also be analysed.

The economic impact of exclusionary behaviour on the market requires a detailed analysis of, among other things, barriers to entry and switching costs. The challenge is to make a distinction between what can be seen as behaviour under normal competition and what can be labelled as abusive practices. In this respect, the OFT (2001) distinguished between conduct that inflicts harm to competition and that which inflicts harm to competitors. Demonstrating harm to competitors is important only when it leads to adverse impacts on consumers. Harm to competitors does not necessarily have an adverse impact on competition. It must therefore be determined whether the conduct represents normal business practice (i.e., lawful competitive behaviour) or abusive behaviour.

Step 3: Issue decision

If no harm to competition can be demonstrated, competition authorities refrain from any intervention. However, if (possible) harm to competition can be proven, competition authorities may impose administrative sanctions, like imposing a fine, prohibiting a proposed merger or acquisition, or requiring additional concessions for the proposed merger or acquisition.

An interesting example of the latter is the proposed merger between the two Swedish banking groups Förenings Sparbanken and SEB in February 2001. The merger of these two banking groups would have created Sweden's leading financial group with market shares in a number of markets in the range of 40–60 per cent. According to the European Commission (2001), the merged entity's large customer base and extensive branch network would have placed it well ahead of its closest competitors in Sweden. In reaction to the preliminary views of the European Commission set out in its Statement of Objections, Förenings Sparbanken and SEB announced in September 2001 that they would withdraw their merger application, claiming that the concessions (e.g., forcing the banks to significantly reduce their market shares) would jeopardise the value of the proposed merger. The European Commission (2001) argued that it should not have been a surprise that it had considered the market as national.

Table 12.4 Relevant geographical market for financial services

National	European	Global
Retail banking & insurance		
	Wholesale banking & insurance	
		Re-insurance
	Stock exchanges	
		Investment banking

To define the market for banking services to households and SMEs as national is standard practice for antitrust regulators worldwide. In previous cases involving banking mergers the Commission has raised concerns where market shares were considerably lower (30–35 per cent). Moreover, in 2001 the UK authorities blocked a merger between Lloyds and Abbey National which presented significantly lower combined market shares (27 per cent for household accounts). The subsequent takeover of Abbey National by the Spanish banking group Banco Santander in 2004 did not raise any competition concerns as these banks were (mostly) active in different countries.

Table 12.4 provides some indications on the relevant geographical market for various financial services. The relevant market for retail banking and insurance is national. Retail banking consists of banking services for consumers (e.g., payment services, consumer credit, and mortgages) and SMEs (e.g., payment services and loans). Retail insurance for consumers and SMEs is also very much a local business with significant differences between countries. The relevant rules for retail insurance products, such as the fiscal treatment, the social security framework, and the liability legislation, are national. The relevant market for motor and health insurance is thus clearly national. Markets for wholesale banking and insurance for large firms are European or even global. Corporate customers are looking for tailor-made solutions for their business and are approached by banks and insurers across Europe. There is a shift to global solutions for more specialised services for large firms. Re-insurance, for example, is a global business. A small group of large re-insurance companies from Europe (in particular Germany and Switzerland) and the United States dominate the global market. Investment banking is also a global business. Leading investment banks – located primarily in New York and London – offer underwriting services and advice for mergers and acquisitions. Finally, the relevant geographic market for stock exchanges is shifting. Not too long ago each country had its own stock exchange where nearly all domestic companies were listed. The market is consolidating at the European (Euronext, OMX) as well as the global level (for instance, the merger between the NYSE and Euronext).

The borderline between geographical markets may in practice be less distinct than is suggested by Table 12.4. An example is the 2007 acquisition of (a part of) ABN Amro by Fortis. In this specific case, the European Commission was concerned that as a result of the transaction corporate customers with a turnover of €2.5 million to €250 million (i.e., SMEs as well as larger corporate customers) would face less competition between banks. As a result, Fortis was forced to sell a part of ABN Amro's commercial banking business in the Netherlands. This example illustrates that the relevant geographical market for large firms can also be defined at the national rather than at the European level.

12.5 Institutional structure

The enforcement of EU competition policy remained largely unchanged from 1962, when a highly centralised authorisation system for all restrictive agreements was established (Monti, 2003a). However, since May 2004 the enforcement system has become more decentralised as the national competition authorities and national courts have become (increasingly) involved in the enforcement of Community competition law. Figure 12.3 gives an overview of the dual legislative and enforcement system in the EU.

Before the introduction of the Community competition law in 1958, most Member States did not have a competition policy regime in place. Competition policy has been established at the Community level, and many Member States created their own legislation and enforcement agencies, while gradually obtaining more enforcement powers originating from EU legislation. This centralised approach in competition policy differs from the enforcement of financial supervision, where supervision has traditionally been organised at the national level. Box 12.4 discusses the issue of decentralisation vs. centralisation in more detail.

Within the current EU competition policy system, the Community institutions (still) occupy a central position. The European Commission enjoys the right of initiative in the legislative process, which confers agenda-setting power to it (Schmidt, 2000). Moreover, as shown in section 12.4, the Commission has specific powers in enforcing Community competition law. The application of EU competition law is supervised by the European Court of First Instance (ECFI) and the European Court of Justice (ECJ). The ECFI is an independent court attached to the ECJ which rules on competition cases in the first instance. Decisions of the ECFI can be appealed to the ECJ.

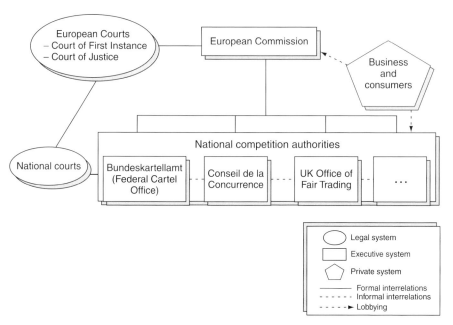

Figure 12.3 Enforcement of EU competition policy
Source: Based on Budzinski and Christiansen (2005)

Effective enforcement of EU antitrust rules requires close co-operation between the Community and national institutions. According to Smits (2005), they have to co-operate in finding evidence for infringements and inform each other about investigations so as to ensure both an efficient division of work and an effective and consistent application of EC competition rules. For this reason, the European Competition Network (ECN) was established in 2004. Within this network, EU competition authorities work together, exchange information, and allocate cases. Monti (2004) argues that the ECN reflects that in an integrated economy collaborative competition enforcement is more effective than isolated efforts. Given the dual structure of EU enforcement, general principles have been established to ensure an efficient division of work (Monti, 2003b):

● as a rule, competition authorities of the Member States will be well placed to deal with cases that have a major effect on the territory of their Member State;
● where a suspected infringement has its main effects in the territory of two or three Member States, these authorities should consider working together on a case;
● where a suspected infringement has larger geographical scope, the Commission is likely to be best placed to deal with a case.

Box 12.4 Which level of (de)centralisation?

The appropriate level of centralisation is an important issue for policy making. National policies offer the flexibility to adapt policies to local circumstances. In addition, policy competition between countries can be beneficial. But when there are externalities (i.e., spill-over effects from one country to another country of national policy) it may be useful to centralise policy making. Another reason for centralisation can be economies of scale. It is, for example, more efficient to examine a merger between two EU-wide operating companies at the central level than to have up to 27 separate examinations by national authorities.

The *principle of subsidiarity* states that matters ought to be handled by the smallest (or the lowest-level) competent authority. Subsidiarity means that a central authority should perform only those tasks which cannot be performed effectively at a more local level. The principle of subsidiarity is enshrined in the Treaty of Amsterdam (Gelauff, *et al.*, 2008).

Figure 12.4 illustrates the degree of centralisation for the three main policy areas in financial services. As discussed in chapter 10, the competent authorities for financial supervision are national. There is some co-ordination within the level 3 supervisory committees, but the national supervisors are still operating on the basis of a national mandate. Large European banks often complain about duplications in the supervision of their European activities. There are discussions to strengthen the legal base of the level 3 committees and to adopt a European mandate forcing national supervisors to co-operate with other EU supervisors and to promote convergence within the EU.

Chapter 11 indicates that national central banks are primarily in charge of financial stability. The lender-of-last-resort function for individual banks is the responsibility of the NCBs. Financial stability is typically an area where externalities are important. The central authority, the ECB, is allowed to contribute to the policies of the NCBs only to promote financial stability. The ECB is slowly expanding its role by maintaining the liquidity of the overall financial system in times of crisis (but not of individual banks) and publishing a Financial Stability Review.

This chapter illustrates that competition policy is highly centralised: the European Commission (DG Competition) is in charge. In 2004, the European Competition Network, consisting of the European Commission and national competition authorities, was created to co-operate and to delegate activities to national authorities where possible.

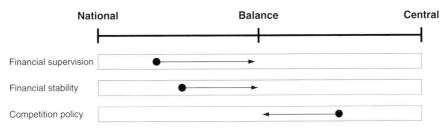

Figure 12.4 Degree of centralisation

> ## Box 12.5 Antitrust policy in the EU and the US
>
> Ginsburg (2005) argues that Sections 1 and 2 of the US Sherman Act cover largely the same ground as Articles 81 and 82 of the Treaty of Rome. Moreover, the US Clayton Act is roughly comparable to the EC Merger Regulation. In practice EU and US competition policy are exhibiting more and more similarities. In this respect, Martin (2005) poses that the EU is moving along the same path trod by US antitrust a quarter century ago: from a reliance on maintaining the ability of equally efficient competitors to compete as a way of getting good market performance towards an explicit, case-by-case assessment of the impact of a business practice on market performance, or of a proposed merger/structural change on expected market performance.
>
> Still, there are important differences between antitrust policies in the US and the EU. According to Rosch (2007), one of the main explanations for these differences is that the policies are based on different schools of thought. While US antitrust policies are based on 'Chicago School economics', those of the EU policies are built on 'post-Chicago School economics'. The basic assumption of the first is that markets are by their nature efficient and that a monopolist will never be able to keep out competitors. Chicago School scholars therefore argue that (i) firms alleged to be engaged in predatory pricing are more likely to be engaged in profit-maximising conduct that is efficiency-enhancing instead of efficiency-impairing, and (ii) even if a firm is trying to engage in predatory conduct, the market is likely to adjust. However, according to post-Chicago School scholars, firms do engage in strategic behaviour to undermine (potential) rivals and active antitrust policies are therefore needed. In addition, Rosch (2007) argues that where the Chicago School tends to advocate a hands-off approach, post-Chicago scholars favour a 'light-touch' regulatory approach. In practice, this entails that EU enforcement agencies challenge certain actions of monopolists, while US agencies and courts rarely (successfully) challenge certain exclusionary practices, such as vertical restraints and predatory pricing.

As for the sanctioning regime, Smits (2005) argues that the absence of a clear regime to impose sanctions for infringements with out-of-state effects is an omission which requires close collaboration among national competition authorities (NCAs). Another element which needs to be remedied according to Smits (2005) is the absence of a common leniency platform, as currently individual applicants need to approach as many authorities as the number of markets that may be affected. However, in 2006 the ECN Model Leniency Programme was introduced. Although it does not provide for a one-stop shop, it diminishes discrepancies and allows for summary applications in case of applications in multiple jurisdictions, notably with the European Commission.

The EU's competition policy is different from that in other countries. Box 12.5 illustrates this by comparing competition policies in the US and the EU.

12.6 Conclusions

Competition policy is one of the pillars of the EU's internal market policy. By combating distortions of competition between firms, competition policy aims to create the preconditions for the proper functioning of markets. Moreover, safeguarding competition is an important instrument to promote further market integration, also within the financial system.

Competition forces firms to become (more) efficient, offer greater choice of products and services, and offer these products and services at lower prices. Ultimately, this gives rise to increased consumer welfare and allocative efficiency. The level of competition is also an important aspect of financial-sector development and, in turn, economic growth. However, firms can benefit from anti-competitive behaviour and may try to scale down competition. The European Commission and the National Competition Authorities therefore aim to:

- eliminate agreements which restrict competition;
- prevent abuse of a dominant position;
- make sure that mergers and acquisitions do not harm competition;
- liberalise monopolistic economic sectors; and
- prevent illegitimate state aid.

As for the prevention of abuse of a dominant position, this chapter discusses a framework for abuse of dominance investigations. One of the elements of this framework is the 'Small, but Significant Non-transitory Increase in Prices' (SSNIP) methodology, which is used to define the smallest market in which a hypothetical monopolist would be able to impose a small but significant non-transitory price increase (the so-called relevant market). Finally, the institutional structure of EU competition policy is explained. It is shown that enforcement of EU competition policy has become more decentralised and the dual enforcement system requires close co-operation between the European Commission and the National Competition Authorities.

NOTES

1. The OECD (1993) defines perfect competition using four conditions: (i) there is such a large number of sellers and buyers that none can individually affect the market price, (ii) there are no barriers to entry and exit, (iii) buyers and sellers are perfectly informed about production and consumption decisions, and (iv) products are homogenous.

2. Under the Lisbon Treaty, which was scheduled to enter into force on 1 January 2009 (see chapter 2), Articles 81 and 82 will be renumbered as Articles 101 and 102.

3. The multilateral interchange fee is a fall-back option, which can be used when the issuing and acquiring banks are not able to bilaterally agree on an interchange fee.

4. Council Regulation (EC) No 139/2004 of 20 January 2004 on the control of concentrations between undertakings.

5. Case 27/76 *United Brands Co and United Brands Continental BV v Commission* [1978] 1 CMLR 429.

SUGGESTED READING

Bikker, J. A. and J. W. B. Bos (2008), *Bank Performance: A Theoretical and Empirical Framework for the Analysis of Profitability, Competition and Efficiency*, Routledge, London.

Monti, M. (2004), Competition Policy in a Global Economy, *International Finance*, 7(3), 495–504.

Motta, M. (2004), *Competition Policy; Theory and Practice*, Cambridge University Press, Cambridge.

REFERENCES

Bikker, J. A. and J. W. B. Bos (2008), *Bank Performance: A Theoretical and Empirical Framework for the Analysis of Profitability, Competition and Efficiency*, Routledge, London.

Budzinski, O. and A. Christiansen (2005), Competence Allocation in EU Competition Policy as an Interest-Driven Process, *Journal of Public Policy*, 25(3), 313–337.

Claessens, S. and L. Laeven (2004), What Drives Bank Competition? Some International Evidence, *Journal of Money, Credit, and Banking*, 36, 563–583.

Claessens, S. and L. Laeven (2005), Financial Dependence, Banking Sector Competition, and Economic Growth, *Journal of the European Economic Association*, 3(1), 179–207.

De Guevara, J. F. and J. Maudos (2004), Measuring Welfare Loss of Market Power: An Application to European Banks, *Applied Economic Letters*, 11(13), 833–836.

Dermine, J. (2005), ING Direct, A Growing Success Story, INSEAD Case Study 05/2005-5282, 1–9.

European Commission (1997), Commission Notice on the Definition of the Relevant Market for the Purposes of Community Competition Law, EC, Brussels.

European Commission (2000), *XXIX Report on Competition Policy*, EC, Brussels.

European Commission (2001), Commission Takes Note of Merger Withdrawal by Swedish Banks (SEB/FSB) (press release), EC, Brussels.

European Commission (2004a), EU Competition Policy and the Consumer, EC, Brussels.

European Commission (2004b), The Internal Market and the Relevant Geographical Market – The Impact of the Completion of the Single Market Programme on the Definition of the Relevant Geographical Market, Enterprise Papers No. 15, EC, Brussels.

European Commission (2007a), Antitrust: Commission Prohibits MasterCard's Intra-EEA Multilateral Interchange Fees (press release), EC, Brussels.

European Commission (2007b), Anti-trust: Groupement des Cartes Bancaires Restricts Competition by Hindering the Issuance of Cards at Competitive Prices (press release), EC, Brussels.

European Commission (2007c), Antitrust: Commission Welcomes CFI Ruling Upholding Commission's Decision on Microsoft's Abuse of Dominant Market Position (press release), EC, Brussels.

European Commission (2007d), Press release on UK rescue aid package for Northern Rock, EC, Brussels.

European Communities (2003), Glossary of Terms used in Competition Related Matters, EC, Brussels.

Gelauff, G., I. Grilo, and A. Lejour (eds.) (2008), *Subsidiarity and Economic Reform in Europe*, Springer, Berlin.

Geroski, P. and R. Griffith (2004), *Identifying Antitrust Markets*, in: M. Neumann and J. Weinand (eds.), *International Handbook of Competition*, Edward Elgar, Cheltenham, 290–305.

Ginsburg, D. H. (2005), Comparing Antitrust Enforcement in the United States and Europe, *Journal of Competition Law and Economics*, 1(3), 427–439.

Martin, S. (2005), U.S. Antitrust and EU Competition Policy: Where Has the Former Been, Where is the Latter Going?, Working Paper in Economics 27, University of Aveiro, Aveiro.

Millward Brown (2008), *BrandZ Top 100 Brand Ranking 2008*, New York.

Monti, M. (2003a), The New Shape of European Competition Policy, Speech given at the Inaugural Symposium of the Competition Policy Research Center, How Should Competition Policy Transform Itself?, Tokyo.

Monti, M. (2003b), EU Competition Policy after May 2004, Fordham Annual Conference on International Antitrust Law and Policy, New York.

Monti, M. (2004), Competition Policy in a Global Economy, *International Finance*, 7(3), 495–504.

Motta, M. (2004), *Competition Policy; Theory and Practice*, Cambridge University Press, Cambridge.

Office of Fair Trading (2001), *The Role of Market Definition in Monopoly and Dominance Inquiries*, OFT, London.

Office of Fair Trading (2003), Assessing Profitability in Competition Policy Analysis, Economic Discussion Paper 6, OFT, London.

Office of Fair Trading (2004), *Abuse of a Dominant Position – Understanding Competition Law*, OFT, London.

Organisation for Economic Cooperation and Development (1993), *Glossary of Industrial Organisation Economics and Competition Law*, OECD, Paris.

Panzar, J. and J. Rosse (1987), Testing for 'Monopoly' Equilibrium, *Journal of Industrial Economics*, 35, 443–456.

Roeller, L.-H. and O. Stehmann (2006), The Year 2005 at DG Competition: the Trend Towards a More Effects-based Approach, *Review of Industrial Organization*, 29, 281–304.

Rosch, J.T. (2007), I say Monopoly, You say Dominance: The Continuing Divide on the Treatment of Dominant Firms, is it the Economics?, paper presented at the International Bar Association Antitrust Section Conference in Florence, available at www.ftc.gov/speeches/rosch/070908isaymonopolyiba.pdf.

Schmidt, S.K. (2000), Only an Agenda Setter? The European Commission's Power over the Council of Ministers, *European Union Politics*, 1(1), 37–61.

Smits, R. (2005), The European Competition Network: Selected Aspects, *Legal Issues of Economic Integration*, 32, 175–192.

Tirole, J. (1988), *The Theory of Industrial Organization*, MIT Press, Cambridge (MA).

Index